THE NEW POLITICAL ECONOMY OF DEVELOPMENT

THE NEW POLITICAL ECONOMY OF DEVELOPMENT

Integrated Theory and Asian Experience

K. Dopfer

M

Softcover reprint of the hardcover 1st edition 1979

First published 1979 by
THE MACMILLAN PRESS LTD
London and Basingstoke
Associated companies in Delhi
Dublin Hong Kong Johannesburg Lagos
Melbourne New York Singapore Tokyo

Typeset in Great Britain by
Santype International Ltd., Salisbury

British Library Cataloguing in Publication Data

Dopfer, Kurt
New political economy of development
1. Economic development
I. Title
330.9 HD82

ISBN 978-1-349-04786-4 ISBN 978-1-349-04784-0 (eBook
DOI 10.1007/978-1-349-04784-0

Contents

List of Tables

List of Figures

Preface

At the present state of development theory, any author seems to be confronted with the choice whether to travel on a well-paved road in a wrong direction or to travel on an unpaved road in (hopefully) the right direction. As far as this author could not avoid making this choice, he unhesitatingly chose the latter option—well aware of the risks involved in such a choice. There are, indeed, good reasons to use the well-paved road of established paradigms in the theory of development, the well-reasoned hypotheses, neatly arranged data, and rigorous methods of empirical testing. There is, for instance, always the hope that the well-paved road will be only a detour that finally arrives at the proper destination—with more rigour and with more substance of the theoretical and empirical statements made.

The author felt reluctant to adopt this optimism. The empirical evidence challenges increasingly not only the validity of single hypotheses, but of the entire set of premises on which these hypotheses are based. Major developmental outcomes—such as increasing socio-economic differentials (asset-, income-, productivity-, etc. differentials), imbalances in ecological development, persistent population pressure and increasing mass poverty—are difficult to predict and to explain within the existing 'paradigm'. Thus, the assumption of a 'productive detour' may well misdirect our entire research efforts in a principal way. It becomes increasingly apparent that only a new road—*a reassessment of the basic set of premises and assumptions*—will secure a somewhat safer travelling given the present state of development theory.

I have the agreable duty to thank all those who contributed to the accomplishment of the work. In particular, I gratefully acknowledge valuable comments made by Professors Michael Braulke (Konstanz), David J. Frederickson (New York), Takao Fukuchi (Tokyo), Emil Küng (St. Gallen), Harvey Leibenstein (Cambridge, USA), Kurt W. Rothschild (Linz), and Mitsuo Sasaki (Tokyo). I further owe a token of gratitude to Mrs Ingrid Seger who typed the manuscript, and, finally, to the Swiss National Science Foundation who supported the study. It goes without saying that for all the inadequacies the reader may encounter on the unpaved road, the author alone is responsible.

Glossary of Symbols

Only symbols used throughout the text are listed.

S_i = System i, where $i = e, s, p, t, c, n$.
- e = economic
- s = social
- p = political
- t = technical (techno-)
- c = ecological (eco-)
- n = population

M^j = System level j
M^{aa} = Macro-macro-level (combining the systems S_c, S_n)
M^a = Macro-level (combining the systems S_e, S_s, S_p, S_t)
M^i = Micro-level (combining the systems S_e, S_s, S_p)
N = Land
R = Non-renewable resources
C = Carrying capacity of environment, or ecosystem (S_c)
$\overline{A}$ = Average consumption and production activities
k = Coefficient expressing impact of $\bar{A}$ on S_c (i.e. N, R, C)
W_K = Welfare at K, where K stands for a specific combination of the variables $\overline{A}$, P, k
u = Social utility
d = Social disutility
P = Population
r_p = population growth rate (in %)
ε_1 = Initial equilibrium phase of population (constitutes first phase in demographic transition, viz. high birth and high death rates)

ε_4 = Ultimate equilibrium phase of population (constitutes fourth phase in demographic transition, viz. low birth and low death rates)

F_i = Production function
= $O_i = f(K_i, L_i, \ldots)$
O_i = Output
K_i = Capital
L_i = Labour
i stands for sector $(s)i$, where $i = 1, \ldots n$

$\bar{F}_1$ = 'Traditional', small-scale sectors, applying specific 'traditional' production and demand functions, institutions and behaviour

$\bar{F}_n$ = 'Modern', large-scale sectors, applying specific 'modern' production and demand functions, institutions and behaviour

Y = Total income

y = Average income

r_o = Total income growth rate (in %)

r_i = Average income growth rate (in %)

Introduction

Though social scientists are usually reticent about making value judgements, probably few would hesitate to say that the problem of development of the less-developed countries (LDCs) is the most pressing problem of our time. However, the common awareness has failed to produce anything like an *unité de doctrine* in the theoretical realm. This is hardly surprising. The problem of alleviating the poverty of the major part of mankind clearly is not an easy one. It took 200 years to overcome the poverty of a relatively small part of mankind, and there will be no ready solutions for accomplishing the rest of the task.

The differences in the theoretical approaches may be due (1) to the different emphases given to explanatory variables, and (2) to different hypotheses explaining the causal interactions among them and their impact on specific developmental outcomes. It goes without saying that (1) and (2) are closely logically interrelated. The choice of the explanatory variables will determine the type of the hypotheses propounded, and a theoretical preconception about the causal nexus among the variables will determine the range of variables to be chosen. Pitfalls may occur in both realms of theory formulation. Shortcomings in one will have repercussions on the other.

It appears that the major theoretical shortcomings have been occurring in category 1, the choice of explanatory variables. Specifically, a mode of theorising has prevailed which tended to give a single variable the rank of a 'critical' explanatory or strategic variable around which the entire process of development revolves. The 'reductionist' approach has been applied to a resource framework excluding behavioural elements, or to a behavioural framework excluding resource relationships. The 'reductionist' approach has even been applied—with worse consequences for the validity of the theory and strategy inferences within the two already reduced theoretical frameworks. This is particularly apparent with regard to the resource-focused approach. While the emphasis was first exclusively on capital formation, it was later almost exclusively on education. There has been increasing recognition that both approaches, like any other 'particularistic' or 'reductionist' approach, inevitably fail to explain the complex nature of the development process. As yet, however, the academic discussion has contributed little to the delineation of a framework which would allow the choice of relevant explanatory variables and a set of plausible hypotheses about their interactions.

This study is an attempt to contribute to the solution of this problem. In doing so, we construct, first of all, a theoretical framework which allows the choice of possibly relevant explanatory variables. This will entail a detailed discussion of some major methodological issues such as the concept of time, 'endogenous' versus 'exogenous' variables, and the impact of the empirical scope on the validity of the theory propounded. We shall then proceed with a discussion of the choice of the variables and the basic propositions about their causal interactions.

An alternative approach would be to begin with a discussion of the existing body of development theories; viz., the grand theoretical designs of the classical political economists of the 18th and 19th centuries. After a description of the theoretical features, a critique would follow, supplemented by a subsequent reformulation of the major aspects and integration into a 'new' theory. Past experience has shown that the descriptive outline of the theories is relatively easy, but that we find difficulties when it comes to the second part of the procedure: the reformulation and integration into a new theory. Far from intellectual incapacity, the reasons lie in the differences pertaining to the levels and rates of change of major variables which constitute that theory. We are, at an early stage of our theoretical inquiry, thrown back to the starting point, confronted with the requirement of clarifying the principal methodological-epistemological position. Hence, it appears to be more economical to start from a 'generalist' view and integrate the various classical hypotheses into the framework at a later stage of the study.

Principally, our analysis is from the outset akin to the classical political economy in its analytical intention, to analyse (1) the 'laws' of accumulation and distribution of the national produce among social classes or individuals, and (2) the 'objective' long-run conditions under which this socio-economic process is bound to operate. This is a reiteration of Ricardo's definition of political economy, and it is a delineation of the two major areas of investigation dealt with in this study (Parts 2 and 3). The political economy is 'new' (as stated in the title) in a sense that it may build on the stock of scientific knowledge which has accumulated since the classical political economists conducted their original studies. The attribute 'new' is furthermore required to draw attention to the fact that the historical context to which our study refers is different from the one the classicists had in mind. While they were occupied with European reality of the 18th and 19th centuries, we deal with the socio-economic development of the contemporary Asian countries. That this must have an impact on the theory formulation will become clear as the study proceeds.

A final word is required, explaining that the study is not in the tradition of the planning approach which could also qualify as a political-economy approach. The reason for this lies less in the subjective preference for a specific regime of state intervention, than in the recognition that in the past a range of sophisticated policy instruments produced unsatisfactory results. Given an impressive stock of policy instruments, the failure can be due only to the inappropriate frame of theoretical reference upon which the application of these instruments is based. If a theory propounds that an outcome X is dependent on a specific level or rate of change in Y, but in reality this relationship does not hold, a policy instrument designed to implement this relationship must necessarily fail to produce the results intended. In fact, the 'success' in the policy implementation positively correlates with the failure of its results. The present situation (in Asia, as in other developing countries) impresses upon us the need to rethink some of the major theoretical positions rather than to formulate 'policies' or improve the planning techniques on the basis of the existing theories.

PART ONE
Scope and Foundations

1 Impact of Regional Scope on Choice and Validity of Theory

While mathematical theorising starts from a set of axioms, social science, including economics, starts from social reality. As in the former a set of axioms determines the range of theorems and hypotheses derived therefrom, so in social science the scope of reality determines the type and validity of the theory, the choice of the explanatory variables, and the degree of generality of the hypotheses. According to the range of phenomena perceived, reality will show different degrees of complexity. The perception may be directed to a single phenomenon, say x or y, or to a set of phenomena combined in classes X and Y of which x and y are part. Focus may be on the structures of the classes, the pattern of change, or on interrelationships between classes. According to the empirical scope, the degree of complexity will differ, and with it the nature of the theory which must explain the respective phenomena. For simple phenomena, a simple theory will do. The behaviour of y may be adequately described by a simple relationship such as $y = f(x)$ (where causality is assumed). Complex phenomena, such as a structured set of elements, require a larger range of explanatory variables, say $y = f(x, \ldots, z)$. The explanation of a function f may require a more general theory, since the variables $a, b, \ldots, e$, which may explain changes in f, lie outside the theory $y = f(x, \ldots, z)$, and constitute yet undetermined exogenous variables. The width of our empirical scope, ranging from simple phenomena to complex ones, determines in a principal way our theorising. Specifically, the choice of Asia as empirical reference frame will necessarily lead to the choice of variables and hypotheses which reflect the degree of complexity of that reality.

Theorising may start from the opposite end—with a theoretical preconception. As the range of empirical phenomena determines the theoretical scope, the theoretical preconception will delineate the choice of empirical phenomena. Both approaches being part of the same epistemological procedure, they apparently must converge. However, this will be true only if the complexity of the phenomenon is due to the 'whole'; it will not be true if the complexity of the whole can likewise be reflected in a segment of the whole. Such an 'aggregation' of phenomena is conceivable if the phenomena extend in space—for instance, if the development problems of the entire Asian region can be faithfully represented by a single country. Granted this be the case, any reference to the whole region will not enhance the complexity of the phenomenon but will constitute a mere multiple of it. If we obtain a theory, the question consequently will arise whether the empirical scope from which this theory is derived is the only one conceivable or whether reference to other empirical phenomena would lead to the same theoretical result—with perhaps less work.

Both a narrowing and widening of the empirical scope present themselves. It is conceivable that a country study could be substituted for the regional approach. Since Asia is understood as a composite of countries with homogeneity sufficient to group them into a single class, all factors making for homogeneity will, in turn, allow for *pars pro toto* conclusions. However, inductive reasoning is rejected here in favour of the deductive approach. There are no *a priori* criteria which would allow us objectively to ascertain which of the inferences are valid in a specific case nor to what extent they are valid. The distinction between 'general' and 'specific' hypotheses can be drawn only if the particular case is related to the 'whole'. Reference to a specific country may serve the purpose of showing the differences between the countries: the limitations of a hypothesis rather than its general validity.

Alternatively, a widening of the empirical scope may be considered. A large body of international data provides useful information for a single case as well. The overall data indicate which bits of information from the particular data set, here Asia, may be qualified as general and which as specific. The same rationale applies here as above. The choice between general and specific hypotheses exists as a viable option only in the context of international data. However, once a theoretical preconception is established by inspection of a broader range of data, the question arises whether it is fruitful to carry the onerously large body of data further. If the data contain general information, the information provided by the two sets of international and regional data will not deviate much. We can therefore just as well rely on the latter set of data. If specific information is considered, the reference to more specific data will be appropriate anyway, since they are inherently better substantiated.

The discussion on the 'wide' approach would not be worthy of much attention in the context of our analysis if it did not bring up the larger issues of the possibility of arriving at a general development theory on the one hand, and of the possibility of inferences from our regional study to other less-developed countries on the other. The issue of the feasibility of formulating a general development theory cannot be judged upon *a priori* reasoning, since the assessment obviously depends on how much generality or, alternatively, how much loss of information we are willing to accept. We may conclude on this topic summarily (further elaboration is beyond the scope of this study) that statements about structure—basic relationships between the explanatory variables and directions of causal links—are likely to be general enough to be equally valid for all less-developed countries. This assumption shall, in turn, serve as a guideline for inferences from our study. Whenever general hypotheses are stated, they may be valid for all less-developed countries, while more specific hypotheses will require further empirical justification from case to case.

After this brief epistemological clarification, it should be stressed that the main concern in our study is explanatory-theoretical rather than descriptive. A development theory valid for Asia is envisaged, not an exhaustive descriptive account of the region. The experience included in this study will serve this purpose. This requires in some instances a widening of the empirical basis—say, reference to early European or Japanese development—and in others an 'inductive' treatment of specific cases.

2 Rationale and Implications of Historical Time

An assessment of development processes requires that we have a predetermined time horizon within which we assume that significant changes occur. Without being rigid, we shall apply a time horizon of fifty years ranging from about 1950 to 2000.

To this time span we relate changes in explanatory variables. On this broad scale, broad changes can characteristically be described, while small changes will not receive enough profile. Variables which describe changes 'in the large' can be referred to as long-run variables; those which describe changes 'in the small' as short-run variables.

A development theory, by its nature, must explain the relationships among long-run variables and allow the formulation of hypotheses about changes in these variables. Static equilibrium theory, which describes marginal changes in the *status quo*, will not serve this purpose. Similarly, economic dynamics may be bypassed insofar as it leaves variables unexplained which actually change within fifty years, such as population, technology, social institutions, and so forth. What are typically exogenous variables in much of contemporary economics (with its focus on short-run analysis) become major explanatory variables in a development theory.

The reference to a specific historical time span, and not merely to an undated period of fifty years, has a principal impact on further theorising. It implies that the development process cannot be viewed as an ahistorical process but as a sequence within a historical continuum. The specific point on the historical time scale at which the development sequence occurs is decisive for the generalisation about the development process. The intended theory for a given region would look different if referred to the year 1880 than it does when referred to the year 1980. Specific processes such as the mode of capital accumulation and appropriation, the emergence of classes, the provision of natural resources, the availability of know-how for the management of enterprises and governments, expectations, ideals, and so forth are related to a unique historical phenomenon the occurrence of which is limited to a specific historically unrepeatable epoch.

Once a historical process, say *X*, occurs, the very existence of *X* will have altered the historical conditions in a way that *X* will not be repeated as *X* but as, say, *X′*, even if the regional-cultural settings are similar. Both the experiences about earlier processes and the changed preconditions caused by that process will make any reoccurrence of the same development process impossible.

Eighteenth- and nineteenth-century Europe, and to a lesser extent Japan, followed a sequence of historical events which could be termed a '*successive sequence*'—*A* before *B*, and *B* before *C*, where *B* in this sequence is not possible before *A*, and *C* not before *A* and *B*. In less-developed countries, a situation exists where in many ways elements from *A*, *B*, and *C* are being combined, and constitute a new type of '*simultaneous sequence*'. The assumption of a 'simultaneous-sequence' type of development will form the basis of the discussion in Part 3.

3 A Holistic Systems View

The set of development variables reaches in its implications and repercussions into a variety of areas. The growth and distribution patterns are dependent on behaviour and institutions in the social, economic, and political contexts. Factors such as resource availability and the environmental carrying capacity are determined by the natural-ecological conditions and the absolute size and growth rate of the population. The variables, even if they are merely of an economic nature, extend far beyond the economic realm as their complex nature and causality is explored.

This suggests that any approach which includes only the economically relevant part of reality must necessarily mis-state the nature of the problem, severely limiting its capability of proposing valid hypotheses. The approach adequate for a comprehensive explanation of the phenomena under discussion is by its very nature a holistic approach. Holism as developed by Bews, and later by Smuts, states that phenomena which are part of a complex environment must be analysed in their property as part of this environment.[1]

Following a holistic approach, the nature of interdisciplinary reasoning will differ from traditional interdisciplinary research. The traditional procedure has been to perceive an economic phenomenon, say $\mathscr{E}$, to formulate the relevant questions in terms of economics, E, to choose the specific scientific ingredients such as available economic theories, methods, and data, e. Then allowance may be made for some non-economic phenomena, ξ, to be included as additional explanatory variables whenever a gap in the theory suggests this to be necessary.

Interdisciplinary reasoning emerging from a holistic view perceives the economic phenomenon, $\mathscr{E}'$, within the overall context of which this phenomenon constitutes part, say $\mathscr{E}'$ in its relation to phenomena ξ', $\ldots, \gamma', \mu'$. Based on this holistic perspective, the relevant theory embraces explanatory variables from the entire environmental context to which the phenomenon pertains. Premises, hypotheses, and empirical data are derived from all relevant sciences.

From a holistic environmental perception, proper methodology encompasses system analysis; phenomena are viewed in their complexity and interrelatedness. Phenomena which expound the characteristics of complexity and interrelatedness are combined into a system. A system is thus defined as an 'aggregation or assemblage of objects (or ideas, or activities) united by some form of regular interaction or interdependence',[2] or simply as a 'set of elements standing in interrelation'.[3] The generalised concept of system allows us to expound *a priori* some basic characteristics of phenomena which are composed according to the characteristics of a system. A principal conclusion will be that a part cannot be understood without knowing its relation to other parts. Consequently, the relations themselves are of prime analytical interest; not the behaviour of the single parts or the co-variation between isolated parts—an emphasis characteristic of the reductionist type of theorising. The question of whether or not to conceive a set of phenomena as a system depends on the assessment of the interrelatedness and interactions of the phenomena, and constitutes both a theoretical and empirical problem. Assessing the phenomenon of development, we start from the assumption, based on broad observation and intuition, that all conceivable developmental variables are interelated in a complex way.[4] The conception of these phenomena as a system is therefore a more valid generalisation of reality than the alternative conception of viewing the variables separately, not allowing for their complex interrelatedness.

We may denote the variables of a system as $\alpha, \beta, \ldots, \mu$, and state that they are in relation R. R represents the system structure. If all variables relate to each other, we may write R as a system of simultaneous differential equations[5] in the form

$$\frac{d\alpha}{dt} = f_\alpha(\alpha, \beta, \ldots, \mu)$$

$$\cdots\cdots\cdots\cdots\cdots\cdots$$

$$\frac{d\mu}{dt} = f_\mu(\alpha, \beta, \ldots, \mu).$$

$f_\alpha, \ldots, f_u$ show how a variable λ of the system is 'determined' by all other variables of that system. $f_\alpha, \ldots, f_\mu$ describe the system behaviour, given a set of variables $\alpha, \beta, \ldots, \mu$. The structure says nothing about where an initial change may occur; nor what time it actually requires to carry out the system changes. By definition, the system above is 'simultaneous', while causality is not.[6] The algebraic expression nevertheless provides a first idea of the overall interrelatedness of the system variables, and may serve as a starting point for the analysis of more complex phenomena.

There is a multitude of sets of related phenomena. Specifically, we have sets comprising economic, social, political, technological, natural-ecological, and population-related phenomena. Consequently we have not merely one system but a set of systems: the economic system (S_e), social system (S_s), political system (S_p), techno-system (S_t), ecosystem (S_c), and population system (S_n). These systems relate to each other in an analogous way as the variables within a single system. Having combined the variables to single systems, we may relate them to each other in the relation **R**. The total set of related systems we may designate as total-system. Similarly, we may write

$$\frac{dS_e}{dt} = F_e(S_e, S_s, S_p, S_t, S_c, S_n)$$

$$\cdots\cdots\cdots\cdots\cdots\cdots\cdots\cdots\cdots\cdots\cdots$$

$$\frac{dS_n}{dt} = F_n(S_e, S_s, S_p, S_t, S_c, S_n).$$

For the systems $S_e, \ldots, S_n$ to be interdependent does not require that all the variables $\alpha_i, \ldots, \mu_i$ of each of the systems be dependent on each other. Since there is 'internal' interdependence within the context of R—say, the social system variables—a dependence of one of these system variables is sufficient to constitute cross-system or macro-dependency. The initial change in a single variable of a system S_i may induce changes in all other variables of system S_i.

The delineation of the general structure of the total-system allows conclusions with regard to the nature and explanatory power of the variables. Changes in one or more variables in one system S_i always depend on both the system-internal relational pattern R_i *and* the relationship between R_i and the overall relational pattern **R** of the total-system. A system S_i is always *open* in relation to other systems. A set of 'exogenous' variables determines the functioning of any single system.

Within the total-system, however, the single system is reciprocally related to other systems, and thus constitutes an 'endogenous' variable. The total-system constitutes a *closed* system, 'self-contained', without undetermined and unexplained exogenous variables. This is an important proposition about the basic system structure. The single systems are understood as being necessarily causally related, not—as the total-system—as self-determined closed systems. This enables us to understand all relevant phenomena in their interrelatedness and causal interactions. None of the systems, say, the social system, is treated as the one crucial element on which development depends. Within the context of the total-system there may be many configurations of *R* and **R**, and initial changes which induce changes in the total-system may occur in any of the systems.

Against our holistic system view, the objection may be raised that it includes variables which are not crucial determinants of the total-system or of the development process. A variable *k* may have such a low degree of interaction with other variables, that the coefficient may be zero or be decreasing over time to converge on zero, and thus the inclusion of the variable *k* does not add anything to the explanation of the behaviour of the system. Similarly, a whole system may have little interrelation with other systems, and may not significantly affect the behaviour of the total-system. The question of the adequate choice of variables or systems is a theoretical as well as an empirical one. At this stage, only a broad preconception of the total-system is required; the final choice of system variables will be treated in the chapters to follow, taking into consideration the partial theories and the empirical knowledge available. As the basic assumption about the total-system we propound that, within the spatial-temporal scope envisaged, all mentioned systems are relevant as determinants of the behaviour of the total-system. This theoretical preconception is a necessary condition for further theorising and for the selection of relevant theories and empirical data. The preconceptional assumption must not be confined to the immediate past or future, but should be viewed in its dynamic implications over the time span suggested. Systems contemporarily irrelevant in their implications for the behaviour of the total-system or of other systems may become relevant in the time span considered. For instance, up to the year 2000, technological change, economic activities, and environmental hazards under the conditions of rapidly deteriorating land-man ratios must be assessed in their interrelatedness and system-wide repercussions. Historically, the population problem would perhaps have taken another turn if the problem had been assessed and consequently anticipated in the context of a systems framework that includes medical progress, cultural values, and so forth as explanatory variables. Today, these variables necessarily have to be integrated into a framework relevant for the explanation of developmental processes.

4 Total-System Behaviour: Principles and Propositions

I. DETERMINISM: HISTORICAL AND *A PRIORI* CONCEPTS

Since the single systems constitute an integral part of the total-system, an isolated treatment of single systems is not adequate for the assessment of the behaviour either of single systems or of the total-system. An idea of the total-system behaviour is therefore instrumental for the assessment of both single- and total-system behaviour. In its general form the problem is, firstly, to what extent the interactions of the total-system are predetermined by 'regularities' or 'laws', and, secondly, to what extent the interactions of the total-system can be voluntaristically varied by man and directed towards a set of goals or objectives chosen from a set of alternatives. This general theoretical preconception is, again, important for the scope of subsequent theorising and for the selection of partial theories and empirical data. On this abstract level, we merely 'flip the switch' for further theorising. Ontological plausibility and broad historical evidence are the scientific criteria.

In pursuit of a classification of relevant explanatory variables, we may fall back upon ontological classifications. Following ontology from Greek to modern philosophy, factors pertaining to ideas and factors pertaining to matter both constitute necessary explanatory variables of any 'total'-system. Philosophies originating from the two ontological entities are materialism and idealism. Materialistic socio-economic theories include Marxism and historical-stage theories; most

'Western' theories, particularly of the neoclassical model-building type, derive from idealism. The assessment of the two sets of theories follows two criteria: first, whether they allow for all relevant variables; second, whether they attach the proper weight to the variables in their property as determinants of the total-system. Departing from the total-system approach outlined, any theory including only the economic system or the economic system in its relation to the social and political systems, while treating other systems as historically irrelevant *ceteris paribus* assumptions, will lead to a lopsided assessment of the long-run development of the total-system. Whether the theories emphasise the voluntaristic aspects stressed by idealism or the deterministic aspects stressed by materialism is irrelevant for the lopsidedness of the historical view as such.

We have been conceiving time as historical time. Propositions which pertain to the attaching of causal weights to the variables must be assessed along the horizontal or time axis, expressing the *diachronic* character of the total-system. To be more explicit, we may designate f as a rule which relates the time x to certain values of development indicators y. Thus x becomes the 'determinant' of f, a result which can be explained only in a context where x is not thought of as assuming simply a sequence of members corresponding to years, $1, \ldots, n$, but represents various sets of specific historical circumstances. To assume x to stand to f in a relationship $x \mapsto f$, it must be redefined as $x_1, \ldots, x_n$, where the subscripts designate points in a specific historical time segment, for instance $x_1 = 1950$, $x_2 = 1951, \ldots, x_n = 2000$.

Using the time concept suggested, the ontological factors mentioned must be viewed within their historical context. The degree of determinism or voluntarism will differ according to the historical context of the factors. It follows that 'general laws', as propounded by both the materialistic and idealistic approaches, cannot be transferred to all historical instances. The concept of transferability, be it the notion of a matter-determined world ('laws' of the material basis) or of a world ruled by the omnipotence of man's ideas and actions, is not feasible irrespective of the validity of its ontological weighting. The 'philosophical' concept we propound is a *relative determinacy* of the total-system: the total-system behaviour is determined not by repeatable 'patterns' (which would lend themselves to theoretical generalisation) but by a specific historicity of the total-system. This is the broader philosophical-epistemological context within which our specific proposition of a 'simultaneous sequence' (see p. 11) prevailing in contemporary less-developed countries must be viewed. (For further discussion see Appendix I, 'Relative determinacy of historical processes: the case of simultaneous sequence development in LDCs.')

II. FINALITY AND EQUIFINALITY

The onto-epistemological position we took with regard to the concept of 'relative macro-determinacy' does not imply a 'law' inherent in the historical process which would yield a 'unique' historical pattern insusceptible to human will. Such a hypothesis would be in principle inconsistent with the behaviour of some of the systems of which the total-system is composed. The economic, social, and political systems clearly exhibit voluntaristic properties. They are composed of human beings—say economic agents, members of political and social institutions, and so forth. The members of any of these systems are apt to act purposefully, with goals in mind and actions to serve them. Given these voluntaristic elements, the behaviour of the total system is characterised by *finality*.

A system is said to have finality if its final state determines the behaviour of the system. Up to this point, the behaviour of the total-system has been assumed to be determined solely by the past behaviour of the system. Specifically, the history of Europe has been viewed to be significantly different from the history of the contemporary LDC, and therefore the future behaviour of the latter has been expected to be different from the former. The distinction between the 'successive-sequence' and the 'simultaneous-sequence' type of development has brought out this difference in the behaviour of the total-system. However, the future behaviour of the total-system is determined not only by its past: the ideas about the terminal state of the system—theoretical preconceptions, ideological visions, a set of normative desiderata, and so forth—will determine the behaviour of the system in the future.

Not all systems have this type of *teleological* finality. For instance, we could think of our human body as having finality since the 'system' moves from an initial state, procreation, to a final state, death. However, this type of finality is different from the finality envisaged here. Once a 'law' or 'growth equation' of a biological entity, such as the human body, is established, we are able to predict the final state, given the information about its initial state and the exogenous conditions on which the system depends. The final state does not determine the behaviour of the system from its initial state on. The final state is itself a result of a deterministic process and there is consequently also a predetermined path back from the final to the initial state of the system.

Finality in its proper teleological sense states rather the opposite: there is a range of alternative final states and accordingly a range of alternative paths to reach these states. The choice of a final state (among various possible final states) as a deliberate act based on a normative vision determines the actual behaviour of the system towards its final state (whether the 'ideal' final state is identical with the one actually reached is irrelevant for the possibility of the choice as such). If the final state were predetermined by a law, freedom of action and the possibility of shaping historical events would have ceased to exist. Development planning and socio-economic policies are meaningless if not conceived in the context of finality. (For a formal presentation of the concepts of finality and related topics see Appendix 2, 'Finality, equifinality, and historically feasible paths.')

III. PREDICTIVE CAPACITY OF SYSTEM THEORIES

Yet undetermined is the 'definite' path which we wish to propound as the most plausible hypothesis. Indeed, it is debatable whether a range of predictions should be theoretically allowed or whether that range of predictions should be narrowed (for instance, to include only the most probable paths). Limitation would be desirable to ensure the predictive capacity and facilitate the empirical testing of the theory. The point may sound trivial, but the implications of that consideration for theory-making in the area of development have been far-reaching. If the predictive quality of a theory depends on the number of predictions, i.e. the number of feasible paths to be assumed to actually occur, then it is sensible to make the number of predictions small. From the viewpoint of an unambiguous formulation and an unambiguous empirical testing of a hypothesis, the 'best' theory will be the one which allows but one single alternative. In this context, any strictly deterministic theory must appear to be superior to any theory that is not strictly deterministic. Without attempting here an excursis into the history of doctrines or the psychogenetic aspects of scientific discovery, it may be safely assumed that this or similar reflections have to a significant extent guided the formulating of development theories. This is true for the grand designs, the 'magnificent dynamics', be they the Marxian historical materialism or the Rostowian view of history as stages of growth.[1] It is equally true for the analytically and theoretically narrower approaches such as the transition theories,[2] including those approaches which try to bring into the development process an element of chance by introducing systems of stochastic differential equations.[3]

Predictions based on the body of deterministic theories are straightforward. A specific historical situation or a state of the total-system is plotted on an overall sequence of periods, stages, epochs, phases, regimes, etc. Once the 'point of identity' is found, viz. once the actual historical situation matches with the point theoretically predetermined on the sequence of periods (this point is assumed to exist *ex hypothesi*), the future path or behaviour of the system is easily predicted, since the theory asserts that any system moves through the postulated sequence of regimes. For instance, in Marxian historical materialism, any society turns from a feudalistic social formation to a capitalistic one, and subsequently is inevitably superseded by a socialist and later communist social formation. A prediction is made by defining the location of an actual system on this overall sequence of social formations. No further reflections on the future path of the system is then required; in fact, any further predictive attempt is considered to be 'metaphysics', based on a lopsided idealistic-voluntaristic philosophy. Similarly, little predictive endeavour is required once we locate a specific society within the context of the Rostowian growth stages. Any society moves inexorably from the stage of feudalism, over a transitional stage to the take-off stage, which is followed by the stage of maturity. In the transition theories which, on the basis of a deterministic resource framework, offer an explanation for the transition from the agrarian regime to the non-agrarian, mainly industrial, regime, an unambiguous prediction is possible once the values of certain variables (sectoral wage rates, population growth rates, innovational intensity, rate of capital accumulation, etc.) are ascertained.

Deterministic theories have the merit of being refutable by a set of contrary facts. If we predict that a system moves from S_0^x to S_1^x, this is an unambiguous statement which can be subjected to empirical scrutiny. Conversely, if we predict that the future state of a system may be either S_1^x, S_1^y, or S_1^z, then the propositional relevance of the theory is diminished. If we predict that a system starting from S_0 may reach any future state S_1, then the theory is hardly a valuable device to predict the future and we could perhaps well dispense with it. Given the close connection between the predictive and deterministic qualities of a theory, it is understandable that an inclination exists to formulate theories as deterministic as possible.

The principal epistemological problem comes in if we contrast the postulate for making a theory relevant and refutable with the actual phenomena to be analysed. They may well not show the degree of determinism which would be desirable from the point of view of formulation and testing a theory. There may be a broad range of alternatives which the system actually may reach in the future. The system may, indeed, have at t_0 the 'option' of moving from S_0^x either to S_1^x, S_1^y, or S_1^z. The indeterministic character, although theoretically unsatisfying, may be inherent in the phenomena analysed.

To narrow the theoretical statement to less than the entire range of possible and/or feasible alternatives is to make a false theoretical statement for the sake of rigour in the theoretical presentation and the subsequent validity test. To the extent that a theory gains in theoretical rigour it loses in validity. There is no inherent necessity (although perhaps there may be a sociological one) to be trapped in the positivist ideal of scientific research or any ontological prejudice (like materialism). It certainly is epistemologically questionable to start first with the choice of the method and then proceed to the problem; it seems more appropriate to consider first the nature of the problem, and then to choose the appropriate method. If so, it is appropriate to state, specifically, first the degree of determinism and the degree of finality respectively, and subsequently to proceed to the choice of the adequate method, the relevant theoretical context, and the body of hypotheses. This may entail a less rigorous exposition and testing of the theory—an unavoidable price for any analysis of complex phenomena.[4] Nevertheless, there may be little co-variation between the plausibility or the acceptance of a theory and the possibility of subjecting the theory to a falsification procedure. It may suffice to mention Darwin's theory of evolution, which has been little subjected to satisfactory empirical testing and yet is widely accepted and useful to further advances in biology. The falsification, in this case, would consist in providing empirical evidence for events which (according to the theory) cannot occur. It seems reasonable to apply the same falsification criteria of 'elimination' also to complex phenomena in the social realm.

Two major propositions emerge from our study up to this point:

First, the process of development is a historical process. It is not necessarily repeated in the same fashion in different historical periods. Past development in a system X usually excludes the repetition of a similar development in another system, say Y or Z, in later historical periods. There is a 'relative macro-determinacy', since we find in any period a unique set of historical variables which determines the behaviour of the system.

Second, the determination of the system is not absolute in the sense that no variant courses of action could occur. The total system is composed of human agents who are capable of thinking of and choosing among various alternatives. This has led to the assumption that the total-system possesses the property of finality.

Both propositions, relative macro-determinacy and finality, exclude the possibility of the total-system's following a single and predeterminable path over the entire sequence of historical periods.

Hence, our cognitive problem is not to search for a generally valid theory of development which, once and for all, could describe in deterministic terms and with claim of *a priori* validity the entire development process. Instead, the analytical endeavour will be directed to seeing how the development process is determined at a historical time, t_x, say in 1980, up to a historical time t_{x+1}, say the year 2000. Clearly, there are significant theoretical and empirical implications of this cognitive view. The theoretical task is to ascertain those phenomena of the total-system which lend themselves to meaningful and relevant generalisation. The working hypothesis must be that the functioning of the total-system is governed by certain 'regularities' or 'laws'. Any theorising becomes futile if this assumption is not made. If, indeed, 'laws' apply to the behaviour of the total-system, a theoretical interpretation of any historical period will be feasible. The 'laws' are possibly more general than the laws stated in the deterministic theories mentioned. But they would not be necessarily deterministic in the sense that only a unique historical path over the entire range of periods could appear. Within this framework a multiplicity of paths is still logically possible and theoretically left open—as, clearly, the proposition of finality implies.

IV. DEVELOPMENTAL FUNCTION: DESIDERATA AND INSTRUMENTALS

In search for general statements about the system behaviour, we introduce a further analytical distinction between 'desiderata variables' and 'instrumental variables'. The two may be combined in the concept of a 'developmental function'. On the left-hand side of this equation appear the desiderata goals, norms, values, outcomes, outputs, etc. On the right-hand side of the equation appear the instrumental variables, production factors, inputs, etc. For instance,

$$\{S_e^D, \ldots, S_p^D\} = f\{S_e^I, \ldots, S_p^I\},$$

where the superscripts D and I designate the desiderata and instrumental variables respectively, while the subscripts designate the specific type of system.

This exposition allows us to locate theoretically the two basic 'laws' which we assume to apply to the total-system behaviour. The first set of laws which rules the behaviour and the change of the values of the system variables pertains to the left-hand side of the equation, the goals, desiderata, etc. Specifically, the question arises whether all norms set to be reached by the system are consistent with certain objective requirements. The second set of laws concerns the feasibility of the causal interactions among system variables designed to reach the desired outcomes. Specifically, the question is whether there are any hierarchical dependencies of one variable set from another. Both sets of laws are closely interrelated; they may be divorced for an analytical instance but hardly as phenomena in their living and dynamic totality. The analysis of the relationships among the variables—of which the set of interactions between the variables of both sides of the equation is only one example—will constitute a major analytical concern of this study.

V. TOWARDS AN EMPIRICAL WELFARE THEORY: MINIMUM AND SUPPLEMENTARY DESIDERATA

We have presented the functioning of the total-system in the form of a system of differential equations (see Chap. 3). In that system any change in a subsystem S_j has been due to changes in all other subsystems $S_e, \ldots, S_n$. The two sides of the equation given may be viewed as representing the two sides of the developmental function (introduced in the last section). Any change in S_j, dS_j/dt, may be interpreted as change in the set of desiderata of the system S_j, whereas the vector functions $F_e, \ldots, F_n$ may be interpreted as representing the kind of change necessary in all systems to bring about a change of the magnitude dS_j/dt. The crucial question with regard to the change of the desiderata is whether they may take any value or rather be limited to values within a specific domain of empirically warranted values only. As stated previously, there will be specific minima pertaining to the values of all systems if the functioning of the total system is to be maintained. These minima constitute a set of 'side conditions' which impose 'side constraints' to any solution. Hence, the solution of the system of differential equations is subject to the conditions

$$\frac{S_e^A}{S_e^M}, \ldots, \frac{S_p^A}{S_p^M} \geq 1,$$

where the superscripts M and A designate the minimum and actual values respectively and the subscripts the type of system. Given numerical values for the variables involved, the relative value for the minima may be expressed for all six systems or the total system respectively as

$$\sum_{i=1}^{n=6} S_i^M \geq 6,$$

where any S_i is subject to the condition $S_i^A/S_i^M \geq 1$. A diagrammatic exposition of the change in the variables of the sub-systems within constraints of minimum desiderata is given in Fig. 4.1. The method used is reminiscent of the method of the 'correspondent points'.[5] On the vertical axis are plotted the values for sets of indicators for all systems V_i, and on the horizontal axis the relevant systems are plotted, S_j.[6] Various development patterns are assumed. To each of them a specific year t_i, e.g. 1970, 1980, 1990, and 2000, is assigned. The entire development path is composed of various development patterns of

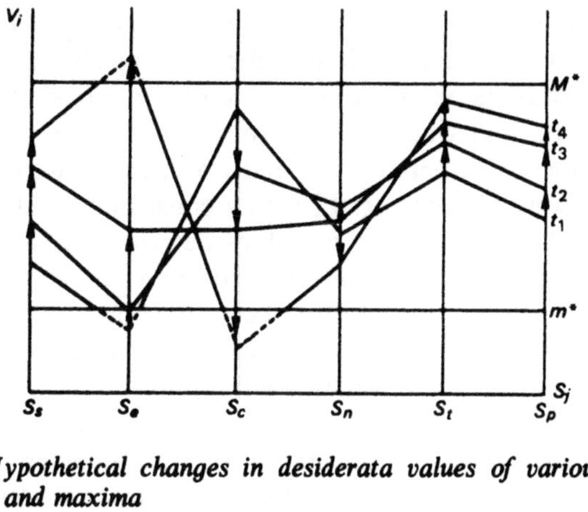

FIG. 4.1 *Hypothetical changes in desiderata values of various sub-systems with minima and maxima*

these periods. The development path must not at any time yield values for any of the systems which fall below the minimum values, indicated by the horizontal line m^*. The direction in the change of the system values is indicated by arrows; for instance, upward arrows are drawn for an increase in the values of the economic system S_e, while downward arrows are drawn for a decrease in the values of the ecosystem S_c. Thus, the hypothetical path in Fig. 4.1 shows that an upward movement in the values of the economic variables corresponds with a downward movement in the values of the eco-variables.

We could operate with the assumption that the minimum value in S_c cannot be reached because other systems attained too high values, and consequently certain maximum values of these systems are exceeded. The maximum value could, for instance, pertain to the economic system S_e; a conflict between an increase in the food production and the ecological balance could account for it—a possibility represented in the figure by the upper horizontal line M^*. This appears a reasonable theoretical inference. However, to say anything specific obviously requires a theory about the causal interactions among the system variables—a theme to be developed in this study.

A specification of the system variables will be made as our study proceeds. Various aspects determine the choice and classification of the system variables. For instance, a classification of the system variables according to their dependency (in the context of a hierarchical ordering; see subsequent section) will have implications on the grouping of the variables.

What shall be brought into clearer analytical focus is the relationship between desiderata and instrumentals. The distinction is not as clear cut as the separation into two sides in the developmental function would suggest. Generally, dS_j/dt describes a change in the system S_j. It will in some instances be unambiguous to determine what variables of S_j are desiderata and what are instrumentals. A case in point is the production function, where output and production factors are neatly separable. However, some variables may constitute desiderata as well as instrumentals. A change in variables determining human welfare can hardly be without effect on the productivity of the humans to which that change in the welfare state (or flow) applies. Welfare factors—say adequate nutritional intake, housing, schooling, medical care, etc.—are desiderata as well as instrumental variables determining those and other desiderata. Hence, it is theoretically important (1) generally to leave open the possibility for the variables to take on a dual nature according to the specific empirical and theoretical context in which they become relevant, and (2) to allow for the possibility of causal reciprocity, viz. not only for the asymmetrical relationship $X \mapsto Y$ (by which causality is defined) but also for $Y \mapsto X$, and hence for the entire relationship

$$X \rightleftarrows Y$$

Our theoretical exposition will be based on this general assumption, rather than on the assumption of strict separability of desiderata and instrumentals with its implied uni-directional causality.

At this point, a definition of development may be attempted. Development shall be defined as any change of the total-system in a desired direction in terms of desiderata of all systems, under the condition that none of the desiderata must take on a value which is below a specific minimum value.

This definition does not yet give any information about how much development has been achieved within a specific period. If statements about the performance are to be made, a scale of measurement must be proposed and its values agreed upon. The problem has a theoretical and empirical side. We shall make at present some theoretical statements, leaving the empirical discussion to the later chapters (which necessarily implies a discussion on the situation in Asia). Theoretically, a division suggests itself into desiderata pertaining to the minimum values and those pertaining to values above the minimum. We shall call the former *M*-desiderata, the latter supplementary or *S*-desiderata.[7] Once we have attached absolute priority to the *M*-desiderata, the constellation

$$\frac{S_e^A}{S_e^M}, \ldots, \frac{S_p^A}{S_p^M} \geq 1$$

becomes a categorical postulate for the development policy. We may assign to *M*-desiderata the value 0, and assign any value below the *M*-desiderata a negative value. The normative proposition then shall be made that any diminution of any negative value has a greater weight than the loss incurred by reducing any value of any *S*-desiderata. We call this type of utility ordering the *lexical* ordering principle.[8] This utility ordering implies a rigorous value judgement, but it is nevertheless a weak value judgement considering the implications when the *M*-desiderata are not reached. To some extent it may be argued that the proposition and a policy oriented towards absolute priority for the M-desiderata have no normative significance at all, since the close connection with the functioning of the systems gives it an objectivity of its own.[9]

Proceeding to the S-desiderata (the choice of additional variables and values above the M-level), we are confronted with intricate value problems. As a starting point we may take the suggested value $S^A/S^M = 1$, upon which the scale for measuring the welfare, utility, developmental performance, etc. is constructed. At $S^A/S^M = 1$, the supplementary utility derived from the desiderata equals 0. Various assumptions with regard to the value of the utility derived from a change in S^A/S^M from the minimum value on may be made.

A first possibility applies to the evaluation of the categories of desiderata. It includes as alternatives, (a) an egalitarian value judgement with regard to the welfare categories, namely the judgement to apply the same welfare weights to all categories, or (b) the pursuit of an inegalitarian line by applying different welfare weights to different categories. Value judgements will always be implied in some way or other when assigning welfare weights. The frequent heterogeneity of the welfare categories entails judgements which can usually not be made on the plane of 'pure objectivity' but include the value judgement of the comparer(s). The leanings may be towards either (a) or (b), granted value judgements are not stated explicitly anyway in favour of either (a) or (b). The second possibility pertains to the change in utility, given an increase in S^A. The marginal utility may (a) decrease as the amount of welfare entities obtained increases, or (b) it may remain constant. Increasing marginal utility is ruled out (a basically sound assumption of economic theory).

The third dimension refers to the social distribution. Since humans live in social contexts (family, community, nation, etc.), a distributional judgement with regard to the distribution of utility among the members constituting social contexts is required. The entire set of possible distributional schemes can be conceived within the two border values of (a) a totally egalitarian and (b) a totally inegalitarian distribution, where in the case of (a) all members would receive the same amount of utility while in (b) only one single individual or group would receive utility while all others would not receive any utility.

The validity of the theoretical statements will *ceteris paribus* depend on the empirical scope of which the theoretical statement is a generalisation. In the so-called 'new welfare economics', theoretical statements about 'reality as such' have been attempted. Given the claim for general validity, the statements are empirically void. The theory posits conjectural choices among hypothetical alternatives by freely-choosing economic agents (consumers, governmental agencies, etc.). Any further substantiation is effectively blocked by the assumption that any further statement will depend on a value judgement. Since scientists *qua* scientists are not allowed to make value judgements, any further theoretical statement cannot be advanced. That the missing theoretical content was due not to the impermissibility of making value judgements but rather to the empirical scope's being too broad to be relevant for meaningful theorising was not considered a worthwhile reflection.

For the sake of relevance, it is desirable to approach welfare from an empirical-historical angle. This will have far-reaching theoretical implications. If the empirical-historical scope narrows (as suggested in this study), the claim for validity narrows. Conversely, what may have been considered to depend on a mere value judgement in a general context may attain objectivity in a narrower context. For instance, it may be expected that people in a specific historical context, say at a level of average income X, with a socio-economic structure Y, and ecological conditions Z, will reach agreement about what their consumption patterns, their needs, desires, etc. are. This does not imply that value judgements would not play any role in determining the needs, desires, etc. It simply means that there is an objective basis underlying those value judgements. It would certainly imply a value judgement to overlook this fact. The objectively ascertained historical context will have the greater theoretical significance the closer the society referred to is to the subsistence level (where the satisfaction of physical needs is of primary importance).

Hence, it is theoretically meaningful to start with the analysis of the empirical-historical contexts, and then to proceed to the problem of choice. The latter must be conceived within the former; and not the opposite way. This will lead to substantiated statements (also) about welfare. There will still be a value-loaded choice problem. But it will be conceived within a specific empirical-historical context which allows objective generalisations about values—previously assumed to depend solely on subjective-arbitrary judgements reflecting the specific 'state of consciousness', psychic property, ethical beliefs, ideological leanings, etc.

The empirical approach to welfare receives its justification also from the side of policy-making. Departing from the formal apparatus of modern welfare economics and the body of empirically void hypotheses it propounds, a rational foundation for development policies and strategies is necessarily lacking. If not the social scientists, who shall develop criteria which allow an 'efficient', rational, and consistent choice of development desiderata and something like an 'optimal' development path? If the social-welfare function is conceived only as an automatically emerging result of undisputed consumer and producer rationality (confined to market contexts), then development becomes a fatally deterministic process. Development theory may perhaps describe and interpret it, but development strategy has ceased to exist (assuming that the absence of any strategy is not a specific type of strategy). In this context, finality has no normative-teleological meaning, merely at best, a probabilistic meaning (a less rigid form of determinism). As our study proceeds, it will become evident that the current processes in Asia do not represent the best of all conceivable worlds. The explicit formulation of a 'new direction' of development—of a set of substantiated normative propositions—is a prerequisite to indicate the better alternatives within the broad range of feasible alternatives.

A final note is needed on the measurement of the development performance. Generally, we do not aim at the formulation of criteria for measuring development *per se*, in order, say, to provide a framework for comparing the development performance of various countries or regions. The emphasis lies on description and explanation. Thus, quantification becomes relevant when it contributes to the exposition of the structure of causal interactions and the formulation of hypotheses.

The delimitation of the analytical task is itself not without implications for the possibilities of measuring the developmental performance. Suffice it to consider, first, that the formulation of social indicators crucially depends on a development theory which allows the rational choice of relevant indicators. Second, closely linked to the intended search for an empirically relevant welfare theory, theoretical statements about evaluations (minimum standards, etc.) to be applied as performance weights critically determine success and failure of any performance measurement. This is true for both the performance measurement directed towards the development of nation-states and (even more so) the performance measurement directed towards international comparisons.[10] Advances in the realm of performance measurement will depend on advances in the realm of theory. Intricate problems such as (still) non-comparable indicators due to differences in needs, the infeasibility of quantifying certain aspects of life such as human freedom, etc., can be resolved (if at all) only on the basis of an improved theoretical understanding.

VI. SYSTEM LEVELS AND HIERARCHICAL DEPENDENCY

The minimum desiderata define the side conditions within which a developmental system is bound to operate. Nothing is yet said about how the system actually operates once the side conditions are given. The second proposition refers to the operation of the system. The total system is composed of various (sub-) systems of very different natures. Thus, there will be differences in the relationships among the systems because of differences between the systems. In the search for a general pattern describing the relationships, empirical evidence brings into focus the concept of system hierarchy. A system hierarchy can be defined as a structure which relates (sub-) systems to each other in a rule of dependency. Various system levels exist which constitute the hierarchical structure of the total system.

We classify the total-system—for reasons which will become clear as our discussion proceeds—into three system levels. They are respectively:

(i) macro-macro-level (M^{aa})
(ii) macro-level (M^{a})
(iii) micro-level (M^{i}).

(i), the M^{aa}-level, includes the systems S_c, S_n; (ii), the M^{a}-level, encompasses the systems S_e, S_s, S_p, S_t; and (iii), the M^{i}-level, the systems S_e, S_s, S_p.[11] Since the hierarchical ordering is in the direction of the sequence (i) → (ii) → (iii), we have a clear dependency ordering. The system levels are related to each other as

$$M^{i} \in M^{a} \in M^{aa}.$$

The 'laws' of the M^{aa}-level are the 'laws' of the M^{a}-level, but not vice versa; and the 'laws' of the M^{a}-level are those of the M^{i}-level, but not vice versa. The 'laws' of the lower level are bound to be effective within the context of the 'laws' of the higher level, and consequently we may conceive the former as sub-set of a set of a higher level.

What is, however, concealed by this notation is the fact that relationships among the system levels exist. Clearly, the property of hierarchical dependency of the system levels does not preclude causal interactions among all systems. The concept of hierarchical dependency must therefore not be confused with mono-causality of the system levels—a possibility ruled out in principle by our propositions about the total-system behaviour.

The political system S_p has been set apart from both the desiderata and the dependency structure. The rationale for this is that S_p has a dual nature. On the one hand, S_p denotes a set of political institutions and behaviour rules S_p^A; on the other hand, it denotes the decisions and actions of the members operating within this structured entity, S_p^B. The former element, S_p^A, constitutes a set of endogenous variables within the total-system. Political institutions causally interrelate with the economic and social institutions. The latter element, S_p^B, must be viewed as an exogeneous variable, since freedom of action is a prerequisite for pursuing a strategy. The proposition of treating S_p^B as an exogeneous variable is one of the most decisive differences between the classical political economy and any modern strategy approach. The classical writers confined the state to minor functions which hardly deserve the notion of a strategy in the modern sense. In less-developed countries, and specifically in Asia today, the government is not expected to be pushed by events but to purposefully influence the events—as, indeed, we have been assuming in our preceding discussion.

While we recognise a hierarchical dependency of the system levels, we do not assert that there is (or should be) a priority of goals, according to the system hierarchy—for instance,

$$D^{aa} > D^{a} > D^{i},$$

where D stands for the 'weight' given to the desiderata, and the $>$-sign would indicate a priority given to the goals of higher levels. Economics has long-assumed a priority of economic goals by treating, say, resource variables as the dependent variables without allowing for repercussions on and the impact of goals pertaining to the eco-system. Similarly, in reaction to the single-focused economic view, the eco-system approach has stressed the priority of the goals pertaining to the eco-system.

However, a minimal *anthropocentric* attitude seems to be advisable. Why should the eco-system goals have priority over the goals of other systems? To state an extreme position, a human or societal value can be attached to the eco-system only if humans or the society exist at all. If we argue in terms of dependency of the goals, we will attach minimal values to the variables of the M^{aa}-level, since a threatening of the M^{aa}-level will also threaten variables of the M^{a}-level. But equally we can say the minimal values must also be assigned to the variables of the M^a-level since, for instance, nutritional intakes below subsistence level will jeopardise the existence of the people, and thus all subsequent levels of the total system—at least, from a human perspective. Our approach is anthropocentric in the sense that we assign minimal values or minimum desiderata to all systems.

The grouping of the systems into system levels allows us to classify the various approaches to development. According to the emphasis given to a specific level, the definition, meaning, purpose, performance evaluation, measurement, etc., suggested in the approaches will differ widely. From an ecological perspective, development will be viewed as processes, activities, etc., in accordance with the ecological laws.[12] From an M^a-level perspective, development will be understood as desired changes in the structure and levels of productive and consumptive activities, changes of socio-economic institutions, etc.[13] Approaching development mainly from the M^i-level, development stands for the full realisation of the human potential.[14]

There is no reason to abandon our holistic approach to development. The above approaches can be integrated in some way or other into our approach. As far as development theory is concerned, a broader scope is useful for bringing into analytical perspective all relevant causal interactions. As far as development strategy is concerned, a holistic view works against the narrow-mindedness and the pursuit of vested interests of politicians, bureaucrats, and other powerful social groups.

PART TWO

Population Dynamics in a Finite World

5 Basic Causal Linkages

Figure 5.1 provides a first clue to the causal interactions between the M^{aa}- and M^{a}-levels. The M^{aa}-level, designated by area A, shows the ratios between population P and the eco-variables land N, non-renewable resources R, and carrying capacity of the environment C. The impact on the ecosystem S_c by population P is expressed by the aggregate ratio P/S_c. The link to the M^{a}-level, embracing area B, is given by $\bar{A}$ and k. $\bar{A}$ stands for average consumption and production activities, and k is a coefficient which expresses the degree to which $\bar{A}$ and P affect S_c (see section on Social Choice in a Finite World, pp. 99–107). $\bar{A}$ and k depend on the M^{a}-systems S_e, S_s, and S_t. The overall eco-ratio $\bar{A}kP/S_c$ exerts feedbacks on the population system—for instance, the Malthusian food-population feedback. The overall eco-ratio exerts, furthermore, feedbacks on the M^{a}-system—for instance, responses to counter the Malthusian threat or adapting production and consumption activities to changed environmental and natural-resource conditions. To some extent, the eco-variables N, R, and C may be altered by policies (as denoted by the broken lines from the systems S_e, S_s, and S_t)—for instance, intensification of new resource recoveries, etc.

Given finite magnitudes in the ecosystem, any increase in number or change in the structure of population will determine changes in the ratios in the M^{aa}-level. Though causally interlinked, this relationship must be distinguished from the 'direct' link between population and the M^{a}-variables as depicted by the links between S_n and S_e, S_s, S_t. The analytical distinction would not be noteworthy did it not shed light on

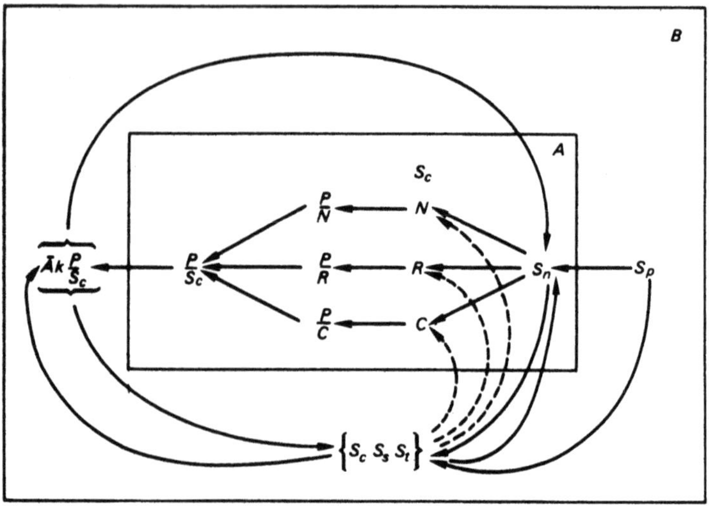

FIG. 5.1 *Causal interactions between M^{aa}- and M^{a}-levels*

S_c = Ecosystem
N = Land (arable)
R = Non-renewable resources
C = Carrying capacity of the environment
S_n = Population system (fertility, mortality)
P = Absolute population size
S_e, S_s, S_t = Economic, social, and techno-systems
$\bar{A}$ = Average consumption and production activities
k = Coefficient expressing impact of $\bar{A}$ on S_c (i.e. N, R, and C)
S_p = Political system
A, B = Areas embracing variables of the M^{aa}- and M^{a}-levels respectively

one of the shortcomings of traditional development theories: the inadequate theoretical and empirical treatment of the M^{aa}-level in general and of the population system specifically. Variables of the ecosystem have often enough been excluded. Emphasis in the early theoretical discussion was on economic variables and magnitudes, say on the rate of investment or the investment pattern conducive to an income-growth rate which would lift up the economy over the critical threshold necessary to sustain long-run development. There has been celebrated discussion as to whether 'balanced' or 'unbalanced' investments would more adequately serve this purpose. S_c-variables such as arable land, non-renewable resources, energy, or ecological factors being excluded, the term 'balanced' logically could not refer to a comprehensive concept of 'developmental balance' conceived in terms of ecological equilibrium, intertemporal distribution of non-renewable resources, and so forth. Similarly, the critique focused on the inadequacy of hypotheses expounded on the basis of the 'pure' economic model; behavioural premises were subject to increased empirical scrutiny and the theoretical relevance of additional hypotheses about investment behaviour, decision-making, or organising capacity was increasingly emphasized. The M^a-models, thus, have been extended. The systems and variables of the M^{aa}-level, however, did not receive the analytical attention they deserve as critical determinants of development. The confined analysis shaped the discussion also when reference was to single variables of the M^{aa}-level, this, again, being the case with regard to population. Among the two mentioned causal links of the population system, only the link to the systems of the M^a-level, mainly the economic and social systems, were analysed, while the 'indirect' link to the variables of the M^{aa}-level was often excluded.

The question arises why the indirect link has been excluded, or whether it should be included. We may assume that the successful development of the Western countries has much influenced the shift from the earlier Malthusian view to the modern approach. This historical experience demonstrated that the Malthusian resource link which in the long run kept the population at a subsistence minimum could be broken by technological and economic progress. A generalisation of this experience would be valid if the empirical values to be attached to the M^{aa}-variables of early Western countries and contemporary Asia were comparable. The stated shift in the analytical interest implies such an assumption. However, insofar as the relevant explanatory variables were excluded, an empirical assessment proving the validity of this hypothesis was *a priori* not feasible; insofar as the variables were treated as *ceteris paribus* assumptions, this proof was explicitly considered unnecessary and was not attempted. The theoretical integration of the M^{aa}-level as a principal constituent of development suggests that the above assumption be discarded in favour of the alternate assumption that there are significant differences in the empirical values and interactions of the M^{aa}-variables in 18th- and 19th-century Western countries and contemporary Asia.

6 Population Dynamics

I. CHARACTERISTICS OF POPULATION SYSTEM

Choosing population as a starting point, the question first arises why population should be conceived as a system. A justification may be simply that individuals relate to each other and that certain 'laws' about this behaviour can be established. Dealing with population, however, we are interested not in human behaviour as such but in the behaviour which affects changes in the number or composition of the population as a whole. The variables describing these changes are fertility, mortality, and migration. Restricting our view to fertility and mortality, it appears that straightforward 'laws' apply which are valid for all types of populations, of humans and other species as well as of non-biological phenomena with the same traits of birth and death.

We may define the change in total population as

$$\Delta P = B - D$$

where, migration being excluded, ΔP denotes change in population over a period of time, B births, and D deaths over that period of time. Relating this absolute change of population to the total population, we get the relative change, and multiplying by 100, we get the percentage change

$$r_p = \frac{100 \cdot B}{P} - \frac{100 \cdot D}{P}.$$

B/P is called the crude birth rate (CBR), D/P the crude death rate (CDR).

We know from the equation on p. 14 that the population system S_n or, specifically, the variables P, B, D, and r_p are determined by the behaviour of all (sub-) systems of the total-system

$$\frac{dS_n}{dt} = F_n(S_e, \ldots, S_n).$$

Empirically, we know that the level and structure of the socio-economic variables, the ecological conditions, the technology applied, the pro- or anti-natalist type of population policy pursued, all affect the behaviour of the variables of the population system. Moreover, the population system itself—the previous growth rates and resulting structures of age, sex, etc.—will, over time, determine the behaviour of the population system.

If we view the population system as being dependent only on the change of variables of the population system itself (excluding the other systems of the total-system), the behaviour of the population system could be described by

$$\frac{dS_n}{dt} = F_n(S_n).$$

Various shapes of this function are conceivable.[1]

An empirical corollary of the logistic curve is the demographic transition theory. This theoretical generalisation of European experience propounds that in a first phase of population growth, both birth and death rates are high, yielding a low growth rate. In the second phase, the death rate falls significantly while the birth rate remains stable, producing a high rate of relative change; in the third, the birth rate drops, reducing the population growth rate; and in the fourth phase, low birth and death rates establish a low growth and eventually zero population growth. According to the growth behaviour of r_p, we may classify the entire demographic process into two types of phases. The first type includes phases with low or zero growth rates. This type embraces the first and fourth of the demographic phases. As $r_p \rightarrow 0$, the system reaches a state of equilibrium ε. Depending on whether it pertains to the first or fourth phase, the equilibrium will have different values for the population and other related variables; we must consequently distinguish between equilibria ε_1 and ε_4. The second type encompasses the second and third phase with high growth rates. The second and third phase constitute the transition proper—the core of the transition theory. The typical shape of the logistic curve is governed by phases two and three. The whole sequence may be written as

$$0 = r_p^{\varepsilon_1} < r_p^a < \cdots < r_p^{k-1} = r_p^k > \cdots > r_p^z > r_p^{\varepsilon_4} = 0.$$

II. PRE-TRANSITION EQUILIBRIA AND ADJUSTMENTS

Population problems are usually viewed as pertaining to the second and third, the *transitional*, phases. Terms such as 'population explosion' dramatically express this view. However, as historical records show, the maintenance of the equilibrium ε_1 was based on a succession of crises and human suffering. Generally speaking, the crises occurred when

$$\frac{O_1}{P_1} > \frac{O_2}{P_2}, \quad \text{since} \quad \frac{O_1}{P_1} \approx e,$$

where O denotes agricultural output and e subsistence level. In this relationship, O was the crucial determinant. Bad harvests occurred in periodical cycles. Given bad transportation and stocks usually sufficient only for one year, a bad harvest over two successive years triggered the crisis. It was in the period t_2 that mortality rose and as a consequence P in the subsequent period t_3 fell, $P_3 < P_2$. Though fertility may have risen from t_1 to t_2 and the increase in P_2 might have put additional pressure on O_2, the crucial determinant in the ratio O_2/P_2 was the sudden decline in O_2 rather than a high P_2. The adjustment mechanism worked over the mortality rate. This was irrespective of whether the population had grown over the initial equilibrium level or not. Since the population at t_1 was at subsistence level, the crisis could, and actually did, occur even at stagnant populations, $P_1 = P_2$. A situation $P_2 > P_1$, due to a rise in fertility, aggravated the crisis but did not trigger it. The cause of death could be starvation as a direct result of the situation $O_i/P_i < e$. It could also be plagues and epidemics which hit the starvation-stricken and weakened population particularly hard at the times of the food crisis.

It appears that human suffering was sometimes greater in the case of famine unaccompanied by subsequent plagues, epidemics, and diseases, since in the latter case the drastic rise in mortality brought concomitant relief to the surviving population. The hypothesis is supported by comparative data on cases where a substantial part of the population died and cases where cannibalism broke out.[2] There seems to have been no positive correlation between the two. London lost 25 per cent, or at least 50,000, of its population in 1361, but cannibalism broke out in 1316. In Paris, people resorted to man-eating in 850, 873, 940, 1007, 1027–29, and 1033, but the great losses in population of 25 per cent and more were in the years 1418 and 1466. In India, famine repeatedly caused heavy death tolls; for instance in Bombay in 1689–90, in Bengal including Calcutta in 1769–70, and in the Baroda, Indore, and Rajputana states in 1899–1900; but cannibalism broke out in 941, 1022, 1033, and 1790–91. However, the question whether there is a positive correlation is indeed a marginal one. It pertains to the speed with which the 'death mechanism' brought the population in balance with the resource basis. What is crucial is the conclusion that recurrent crises force a population to stagnate at an equilibrium position, say, ε_1^*, where the asterisk stands for a specific level of resources (natural resources and technology) available to support a population P^*.

The conclusion suggests that population equilibrium has no intrinsic normative quality which would make an equilibrium *a priori* desirable. It may be desirable, or it may not. Consequently, the critical problem is not to conduct the population development into an equilibrium state *per se* but into an equilibrium state which is desirable.

III. DEMOGRAPHIC TURNING POINTS

Today all societies of the world, except perhaps a few tribal communities, have passed through the ε_1 phase and succeeded with the population 'take-off'. The causes for the rise of r_p have been the drop in mortality rates due to medical advances, persistently high fertility rates at levels similar to the ε_1 phase, and technical progress able to cope with the increased demand for food. This causal mechanism of the transitional phase is very much the same all over the world. Asian experience resembles that of the other less-developed regions, and the experience of both resembles that of the now-developed regions. There are, however, differences pertaining to (1) the timing of the turning point from the ε_1 phase to the transitional phase, (2) the values of P, r_p, or the time in which absolute changes are accomplished, and (3) the length of the transition period extending from the take-off point to the equilibrium state ε_4.

The population take-off of the European countries may be set between 1700–1800, coinciding with the emergence of the Industrial Revolution.[3] Though there are marked variations in the timing of the

TABLE 6.1 *World population at each half-century, 1750–1950, and at each decade 1900–70, distinguishing currently more-developed from currently less-developed regions*

	Population (millions)			Annual rate of increase since preceding date (per cent)*		
Year	World	More-developed regions	Less-developed regions	World total	More-developed regions	Less-developed regions
(a) by half-centuries						
1750	791	201	590	—	—	—
1800	978	248	730	0·4	0·4	0·4
1850	1262	347	915	0·5	0·7	0·5
1900	1650	573	1077	0·5	1·0	0·3
1950	2486	858	1628	0·8	0·8	0·8
(b) by decades						
1900	1650	573	1077	—	—	—
1910	1775	650	1125	0·7	1·3	0·4
1920	1837	682	1155	0·3	0·5	0·3
1930	2044	759	1285	1·1	1·1	1·1
1940	2267	821	1446	1·0	0·8	1·2
1950	2486	858	1628	0·9	0·4	1·2
1960	2982	976	2006	1·8	1·3	2·1
1970	3635	1090	2545	2·0	1·1	2·4

* Exponential rates.

Source: *Demographic Trends in the World and its Major Regions, 1950–1970*, prepared by the United Nations Secretariat World Population Conference, 1974, preliminary text, 60/BP/1; figures for 1750–1900 according to J. D. Durand, 'The Modern Expansion of World Population', *Proceedings of the American Philosophical Society*, vol. 3, no. 3, 22 June 1967. Figures for 1920–70 according to various issues of the United Nations Demographic Yearbook, with adjustments where needed for consistency. Figures for 1910 are rough interpolations, taking into account population losses due to war and epidemic in 1910–20.

TABLE 6.2 *The rate of population growth in Western European countries (annual average percentage increase)*

Country	1700–1750	1750–1800	1800–1850	1850–1910	1910–1940
England/Wales	0·2	0·7	1·8	1·6	0·5
France	0·1	0·6	0·7	0·2	0·1
Holland	0·7	0·8	0·8	1·5	1·7
Belgium	0·8	0·7	0·9	1·2	0·4
Sweden	—	0·6	1·0	1·0	0·5
Scotland	0·6	0·5	1·6	0·9	0·4
Ireland	0·6	1·1	0·6	0·6	0·1
Denmark	—	0·3	1·6	1·4	1·0
Finland	—	3·0	1·2	1·6	0·6
Norway	0·4	1·0	1·3	1·0	0·8

Source: N. Trantner, *Population since the Industrial Revolution: The Case of England and Wales*, p. 43.

transitions and in the values for r_p from one country to another, the general pattern shows remarkable uniformity (Table 6.2).

In most Asian countries the turning point from the ε_1 phase to the transitional phase may be set somewhere around 1800. The dating is even more unreliable, since census-taking was less systematic in Asia than in Europe (where church cadastres existed). The differences among the countries appeared to have been more distinct in Asia than in Europe (Table 6.3). While India's population growth rate stood between 1800 and 1850 at 1·1 per cent and the rate of the Philippines at 1·4 per cent, Thailand had zero population growth and Burma and Ceylon only half the rate of India and the Philippines. Java and Madura, where most of Indonesia's people were living, had the most burgeoning population, with rates at 1·8 per cent between 1800 and 1850, and 2·1 per cent between 1850 and 1900. In 1830, Java's population was about 7 million people; in 1840, 8·7; 1850, 9·6; 1860, 12·7; 1870, 16·2; 1880, 19·5; 1890, 23·6; and 1900, 28·4—an average increase during 70 years of approximately 2 per cent.[4] The population of Malaya and Singapore increased half a century later at a rate of 2·9 per cent, surpassing the population growth rate of Java and Madura by about 1 per cent. Inspection of the global data (Table 6.1) shows that some Asian countries (particularly those under early colonial rule) were forerunners in the population take-off among the less-developed countries. The average rate for the less-developed regions of the world of 0·4 per cent in

1800, 0·5 in 1850, and 0·3 in 1900 is exceeded by all Asian countries mentioned (Table 6.3). The rates of the Asian countries were already higher than those of Europe between 1850 and 1900, the period when Europe's demographic transition was at its peak. No European country reached in that period the 2·9 per cent growth rates of Malaya and Singapore or the 2·1 per cent growth rates of Java and Madura. England came closest, with a growth rate of 1·8 per cent.[5]

TABLE 6.3 *Broad estimates of population growth, 1800–1960, and of population size in 1800 and 1960, selected Asian Countries*

	Annual growth of population (per cent)				Size of population (millions)	
Country	1800–1850	1850–1900	1900–1950	1950–1960	1800	1960
Undivided India	1·1*	0·4†	0·9	1·8	125·0	524·3
Ceylon	0·6	1·2	1·3	2·4	1·6	9·9
Burma	0·6	1·1	1·2	1·4	(4·5)	21·5
Malaya and Singapore	1·0	2·9	2·2	3·2	(0·3)	8·5
Thailand	0·0	0·6	1·8	3·1	(6·0)	26·3
Vietnam, Cambodia, Laos‡	0·3	1·4	1·3	1·9	(7·0)	36·0
Philippines	1·4	1·4	2·1	3·1	(1·7)	27·8
Java and Madura	1·8	2·1	1·1		4·0	
Rest of Indonesia	0·6	1·0	1·9	2·0	4·5	93·5
Total	1·0	0·7	1·0	2·0	155	748

* 1800–1871

† 1871–1901

‡ The figures refer to the whole territory of the former French Indo-China, including North Vietnam.

Source: Gunnar Myrdal, *Asian Drama*, vol. 1 (Harmondsworth: Penguin Books) p. 435; for a listing of the sources used, see p. 1396.

After the turn of the last century, the population growth slowed down in the less-developed regions as a whole and in Asia in particular. While in 1850 the population growth-rate of the less-developed regions was 0·5 per cent, it stood in 1920 at 0·3 per cent. Middle South and South-East Asia's population grew in the two decades between

1900 and 1920 by an average rate of only 0·3 per cent (Table 6.4), a drastic decline when contrasted to the rates between 1800 and 1900 (Table 6.3). It appears that this growth pattern contradicts the notion of a continuous demographic transition. Indeed, empirical evidence suggests the hypothesis that Asia and probably most other less-developed countries (at least in average; see Table 6.1) experienced two or more turning points from a state near population equilibrium to the transition. Further historical inquiry into the population behaviour of that time may provide a differentiated picture on the changes in fertility and mortality rates and of the underlying causes. Our interest focuses on the second population 'revolution'; the first 'revolution' is relevant for the present demographic situation insofar as it produced a high absolute population for the second 'revolution' to start with.

TABLE 6.4 *Population of major Asian regions: average annual increase 1900–80* (%)

Region	1900–1920	1920–1930	1930–1940	1940–1950	1950–1960	1960–1970	1970–1980
Asia: total	0·5	0·9	1·0	0·8	1·9	2·2	2·3
East Asia	0·5	0·7	0·7	0·5	1·6	1·8	1·7
Mainland and other	0·5	0·6	0·7	0·3	1·7	1·9	1·7
South Asia	0·3	1·2	1·4	1·2	2·2	2·7	2·8
Middle South Asia	0·3	1·1	1·3	1·3	2·0	2·6	2·8
South-East Asia	0·3	1·6	1·7	1·0	2·8	2·8	2·9

Source: *Demographic Situation in Relation to Factors Effecting Population Change*, Second Asian Population Conference, Tokyo, 1972. (United Nations publication, POP/APC.2/BP/1, 1972) p. 33 (selected data).

The second demographic transition started not only with significantly higher absolute values; the relative changes which apply to these values also significantly accelerated. The turning point for both the less-developed regions as a whole (Table 6.1) and the Asian regions (Table 6.4) can be set at approximately between 1920 and 1930. The growth rate for all less-developed regions rose from 0·3 per cent in 1920 to 1·1 per cent in 1930, while it rose in the Asian countries from

0·5 per cent between 1900 and 1920 to 0·9 per cent between 1920 and 1930. The empirical picture more closely resembles the pattern of the less-developed regions when East Asia is excluded. Middle South and South-East Asia's growth rates increased from 0·3 per cent between 1900 and 1920 to 1·1 and 1·6 per cent respectively between 1920 and 1930. From the second turning point on, the population growth rates constantly increased up to the period 1970–80. The increase in the growth rate was particularly notable in the period from 1940–50 to 1950–60, when the growth rates for Middle South Asia approximately doubled and the growth rates for South-East Asia approximately tripled. In both areas, the growth rates further increased during the following two decades. In the decade 1970–80, Asia's population growth rate is assumed to have reached its peak. As a region Asia is assumed to have a rate of 2·3 per cent, Middle South Asia of 2·8 per cent, and South-East Asia of 2·9 per cent.

The rapid acceleration of the population growth rate deserves closer attention. The breaking-down of the growth rate is important for both the assessment of the population projection and for the evaluation of the possibilities of successfully pursuing a population policy.

The *specificum* of the Asian transition after the Second World War as compared to earlier transitions and to the transitions of the European countries appeared to be (1) an exceedingly rapid fall in death rates, and (2) little change in the birth rates. Within about two decades, the CDR fell in Burma by 19·0 per 1000 population, in India by 13·9, in Sri Lanka by 13·6, and in Thailand by 9·5, while the CBR increased in Burma by 3·2 births per 1000 population and in Thailand by 6·7, whereas in India it decreased by 7·7 and in Sri Lanka by 4·2 (Tables 6.5 and 6.6). The rapidity with which the decreases in mortality came about becomes apparent when we compare the death rates of a single Asian country with a European country and determine the period in which the same fall in mortality took place in Europe. A comparison between Sri Lanka and England (Table 6.5) reveals that in England it took about a century for the death rate to fall 9·4 from 21·4 to 12·0, while Sri Lanka's death rate fell 13·6 within little more than two decades, from 21·5 to 7·9 deaths per 1000 population. The birth rate in the same period fell in England from 35·2 births per 1000 population to 14·9, while in Sri Lanka it fell from 35·9 to 31·7. When England's birth rate of 31·4 in 1886–90 approached that of Sri Lanka in 1968, its death rate still stood at 18·9, whereas in Sri Lanka it was below 8·0. Before the Second World War England's death rate of 12·0 was still 4·1 higher than Sri Lanka's of 7·9 in 1968.

TABLE 6.5 *Birth rates and death rates in England and Wales, 1841–1938, and Sri Lanka, 1945–69*

England and Wales			Sri Lanka		
Period	Crude birth rate	Crude death rate	Period	Crude birth rate	Crude death rate
1841–45	35·2	21·4	1945	35·9	21·5
1846–50	34·8	23·3	1946	37·4	19·8
1851–55	35·5	22·7	1947	38·5	14·0
1856–60	35·5	21·8	1948	39·7	12·9
1861–65	35·8	22·6	1949	39·1	12·3
1866–70	35·7	22·4	1950	39·7	12·4
1871–75	35·7	22·0	1951	39·8	12·7
1876–80	35·4	20·8	1952	38·8	11·8
1881–85	33·5	19·4	1953	38·7	10·7
1886–90	31·4	18·9	1954	35·7	10·2
1891–95	30·5	18·7	1955	37·3	10·8
1896–1900	29·3	17·7	1956	36·4	9·8
1901–05	28·2	16·1	1957	36·5	10·1
1906–10	26·3	14·7	1958	35·8	9·7
1911–15	23·6	14·3	1959	37·0	9·1
1916–20	20·1	14·4	1960	36·6	8·6
1921–25	19·9	12·1	1961	35·9	8.0
1926–30	16·7	12·1	1962	35·7	8·5
1931–35	15·0	12·0	1963	34·4	8·7
1936–38	14·9	12·0	1964	33·2	8·8
			1965	33·1	8·2
			1966	32·3	8·3
			1967	31·6	7·5
			1968	32·0	7·9
			1969	31·7	—

Sources:

For England: N. Trantner, *Population since the Industrial Revolution: The Case of England and Wales*, p. 53; Crude birth-rates 1841–45 to 1876–80; D. V. Glass, 'A Note on the Under-Registration of Births in Britain in the Nineteenth Century', *Population Studies*, vol. 5, no. 1, 1951–52. All other statistics calculated from data on the estimated mid-year size of the population, births and birth rates, deaths and death rates given by B. R. Mitchell and P. Deane, *Abstract of British Historical Statistics* (London: Cambridge University Press, 1962) pp. 8–10, 29–30, 34–5, 36–7.

For Sri Lanka: Comparative Study of Mortality Trends in ECAFE (ESCAP) Countries, Asian Population Studies Series, no. 14, E/CN.11/1108 (Bangkok: United Nations, 1973) p. 71.

TABLE 6.6 *Changes in birth and death rates of selected Asian countries, 1940s to 1960s*

	Crude birth rate (per 1000)			Crude death rate (per 1000)		
Burma	37·2 (1948)	40·4 (1968)	+3·2	31·9 (1948)	12·9 (1968)	−19·0
India	28·0 (1945)	20·3 (1963)	−7·7	22·1 (1945)	8·2 (1964)	−13·9
Indonesia	26·5 (1952)	24·0 (1962)	−2·5	14·6 (1952)	11·0 (1962)	−3·6
Rep. of Korea	18·7 (1948)	17·1 (1966)	−1·6	9·0 (1947)	4·7 (1967)	−4·3
Philippines	28·9 (1946)	26·5 (1969)	−2·4	15·1 (1946)	6·8 (1969)	−8·3
Thailand	25·9 (1945)	32·6 (1969)	+6·7	16·5 (1945)	7·0 (1969)	−9.5

Source: *Comparative Study of Mortality Trends in ECAFE (ESCAP) countries*, Asian Population Studies Series, no. 14, E/CN.11/1108 (Bangkok: United Nations, 1973) pp. 58, 60–3, 70–2.

IV. TRANSITION SCENARIOS

The questions arise: (1) when will the turning point in r_p, $r_p^{k-1} = r_p^k$, set in, that is, the growth rates start declining? and (2) at what speed will r_p decline, or, alternatively, what will be the length of the time period between r_p^k and the beginning ε_4? Given the initial population P_k at t_k, the absolute population P at the end of the transition or at the beginning of ε_4 at the time t_4 will depend on (1) and (2).

Following the median variant of the UN projections (Tables 6.4 and 6.7), the turning points for r_p of Asia are assumed to be between 1960 and 1980. The mainland region, of which the major population is that of the People's Republic of China, is estimated to have reached the turning point in the 1960s with a maximum growth rate of 1·9 (Table 6.4). The growth rates for South Asia are estimated to start declining from 1970–75 on: Middle South Asia from a maximum rate of 2·8 and South-East Asia from a maximum rate of 2·9 (Table 6.7). The timing of the turning point for South Asia coincides with that of the less-developed countries as a group, which reach a maximum rate of 2·5 between 1970 and 1975. Following the UN projections, the present decade appears to be one of a demographic breakthrough. The phase

TABLE 6.7 *Total world population and annual rates of growth by region, 1965–2000 (medium variant)*

Area and region	Population (in millions)								Annual rates of growth (%)						
	1965	1970	1975	1980	1985	1990	1995	2000	1965–1970	1970–1975	1975–1980	1980–1985	1985–1990	1990–1995	1995–2000
World total*	3209	3632	4022	4457	4933	5438	5961	6494	2·0	2·0	2·1	2·0	1·9	1·8	1·7
More-developed regions*	1037	1090	1147	1210	1275	1336	1396	1454	1·0	1·0	1·1	1·0	0·9	0·9	0·8
Europe	445	462	479	497	515	533	551	568	0·8	0·7	0·7	0·7	0·7	0·7	0·6
Less-developed regions*	2252	2542	2874	3247	3658	4102	4565	5040	2·4	2·5	2·4	2·4	2·3	2·1	2·0
East Asia	852	930	1011	1095	1182	1265	1346	1424	1·8	1·7	1·6	1·5	1·4	1·2	1·1
Mainland region	713	779	840	919	992	1064	1134	1201	1·8	1·7	1·6	1·5	1·4	1·3	1·1
Japan	98	103	110	116	121	125	129	133	1·1	1·2	1·1	0·8	0·6	0·6	0·6
Other East Asia	41	47	53	60	68	76	83	91	2·5	2·5	2·5	2·4	2·2	1·9	1·7
South Asia	981	1126	1296	1486	1693	1912	2134	2354	2·8	2·8	2·7	2·6	2·4	2·2	2·0
Middle South Asia	665	762	875	1001	1137	1280	1424	1565	2·7	2·8	2·7	2·5	2·4	2·1	1·9
South-East Asia	249	287	331	380	434	492	550	608	2·8	2·9	2·8	2·7	2·5	2·2	2·0

* The total for the world, more-developed and less-developed regions have been slightly adjusted to take into account the discrepancies between international immigration and emigration assumptions.

Source: *World and Regional Population Prospects*, World Population Conference, 1974, Symposium in Cairo, 1973, preliminary text, 60/BP/3, table 1 (selected data).

of accelerating growth rates comes to an end; that of continuously declining growth rates sets in. The relative increase of Asia's population is assumed to slow down from 2·3 to 1·6 per 1000 in the period from 1970 to 2000. East Asia's population growth rate will fall from a comparatively lower rate of 1·7 to 1·1, while South Asia's growth rates will fall from 2·8 to 2·0 in that period. The decline in the growth rates is assumed to be 0·9 for both Middle South and South-East Asia. When compared to the less-developed regions as a group, the rates of South Asia show the closest resemblance. The growth rates slow down slightly faster in South Asia, but the rates in both groups are 2·0 in the year 2000.

The decrease in the rates of relative change does not preclude significant additions in the absolute number of people. The numerical additions keep increasing in Asia as a whole until 1980–90 (Table 6.9), whereas in Middle South Asia and South-East Asia, a decline in the absolute growth rate sets in only after 2000. The numerical increase in Asia as a whole between 1990 and 2000 is projected to be six times higher than the increase between 1900 and 1920. More striking are the regional differences. In the mainland and adjoining regions, the increase in the absolute numbers triple, while in Middle South Asia the absolute additions are twelve times and in South-East Asia eleven times higher when compared with the decades at the beginning and at the end of this century. Half of the additions to the world population between 1990 and 2000 will come from Asia. This growth pattern gives East Asia a population of 1·4 billion in the year 2000, with 1·2 accruing to the People's Republic of China and other mainland countries; Middle South Asia 1·6; and South-East Asia 0·6 billion (Table 6.7).

The length of the transitional phase depends on the initial levels of r_p and their rates of decrease. While the initial levels are known, the rates of decrease must be estimated. A decrease in r_p depends on a decrease in the birth rate, provided the death rate remains unchanged or falling. The birth rate is a function of (a) the fertility or net reproduction rate and (b) the age structure of a population. Projections include estimates of both. Estimates of (a) rest on assumptions about the response of population to family programmes (acceptor rate, etc.) and the impact of the socio-economic processes on fertility behaviour. Estimates of (b) are less conjectural, since both the present age structure, which is known, and the future fertility rates determine the future age structure.

The age structure of Asia's population carries the momentum of high birth rates (Table 6.10). In 1965, South Asia had 43 per cent of its population in the age bracket between 0 and 14 years—a direct result

TABLE 6.8 *Crude birth and death rates by region, 1965–2000 (medium variant)*

	Crude birth rates (per 1000)							Crude death rates (per 1000)						
Area and region	1965–1970	1970–1975	1975–1980	1980–1985	1985–1990	1990–1995	1995–2000	1965–1970	1970–1975	1975–1980	1980–1985	1985–1990	1990–1995	1995–2000
World total	33·8	33·2	32·1	30·9	29·0	27·0	25·1	14·0	12·8	11·6	10·5	9·6	8·7	8·1
More-developed regions	18·6	18·9	19·5	19·5	18·7	17·8	17·5	9·1	9·2	9·3	9·4	9·6	9·4	9·6
Europe	18·0	17·9	17·9	17·9	17·6	17·2	16·9	10·2	10·3	10·4	10·6	10·7	10·3	10·5
Less-developed regions	40·6	39·0	37·0	34·9	32·5	29·9	27·4	16·1	14·3	12·5	10·9	9·6	8·5	7·6
East Asia	31·5	29·1	27·0	25·1	22·8	20·9	19·4	14·0	12·3	11·0	10·0	9·2	8·5	8·1
Mainland region	33·0	30·1	27·8	25·9	23·4	21·4	19·6	15·1	13·2	11·8	10·5	9·5	8·7	8·1
Japan	18·0	18·6	18·1	15·9	14·9	14·9	15·4	7·0	6·6	6·8	7·5	8·4	9·0	9·8
Other East Asia	36·3	34·3	32·9	31·2	28·2	24·6	22·3	11·0	9·4	8·2	7·1	6·2	5·6	5·3
South Asia	44·3	42·9	40·0	36·9	33·7	30·0	26·7	16·8	14·8	12·7	10·9	9·4	8·1	7·1
Middle South Asia	44·4	42·9	39·8	36·6	33·3	29·6	26·2	17·2	15·1	13·1	11·2	9·6	8·3	7·3
South East Asia	44·2	42·6	39·9	36·9	33·7	30·1	26·7	16·1	14·1	12·1	10·4	8·9	7·7	6·8

Source: *World and Regional Population Prospects*, World Population Conference, 1974, Symposium in Cairo, 1973, preliminary text, 60/BP/3, table 2 (selected data).

TABLE 6.9 *Increases in the population of the world and Asian regions, 1900–2000 (in millions)*

Region	1900–1920	1920–1930	1930–1940	1940–1950	1950–1960	1960–1970	1970–1980	1980–1990	1990–2000
World total	209·9	208·7	226·4	190·7	495·9	653·6	832·1	989·7	1055·5
More-developed regions	110·6	85·2	62·8	37·1	118·3	114·4	119·7	126·8	117·0
Less-developed regions	99·3	123·5	163·6	153·5	377·6	539·2	712·5	862·9	938·4
Asia total	84·5	94·2	117·9	135·7	275·9	385·3	497·4	535·5	527·3
East Asia	56·1	37·8	43·0	56·7	115·8	144·4	165·2	161·2	152·3
Japan	11·5	8·5	7·5	18·2	18·2	10·3	12·8	8·8	7·7
Mainland and other	44·5	29·3	35·5	38·5	90·4	134·1	152·3	161·1	144·7
South Asia	28·3	56·5	74·9	79·0	155·1	240·9	332·2	374·3	375·0
Middle South Asia	21·5	37·7	51·3	56·8	109·2	173·5	239·2	263·8	263·8
South-East Asia	6·9	18·7	23·7	22·2	45·9	67·4	93·1	110·5	110·5

Note: Because of rounding, totals are not in all cases the sum of the parts.

Source: *Demographic Situation in Relation to Factors Effecting Population Change*; Second Asian Population Conference, Tokyo, 1972 (United Nations publication, POP/APC.2/BP/1, 1972) p. 31 (selected data).

TABLE 6.10 *Percentage age distribution of major areas, 1965, 1985, and 2000 (medium variant)*

Region	1965	1985	2000
More-developed regions			
0–4 years	9·5	9·3	8·4
5–14 years	18·6	16·9	16·5
15–64 years	63·0	63·4	63·7
65 + years	8·9	10·4	11·4
Less-developed regions			
0–4 years	15·9	14·8	12·3
5–14 years	25·7	25·0	22·8
15–64 years	55·1	56·4	60·3
65 + years	3·3	3·8	4·6
East Asia			
0–4 years	12·9	11·0	9·1
5–14 years	24·0	20·6	17·9
15–64 years	59·0	63·1	66·0
65 + years	4·1	5·3	7·0
South Asia			
0–4 years	16·9	15·5	12·0
5–14 years	26·1	26·5	23·3
15–64 years	54·0	54·6	60·5
65 + years	3·0	3·4	4·2

Source: *World and Regional Population Prospects*, World Population Conference, 1974, Symposium in Cairo, 1973, preliminary text, 60/BP/3, table 4 (selected data).

of the high growth rates of the past. The advanced age structures of East Asia still had 36·9 per cent of their population in the age bracket between 0 and 14 years as compared to the more-developed regions with 28·1 per cent. If the growth rates of the medium-variant projection are taken (Table 6.8), East Asia in the year 2000 will have 27 per cent of its population in the pre-school and school-age bracket, a decline of 9·9 per cent from 1965. However, the shift is mainly to the population of working age between 15 and 64, which now comprises 66 per cent as compared to 59 per cent in 1965. It follows that the 'fertility bracket' still encompasses a large part of the population, while the 'mortality bracket' comprises a relatively low proportion of the population. The age distributions for East Asia look similar to those of South Asia, although it follows from the lower growth rates in the past that they will have reached a more advanced state than the latter.

The question arises as to when the transition to the ε_4 phase begins. It should be clear from the preceding discussion that a net reproduction rate which under 'ideal' conditions would yield zero population growth does not do so under conditions of an unfavourable age structure. It may be asked what growth pattern would emerge if under the present age structure various hypothetical fertility rates were attained. Table 6.11 reproduces computations of hypothetical transitions under the assumption of a net reproduction rate of 1·0 at specified future dates. Only the hypothetical paths which correspond with the mentioned growth rates of the UN medium-variant projection are taken from the original tables. Mainland East Asia, which is predicted to have a 1·1 per cent growth rate in the year 2000, must according to the computations accomplish a net reproduction rate of 1·0 in 1980–85. This, at least, is the assumption applied in the UN projection. The ε_4 phase will be approached in the year 2075, with a maximum population of 1,362,006,000. The numerical addition from 1965–70 to 2070–75 would be, on the assumption of the mentioned rapid fall in the net reproduction rate, 589,004,000. For Middle South Asia a net reproduction rate of 1·0 is assumed to be reached between 2045 and 2050, and in South-East Asia between 2015 and 2020. The maximum populations in 2075 would stand at 2,893,000,000 and 838,100,000 respectively.

Projections are hypothetical paths. The critical question is to what extent it will be possible to curb fertility and accomplish the replacement levels. The answer is not straightforward, since there are numerous causal interactions and repercussions between the population growth 'mechanism' itself and the population and other development variables. Recall, for instance, the fact that any decrease in the fertility rate has a favourable impact on the age structure of the population in a later period—which will, in turn, affect the birth rates, in addition to the lower fertility rate in a subsequent period. The compound effects may occur in each of the periods anew and may be accumulated in an exponential fashion. The same reinforcing process works in reverse if the fertility rate is on the increase. Besides this clockwork mechanism of the population growth, various causal interactions between fertility of various periods and between fertility and mortality exist. Fertility depends on the level and the rates of change of a complex composite of socio-economic variables, and fertility may at the same time be a factor hampering favourable socio-economic

TABLE 6.11 *Hypothetical transitions in Mainland East, Middle South, and South-East Asia, net reproduction rates (NRR) of 1·0, various dates, 1980–85 to 2020–25*

Periods by period of NRR of 1·0	Population (in millions)*	Annual growth (%)†	Vital rates (per 1000)†		Life expectancy at birth (years; female)	Reproduction rates	
			Births	Deaths		Gross	Net
In 1980–1985:	*Mainland East Asia*						
1965–70	773·2	2·09	35·5	14·6	52·0	2·40	1·79
1980–85	940·9	0·90	19·4	10·4	59·0	1·21	1·00
1995–2000	1089·9	0·97	19·4	9·6	64·5	1·13	1·00
2015–20	1243·0	0·48	15·0	10·1	70·0	1·07	1·00
2045–50	1338·8	0·11	13·7	12·7	74·0	1·03	1·00
2070–75	1362·6	0·01	13·5	13·4	74·0	1·03	1·00
In 2020–2025:	*Middle South Asia*						
1965–70	735·1	2·67	42·1	15·4	50·0	3·00	2·17
1980–85	1069·6	2·50	35·6	10·6	57·5	2·47	2·01
1995–2000	1505·1	2·18	29·8	8·0	63·5	1·94	1·70
2015–20	2098·5	1·33	20·1	6·8	69·0	1·24	1·15
2045–50	2709·0	0·57	14·8	9·1	73·5	1·04	1·00
2070–75	2893·0	0·11	13·8	12·7	73·5	1·04	1·00
In 2000–2005:	*South-East Asia*						
1965–70	288·1	2·89	43·1	14·2	52·0	3·00	2·26
1980–85	415·8	2·32	32·7	9·5	59·5	2·18	1·83
1995–2000	549·6	1·59	23·1	7·2	65·5	1·37	1·23
2015–20	690·3	1·05	17·6	7·1	71·0	1·06	1·00
2045–50	817·7	0·30	14·0	11·0	74·5	1·03	1·00
2070–75	838·1	0·06	13·5	12·9	74·5	1·03	1·00

* Total populations estimated from projected female populations.

† Vital rates and percentage changes, female populations.

Source: Tomas Frejka, *Alternatives of World Population Growth* (New York: Population Council, 1973) monograph selected tables).

processes. The reciprocal effects are cumulative; a decrease in fertility may cause an increase in average output, and the latter may 'feed back' to fertility, causing an additional fertility decrease. A projection to be valid in a rigorous sense presumes a theory which encompasses all the relevant explanatory variables, exhibits all relevant causal links, and propounds meaningful hypotheses about them. Even if such a theory is granted to exist, a theory which serves for prescription would question the validity of the prediction, since the prediction of strategic intervention, such as various types of population policies, precludes the choice of alternative strategies which may, as development proceeds, prove to be more effective. The prediction then would again be hypothetical, not deterministic in any sense. The assessment ultimately must rest on empirical conjectures, subjective evaluation, and intuition, on which these can systematically be based. As predictive starting points the medium-variant projections serve the purpose. Whether the transitions can be completed before or after the time estimated does not affect the general conclusion that the absolute additions of the number of people and the maximum populations at ε_4 will be large compared to the populations at present. Though general, this is a crucial conclusion with regard to the further assessment of the M^{aa}-variables.

7 Population Densities

I. OVERALL DENSITY INDEX

Of the three sets of M^{aa}-ratios, the relationship between population and available land seems theoretically least problematical. Assuming that new land will not be discovered, land is fixed and changes in the ratio become a function of changes in population. The relationship can be written as P/N, where N denotes the land, or any other resource which is considered to remain fixed (see Fig. 5.1). Emphasis must be given to the fact that it is not the relative change of r_p but the change in the absolute value P, say $P_n - P_0$, which determines the change in the ratio. Thus, the increase from 86 to 154 per sq. km. in the average population density in Asia from 1970 to 2000 (Table 7.1) is a function of the increase in the absolute number of the population in that period (Table 6.7).

The overall density index allows some general inferences with regard to the magnitude of the changes in the ratios, while for the assessment of specific forms of population pressure it is not a meaningful measure. First, the index, being an average, excludes information about the range of data. Consider the density of the Republic of Korea with 601 per sq. km. compared with that of Laos with 25 per sq. km. in the year 2000 (Table 7.2). Second, within countries the population is unevenly distributed, due to a large extent to an uneven distribution of the resources or land-use ratios. Consider Indonesia, where about two-thirds of the population is clustered in Java, while the rest of the hundreds of islands are very sparsely populated. Third, the overall

TABLE 7.1 *Average population densities per sq. km., Asia, 1970–2000*

	Total population per km²		Rural population per km²
Year	Total area	Arable land	Arable land
1970	86	494	370
1975	96	554	406
1980	108	618	438
1985	120	687	466
1990	131	752	484
2000	154	884	500

Source: *Demographic Situation in Relation to Factors Effecting Population Change*; Second Asian Population Conference, Tokyo, 1972 (United Nations publication, POP/APC.2/BP/1, 1972), p. 49 (selected data).

TABLE 7.2 *Average population densities per sq. km., various Asian countries, 1970, 1980, and 2000*

Country	1970	1980	2000
Burma	41	52	78
Ceylon	192	243	337
China, People's Republic of	79	93	121
China, Republic of	390	484	626
Hong Kong	4168	5314	6735
India	170	220	331
Indonesia*	64	85	137
Japan	280	315	359
Korea, Democratic People's Republic of	115	151	228
Korea, Republic of	326	415	601
Laos	13	16	25
Malaysia	32	43	66
Nepal	80	100	151
Pakistan	145	202	313
Philippines	127	180	308
Singapore	3508	4408	5922
Thailand	70	97	156
Vietnam, North	133	162	236
Vietnam, South	103	125	185

* Data related to agricultural and arable land, excluding West Irian.

Source: *Report* and *Selected Papers* of the Regional Seminar on Ecological Implications of Rural and Urban Population Growth, Asian Population Studies Series, No. 10 (Bangkok: United Nations, 1971), p. 45 (selected data).

TABLE 7.3 *Average population densities per sq. km., selected Asian countries, 1970–2000*

Country	Year	Total population per km²			Rural population	
		Total area	Agricultural land	Arable land	Agricultural land	Arable land
China, People's Republic of	1970	81	268	702	204	532
	1975	88	292	763	216	564
	1980	95	316	827	227	593
	1985	103	343	898	236	618
	1990	109	364	951	237	619
	2000	123	409	1069	239	625
India	1970	170	321	347	257	278
	1975	194	366	396	288	313
	1980	220	415	449	315	341
	1985	247	467	506	336	364
	1990	275	519	562	353	382
	2000	331	625	677	356	386
Indonesia	1970	64	951	1147	781	943
	1975	74	1101	1328	886	1069
	1980	85	1266	1527	978	1180
	1985	97	1442	1739	1055	1273
	1990	110	1644	1983	1124	1356
	2000	138	2054	2478	1233	1487
Philippines	1970	127	405	446	277	304
	1975	151	482	530	318	350
	1980	180	575	633	360	396
	1985	213	681	749	401	441
	1990	245	781	859	430	472
	2000	308	984	1082	459	504
Korea, Republic of	1970	326	1372	1384	823	830
	1975	368	1548	1561	874	882
	1980	415	1745	1760	924	932
	1985	466	1963	1980	940	948
	1990	511	2150	2169	927	935
	2000	601	2529	2551	872	880
Laos	1970	13	187	373	158	317
	1975	14	213	426	179	358
	1980	16	244	488	200	401
	1985	19	278	556	225	451
	1990	21	310	620	243	486
	2000	25	374	749	281	561

Source: *Demographic Situation in Relation to Factors Effecting Population Change*, Second Asian Population Conference, Tokyo, 1972 (United Nations publication, POP/APC.2/BP/1, 1972), pp. 50–2 (selected tables).

TABLE 7.4 *Land utilisation in Asia (total and per capita) in 1970*

Sub Regions	Land area		Arable land		Permanent meadows and pastures		Forested land		Other land	
	Total mill. hect.	*Per capita* hect.	Total mill. hect.	*Per capita* hect.	Total mill. hect.	*Per capita* hect.	Total mill. hect.	*Per capita* hect.	Total mill. hect.	*Per capita* hect.
Total Asia	2663·0	1·3	458·8	0·2	488·8	0·2	528·5	0·2	1186·9	0·6
South Asia	442·2	0·6	197·1	0·3	16·2	—	72·8	0·1	155·1	0·2
East and South-East Asia	445·6	1·4	71·0	0·2	17·2	0·1	278·1	0·9	79·3	0·2
Japan	37·0	0·4	5·5	0·1	0·9	—	25·6	0·2	5·0	—
China	956·1	1·1	110·3	0·1	177·0	0·2	76·6	0·1	592·2	0·7

Source: *Population and Food Supply in Asia*, Second Asian Population Conference, Tokyo, 1972 (Background Paper, FAO/ESS/72/Misc. 4, Rome, 1972), table 8 (selected data).

ratio does not provide information about the quality of the land and the various forms of land-use. Generally, the index can be made more meaningful by dissecting the values in the denominator and numerator. The denominator can be classified according to its use—for instance, into habitable versus unhabitable land, rural versus urban, and arable versus nonarable land (Tables 7.3 and 7.4). The numerator can be broken down to its 'structural' criteria—age structure, sex composition, and sectoral distribution. Population pressure is then defined as an increase in one of the sub-ratios in the context of specific overall conditions.

II. DISPERSION: SIMULTANEOUS TRENDS TOWARDS URBANISATION AND RURALISATION

The distinct features of the population dispersion in Asian countries are the rapid increase in the urban areas relative to the rural areas and the rapid absolute increase in both areas. In Asia as a whole, the urban population is expected to increase from 25 per cent to 43·5 per cent of the total population between 1970 and 2000, with the rural part decreasing concomitantly (Table 7.5).

TABLE 7.5 *Population estimates and projections, Asia, 1970–2000 (total, urban, and rural)*

	Population (in thousands)								
			Urban			Rural			
Year	Total	Average increase (%)	Number	%	Average increase (%)	Number	%	Average increase (%)
1970	1975537	—	494461	25·0	—	1481076	75·0	—
1975	2214190	2·3	589519	26·6	3·7	1624671	73·4	1·9
1980	2472908	2·2	720538	29·4	4·1	1752370	70·6	1·5
1985	2748696	2·1	886983	32·3	4·2	1861713	67·7	1·2
1990	3008661	1·8	1074653	35·7	3·9	1934008	64·3	0·8
2000	3535692	1·6	1537012	43·5	3·6	1998680	56·5	0·3

Source: *Demographic Situation in Relation to Factors Effecting Population Change*, Second Asian Population Conference, Tokyo, 1972 (United Nations publication, POP/APC.2/BP/1, 1972), p. 55.

In the urban areas the relative rates of increase stand at a strikingly high rate of 3·7 per cent in 1975, further increase up to a maximum of 4·2 per cent in 1985, and still stand at 3·6 per cent in the year 2000. While in the early phase the growth rates apply to the relatively small urban section of the total population, in the year 2000 the 3·6 per cent relative rate of change applies to 43·5 per cent of the total population. The present urban growth rates produce the future urban problem. Even a rapid decrease in the urban growth rate two decades from now would yield large absolute increases in the population of the urban areas. In rural areas the situation is the reverse. The comparatively low rate of increase of 1·9 per cent in 1975 applies to 73·1 per cent of the total population, which yields a large absolute increase in the rural population. However, because of the constant decrease in the growth rate of the rural population, not only the lower growth rate of 0·3 per cent but also, as a result of the preceding relative increases, a smaller proportion of the total population of 56·5 per cent determines the absolute increase in the year 2000. Given approximately the same initial values of the urban and rural populations in the year 2000, the twelvefold value of the relative rate of change in the urban areas lends support to the hypothesis that the huge population problem is mainly an urban problem.

The salient feature, however, of the urban-rural transformation of Asia is the high rate of increase in both areas. Viewed against this fact, the increase in the rural population, although decreasing, appears to deviate more from the historically known patterns of transformation than the high urban rates. In Europe during the 19th century, rural populations fell both in relative and in absolute terms (Table 7.6). In 1851, 48 per cent of England's population was rural, while it was 22 per cent in 1911. The absolute number decreased from 9 million to 8 million in that period. Similar, although not so distinct, was the decrease in the rural population in France and Germany. Inversely, the urban population increased by 20–30 per cent, and the absolute urban populations doubled or tripled in the European countries in the period 1851–1911. Because of the persisting population increase, Asia has the worst of both worlds. The people living in urban areas will triple in half of the time, while the number of people living in rural areas still will increase by 35 per cent (Table 7.5). Thailand, Indonesia, and the Philippines will have annual rates of increase for the urban population of 4–6 per cent from 1970 to 2000, but the rural population will still approximately double in that period.

Assessing the welfare impact, the increasing densities will adversely affect psychic well-being, determined as it is by adequate living and recreational space. In cases where the negative effects can be compensated for by improved socio-economic conditions, such as improved housing and public utilities, the negative effects will be on the diminished provision of resources for the production of other commodities. In most cases the density effects on welfare cannot be mitigated by increasing socio-economic development, since space is *qua* space a welfare entity which cannot be improved by better provision of other commodities. The welfare derived from this variable can be improved only, *ceteris paribus*, by decreasing the density. Given high and increasing densities in all sectors of the economy the situation is more or less one of a zero-sum game where benefits in one sector presuppose losses in another. Irrespective of the impact on socio-economic development, decreases in the population growth rate will have a favourable effect on welfare.

TABLE 7.6 *Urban and rural populations in selected European countries, 1850–1911 (figures rounded off)*

Country	Years	Total population (in millions)	Rural population		Urban population	
			(millions)	(%)	(millions)	(%)
England and Wales	1851	18	9	48	9	52
	1881	26	8	31	18	69
	1911	36	8	22	28	78
United Kingdom	1851	26	14	52	12	48
	1881	33	12	37	21	63
	1911	46	13	27	33	73
Germany	1871	41	26	64	15	36
	1891	49	23	47	26	53
	1911	65	26	40	39	60
France	1851	36	27	75	9	26
	1886	38	24	64	14	36
	1911	40	22	56	18	44

Source: J.-P. Rioux, *La Révolution industrielle, 1780–1880* (Paris: Éditions du Seuil, 1971), p. 148 (selected data).

8 Long-Run Capacity of Agriculture

I. COMPARATIVE DYNAMICS: 18TH- AND 19TH-CENTURY EUROPE AND CONTEMPORARY ASIA

Already, broad empirical contours of early Western and contemporary Asian agricultural development provide sufficient evidence to support the hypothesis of unfavourable levels and changes in the ratios of the M^{aa}-variables of the Asian as compared to the Western countries.[1] Europe, for instance, in the 18th and 19th centuries had sufficient land 'to start with'. Extensive cultivation as a means of enhancing agricultural output was feasible and, in fact, was an important factor in securing sufficient food for the additional population. Land clearance continued in Eastern Europe, where most areas did not reach saturation, as far as population at the prevailing level of technology was concerned, until late in the 19th century. Only since the beginning of the present century has land clearance ceased to be of major importance as a means of enhancing agricultural output.[2] In Western Europe the extensive method of land cultivation which was characteristic of the two-field system offered large reserve capacities for increases in agricultural output once the shift to the three- and four-field system was accomplished. In France, England, and Saxony in 1760, half of the land cultivated had to be sacrificed as fallow land under the two-field system. With the subsequent change to the three- and four-field system, the percentage of fallow land constantly fell over the following 150 years to an intangible level (Table 8.1). In East-Elbian Prussia from 1815 to 1864, the area under cultivation more than

TABLE 8.1 *Arable land used as fallow land, selected European countries, 17th–19th centuries*

France		England		Saxony	
Period	% of fallow land	Period	% of fallow land	Period	% of fallow land
1760	50	1812	20	1657	38
1790	40	1831	14	1713	32
1840	27	1866	6	1760	34
1852	20	1891	3	1800	3
1892	13				

Source: Bairoch, Paul, 'Le rôle de l'agriculture dans la création de la Sidérurgie moderne', *Revue d'histoire économique et social*, 1966, no. 1.

doubled, from 5·5 to 12 million hectares, while in Posen the share of arable land cultivated rose in the same time span from 11·9 per cent to 60·6 per cent, and in Pomerania from 15·5 per cent to 52·3 per cent of the total land area.[3] In Europe, at the time when land clearance was still feasible, the production functions could be shifted upwards (due to improvements in agro-technology, transportation, communications, etc.), yielding a rapidly increasing surplus which supported industrial development—itself, in turn, of major importance in sustaining the growth of the agricultural surplus (see Part 3, Ch. 14 and 15). Around 1900, when land clearance ceased to be of major importance, the accumulated advances in productivity easily compensated for the exhaustion of reserves of virgin land or the increasing density of population per arable land unit. Population growth had lost its momentum, and the question of whether the law of diminishing returns would have affected the agricultural return in Europe ultimately became an academic one.

A prediction of the impact of the M^{aa}-variables on agricultural performance in Asia depends naturally on more imponderable factors than the historical description of the respective traits of European agriculture. Let us, first, focus again on the feasibility of further extending the proportion of cultivated land to arable land or of arable land to total land available, and, second, discuss the prospects of increasing the returns per unit area from the presently and newly cultivated land. To put the discussion into proper perspective, the specific climatic and soil conditions upon which Asian agriculture is based must first of all be duly stressed. Asia belongs climatically to the tropical or sub-tropical climate, except for some highland areas, northern China and northern Japan.[4] The seasons are determined by the frequency of rainfall rather than by variations in temperature. The average monthly temperatures vary between 60° F and 80° F. In contrast, the monsoon rains are unevenly distributed, with peaks usually in the summer months and little rain the rest of the year (Fig. 8.1).

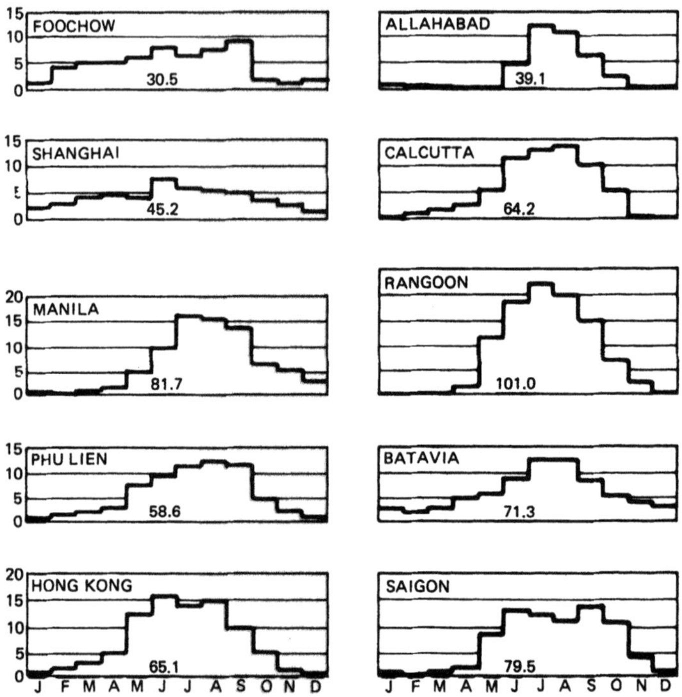

FIG. 8.1 *Seasonal distribution of rainfall at selected stations in Monsoon Asia (in normal inches)**

* Basic data from World Weather Records (Washington, DC: Smithsonian Misc. Coll., vol. 79, 22 Aug. 1927, and vol. 90, 18 May 1934); for China, from G. B. Crassey, *China's Geographic Foundations: A Survey of the Land and its People* (New York: 1934).

[a] Note different arrangement of months, applying to Batavia only.

Source: Wickizer and Bennett, *The Rice Economy of Monsoon Asia*, Food Research Institute, Stanford University, 1941.

The soils are acid aluminium- and iron-bearing soils, except those of northern China and western India, which are basic, that is calcium-bearing, soils. The crop best suited to the climatic and soil conditions of monsoon Asia is rice. Rice endures the seasonal variations of rainfall and heat, resists tropical diseases remarkably well, and can be stored without losses in the hot and humid climate. Rice prefers the acid or aluminium- and iron-bearing soils prevalent in monsoon Asia, while alternative crops such as wheat prefer basic soil.

The quality of the tropical and sub-tropical soils differs widely. At one extreme there are the inherently infertile laterised and podzolised soils, at the other the alluvial and recent volcanic soils which are rich in mineral and organic compounds (Fig. 8.2).

The differences in the quality of the soils have a decisive impact on the method of cultivation. In the areas with laterised and podzolised soils, shifting cultivation—a method where the bush is slashed and burned, and after a harvest or two the soil is allowed to revert to jungle again to restore the organic and mineral fabric necessary to grow plants—is most common. In the areas with alluvial and volcanic soils, transplanting—a method where young rice shoots are taken from a nursery and set out in a larger field to grow—is dominant (Fig. 8.3).[5] The type of agriculture in less-fertile areas is typically extensive, while in the fertile areas it is intensive; for instance, in Borneo, where the soil is podzolised, shifting cultivation is dominant, while in Java, where the soil is rich in mineral and organic compounds, transplanting prevails. Not only do the soil conditions determine the type of cultivation, but, in turn, the type of cultivation and the intensity with which it is applied have a significant impact on the long-run soil fertility. The relationship of reciprocal causation is particularly apparent in areas where the soil is already inherently infertile and shifting cultivation must be applied. If the fallow periods are shortened because of increased food requirements, the soil may not have the time to build up the necessary mineral and organic compounds, and a process of leaching followed by rapid laterisation or podzolisation may set in. The decrease in the returns from the soil will increase the necessity of further shortening the fallow period, further increasing the laterisation and podzolisation processes, and further decreasing soil fertility. Both population pressure and the cumulative repercussions from the soil reactants promote a process of accelerated soil erosion which in many cases does irreparable damage to the ecological balance. In parts of the Philippines, Borneo, and southern China, the dead soil to a large extent stems from the breaking of the ecological rhythm.

FIG. 8.2 *Soil regions*

Source: J. E. Spencer and William L. Thomas, *Asia, East by South: A Cultural Geography* (New York: Wiley, 1971), p. 240.

In view of the ecological equilibrium required to sustain plant life in the tropics, the extension of cultivated land—as a means of increasing agricultural production—appears to be highly risky in terms of sustained soil fertility and in many cases unfeasible from the beginning

FIG. 8.3 *Major locations of transplanting and shifting cultivation*

Source: Lucien M. Hanks, *Rice and Man: Agricultural Ecology in South-East Asia* (Cornell University Press: 1972), p. 26; based on J. E. Spencer, *Shifting Cultivation in Southeastern Asia.*

in view of the foreseeable consequences. The argument pertaining to the shortening of the fallow periods applies *mutatis mutandis* also to the clearing of virgin forests, which might be considered as reserves for extensive cultivation. In the tropical climate, with its torrential rainfall succeeded by dry heat and winds, a precarious ecological equilibrium exists among various types of vegetation. It seems that clearing the virgin rain forests may not only yield low marginal returns, but also, above all, impair the fertility of land already cultivated owing to changes in climate and increased soil erosion.[6] Clearing the tropical rain forests will be ecologically most disastrous where the forests *qua* commodity timber are slashed, and the denuded land is not reforested or agriculturally used. To remain fertile, tropical soil of the non-alluvial or volcanic types requires plants and trees constantly to return to the soil to restore fertility; if this process is interrupted by forest denudation, the consequences in the form of laterisation and podzolisation are the same as in the case where the fallow periods are not adjusted to the rhythm the soil needs to restore its organic and mineral basis. If the increasing nutritional demands in Asia are to be met in the long run, maintaining the substance of the potentially arable land clearly constitutes the ecological minimum requirement.

Given the limitations in the extension of the cultivated area, the future increases in agricultural output will critically depend on the productivity gains of the already cultivated lands and, as such, on the fertility potential of the alluvial and volcanic soils. It is no mere accident that the fertile areas—like river valleys and deltas, and areas with recent volcanic soil—are densely populated, while laterised and podzolised areas are sparsely populated. Thus, Java contains about two-thirds of the Indonesian population on 30 million acres, whereas Borneo, with four times the area, has only a few percentage points of the total population. Seventy-five per cent of the soil of Java consists of fertile lavas, or colluvial and alluvial deposits derived from such lavas, while Borneo's soil consists of elder sedimentary rocks and podzolised earths which are inherently infertile.[7] Given the density differentials, most of the fertile land is already under cultivation and the densities per acre of cultivated land are high. Consequently, the assumption that little productivity can be gained by increasing agricultural labour per unit of the most fertile areas is sound. Reverting to our theoretical discussion (see Appendix 3), we may assume that in most fertile areas the hypothetical maximum output d^* can never be reached because the population employed in such areas is already beyond the density level D_y. Thus, even when the production functions are shifted upwards to the maximum function F_5, the marginal returns to labour (not of the technology-related inputs which induce the shift in the production functions) are bound to be increasingly negative.

The hypothesis is supported by the fact that water—the major natural 'intermediate' input factor—is critically scarce. Water is, naturally, intrinsically linked to the fertility of the soil. To produce a ton of rice, 4000 tons of water are needed.[8] Although the seasonal regime of rainfall suits the biological requirements of the rice crop well, the monsoon rains are subject to great and unpredictable variations, bringing floods in one year and droughts in another. Irrigation, drainage, and flood control are often prerequisites for the methods of broadcasting—the watering of settled fields in order to provide nutrients to the soil—and multiple cropping—an annual sequence of two to three crops grown on the same plot—and planting of high-yield varieties. Water, however, remains a scarce production factor in the tropics. The monsoon rains not only vary but also come in the hot summer season where the evaporation and evapotranspiration coefficients are as high as 30 per cent, restricting the actual use of the rain. The water supply is further aggravated in areas already less fertile, where the soil permeability shows a higher coefficient of surface run-off, which also may amount to up to 30 per cent of the total rainfall.[9] In short, water, as well as the carrying capacity of the soil, may constitute a critical limitational factor which precludes further intensification of cultivation.

II. POLITICAL AND SOCIO-ECONOMIC RESPONSES REQUIRED

A concluding evaluation of the productivity potential will depend on the provision of new inputs such as fertilisers, biological innovations (high-yield varieties), energy inputs, and mechanisation, as well as the willingness of the cultivators to adopt improved technologies (extension services, etc.)—all of which depend on the response of the economic, social, and political systems. Both sets of variables—the M^{aa}- and M^{a}-variables—are causally interrelated, and the assessment of either of these must remain highly tentative unless the reciprocal interactions are allowed for. If the impact of the density, climatic, and soil conditions on the future agricultural performance is analysed, the analytical endeavour cannot be directed towards a definite statement about the future agricultural potential, but rather towards outlining the changes in the M^{aa}-variables, and on the assumptions about the major responses which are required from the socio-economic and political systems to cope with the changes in the variables of the M^{aa}-level. Actual responses may or may not be forthcoming from the socio-economic system, affecting the outcomes and the conditions under which they are accomplished. The causal interactions such as changes in M^{aa}-variables and the response of the socio-economic and political systems can be viewed only as a process of continuous causal interactions. The initial hypotheses of a hierarchy among system levels nevertheless make it necessary and possible to evaluate the changes in the

M^{aa}-variables independently insofar as they constitute the 'conditional' or 'limitational' variables as a consequence of their belonging to an upper level of the hierarchy. The main conclusion to be drawn from the preceding discussion is that the changes in the variables of the M^{aa}-level affecting the ecological conditions of agriculture will require continuous efforts from the socio-economic and political systems if a satisfactory social-welfare function, i.e., minimum nutritional intake, is to be met. A discussion of these topics will constitute the theme of Part 3.

9 Non-Renewable Resource Basis for Industrialisation

I. NON-RENEWABLE RESOURCE SUPPLY CAPACITY AS A FUNCTION OF RESERVES AND POLITICAL-ECONOMIC POWER

The evaluation of feasible paths of industrial development is prejudiced by the preceding analysis, which has emphasised the importance of agricultural development. We shall depart from this postulate later when dealing with the socio-economic processes in the subsequent chapter. Here the question arises—on the plane of the M^{aa}-level—of what the conditions for industrialisation are in terms of availability of natural resources and carrying capacity of the ecosystem.

The distinction is usually drawn between renewable and non-renewable natural resources. As the preceding discussion has shown, the distinction is relative. Water is renewable but may be critically scarce. A non-renewable resource may be absolutely limited and, worldwide, be near exhaustion but not relevant for a country at its level or prospects of development, or it may be later supplanted entirely. However, the distinction is meaningful in a number of specific historical instances—this being the case in contemporary Asia. A high proportion of the exhaustible resources constitute unalterable input factors critical for industrial development.

As far as the renewable or non-exhaustible resources are concerned, land and water will become scarce relative to the increasing demand and, depending on the efficiency of the resource management, eventually set an upper limit to further development. The preceding discussion has stressed the impact of relative resource scarcity on agricultural development; but inasmuch as the overall supply of resources is scarce, the limitations naturally apply also to industrial development. The relative choice between the two sectors cannot meaningfully be treated in a formal way which would offer *a priori* conclusions, since different levels and structural features of the industrial development at specific resource conditions will differently affect the use and future supply capacity of the renewable resource basis. Technology may increase fresh-water supply, and it may also accelerate its use. A statement about the relative choice in resource distribution is feasible on the basis of the previous section insofar as the supply conditions of the agricultural sector will suggest a priority for agricultural development. A conclusive statement will depend on the type of industrial development, which may or may not promote resource-saving activities (substitution of resources by capital and labour) and new investment (irrigation systems, desalination of oceanic reserves, industrial production with little cooling water, etc.).

While renewable resources permit a development process to be sustained *ad infinitum* (although eventually at a maximum point), exhaustible resources do not have this intrinsic quality. By definition, their finite stocks are being exhausted as they are used. At any time t the stock available for future production X_t depends on the initial stock X_0 and the stock of resources already used up from the beginning of the production up to t, U_t,

$$X_t = X_0 - U_t.$$

The past resource-use U_t depends on the time span from the beginning of the resource extraction to t and the rate of extraction r in that period. X_0 being a constant, changes in X_t are determined by the time span and rate of past resource recovery. The rate at which X_t will be extracted depends on the assessment of X_0 (known reserves versus actual reserves) and the need for that resource (e.g. with possibilities of substitution) in the future. If the resource is recognised as a bottleneck for future production, r will tend to decrease (for further discussion, see sec. on Choice Criteria and Choice Variables, pp. 99–102). The length of the time span between the point of inflection of r and the final state of exhaustion of the resource will depend on the level and decrease of r. As stated in the discussion on the logistic curve, we have an initial phase where the resource recovery or the U_t-curve follows an exponential path, and a second phase where the path of resource recovery approaches an upper asymptote given by X_0; at period of exhaustion we have $X_0 \approx U_t$; $X_t \approx 0$.[1] (For an explanation of exponential and logistic growth paths see Chapter 6, fn. 1, pp. 307–308.)

The resource availability for a nation-state at time t until the exhaustion of the resource depends on the stock of global reserves X_t^Z and the capacity of the nation-state to secure a share of the global stock. The size of X_t^Z will depend on the initial stock of global reserves X_0^Z and the accumulated past resource consumption U_t^Z. For the regional distribution of X_t^Z between Asia and the rest of the world according to the actual consumption of or ability to compete for resources in the future, we have

$$X_t^Z = X_t^A + X_t^E,$$

where the letters A and E stand for Asia and the rest of the world respectively. The availability of resources for Asia may specifically be written as

$$X_t^A = u_0 - \int_0^t \dot{v}\, dt + x_0 - \int_0^t \dot{y}\, dt,$$

in simplified notation

$$= (u - v) + (x - y),$$

where u stands for the national resource reserves of Asian countries, v for accumulated resource exports, x for global resource reserves (Asia excluded) and y for accumulated resource use of the world (Asia excluded). Thus, the resource availability for Asian countries depends, generally, on the global resource reserves X_t^Z and, specifically, on the national resource basis u, as well as on the capacity to compete for resources of non-Asian countries and the economic necessity for the Asian countries to export resources. Both the distribution of stocks and of the political-economic power to control the stocks (purchasing capacity, bargaining power) determine the availability of resources for a nation.

II. ECONOMIC IMPLICATIONS OF 'DELAYED ENTRY' IN RESOURCE EXHAUSTION

For an assessment of the size and distribution of the global resource reserves, a distinction must be made between mineral resources and fossil fuels. As for mineral resources, neither the global stocks nor the stocks of the Asian region show signs of imminent exhaustion. This is true not only for metals abundant in the continental crust, such as iron and aluminium, but also for metals which constitute only 0·1 per cent or less of the continental crust, such as copper or lead. It has been estimated that the existing mineral resources are approximately 5 million times greater than the proven mineral resources.[2] Considering the nearly inexhaustible stock of mineral resources, the critical question does not appear to be one of the absolute size of the stocks but one of their economical recovery. Even when technical solutions are conceivable, the resource recovery may be infeasible in economic terms. A rich country may be able to extract resources with expensive technology; a poor country may not have this option. The stock of actual reserves in economic terms, therefore, shifts according to the capacity and willingness to pay the costs for the recovery of additional resources. The future costs for the resource recovery depend on the quality of the ores presently used and the rate of decrease in the quality of ores as the resources are extracted.[3] The grade of ores presently used is generally high; that of iron is about 60 per cent and that of aluminium about 30 per cent. The quality of the ores and the recovery costs can be expected to be inversely proportional to each other. To recover an amount of metal from ore which is, say, one-tenth of the former quality, ten times more raw ore must be mined at costs ten times the initial costs. Increased costs of recovery may be faced first in metals which are relatively scarce, such as copper, which constitutes only about 0·0058 per cent of the continental crust. The acceptable quality of copper would have to be reduced by a factor of 100 if ordinary rocks were to be used as raw ore, while for iron ore, ordinary rocks could be used as raw ore if the acceptable ore quality were lowered only by a factor of about 4.[4] Considering the amount of absolute existing reserves in relation to the demand for each metal, the future problem appears to be not one of absolute scarcity or the exhaustion at a foreseeable doomsday, but of the capability of a nation-state to pay a price for resources such as copper, lead, zinc, etc., which is likely to be a multiple of the present price.

Reverting to our *problemstellung*, the question arises as to what extent the developing countries of Asia will be affected by higher prices for mineral resources. The outcome will depend on the behaviour of the variables u, v, and $x - y$; in other words, on (1) the size of national reserves, (2) the need to export national reserves, and (3) the capacity to import mineral resources that are not available within national boundaries. Pertaining to (1), Asia may be expected to contain a portion of the world mineral reserves proportionate to its land mass. In terms of actual resource reserves for future consumption, she will be better off than other regions which have already consumed a comparatively large portion of their finite resource stock.[5] This will provide Asia with a 'cushion', delaying the eventual effects of price increases for mineral resources. The production figures are low, not only for abundant metals such as iron but also for scarce metals such as copper, lead, and zinc, where bottlenecks will first occur. The world production of copper in 1968 was 5,293,360 tons, while in the ESCAP region, excluding the People's Republic of China, it was 378,611 tons. For nickel ore the figure for world production was 483,000 tons as compared to 45,247 tons in the ESCAP region.[6] Generally, the presently low production figures for mineral resources give Asia a comparative advantage in terms of resource availability in the future.

Whether the advantage turns out to be also an economic one depends on (2), the necessity of exporting national resources in order to finance development and/or to secure decent current levels of consumption. Countries with a national resource basis are poor (as are those without a national resource basis), and there is the obvious need and willingness to use the natural riches as a means of financing development or, at least, of securing the minimum sustenance for a rapidly growing population. The production structures are historically based. They are usually biased in favour of mineral exports by the existing international division of labour and/or by the patterns inherited from the colonial past. The differentials in production costs between countries with high and low quantities of accumulated past recovery and resulting low and high qualities of remaining ores reinforce the existing exchange pattern and the reliance on mineral-resource exports. As production costs in the rest of the world tend to rise faster than those in Asian countries, the latter enjoy a seller advantage which suggests further reliance on those exports. Higher world price levels may diminish the export quantity, but the capacity of the industrialised countries to pay for the desired resources and the competitive structure of the world economic order have not, in the past, led to any effective curtailment of the mineral resource demand from the industrialised countries, and this trend is likely to continue into the foreseeable future. However, as development proceeds, the comparative advantage will gradually diminish. The costs of mineral-resource recovery will increase and establish a level of production costs and prices which will make it increasingly difficult for the developing Asian countries to secure the necessary resources for national development in the long run. While developed countries may be able to pay the price and to consume the resources at only slightly reduced rates, developing countries, among them naturally the poorest, may not be able to pay the price or bear the costs for the required resources, impeding their economic development. While exports of mineral resources may for the present permit increase in and improve the capital basis of an economy, the higher costs of resource recovery will impede the benefits from the increased and improved capital stock, and may possibly outweigh the former benefits. It cannot definitely be said which of the mineral resources will experience rapid increases in costs of recovery in a country. The present state of geological forecasting would make it a highly speculative undertaking, and the export demand is equally unpredictable since it depends on the feasibility of substituting mineral resources, on reshaping the world order and the complexity of exchange prices, and on the overall development of the industrialised countries—which is not amenable to meaningful forecasts for these countries themselves, much less for the Asian countries. What generally can be said is that the exports will shorten the time span in which national resources can be consumed at a cost similar to that of the industrialised countries when they underwent early industrialisation—making the development process for the former comparatively more expensive and some development paths possibly altogether infeasible.

The argument pertaining to (3) holds more directly if an Asian country does not have a national resource basis or relies on imports for at least some resources. The less-developed country is destined to consume $x - y$, a variable which explicitly takes account of the strong competitive position of the industrialised countries. At given world market prices, the industrialised countries will be able to more or less fully ensure their necessary share of y. Thus, the feasibility for the developing countries of consuming resources is largely determined by the global stock of resources and the demand from industrialised countries—and less by their own demand and bargaining position. This relationship may be obscured as long as world prices are still comparatively low and the developing countries can satisfy their resource demand at that price level. The restriction for the developing countries will nevertheless work as soon as this reserve margin is used up and prices start rising. In that phase the industrialised countries will be able to pay the price and safeguard the resources, while the developing countries will have to curtail their resource consumption and/or forego alternative consumption (which has high marginal utility and constitutes high opportunity costs). These theoretical considerations are supported by the empirical fact that the present resource consumptions of the industrialised countries and the developing countries stand in a relation of about 10 : 1, and that for the foreseeable future the resource-use follows an exponential path, indicating little likelihood of turning to the second phase of a logistic path.

III. ENERGY CONSTRAINTS, TIME PREFERENCE, AND RISK OF NON-CONVENTIONAL SOLUTIONS

The development of reserves and the consumption of fossil fuels as the second major category of non-renewable resources dramatically confirms the relevance of the preceding considerations. What is merely conjectural in the sector of mineral reserves has already been subject to lively experience in the sector of fossil fuels. Fossil fuels such as coal, oil, and natural gas were formed from living matter. The reserves are limited by the relatively short geo-genetic period in which the plant and animal transformation took place. The differences in quality are less pronounced than in minerals, and a 'stretching' of the final point of exhaustion by increasing the amounts of capital and labour expended on recovery is less feasible—although tar sands and oil shales offer a certain reserve 'cushion'. The present total reserves X_t^Z of coal are estimated at about $6–8 \cdot 10^{12}$ tons, that of petroleum at about $2 \cdot 10^{12}$ barrels (equivalent to $0{\cdot}35 \cdot 10^{12}$ tons of coal) and that of natural gas at about $157 \cdot 10^{12}$ m^3 (equivalent to $0{\cdot}23 \cdot 10^{12}$ tons of coal).[7] As a rough indication of the distribution, petroleum—which, because of its convenience and its economical application assumes a strategic position in the production and consumption process—amounts to only about one-twentieth of coal reserves.

Total world energy consumption has grown at a compound average annual rate of 5·1 per cent between 1950 and 1970, yielding an absolute annual consumption level of 6,843 million metric tons of coal equivalent (m.t.c.e.) in 1970. Assuming the same rate of increase in consumption within this decade, the total world consumption of energy will amount to 11,253 million m.t.c.e. in 1980. The consumption estimates up to the year 2000 will depend on the assumptions made about the consumption behaviour of nations, technological advances, changes in the world economic order, differential levels and rates of economic development, and as such on the specific emerging development pattern assumed to underlie the projection. If an exponential trend is assumed, the total world energy consumption will reach 30,216 million m.t.c.e., if a logistic trend is assumed it will reach 28,086 million m.t.c.e. in the year 2000.[8] Out of the total energy consumption, petroleum and natural gas increased over the last two decades between 8 and 9 per cent per annum as compared to about 5 per cent in coal. At the end of this decade, petroleum will have consolidated its lead, comprising 75 per cent of total energy consumption. The relatively low value for X_t^Z assigned to petroleum at present is due not only to the comparatively low initial global reserves X_0^Z, but also to the high accumulated volume of petroleum consumption from the past to the present, U_t^Z. The projection of $X_{1970}^Z - X_{2000}^Z$, that is, the accumulated total energy use of three decades up to the year 2000, will reach $500 \cdot 10^9$ m.t.c.e.[9] It goes without saying that the relatively low share of petroleum in the total fossil-fuel reserves and the high rates of increase in petroleum consumption will lead in the foreseeable future to a situation where petroleum will be critically scarce. The immediate effect will be continuous price increases and an overall decrease in the growth rates of consumption. Assuming that the rates of increase can on the average be divided in half (which would require continuous readjustments of most economies), the ultimate reserve would nonetheless be exhausted before the end of the next century.

The question whether the energy supply constitutes an imminent threat to the development of the economies of Asia appears again to be an economic one. The close frontier of absolute exhaustion may be expected to have effects on the price and consumption of fossil fuels in Asia. The specific situation will emerge from the dynamics of the variables u, v, and $x - y$.

The global reserves of fossil fuels are less evenly distributed than the mineral reserves. As Table 9.1 reveals, Asia (without Oceania) contains $6{,}200 \cdot 10^{12}$ kWh out of a total of $70{,}850 \cdot 10^{12}$ kWh—less than one-tenth. The ratio for petroleum alone is again about 1 : 10—$320 \cdot 10^{12}$ kWh to $3{,}330 \cdot 10^{12}$ kWh. The resource basis appears even more unfavourable for Asia if the regional populations are related to the regional fossil-fuel reserves. Table 9.2 provides comparative data for the absolute existing amount of petroleum *per capita* in various regions in the world. The ratio for Asia contrasts with those of all world

TABLE 9.1 *Crude estimate of ultimate resources of fossil fuels*

Country/ region	Coal		Petroleum		Tar sand and oil shales		Natural gas			Total
	10^9t	10^{12}kWh.	10^9bbls	10^{12}kWh.	10^9bbls	10^{12}kWh.	known* 10^{12}ft^3	ultimate* 10^{12}ft^3	ultimate* 10^{12}kWh.	10^{12}kWh.
Asia	681	5600	200	320	90	140	70	490	140	6200
USA	1486	12000	200	320	600	950	270	1900	570	13840
Canada	610	4900	95	150	300	480	54	380	110	5640
Latin America	14	100	225	360	50	80	73	510	150	690
W. Europe	337	2800	20	30	70	110	163	1140	340	3280
Comm. countries	4310	35200	500	800			558	3900	1170	37170
Middle East			600	950			344	2400	720	1670
Africa	109	900	250	400	100	160	190	1340	400	1860
Oceania	59	500								500
Total	7600	62000	2100	3330	1210	1920	1720	12000	3600	70850

* The geographical distribution of ultimate gas reserves, unlike that of ultimate petroleum reserves, is not known; hence the estimated total ultimate reserve of 12,000 × 10^{12} ft^3 has been assumed to be distributed in proportion to known reserves.

Source: H. Hoog, in *Electriciteit in onze toekomstige energievoorziening*, p. 13, quoted in Ruyter van Steveninck, *Energy Consumption and Production-Trends and Forecasts*, 1973, mimeo, p. 11.

TABLE 9.2 *Energy resources per capita of the world by regions*

Region	Absolute existing amount of petroleum (100 tons of coal equivalent)	Absolute existing amount of uranium (U_3O_8) (kg.)
North America	15·6	3·2
Central and South America	8·9	—
Europe	1·5	0·4
Soviet Union	3·8	0·6
Asia	0·2	—
Africa	6·8	0·2
Australia and New Zealand	2·1	2·0
Middle and Near East	26·6	—

Source: Y. Kaya and Y. Suzuki, *Global Constraints and New Vision for Development* (Tokyo: 1973), mimeo, p. 78.

regions—least with the ratio of Europe with 7, and most with that of the Middle or Near East with 133 times the *per capita* oil reserves of Asia. Given the small value for u, the overall capacity to export a part of u is equally small. However, what may not be small is the annual absolute rate of exports $\dot{v}$. Here, $\dot{v}$ is a dependent variable of $u - v$ only if the time horizon in which exports are undertaken, T, is assumed to be given. But T may equally be the dependent variable of $\dot{v}$, with $\dot{v}$ being a variable dependent of policy decisions. It is realistic to view $u - v$ in practice as an outcome of *ad hoc* policy decision about $\dot{v}$ and not as a pre-assessed value which could be forecasted or ascertained in welfare-theoretical terms. An assessment of $u - v$ would require a reliable evaluation of u at the time of the assessment, and, provided this can be obtained, it would also require an evaluation of the contribution oil exports can make to national development—broken down into various periods (e.g. years), including a discounting scheme containing estimates about the development forgone because of diminished oil supplies in future periods—and finally an evaluation of the possibilities of substituting alternative energy resources for oil. The difficulties in objectively ascertaining the value of $u - v$ and in providing a rational basis for $\dot{v}$ and/or the time span in which exports are feasible, largely deprive the policy-maker of an objective basis. It usually lends justification to a high value for $\dot{v}$.

As is evident from the nature of $\dot{v}$ as a policy variable, $\dot{v}$ varies according to the policy pursued and the external conditions under which it is bound to operate. The external conditions are given by an export price p (mostly world market price). Changes in the export earnings $\dot{v}p$ are linearly related to changes in the export price p (provided the export quantity $\dot{v}$ is constant). Given a long-run tendency of p to increase, the policy responses may be either (1) to linearly decrease $\dot{v}$ in order to sustain a constant value for $\dot{v}p$, (2) to keep $\dot{v}$ constant and correspondingly increase $\dot{v}p$, or (3) to increase $\dot{v}$ and over-proportionally to increase $\dot{v}p$.

Hypothesis (1) to be valid presupposes on the side of the exporting countries a very high level of p, since the need to finance development over export earnings is generally high. The share of oil in the total exports of Indonesia is over 40 per cent (1971), but the ratio of total exports to the GNP is exceedingly low.[10] The second presupposition for the hypothesis to be valid is that the importing (overwhelmingly industrialised) countries accept a high price as well as quantitative restrictions. A decreasing consumption may be a market response to the high price; but it may equally be a result forced upon them by the exporting countries which consider a restriction on $\dot{v}$ as desirable, given the high level of p. The oil crisis of 1973–5 has shown that under the established national economic systems and world economic order, the capacity to absorb a high level of p for natural resources has an upper limit which cannot be exceeded without causing disruption in the industrialised countries and subsequent repercussions on the developing countries—incurring considerable welfare losses (often) in both. A precise estimate of the price at which $\dot{v}$ will decrease cannot be given here, and probably not at all. It would presume, as stated earlier, the evaluation of a complex entity composed of national preferences, changes in the world economic order, and resource-reserve conditions. However, for the purposes of our inquiry the hypothesis is sufficient and plausible that—under conditions of a conceivably high break-even price at which the Asian countries would be willing to curtail $\dot{v}$, and the economic and political power of the industrialised countries to set an upper limit to p near a point where a drastic curtailment of energy consumption (in quantitative terms) is not needed—p will not reach the break-even point as assumed in (1) where $\dot{v}$ is reduced and $\dot{v}p$ maintained over an extended period of time. This theoretical consideration is supported by the energy policy of the South-East Asian countries and of the People's Republic of China, which are intending to boost oil exports. It is foreseeable that the Asian oil-exporting countries will within the next two decades encounter a state of quasi-exhaustion in which oil is available but only under a regime of quantitative restrictions and high prices. The situation closely resembles the mineral situation, being different only in the 'timing' of the price pressure. The impact of this process on economic development will depend on the feasibility of securing sufficient quantities of foreign petroleum at economically bearable prices (already a necessity for non-oil-producing Asian countries) and the prospects of substituting alternative energy sources.

In assessing $x - y$, it must first of all be recalled that the present relationship between total oil consumption of the industrialised and developing countries is about 10 : 1. Apart from the disproportion in absolute values (the developing countries as a whole have about 4–5 times the population of the industrialised countries) the differential rates of the relative increase change in favour of the industrialised countries. As economies grow, the ratio between the relative change in the average energy consumption and in the average GNP increases. As an outstanding example, between 1920 and 1960 the *per capita* energy consumption of the United States showed an average annual increase of 0·7 per cent, while the average GNP increased at a rate of 1·8 per cent. In the decade 1960–70 this trend was reversed, with a 3·0 per cent annual increase in average energy consumption as compared to a 2·7 per cent annual increase in the average GNP.[11] The share of oil in the total energy consumption has been, as stated earlier, constantly increasing. As y and p increase, difficulties and, at the very least, costs of satisfying the demand from $x - y$ increase. In a case of absolute constraints, the only way out is the resort to the national resource basis u. The preceding discussion has nonetheless revealed that $\dot{v}$ has the long-run tendency to increase or, at least, not to decrease significantly. In consequence, u approaches exhaustion at an exponential rate at a time when $x - y$ may be critically scarce. The reliance then on u will either be infeasible or necessarily costly.

The possibility of overcoming the problem of oil exhaustion depends on the feasibility of replacing oil with alternative sources of energy. Specifically, it depends on the capacity to make new energy sources technically feasible and to finance substitution processes. First of all, switching to another conventional energy material must be considered. Coal stands out as a major substitute. India currently produces about 80 per cent of its energy from coal. The major disadvantage of coal lies in its specific use and with its conceivably unfavourable impact on production and consumption processes. Substitutes from coal in the form of synthetic gas and oil are not yet available.[12] They are expected to be expensive in terms of capital investment as well as in the quantities of coal needed to produce an equivalent of energy substitutes—further accelerating the exhaustion of coal. Coal, nevertheless, may be a 'cushion' for a few decades to come, although probably a more expensive one than usually considered and with costly repercussions on production and consumption processes. As will be stated in the subsequent section, the environmental carrying capacity will set an upper limit to the pollution from energy, and the composition of energy sources must be adjusted in consideration of this constraint.

Other major substitutes for coal are hydroelectric and nuclear power. The potential of both energy sources is considerable. Only about one-third of the potential sites for generating hydroelectric energy are used on a global scale; $25 \cdot 10^{12}$ kWh are still unused.[13] The potential electricity generating capacity in Asia must be assumed to be higher than the world average. Reliable estimates are not available, but electricity being basically a non-tradable commodity, the potential capacity is yet untouched in view of the low domestic use. The critical factor lies in the fact that hydroelectricity constitutes only about 2 per cent of the overall energy presently used and that, say, tripling the presently used capacity would not significantly change the overall energy situation. A basic requirement for meeting the energy demand by increasing hydroelectric power would be the availability of enormous capital (since hydroelectric power is very capital-intensive), which naturally is critically scarce in developing countries.

Atomic energy encounters the fewest constraints imposed by the finiteness of the natural-resource basis. No resource category, however, demonstrates so clearly that the availability and the scarcity of natural resources depend on technical, economic, social, and political factors. The total reserves of U_3O_8 are estimated to be $80 \cdot 10^6$ tons at a price of \$6·00 per pound, and to be more than 10^9 tons if a price if \$10·00 per pound is accepted.[14] Depending on the capacity and willingness to pay, the U_3O_8 reserves will thus vary within a considerable margin. More pronounced even are the differences in the potential energy supply when the application of different technologies is considered. Breeder reactors are 50–100 times as efficient as light-water reactors.[15] Estimates of the total reserves and the increases in the recovery costs are of an entirely different relevance according to the technologies assumed to be applied. The actual use of the conventional reactors (and more so of the breeder reactors, which are not expected to come into use before the 1990s) will depend on solving the technical problems of safeguarding against accidents, explosions, and sabotage and of disposing of radioactive waste. The problems are imminent economic ones, since any application of technical solutions to the mentioned problems will increase the price of energy. Capital investment per installed kW of nuclear energy (conventional reactor) amounted to $120 in the 1960s and is estimated to be $400 in the 1970s. The price will further increase as awareness of the potential dangers of nuclear reactors and pressure for safety measures mount.

A conflict arises between the economical use of nuclear power stations and the avoidance of risk. It will be solved differently according to the values attached to the two factors. A society with a high level of average incomes will attach comparatively low values to the marginal utility of additional consumption, while estimates of the risk probability will be biased upwards, and the values assigned to the marginal utility of safety are likely to be high. In contrast, low-income countries such as the developing countries of Asia have a high marginal utility of consumption (or a high disutility of forgone consumption) and a social consensus for applying rigorous and expensive safety standards may be difficult to find. Although the danger of applying low-safety equipment is imminent (granted no international standards which can be effectively enforced), the actual application of high-risk reactors may be rendered difficult because much of the sophisticated equipment must be imported (at least for the time being) from countries with high safety standards. This will, however, diminish the possibility of solving energy problems on the basis of non-conventional energy—a solution which may be required in view of the constraints set by conventional energy.

10 Carrying Capacity of the Ecosystem

1. POLLUTION FROM AGRICULTURE

The ecosystem—defined as a complex web of interrelating circular flows such as oxygen, nitrogen, phosphorus, hydrogen, and carbon cycles—constitutes the third major constraint to the functioning of related systems. A brief general-theoretical exposition of the basic relationships constituting the phenomenon has been given in Appendix 4, 'Major causal linkages between ecosystem and related systems'. In the following, a specific account of the pollution effects and constraints to the ecological carrying capacity in both the sectors of agriculture and industry shall be given.

Pollution effects from agriculture originate from (1) extensive and (2) intensive land cultivation. Both extensive and intensive cultivation may occur simultaneously, compounding the detrimental effects on the ecosystem and human well-being.

Pertaining to (1), our earlier discussion has revealed the intricate causal nexus between extensive agriculture and the ecosystem. The occupation of virgin lands, such as the denudation of rain forests, and the shortening of fallow periods lead to laterisation and podzolisation of the soils. As the forests are cut down, heavy tropical rains are no longer stored in the soil but instead quickly erode it. The mineral and organic compounds vital to plant life are washed away. Silt loads of large rivers often become excessive and elevate the river-beds, increasing the risk of flooding. The effects on the ecological processes once initiated are often irreversible. In some countries, though—for instance, China (where the denudation of forests started over 3000 years ago)—reforestation programmes have been launched. They are costly in terms of developmental opportunity costs, have long 'gestation' periods, and are burdened with the risk of total failure because of the persisting counterforces of nature, such as wind erosion, torrential rainfalls, floods, etc. The effects of the degraded soils on the productive performance of the agricultural sector vary according to the progress in soil destruction, encompassing losses from lower average yields, inferior quality of innate crops, shifting to inferior crops, and the complete extinction of cultivated crops.

If the ecological basis for agriculture is not to be jeopardised and agricultural returns are to be sustained or increased, resorting to intensive agriculture—the 'shifting upward' of production functions as implied in (2)—is instrumental. In order to clarify the argument, let us write a set of production functions $F_2, \ldots, F_m$ in the explicit form:

$$F_2 \rightarrow O_2;\ \pi_2 = f(a_\alpha \cdots a_\gamma)$$
$$F_3 \rightarrow O_3;\ \pi_3 = g(a'_\alpha \cdots a'_\gamma;\ \alpha_\phi \cdots a_\nu)$$
$$\cdots\cdots\cdots\cdots\cdots\cdots\cdots\cdots\cdots\cdots\cdots\cdots$$
$$F_m \rightarrow O_m;\ \pi_m = h(a^m_\alpha \cdots a^m_\gamma;\ a^m_\phi \cdots a^m_\nu)$$

We start with production function F_2, assuming some past progress; the subscript 1, which would stand for the agricultural sector, and the one indicating the specific pollutant under consideration have been dropped throughout. We have two types of input factors: those used in all production functions, $a_\alpha \cdots a_\gamma$; and those used only in the 'new' production functions, $a_\phi \cdots a_\nu$. The distinction depends on the degree of generality we wish to attach to the notion of input or production factor. If we intend a general statement about production processes, the classical production function including the factors land, labour, and capital may well describe both output functions. The explicit statement of 'new' production factors may not be required. In our case, we wish to analyse the pollution π caused by additional input factors. Consequently, the input factors must be specified in terms of their contribution to pollution. Specifically, they may be subdivided into biological fertilisers versus chemical, solar energy versus fossil fuels, natural plant resistance versus pesticides, etc. In F_3, the 'new' polluting input factors are $a_\phi \cdots a_\nu$. The 'old' input factors $a'_\alpha \cdots a'_\gamma$ will also include pollutants, but of a different type. They will include pollutants deriving from extensive cultivation rather than those from intensive. The different types of pollutants make it difficult to compare pollution effects when shifting from the extensive-oriented production function F_2 to the intensive-oriented production function F_3. In quantitative terms, the hypothesis is plausible that in F_3 the pollution originating from extensive cultivation will remain constant while the additional input factors making for the difference between O_3 and O_2 will add to the overall pollution. The subsequent question is how the pollution varies when a shift from F_3 upwards is accomplished. Any pollution from F_3 upwards is, in principle, derived from intensive cultivation. Generally, we have the possibilities

$$O_3 : \pi_3 \gtreqless O_4 : \pi_4$$
$$\cdots\cdots\cdots\cdots\cdots\cdots\cdots$$
$$O_{m-1} : \pi_{m-1} \gtreqless O_m : \pi_m .$$

The sign < would mean that the output increases over-proportionally to pollution; > would mean that pollution increases over-proportionally to output; and the equal sign would indicate proportionality in the development of the two variables. The hypothesis that > constitutes the most likely path in the long run may claim highest plausibility. Consider that the 'law' of decreasing marginal returns implies—if only constant average returns are set as performance standard—increasing marginal inputs. Since 'new' inputs are pollution-prone the ratio between polluting inputs and total inputs will increase as 'new' inputs are used.

The effects of pollutants from agriculture depend on the type of pollutants and on the 'sensitivity' of the entities subject to that pollution. Pollution from intensive agriculture must be attributed to a comprehensive set of inputs, encompassing high-yield varieties (HYV) such as the IR-8, chemical fertilisers, pesticides, mechanisation-related inputs, water irrigation, and fossil fuels—all of which characterise the new factor mix of the 'green revolution'. Each of these input factors has its specific pollution potential and effects. HYVs allow multiple cropping; but the shortening of the growth cycle requires more fertilisers, which can be applied in sufficient quantities only as chemical fertilisers. Although nitrogen and phosphorus multiply the yield in the short run, they encroach upon the organic compounds of the soil in the long run, contaminate rivers enduringly, eutrophicate lakes, and pollute oceans, affecting fish catch, water supply, recreational opportunities, human health, and environmental aesthetics. HYVs are highly susceptible to parasites and diseases. Pesticides (bactericides, herbicides, fungicides, acaricides, insecticides, etc.) must be disseminated in huge quantities. Pesticides accumulate in the ecosystem and are harmful to human health (genetic mutation, carcinomas). The parasites usually become resistant to the initial doses while the natural enemies die, both enhancing the requirements for additional pesticides and accelerating the accumulation process. Salination and waterlogging will under certain ecological conditions turn fertile alluvial soil into inherently infertile soil; for instance, in Pakistan half of the land watered by the Indus is infertile. Tractors are often required to reduce the peak human and animal labour load, which has grown tremendously as the result of multiple cropping; consumption of fossil fuels consequently increases. What had been a cyclic process with renewable and non-polluting (solar) energy became a cyclic process highly dependent on polluting, exhaustible energy.

The effects of each pollutant on the ecological basis of agriculture and human health are difficult to define (due to the multiplicity and cumulation of causes and effects in the ecosystem) and, even more, to measure empirically. Standards of 'permissible' pollution and (ordinal or cardinal) scales for measuring the effects are yet in the infancy of their scientific development. However, key eco-variables such as the delicate organic and mineral fabric of soils, the long residence time of large rivers, uneven soil-fertility distribution, and the subtropical and tropical climates with their cycles of torrential rainfall and dry heat lend enough support to the hypothesis that the carrying capacity of the ecosystems of Asia is considerably lower than that of the now-industrialised countries of the temperate zones.

Given the ecological constraints, the extent of actual pollution will depend on the size of the input factors and the pollution coefficient $\bar{\pi}$ assigned to each of these. The two magnitudes may be non-linearly related to each other; for instance, large irrigation projects will produce salination and waterlogging, while small irrigation projects will not affect the soil at all. Most input factors such as fertilisers and pesticides are divisible. Size variation and marginal substitution according to the effect on $\bar{\pi}$ appear to be feasible. However, there is to some extent also a functional interdependency of the input factors; unless an entire input 'package' is used, improvements in the output performance may be nil. As a consequence, 'clean' input factors can only to a limited extent be substituted for polluting input factors. Analogously, the total input 'package' has a scale which equals the scale of the input factor with the largest scale, for instance 'tractor-scale'. The inputs, though divisible and seemingly scale-neutral, are biased towards large-scale operations.[1] Pollution is bound to increase if the indiscriminate spraying, overkill, and increased disease-vulnerability to which large-scale operations lend countenance are not countered by ecological adjustments.[2]

In summary, we have increases in 'marginal pollution' as a concomitant of increases in factor inputs, functionally indivisible 'factor packages' with resultant 'pollution packages', a large-scale bias which compounds pollution, and, above all, the minimum nutritional intake requirements of the population. Given these 'fixed' variables, future pollution caused by agricultural activities must be understood as a dependent variable of population growth, and hence can be curbed only by decreasing population growth.

II. POLLUTION FROM INDUSTRY

The second major source of pollution is non-agricultural activities, encompassing industrial (including service) activities and transport. Although the specific causes of pollution differ accordingly, the pollutants produced by the various activities are of the same type: CO, SO_2, tetraethyl lead, dust particles, water contaminants, solid waste, and noise. This must be attributed to the fact that fossil fuel constitutes a substantial input factor of all non-agricultural activities, and is a heavy polluter. The specificum of the prevalent pattern of industrial development is not only the shift from A_1 to A_2 activities but also a shift from non-polluting inputs to polluting inputs—in terms of the preceding discussion, from $a_\alpha, \ldots, a_\gamma$ to $a_\phi, \ldots, a_\nu$ within A_2 and other non-agricultural activities (see Appendix 4).

The effects of non-agricultural pollution are determined, *ceteris paribus*, by the concentration of activities. With respect to concentration, non-agricultural pollution differs from agricultural pollution. The latter is dispersed by its very nature because of the reliance on a comparatively large land area. Non-agricultural pollution is concentrated in high-density urban areas. The effects of high concentration are, first, that the original effects are compounded because the effect of a pollutant may increase non-linearly and because of the multiplicity and cumulation of the effects of several pollutants, and, second, the urbanisation *qua* urban system produces specific types of pollutants and effects.

Specifically, air pollution includes pollutants from industrial activities and transport, both of which are heavily concentrated in urban areas. In average terms, energy consumption is still low in Asian developing countries compared to that of the industrialised countries. It will be recalled that the global distribution is 1 : 10 in favour of the industrialised countries (all LDC included). However, it is precisely the low absolute level of energy-use which permits high relative growth rates that rapidly lead to increased pollution in the confined territories where the activities are concentrated. As the earlier discussion has shown, there are few substitutes for fossil fuels in the foreseeable future. Unless costly anti-pollution devices (which increase the consumption of non-renewable energy resources) are installed, pollution is bound to increase at an accelerating pace. Water pollution even more than air pollution shows the dual nature of urban/non-agricultural pollution. On the one hand, toxic matters are the product of industrial activities. Rivers, lakes, and, increasingly, oceans are toxified, impinging upon the fresh-water supply, fish catch, and agricultural production, compounding the effects that emanate from that sector itself. The Japanese Minamata case (where hundreds of people died or were crippled) may be a portent of some of the future pollution problems of this type in developing countries. It shows that the release of toxic matter is indeed susceptible to control and monitoring; but also that the marginal benefits derived from the non-use of anti-pollution devices are rated highly and eventually are given priority over environmental protection. On the other hand, water pollution is intrinsically linked to urbanisation. A water system, to meet satisfactory sanitary standards, needs a sewage system. In Asian countries, septic tanks and latrines are used instead. In the Manila area, for instance, only about 12 per cent of the people are served by sewers.[3] The inadequacy in the provision of sewage facilities compounds the water pollution generated by industrial activities, creates nuisance, and, in tropical and subtropical climates, is frequently the focus of epidemics. Similarly, solid wastes are accumulated in urban areas at high rates. Industrial activities combined with consumption activities of concentrated populations produced, for instance, a daily average of refuse of the order of 1,200 tons in Manila in 1968.[4] Accumulated refuse has a strong bearing on the fouling of land (which is becoming increasingly scarce), serves as a breeding ground for rats, insects, etc., and creates a nuisance both visual and olfactory.

III. QUANTITATIVE ACCOUNT OF POLLUTION POTENTIALS AND CARRYING CAPACITY

In view of the broad diversity of causes and effects of pollution, any general statement about the impact of the total activities on pollution, and the impact of the total pollution on the total ecosystem, must be based on a number of broad assumptions. However, some quantitative idea of the total pollution volume and effect will be necessary if economic and population (particularly dispersion) policies are to be shaped accordingly. Two magnitudes are foremost relevant for an overall assessment of pollution: first, the total pollution volume, and, second, the carrying capacity of the ecosystem. The total pollution volume—for instance, total CO, SO_2, or tetraethyl-lead content in a confined territory—could be ascertained by aggregating the single pollutants. While, theoretically, the problem of a system with many non-linear functions could eventually be tackled by 'transforming' them into linear ones with more or less damage to the validity of the results, the empirical problem is insurmountable at the present state of classifications and data-gathering. An alternative approach is to estimate the aggregate magnitudes; for instance, on the basis of cross-national comparisons. This approach has been followed by a report of the United Nations Secretariat for Asia and the Far East (ESCAP).[5] The total pollution volume, called the index of pollution potential (IPP), is defined as a function of the population density (P/k) and the density of the gross national product (GNP/N), both per same unit of area. For IPP then the formula $IPP\sqrt{(P/N)^2 \,.\, (GNP/P)/k}$ is obtained, where k is a constant, $k = 100$, and the latter term represents the average GNP. Instead of relying on a pollution coefficient based on estimates of all relevant pollutants, the IPP of the United States (13·3) has been used as a standard to estimate the magnitude of total pollution. Two more reference standards are introduced, one being the Japanese IPP, which is about seven times higher than that of the United States, and the other a reference standard which is based on the assumption of a doubling of the *per capita* income by the year 2000. The absolute figure for population density in the United States is 22 persons per sq. km. and for the average income about $3,680. In Table 10.1, Col. 1 (Col. 3 in Table 7.2 divided by 22·0) shows that by the year 2000 most Asian countries will have a density level several times higher than that of the United States today. Consequently, relatively higher pollution levels must generally be expected, whatever comparative standards of development are applied. If by the year 2000 the Japanese standard (Col. 7) is assumed, all Asian countries (except Laos) will have a considerably higher IPP than that of the United States today. Pollution potentials of the Republic of Korea and of Taiwan will be 16 and 15 times, those of Sri Lanka, India, Pakistan, and the Philippines about 7 times, and that of Indonesia 3 times the standard value of the

TABLE 10.1 *Crude measurement of intensity of pollution (IPP) in countries of the ESCAP region*

	Per capita income[a]				Index of pollution potential (IPP) + 100					
	Density Asian countries[b] (1)	Current[c] level (2)	% of Japan (3)	% of United States (4)	1970 $\sqrt{(1)^2 \times (5)}$ (5)	By 2000 *per capita* income doubles $\sqrt{(3)^2 \times (5) + (5)}$ (6)	Current Japan standard $\sqrt{(3)^2 \times \$1082}$ (7)	Current US standard $\sqrt{(3)^2 \times \$3680}$ (8)	Current Japan standard $\sqrt{(2)^2 \times \$1082}$ (9)	Current US standard $\sqrt{(2)^2 \times \$3680}$ (10)
Burma	3·54	63	5·8	1·7	3·3	8·8	25·6	27·9	17·1	31·5
Ceylon	15·32	140	12·9	3·8	22·7	56·4	110·9	204·4	79·9	147·4
China, People's Republic of	5·50	80	7·4	2·2	7·1	15·3	39·8	73·4	30·6	56·4
China, Republic of	28·45	238	22·0	6·5	60·2	136·6	206·0	379·8	159·5	294·2
Hong Kong	306·14	313	28·9	8·5	737·4	1685·1	2215·4	4085·7	1748·0	3223·6
India	15·05	81	7·5	2·2	15·3	42·1	108·9	200·8	72·3	133·5
Indonesia	6·23	94	8·7	2·5	6·2	18·8	45·1	83·1	27·9	51·6
Japan	16·32	1082	100·0	29·4	92·1	167·0	118·1	217·8	103·6	191·1
Korea, Democratic People's Republic of	10·36	—	—	—	—	—	75·0	138·3	49·7	91·6
Korea, Republic of	27·32	146	13·5	4·0	39·4	102·7	197·7	364·6	136·5	251·8
Laos	1·14	59	5·5	1·6	1·0	2·7	8·2	15·2	5·3	9·7
Malaysia	3·00	283[e]	26·2	7·7	5·4	15·7	21·7	40·0	14·1	26·1
Nepal	6·86	94	8·7	2·6	7·8	20·7	49·7	91·6	32·9	60·7
Pakistan	14·23	123	11·4	3·3	16·1	49·1	103·0	189·9	66·4	122·5
Philippines	14·00	259	23·9	7·0	20·4	70·1	98·8	186·8	59·2	109·2
Singapore	269·18	584	54·0	15·9	847·7	2023·9	1948·0	3592·5	1450·0	2674·0
Thailand	7·09	140	12·9	3·8	8·3	26·1	51·3	94·6	31·9	58·8
Vietnam (North)	10·68	—	—	—	—	—	77·3	142·6	53·3	98·3
Vietnam (South)	8·41	119[f]	11·0	3·2	11·2	28·5	60·9	112·2	41·1	75·8

Source: *Report and Selected Papers* of the Regional Seminar on Ecological Implications of Rural and Urban Population Growth, Asian Population Studies Series, no. 10 (Bangkok: United Nations, 1971), p. 45 (selected data).

Note: A dash indicates that either no data were available, or the data available were considered particularly deficient.
The data for the densities used for the computations in cols. from (8) to (10) can be found in table 7.2.

[a] Source: United Nations Statistical Yearbook, 1967 (New York, 1968).
[b] For average population densities per sq. km., see table 7.2.
[c] Source: *Population and Family Planning: A Factbook* (New York: Population Council, July, 1970).
[e] Excludes Sabah and Sarawak.
[f] At market prices (instead of factor cost).

United States of 13·3. If a doubling of the average incomes by the year 2000 is assumed (a sounder assumption), the pollution potentials of most Asian countries still amount to a multiple of that of the United States today (Col. 6). To reckon but a few percentages of the exercise, Malaysia will have 118 per cent of the pollution potential of the United States today (or 18 per cent more), Indonesia 142 per cent, Thailand 197 per cent, India 316 per cent, Sri Lanka 424 per cent, the Philippines 528 per cent, the Republic of Korea 773 per cent, and Taiwan 1028 per cent.

Objections will be raised that the comparative development standards are highly hypothetical and that Asian developing countries are most unlikely to reach them by the year 2000, if ever at all. Admittedly, it is unlikely that most Asian countries will ever reach the American *per capita* income standard. However, focusing on that objection tends to blur a more relevant conclusion. It is conceivable that most Asian countries will reach a doubling of their *per capita* incomes, and some a tripling or quadrupling. The decisive point is that none of these standards is likely to be reached by the year 2000 but at a later date. Confronted with significant additions in the absolute number of people (Table 6.9) and replacement levels reached some time in the middle of the next century (Table 6.11), the populations will be a multiple by the time the higher income standards will be reached. Thus, the scenarios underestimate rather than overestimate the actual pollution potentials.

The magnitudes of the IPP must be related to a scale the extreme upper value of which constitutes the 'carrying capacity' of the ecosystem. The pollution effect is measured as the ratio 'pollution level' over 'carrying capacity' of the ecosystem. Any value above 1·0 will signify ecological disaster. The notion of the 'carrying capacity' of the ecosystem may not claim much precision,[6] but this does not preclude its relevance.

In view of the preceding discussion, it appears to be useful to divide the ecosystem into urban and rural ecosystems. The values of the above 'eco-ratio' then apply to either of the two sub-ecosystems. It may be conjectured that if the value for one sub-system has exceeded the limitational value of 1·0, the other sub-system is likely also to be significantly affected because of interdependencies of the two sub-systems. We admittedly know little about the causal relationships of the eco-variables. It shall suffice at this juncture to infer from the earlier discussion that both urban and rural sub-systems are apt—in view of the tropical and subtropical climates, soils, and vegetations—to have a lower ecological carrying capacity than those of the now industrialised countries of the temperate zones. The 'margin' for pollution (which the Asian countries still enjoy due to their low average income levels) will be partly vitiated by the lower carrying capacity of their ecosystems.

11 Social Choice in a Finite World

I. CHOICE CRITERIA AND CHOICE VARIABLES

The principal hypothesis about the behaviour of the total-system has been propounded in the notion of 'relative macro-determinacy'. The preceding analysis lends the general statement of 'macro-determinacy' a dual concrete-historical meaning. First, all variables (population, total economic activities, etc.) related to finite M^{aa}-variables (land area, non-renewable resources, environmental carrying capacity) constitute ratios which follow a logistic developmental pattern in the long run. Second, the ratios which are constituted by the M^{aa}-variables of the ecosystem and the population system are higher in contemporary Asia than the ratios at similar development levels in 19th-century Europe and North America. The term 'relative' assigned to the notion of 'macro-determinacy' underscores that the behaviour of the total-system is not absolute in the sense that it would be entirely determined by a unique empirical shape of the logistic curve. The systems which compose the M^{a}-level are causally interrelated with the systems of the M^{aa}-level. The M^{a}-systems have the capacity to learn, to act purposefully, adjust, respond. This quality, however, is subject to constraints imposed by the M^{aa}-variables—the constituents of macro-determinacy.

Since the system levels are ordered in a hierarchy, the adjustment has to come from the systems that compose the lower levels in the total-system hierarchy. Reverting to Fig. 5.1, the major constraints are generalised in the relationship

$$\frac{\bar{A} \cdot P}{S_c} \cdot k \leq 1$$

where $\bar{A}$ designates the level of average consumption and production activities, P the level of population, and k an 'aggregate' coefficient which allows for the 'degree' with which $A \cdot P$ relies on S_c, S_c, standing for the composite of finite magnitudes of the ecosystem. $\bar{A}$, P, k are the policy variables. S_c is a constant in the long run, although there may be considerable flexibility when empirical values are assigned to S_c; for instance, new reserves of exhaustible resources may be discovered and the limit of ultimate exhaustion be shifted into a more distant future. The range of feasible paths for $\bar{A}$, P, k is defined, on the one hand, by the present ratio $\bar{A} \cdot P \cdot k/S_c < 1$, and, on the other hand, by the 'upper boundary' $\bar{A} \cdot P \cdot k = S_c$, or $\bar{A} \cdot P \cdot k/S_c = 1$. Within this range, the development choice is reduced to a principal choice between 'more population' or 'more development' (assuming k constant). Any increase in P will impede increases in $\bar{A}$. Once the choice between P and $\bar{A}$ is decided and/or analytically kept constant, the second gross choice is between various paths for $\bar{A} \cdot k$. The choice of the 'optimal' path clearly involves a complex valuation problem. The range of paths is 'objectively' given, but the empirical shape of the paths (logistic; exponential with sudden 'step' at disaster threshold; various combinations of $\bar{A}$, P, k) is open to deliberate political action.

Thus, the problem arises which criteria to apply to solve the dynamic choice problem. In a formal exposition, the problem may be defined in terms of utilities and disutilities derived from the composite of variables that constitute the development process. At any combination of $\bar{A}$, P, k a welfare-functional

$$W_K = u_K - d_K$$

is obtained, where u designates social utility, d social disutility, and K a specific combination of the variables $\bar{A}$, P, k. The change in W over the entire range may be described by the functions f and g for u and d respectively

$$W(K) = f(K) - g(K).$$

For the marginal social welfare accordingly

$$W'(K) = f'(K) - g'(K).$$

The mathematical inconvenience of having two independent variables can be settled by interpreting d as negative social utility.

The critical problem arises of assigning 'actual' values to u and d—the empirical determination of $f(K)$ and $g(K)$. No theoretical analysis can dispense with value judgements if a definite statement about the empirical shape of the paths is to be attempted. Evaluations in a genuine normative-political sense are required. However, two assumptions about the empirical values of u and d are plausible on *a priori* grounds; hence, the problem of choice has some 'objectivity'. First, utilities and disutilities have a different meaning according to whether they are applied to subsistence or to anything above subsistence, say supplementary utility. Where u and d pertain to survival they have an absoluteness of their own (see discussion in Chapter 4,V). The empirical value assigned to it is infinite, viz. marginal utility (or disutility) at subsistence (or suffocation point) is $+\infty(-\infty)$. This assumption implies that the optimal solution never touches these two corners. We shall revert to this problem. At this juncture it is sufficient to bear in mind that the choice between absolute subsistence utilities and supplementary utilities on the locus of an indifference curve is unrealistic. Nobody wishes to 'trade-in' his life for any other commodity. The type of utility ordering is *lexical*, that is, A must be fully satisfied before B is satisfied. The second assumption refers to the shape of u and d within the confines of the 'limitational' values. It combines the assumptions (1) that the marginal utility is decreasing, and (2) that the marginal disutility is increasing, both as $\bar{A}$ is increasing. The 'law' of decreasing marginal returns is a standard assumption in economics which—in its long-run application—is sound. However, later discussion will reveal that various patterns of income distribution and commodity compositions will yield different shapes of the marginal-utility curve. The assumption about disutility is a different matter. In fact, the different nature and causal unrelatedness suggest a distinction in the denotation between u and d (precluding the use of negative utility). Disutility categories pertain to the M^{aa}-ratios. They vary as the M^{aa}-ratios vary. The empirical shape of d—as the composite effect of the deteriorating ratios—may be assumed to describe in an early development phase a flat, perhaps constant, curve which sharply increases from a certain development level on. The reasons for this are 'objective', as well as being due to the application of different evaluations. In an early phase the disutilities resulting from deteriorating M^{aa}-ratios may be objectively small. A change in the ratio of arable land to population may not significantly affect agricultural productivity if the absolute level to which this change applies is low. Analogously, changes in the level of pollution will hardly be objectionable if the absolute pollution level is still low. On the contrary, if relative changes are applied to high values of the ratios the disutility may sharply increase. Consider the disturbance of the ecological equilibrium and the encroachment on human health and well-being once the M^{aa}-ratios are near the 'critical' levels of the environmental carrying capacity or of permissible emissions. A tendency of the disutility curve to further shift upwards as an initial development level is exceeded results from the changed attitude of policy-makers towards the assessment of the M^{aa}-ratios. Once the M^{aa}-ratios are seen as a bottleneck, any additional reliance on those will be felt as constituting increased marginal disutility. A case where the 'attitude change' appears to be the only evaluation criterion is that of the exhaustible resources. Only the awareness of absolute limitations, in fact, permits further development to be perceived as a process where social disutilities accrue. The actual disutility curve may be more favourable, since the changed evaluation will induce processes of resource substitution. The built-in bias may, indeed, let the *d*-curve shift on its lower initial level. (A formal presentation of marginal social utility and marginal social disutility schedules as they determine net social welfare given various levels of socioeconomic activities and population is given in Appendix 5, 'Social welfare in a finite world—a formal presentation'.)

II. EVALUATIONS PERTAINING TO POPULATION SYSTEM

The relationship $(\overline{A}k/S_c)\ P$ shows that population growth burdens society with social disutility. Interpreting the generalisation propounded in that relationship, we have to keep in mind that it pertains to the specific empirical situation of Asia. However, even within this empirical confinement, the conclusions are not as neat as they may appear at first sight. The policy inference that population growth must be curtailed is, in principle, of course, sound. Whenever the general development desiderata include an increase in average material well-being, a reduction of population growth will contribute to the attainment of this desideratum. Given a decrease in population growth, the marginal social disutilities will increase less rapidly or remain constant, and higher marginal net utilities for $\overline{A}$ will be attained. The question, however, arises whether $\overline{A}$ constitutes the only relevant welfare variable. Such affirmative assumption would not be plausible at all, since parents obviously derive utility from their children. Thus, the intrinsic value of children must be included in the welfare assessment.

The individual welfare function—that is, utility derived from all children belonging to a single family—may be written as

$$w = \sum_{i=1}^{n} \bar{u}_i ,$$

where $\bar{u}$ is the average net utility (e.g., benefits minus costs, satisfaction minus dissatisfaction).

Assuming the community has heard of the Cambridge School and agreed upon that transformation, the social-welfare functional may be written as

$$\begin{aligned} W_n &= \left(\sum_{i=1}^{n} \bar{u}_i\right)_1 + \cdots + \left(\sum_{i=1}^{n} \bar{u}_i\right)_m \\ &= \sum_{i=1}^{m} w_i \end{aligned}$$

The utility $\bar{u}$, as well as the number of children n, will differ among families; but for convenience we take the average utilities derived from the first, second, ..., n-th child, and the average family size of the community.

The individual utility $\bar{u}$ may be dissected according to its specific causes into (1) psychic utility, (2) 'social acceptance' utility, and (3) economic utility. Instances for (1) are the intrinsic value of family life, of watching children growing up, the satisfaction of knowing how one's own children look, of keeping the family name, etc. The number of children required to enjoy psychic utility may be set at 2–3 children, with probably marginal utility approaching zero thereafter.

Utility derived from (2) depends on the ratio between actual family size and socially 'ideal' family size. The latter depends on the prevailing norms of the social system. In a traditional society, fertility is assigned a high value to which women must submit. As a family keeps up to the 'ideal' large family size, it will derive utility from social acceptance (or avoid disutility from social non-acceptance).

Economic utility, as stated in (3), can be derived from children *qua* labour and old-age security. Clearly, if the production function and social-security systems are of a type that children are not needed to generate a desired outcome, the family size will be determined only by (1) and (2). Economic utility of children is, indeed, identical with economic utility derived from $\bar{A}$ to the extent that $\bar{A}$ is generated by children. The economic utility thus ranges from zero (when children do not contribute to the generation of $\bar{A}$) to infinite (when children would help to enable survival production).

Given an 'optimal' family size of 2–3 children pertaining to (1) and a decrease in the family size as $\bar{A}$ increases, the key variable appears to be (2). However, categories (2) and (3) are intrinsically causally interrelated. As a small family size becomes desirable in economic terms, a conflict between (2) and (3) unavoidably will temporarily emerge; but social norms are strongly rooted in economic considerations (particularly in societies at low consumption levels). A change of social norms toward a small family size may be expected as the economic advantages of a small family size become apparent. Historical records provide evidence that religious beliefs (a major non-economic element of norms guiding social behaviour) have had little impact on the fertility decisions of people. The assumption of factor (3) being preponderant in the determination of fertility behaviour receives empirical support from the negative correlation (cross-cultural and intertemporal) between fertility rates and $\bar{A}$.[1]

The population dilemma comes into clear focus if we contrast individual and social utilities at various levels of development. The individual utility of children beyond 2–3 children is larger the lower $\bar{A}$ is. There is a negative correlation of $\bar{u}$ to $\bar{A}$, since the reliance on a child increases as $\bar{A}$ decreases and *vice versa*. The social utility of children beyond the second or third child, or of population growth, is lower the lower $\bar{A}$ is—be it due to socio-economic or M^{aa}-constraints. Social disutility will decrease if the growth in $\bar{A}$ can cope with the population growth rate. Specifically, the negative correlation between $\bar{A}$ and the population growth rate will support the demographic transition, establishing a low population growth rate. In terms of our discussion in Appendix 5, the d'-curve will shift eastward as development proceeds, allowing a higher net welfare for any $\bar{A}$ and a higher value for the state $\bar{A}_x$ (beyond which any further development generates a decrease in welfare).

The general relationship between individual optimum W_n and social optimum W^* for a specific family size may be written as

$$W_n \gtreqless W^*.$$

In a trade-off free state we have

$$W^* - W_n = D = 0,$$

where D denotes the difference between social and individual optimum at a given family size of the total population. D will be larger as the levels of $\bar{A}$ decrease, or D is converging to zero as development proceeds,

$$D_1 > D_2 > \cdots > D_n = 0,$$

where 1 ... n denote increasing values for $\bar{A}$.

Two inferences may be drawn from this relationship. First, population policies will encounter more resistance (on grounds of economic rationality from the parents) the lower $\bar{A}$ is. The need to pursue a rigorous population policy decreases as $\bar{A}$ increases, since D is negatively correlated with $\bar{A}$. Second, the marginal social disutilities of a high population growth rate will be larger the lower $\bar{A}$ is. The resistance to fertility-decreases will diminish as $\bar{A}$ increases until $D_n = 0$ is reached, the state of no resistance at all.

III. EVALUATIONS PERTAINING TO THE *k*-COMPONENT

The values for $\bar{A}$, finally, depend on k, the structure of consumption and production activities. As k decreases, less marginal disutility accrues to society at the same level of $\bar{A}$, and the maximum for $\bar{A}$ is established, *ceteris paribus*, at a higher level. It is obvious that consumption and production activities that conserve non-renewable resources and minimise pollution constitute the strategic focus; a specific pattern of consumption and production activities adjusted to the upper hierarchical level of the M^{aa}-variables should emerge.

The critical policy problem is to make the disutilities expressed in k comparable, and to scale them. The designation of minimum and maximum values and the measuring scale will depend on geological, biological, and medical assessments, as well as on normative-political evaluations. Given these qualifications, the chances of establishing an empirically meaningful (cardinal or ordinal) 'social disutility function' appear dim at present. For a crude solution to the 'empirical-choice' problem we may rely on minimum standards.[2] Any path of $\bar{A}$ (from $\bar{A}_{min}$ on, see Appendix 5) that would not interfere with the minima for k

would be desirable. Clearly, major evaluation problems remain unresolved. First, all evaluations 'in between' which do not refer to the extreme situation where k is at a minimum are not dealt with in this framework. Second, the minimum values of some variables cannot be attained without stating mere value judgements. Consider the choice between the energy use in favour of present generations at minimum consumption standards, and that of future generations at minimum consumption standards. The stipulation of the discounting factor may decide over the survival of more or fewer people in future generations.[3] The actual political choice may be unambiguous. The present government intends to stay in power; therefore, $\bar{A}$ will never be smaller than $\bar{A}_{\min}$ for the present generation—if only a specific time-preference constitutes the constraints. The 'in-between' evaluation problems—more industrial development and pollution or less of both; lower nutritional intakes and pollution but higher consumption of industrial commodities, or the reverse; high population growth and 'happiness for the largest number' of potentially born and early constraints of the ecosystem, or preference for lower eco-ratios and higher welfare for a smaller number of people; and so forth—are unresolvable if no additional criteria are introduced.

It is the implied conclusion of the preceding discussion that the principal criteria for a rational choice among long-run alternatives must come from the M^{aa}-level. The choice is among various paths or states of the M^{aa}-variables, say $X_1, \ldots, X_n$, where $1, \ldots, n$ denote various states of X. The choice is not among variables, say $a, \ldots, m$ within a state X_*. The choice of premises which lead to the desired outcomes $a', \ldots, m'$ does not include a rational choice among a range of long-run alternatives $X_1, \ldots, X_n$. By no means is X_* the only long-run alternative, nor is it likely (though possibly) the optimal one in terms of a deliberately directed path of the total-system. If X_* implies a state where consumer and producer sovereignty constitute the premises, or, similarly, if it describes a state where governmental planners operate in a narrowly defined context of economic rationality and short-run calculus, a specific developmental path characteristic of those premises will emerge. Whether an *a priori* choice of a state X_* or a choice of any other state X_n is feasible without assessing the entire range of alternatives $X_1, \ldots, X_n$ depends on the historical conditions of the M^{aa}-level. Our analysis suggests that in Asia those conditions are such that the priority of the higher hierarchical level gains momentum, and the choice must be among the developmental alternatives $X_1, \ldots, X_n$ if no conceivably undesirable paths of the total-system are to result.

A first step towards the choice among long-run alternatives has been the statement and empirical assessment of some of the key long-run variables. The empirical assessment has been a dual one. First, the finiteness of the key variables—arable land, non-renewable resources, and carrying capacity of the ecosystem—has been made explicit. Second, corresponding M^a-variables have been related to the M^{aa}-variables resulting in eco-ratios. The long-run behaviour of the eco-ratios depends on both the initial and final state of finite magnitudes of the M^{aa}-level and the change in the M^a-variables which are partly open to deliberate decisions and actions. It is the dual character of the eco-ratios which constitutes the choice problem. If a development theory intends to predict, a rational explanation of the specific values which Asian people of different social classes and the government assign to the relevant variables must be given. Not only do the scanty empirical data with which the M^{aa}-variables were described make such scientific undertaking overly ambitious but also, and above all, the hypotheses about the evaluations will hardly justify such endeavour at the present state of knowledge offered by the social sciences. Our procedure has been to state the conjectural choice among empirically feasible alternatives. This has been a step beyond the formal choice rationale of contemporary economics, which is non-empirical and non-historical. The conjectural choice has been conceived here within an empirically and historically confined context. A conclusive statement in terms of strategic inferences will depend on the further assessment of the M^a-variables, to which we shall now turn.

PART THREE

Theoretical and Empirical Outline of Major Socio-Economic Processes

12 Dissected System Structure and Sectoral Relationships

The macro- or M^a-level of the total developmental system encompasses the economic system S_e, social system S_s, political system S_p, and techno-system S_t. The composite of M^a-systems constitutes a lower stratum in the hierarchical order of the total-system; it encounters the absolute constraints of the M^{aa}-level. However, there is a wide range of feasible paths for the development of the M^a-systems. The agents which are part of the M^a-systems have the capacity to act purposefully and to direct the systems in a desired direction. Given differences on normative issues, unequal capacity to implement policies, and differing levels and rates in the variables of the M^{aa}-level, it is quite natural that different structures of the economic, social, political, and techno-systems emerge. It is reasonable to assume that the system structure will be more differentiated and complex as the levels of the variables which compose the system grow higher; inversely, the structure will be the more homogenous and undifferentiated the lower the levels of the system variables.

Various structures of the M^a-systems which historically emerged may be defined in terms of a dual-system structure—for instance, the dualism between agriculture and industry, modern and traditional, or rural and urban. The dissected parts of the system structure constitute sectors. We have, for instance, the modern sector of system S_i, S_i^M, and the traditional sector S_i^T. S_i^M and S_i^T are called (sectoral) sub-systems. A composite of all relevant sub-systems constitutes a sector of the total-system (defined in terms of M^a-systems). For instance, S_e^T, ..., S_p^T designates the traditional sector, and $S_e^M, \ldots, S_p^M$ the modern sector of the developmental system.

Two basic types of sectoral relationships exist: (1) intrasectoral relationships comprising all sub-systems of one sector; and (2) intersectoral relationships comprising relationships between sub-systems of different sectors. The specific intrasectoral relationships may be expressed for the sectors M and T with two different sets of functions, f^i and g^i. The behaviour of the sectors composed of the systems S_e, S_s, S_t, and S_p may be described as follows:

$$
\begin{array}{ll}
\text{Sector } T & \text{Sector } M \\
\dfrac{dS_e^T}{dt} = f^1(S_e^T, \ldots, S_p^T) & \dfrac{dS_e^M}{dt} = g^1(S_e^M, \ldots, S_p^M) \\
\cdots\cdots\cdots\cdots\cdots\cdots & \cdots\cdots\cdots\cdots\cdots\cdots \\
\dfrac{dS_p^T}{dt} = f^4(S_e^T, \ldots, S_p^T) & \dfrac{dS_p^M}{dt} = g^4(S_e^M, \ldots, S_p^M).
\end{array}
$$

The simplest form of intersectoral relationship is the single-system relationship

$$S_i^T \rightleftarrows S_i^M .$$

The effects of intersectoral relationships on the total-system depend also on the intrasectoral relationships. Even a simple single-system interrelationship may be highly significant for the behaviour and outcomes of the total-system if the pattern of intrasectoral relationships, as stated in (1), induces cumulative repercussions in the total-system. The intersectoral relationships will become more complex if we assume, for instance, a determination of a single system of sector T by more or all systems of sector M, say

$$\frac{dS_e^T}{dt} = h(S_e^M, \ldots, S_p^M).$$

Changes in any sub-system of sector M may induce changes in the sub-system S_e^T. Assuming reciprocal relationships, a change in S_e^T may effect changes in any of the sub-systems of sector M, making for another set of differential equations. As in the single-system intrarelationships, multiple causation will be induced by intersectoral relationships in both sectors. A highly complex state of causal interactions will be reached if each sub-system of sector T is assumed to be linked with each sub-system of sector M. The total-system behaviour is then determined by three sets of functions: $f^1, \ldots, f^4$, describing the intrasectoral relationships of the sector T; $g^1 \ldots, g^4$, describing the intrasectoral relationships of the sector M; and $h_e^1, \ldots, h_e^4, h_s^1, \ldots, h_s^4, \ldots, h_p^1, \ldots, h_p^4$, describing the intersectoral relationships between T and M. The latter set of equations must be conceived of as being composed of two sub-sets of equations, one describing the intersectoral relationships $T \mapsto M$, the other $M \mapsto T$. The complex behaviour of the total-system encompassing all sub-systems of the two sectors may be expressed as follows:

Sector T		Sector M
	Type of relationships	
intrasectoral T	intersectoral	intrasectoral M
$f^1, \ldots, f^4$	$h_e^1, \ldots, \ldots, h_p^4$	$g^1, \ldots, g^4$

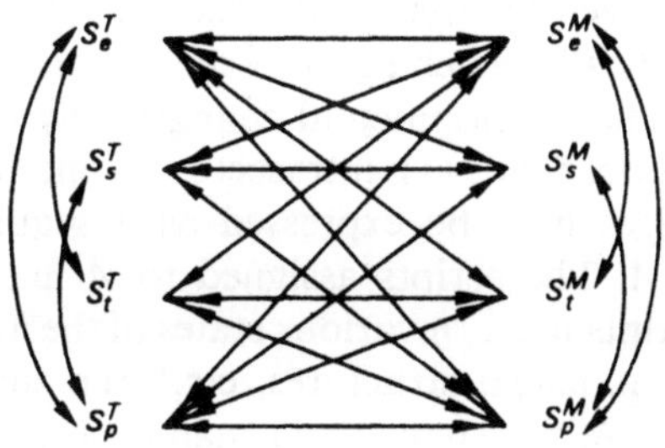

More generally, we may write for the total composite set of relationships

$$\dot{S}_r^K = F_r^K(S_e^T, \ldots, S_p^T, S_e^M, \ldots, S_p^M) \qquad \begin{array}{l} K = M, T; \\ r = e, \ldots, p. \end{array}$$

The subsequent analysis of Part 3 will attempt to give some specific meaning to the complex vector function F_r^K.

13 A General Theory of Transition

Development may be defined as the change of the total-system in a desired direction. Given the dissected structure, development may be defined, more specifically, as changes of the sectoral sub-systems in a desired direction. The developmental changes may be—analogous to the types of relationships—(1) intrasectoral, and (2) intersectoral. Intrasectoral changes may be expressed as a sequence of different states of a sector A. The scripts assigned to A may denote specific states: the superscripts $a, \ldots, n$ various states of the M^a-systems (production, consumption, social structures, etc.), the subscripts $\alpha, \ldots, \phi$ various states of the M^{aa}-systems (land-man ratios, non-renewable resources, etc.). The set of all possible states is defined by the cartesian product. The single sequence may be written as, e.g. $A^a_\alpha, \ldots, A^n_\phi$.

Historically, in an early phase the total-system is composed of a single agrarian sector with but few artisan activities besides. In the absence of a dynamic industrial sector, developmental changes are confined to intrasectoral changes within the agrarian system. An initial cause of changes may stem from (a) the M^{aa}- and (b) the M^a-levels. Changes in population and agricultural man-land ratios may force a response of the M^a-systems. Any change from, say $\alpha \rightarrow \beta$ has a set (which consists sometimes only of a single element) of alternative responses from the M^a-systems. The minimum response for a society at subsistence is to offset the loss in average consumption due to population increases by an equivalent increase in production.[1] The initial causation may stem from the M^a-level, for instance $A^b_\beta \rightarrow A^c_\beta$. A subsequent shift $\beta \rightarrow \gamma$ may be induced if the agricultural surplus suffices to sustain additional population. A change in the M^{aa}-level, namely fertility increases and/or mortality decreases, may offset the original political intention of generating an additional surplus. Whether the population response of the large bulk of farmers leads to a fatalistic attitude on the side of the ruling class or to the reinforcement of political action in subsequent periods depends on the specific socio-economic conditions prevailing in a society. The ruling class may consider enjoying more luxurious consumption. Or it may consider making war against neighbouring countries, keeping a larger standing army to oppress potential resistance, or developing a priest class to legitimise the established power. Causation impulses from the M^{aa}- and M^{a}-levels may both induce a sequence of alternate states in the agrarian system, say $b \rightarrow c$, $c \rightarrow d, \ldots, g \rightarrow h$.

An impressive historical instance of the adjustment of the socio-economic system to changes in the land-man ratio is Java's Sawah system, which prevailed after the arrival of the Dutch. While medical progress brought a burgeoning population, the foreign-enclave sector simultaneously failed to support the indigenous agriculture. As a result the traditional agrarian regime developed in all its delicate nuances, with efforts directed toward more careful land preparation, pre-germination, transplantation, razor-blade harvesting, double-cropping, and terrace flooding. The wet-rice cultivation of Java lent itself to maintaining constant (positive) marginal labour productivity which absorbed the additional population. This process of over-elaboration of detail within a basically unchanged system has been aptly called *involution.*[2]

The ultimate state of the self-contained agrarian regime lies at a point where a maximum production function F_* at a maximum population P_* for a confined territory is reached (see App. 3, pp. 291–95). F_* and P_* are determined by the laws of the agrarian regime. Any expansion beyond F_* and P_* requires the transition to an industrial sector. The necessity for transition results, first of all, from the more productive inputs and factor combinations afforded by the industrial sector. Modern inputs such as chemical fertilisers, high-yield varieties, transportation facilities, mechanical equipment, and energy typically presume an industrial sector. Second, the agrarian regime runs into stagnation at an early stage once the demand for food is satisfied. The shift to commodities with high-income elasticities of demand at the saturation level of the agrarian system constitutes a prerequisite for the development beyond the consumption maximum of the agrarian system.

The necessity of a transition from the agricultural to a dynamic industrial sector in the context of the overall development has led to the mistaken view of the transition process as a strictly deterministic process. This obscures the equally instrumental question of what type of transition should or can be accomplished in a specific historical situation. In the context of 18th- and 19th-century European development, this question was irrelevant. The transition was 'orderly', following a 'successive-sequence'-type path. Given the sectors A, B, C, we have B after A, and C after B, with no major alternatives for either of the transitions. The transitional scenario is entirely different in contemporary Asia. The compounded historical experience offers a large range of hypothetical transitions. Whether all are feasible, and which are 'better' than others, are questions as crucial as the discernment of the significance of the transition as such.

The highly complex choice pattern for transitional alternatives will be made apparent with the exposition in Fig. 13.1. We shall start with successive-sequence-type transitions of a country or country-group X. A designates the agricultural, and B the industrial sectors. The emerging sequence of states of the industrial sector is $B^a_\beta \rightarrow B^b_\gamma \rightarrow \cdots \rightarrow B^n_\phi$. The subscripts $\beta, \gamma, \ldots, \phi$ represent the unique historical M^{aa}-conditions of X. Historical experience in terms of M^a-variables is described by the succession of $a, b, \ldots, n$ which express the socio-economic features of the various states of the B-sector. Similarly, the analysis may focus on the A-sector, describing the sequence of transitional states $k, \ldots, q$.

The successive sequences $k, \ldots, q$ and $a, \ldots, n$ constitute the range of transitions as compounded historical experience which becomes relevant (conveyed more or less faithfully by cross-cultural communications, ideals, expectations, political programmes, etc.) for the country-group Y when it undertakes its transition. The range of 'simultaneous' alternatives in the historical period 2 is depicted by $\bar{B}^{a'}_{\gamma'}, \bar{B}^{b'}_{\gamma'}, \ldots, \bar{B}^{m'}_{\gamma'}$ in the second part of Fig. 13.1. A transition is said to occur if intersectoral relationships between $\bar{A}^i_\gamma$ and any of the $\bar{B}$s exist; or, generally, intersectoral relationships exist between A and B. This implies that a transition does not occur if intersectoral relationships do not exist. In that case, intrasectoral relationships in the B-sector, reminiscent of those in the A-sector, may exist and constitute a self-contained development of the B-sector. If the A- and B-sectors develop independently, but following their own 'laws' lack any dynamic intersectoral interactions, the transitions shall be called quasi-transitions.

In qualifying the term 'transition' we must add that the states in either A or B or both sectors change as time progresses, say $\bar{B}^{a'}_{\delta'} \rightarrow \bar{B}^{b'}_{\varepsilon'}$ from

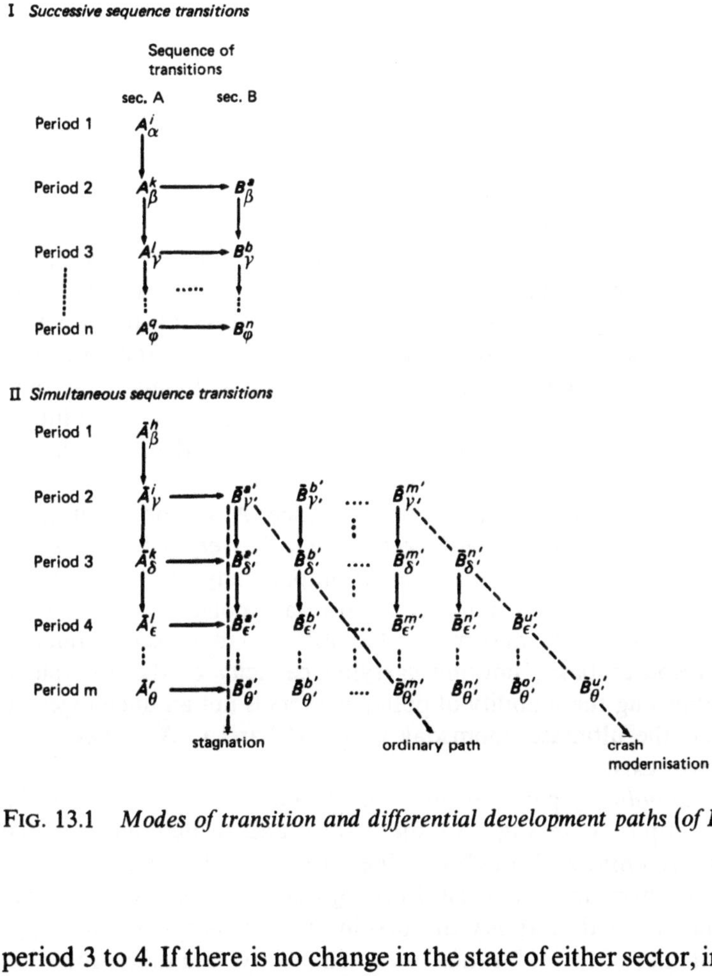

FIG. 13.1 *Modes of transition and differential development paths (of B-sector)*

period 3 to 4. If there is no change in the state of either sector, intersectoral changes nonetheless exist; but the system is at equilibrium. An example will be a country which has reached a state of 'maturity'. The same subscript in each period, say γ' in period 2, for all $\bar{B}$s indicates that the choice exists only in terms of the M^a-variables and not of the M^{aa}-variables—for instance, a choice of technologies but not of various land-man ratios. This does not, however, preclude the possibilities that the socio-economic variables may affect the M^{aa}-variables over the entire time span 2, ..., m—say the relationship between socio-economic variables and the recovery of non-renewable resources. All transitions available at period 2 may be written as

$$
\begin{aligned}
\bar{A}^i &\rightarrow \bar{B}^{a'} \\
\bar{A}^i &\rightarrow \bar{B}^{b'} \\
\vdots &\cdots \vdots \\
\bar{A}^i &\rightarrow \bar{B}^{m'}
\end{aligned}
$$

Similarly, the transitions available in period 3 are given by the same transition sequence plus the new 'experience' of the X-countries, $\bar{B}^{n'}$. The hypothetical transitional patterns for the total time span $2, \ldots, m$ are defined by the initial alternatives at period 2 plus the new experience of X up to u'. The long-run strategic problem consists in choosing the 'vertical' transitional path out of the total of all available transitions. The choice problem thus conceived suggests that the foresight for policy-makers of Asia should include not only their own development but also that of the Western countries, since the future states $B^m, \ldots, B^u$ may offer relevant experience for their own future transitions.

Various transition strategies can be chosen. A first option may be the transition to a state $\bar{B}^{a'}$ with no change in $\bar{B}$ over all periods $2, \ldots, m$. The cause of this choice of a stagnation path may lie in the inability of the policy-makers to conduct appropriate policies or it may be forced upon them by maxima of the M^{aa}-variables (constraints of natural-resource basis, limiting carrying capacity of the ecosystem, etc.). Supposing the inability of policy-makers is not an unchangeable state, and the ultimate doomsday is not at hand in Asia, two basic alternatives exist.

First, an *ordinary* path, for instance $\bar{B}^{a'}_{\gamma'} \rightarrow \bar{B}^{b'}_{\delta'} \rightarrow, \ldots, \rightarrow \bar{B}^{m'}_{\Theta}$. For the sake of simplicity, in Fig. 13.1 the arrows and related states of the A-sector are omitted throughout. The ordinary path constitutes a following of European experience. Two objections may be raised against the feasibility or desirability of pursuing an 'ordinary-path strategy'. The dynamics of the M^{aa}-ratios in contemporary Asia differ from that of 18th- and 19th-century Europe; and some features of the 'old' development may not be repeatable, and if so, only at high cost. Technologies of early vintages available to the Asian countries today have embodied the accumulated experience of all vintages up to the present. The ordinary path is unlikely to be the most efficient one, if feasible at all. Two sub-types may be distinguished: (a) The delayed path, for instance $\bar{B}^{a'}_{\gamma'} \rightarrow \bar{B}^{a'}_{\delta'} \rightarrow \bar{B}^{b'}_{\varepsilon'} \rightarrow, \ldots, \rightarrow \bar{B}^{b'}_{\Theta}$. The rationale for pursuing a strategy which favours this path may lie in the failure to implement successfully an ordinary path strategy or anything beyond. (b) The accelerated ordinary-path, for instance $\bar{B}^{a'}_{\gamma'} \rightarrow \bar{B}^{b'}_{\delta'} \rightarrow \bar{B}^{n'}_{\varepsilon'} \rightarrow, \ldots, \rightarrow \bar{B}^{o'}_{\Theta}$.

The deviation from the ordinary path may also be inspired by an initial failure of following it or stem from considerations at the very beginning which show the ordinary path to be infeasible or non-optimal. In both paths, (a) and (b), the direction of the transitions may change in the course of the entire transition in the periods from 2, ..., *m*.

The second type refers to a crash-modernisation strategy, $\bar{\bar{B}}^{m'}_{\gamma'} \rightarrow \bar{\bar{B}}^{n'}_{\delta'} \rightarrow \bar{\bar{B}}^{o'}_{\varepsilon'} \rightarrow \bar{\bar{B}}^{u'}_{\Theta'}$. This regime may be rooted in the socio-economic structure inherited from the colonial past. The industrial or agro-industrial sector, which initially constituted a foreign-enclave sector, is now linked to other sectors of the economy.[3] Given a colonial or neo-colonial heritage, as in India, Indonesia, the Philippines, or Malaysia, intersectoral relationships, when relying only on the agricultural and former enclave sector, will be weak. The intrasectoral changes tend to continue in the two sectors according to the 'laws' with which they started. The other possibility is the crash-modernisation strategy proper—not out of historical necessity but as a deliberate policy decision. The crash-modernisation strategy, whatever its historical origin or motivation, faces the principal dilemma that the 'developmental distance' between the states of the two sectors is very large. Consequently, the transitions resulting from the momentum of upward-tending intersectoral changes will encounter various inconsistencies. The major dangers inherent in a crash-modernisation strategy are (1) the absence of synchronisation of the needs of the two sectors, and (2) the tendency to self-contained invert development as defined by intrasectoral changes. (1) and (2) clearly reinforce each other. We propound the hypothesis that the development in Asia is largely characterised by a type of crash-modernisation strategy or by an accelerated ordinary-path strategy beyond a dynamic optimum which would allow the interplay of the large traditional agricultural and the industrial sectors.

The strategies pursued constitute a triad: (1) forced modernisation, (2) forced industrialisation and (3) forced urbanisation. The 'modernisation ideal' has been seen to be a constituent feature in the value system prevailing in contemporary Asian societies.[4] Theories which bluntly propound the transition from traditional activities and ways of life to modern ones as the crucial momentum for development give strategic support to the modernisation ideal.

The forced-industrialisation component (2) in the strategies pursued, is causally and logically interlinked with (1). The industrial sector is usually conceived as 'modern'. As the choice among a wide range of transitions, however, it is clear that 'modernity' has various facets of which the sequence $\bar{\bar{B}}_{\gamma'}^{m'} \rightarrow, \ldots, \rightarrow \bar{\bar{B}}_{\Theta}^{u'}$ constitutes only one among many. An extreme position was taken by the Indian planners in the 1950s. Planning was by and large based on the one-sector, capital-focused, Harrod-Domar-Mahanalobis model, which gives industry and capital investment absolute priority. The two-sector models, although more balanced in overall outlook, inherited the bias towards modernisation. Priority was subsequently given to the 'modern' industrial projects, or what were considered as such. Little attention was given to the impact on intersectoral relationships, the specifics of traditional agriculture in its relation to the industrial sector and the socio-economic basis on which the industrial sector should rely and develop.

The hypothesis (3) that urbanisation has been forced will appear to be the least convincing component in a strategy said to be biased. Various countries, such as the Republic of Korea, the Philippines, and India have launched programmes to 'ruralise' the country. At the same time, however, the 'ruralised' cities—namely the slums—are eradicated, with some vague ideal of a 'modern' or 'clean' city in mind. Well-composed decentralisation policies have nowhere been successfully conducted, while the social services in the cities continue to receive favoured attention over those in the rural areas. The strategy pursued often may not have been implying any intention of forced urbanisation; but urbanisation as a causally closely interlinked phenomenon (at least under the present socio- and political-economic system) is a necessary concomitant of modernisation and industrialisation, both of which have been largely forced.

Since the beginning of the 1970s, there has gradually been a change of wind in the assessment of the principal problems and strategies. The basic structure of largely unrelated agricultural and industrial sectors has meanwhile historically emerged. It constitutes the central strategy problem, still little understood and resolved. The subsequent discussion attempts, first, to offer some causal explanation of the developmental system in operation, and, second, by doing so, to design the major empirical outcomes.

14 In the Theoretical Mainstream

I. CLASSICAL AND NEOCLASSICAL THEORY AS DESCRIPTIVE AND NORMATIVE THEORIES

The classical and neoclassical theories constitute the intellectual backbone of the 'forced' strategies. Economists adhering to this impressively consistent body of hypotheses may object to the imputation that their theory has normative implications. At least, the choice of the theory as a strategic device would be considered to be strictly independent from the theory which is understood as being descriptive-explanatory. Such response would faithfully accord with the old tradition (which was brought to a climax in the 'new welfare economics') that economics has to describe what *is* and not to prescribe what *should* be. By no means is the economist *qua* economist in a position to make value judgements or to draw policy inferences from his descriptive-explanatory insight. Besides the evident fact that this itself implies a value judgement, the view suggests an 'objective' science. It may suffice in the context of this study to stress that the classical and neoclassical theories, once stated, are not without normative implications. By propounding, first, that the body of the classical and neoclassical hypotheses explains European history, and, second, that this experience may be telescoped in Asia, the original descriptive-explanatory theory has normative implications. Clearly, if development is desirable, and the corresponding expectations rely on the blueprint of Western experience, the proposition that a repetition of Western experience is feasible along the lines propounded by classical and neoclassical theory can hardly fail to have strong bearings on policy-making. Though the theory itself makes no allowance for a governmental sector and rests basically on the premise of freedom from state intervention, it serves as a basis for intiating processes along those described in the theory. What is described as an automatic process of self-regulating market forces becomes a process which is anticipated by policy-makers and reinforced with deliberation and rigour. Hence, we have forced strategies based on the Western paradigm of development.

In the following, the salient features of the 'Western model' shall be highlighted, before assessing its validity as an explanatory tool for contemporary Asia.[1] Structurally, the model is composed of two sectors—an advanced-industrial and a backward-agricultural sector. Institutionally, the advanced-industrial sector is dissected into a profit-earning capitalist class and a wage-earning labourer class. The backward-agricultural sector plays a passive role, and its functioning does not come into clear theoretical focus (at least in the modern version of the theory). Development is defined as the growth of the relative share of the advanced-industrial sector: the transition from the backward-agricultural to the advanced-industrial sector. The prime mover of the advanced sector, and, thus, the generating force of the developmental transition itself, is the profit-seeking and capital-accumulating entrepreneur.

Development as output growth of the advanced sector is determined by (1) the initial size of the advanced sector, (2) the share of profits π on the total produce $\pi + w$ of the advanced sector, $\pi/\pi + w = \pi/O^I$, (3) the portion of savings from profits, S/π, where $\pi = C^I + S$, C^I being the consumption of capitalists, and (4) the portion of capital actually invested from the savings fund of the capitalists, I/S. An increase of the output in one period (where the subscripts for time have been dropped throughout) may be written in explicit form as

$$\Delta O^I = O \cdot \frac{O^I}{O} \cdot \frac{\pi}{O^I} \cdot \frac{S}{\pi} \cdot \frac{I}{S} \cdot \frac{1}{k} \cdot \qquad (1)$$

I/S does not appear explicitly in the model; thus, $I/S = 1{\cdot}0$. It is a convenient device to remind us that the model excludes real-money imbalances such as inflationary or deflationary gaps (due to negative savings, deficit spending, hoarding, external imbalances, etc.). An output increase then becomes solely dependent on savings S of the capitalists and the intensity of the technology applied as expressed by the capital-output ratio k. Hence, for equation (1) we have

$$\Delta O^I = \frac{S}{k}, \tag{2a}$$

for the relative rate of change

$$\frac{\Delta O^I}{O^I} = \frac{S/k}{O^I}, \tag{3}$$

and for the percentage change

$$r_o = \frac{S/k}{O^I} \cdot 100. \tag{4}$$

The result is reminiscent of the Harrod-Domar model. The difference from the classical and neoclassical models exists in the assumption of the latter that ΔO depends only on O^I and not on the total output O. The classical and neoclassical theory appears to be, at this stage of the argument, a mini-one-sector model. Equation (2a), therefore, may well be written as

$$\Delta O = \frac{S}{k}, \tag{2b}$$

where S/k pertains only to the advanced sector.

The classical and neoclassical models differ in their empirical assumption about changes in $k = 1/k^0$ over time. The classicists assume that k falls in the course of development (technical progress etc.), the neoclassicists[2] that it remains constant. The consequences may be demonstrated by differentiating equation (2a) with respect to time. For the classical version we get

$$\frac{dO}{dt} = \left(-S\frac{dk}{dt} + k\frac{dS}{dt}\right)\frac{1}{k^2}, \tag{2c}$$

for the neoclassical version

$$\frac{dO}{dt} = \frac{1}{k}\frac{dS}{dt}. \tag{2d}$$

As $dk/dt = 0$, the term drops out. While in the classical model a decrease in the savings rate may be offset by a falling capital-output ratio, such decrease must, *ceteris paribus*, lead in the neoclassical model to a fall in the output growth rate. The neoclassical model brings out most clearly the dominant role the savings rate has to play in the 'Western paradigm'. The implications, positive-analytical as well as normative, are far-reaching. Since the savings rate depends, *ceteris paribus*, on π/w, any increase in π/w will increase the savings rate—hence the postulate that wages be as low as possible if the objective is to develop a country as rapidly as possible. Income inequality becomes a *conditio sine qua non* of development.

A weak link, as generally in economics, is the investment function as expressed in S/π or in I/π. A psycho-genetic explanation has been that capitalists are simply prone to accumulating for the sake of accumulation; or that they are seeking social approval. Another rationale has been assumed to consist in the 'pressure' which various bottlenecks (e.g. shortages of resources) exert on investment behaviour encompassing capital accumulation and inventiveness of the entrepreneur.[3] Finally, the very existence of the modern sector itself has been credited with the rank of the pace-setter for additional investment (increasing 'ability to invest').[4] Irrespective of the causal explanation, the empirical statement about the behaviour of capitalists is decisive: that they save and invest a large portion of their profits, and therefore justify a high π/w ratio for the sake of development. As development proceeds, the size of the advanced-industrial sector increases, and with it the effect on growth of investment. The smallness of the advanced-industrial sector is the most critical impediment to development, and the need to squeeze the π/w ratio until the subsistence minimum of the labouring class is reached becomes an imperative.

The economic feasibility of keeping down the π/w ratio depends in the long run on (1) the need to pay a specific wage level, and (2) the capacity to channel agricultural surplus into the advanced-industrial sector. As for (1), the classicists propound that in the initial phase of disguised unemployment, the wage rate will equal an institutional wage rate, while in a state where the labour surplus is absorbed and competitive market forces exert pressure on the labour-demanding entrepreneurs, the wage rate will equal the marginal labour productivity. The neoclassicists assert that there is no disguised unemployment in traditional agriculture, and that the wage rate is equal to the marginal labour productivity throughout. Since this argument applies only to the first (labour-surplus) phase of the classical theory in which the wage level is near subsistence anyway, the dispute is not of paramount importance. The savings rate is not much affected by the difference between marginal productivity of the least-productive labour in the traditional-agricultural sector (which must receive at least the subsistence minimum to survive) and the institutional wage (which assumes that subsistence minimum).

As development proceeds, the capitalists must pay wages according to the marginal labour productivity. As a consequence, the π/w ratio, the savings, investment, and output growth rate are declining. Hence, the existence of (2), the agricultural surplus, becomes important for sustaining development. The total agricultural surplus is defined as

$$S^A = O^A - C^A \tag{5a}$$

$$= [(\lambda\eta) - c]P^A, \tag{5b}$$

where S^A denotes the total surplus of the agricultural sector, O^A its total output, C^A total self-consumed agricultural commodities, λ average labour productivity in agriculture, η employment rate L^A/P^A in agriculture, where $\eta = 1$ denotes a hypothetical situation where the entire population is engaged in agricultural activities, and c average self-consumption in the agricultural sector.

An increase of O^A depends on the innovation intensity of the agricultural sector and the terms of trade (defined in units of industrial goods per units of agricultural goods). The innovation intensity will depend on modern technology inputs from the industrial sector. The relative purchasing power of the agricultural sector will depend on favourable terms of trade. If the terms of trade are such that any ΔS^A is absorbed by the industrial or governmental sector, the intermediate inputs and innovation intensity (as far as attributable to intermediate inputs) will remain at a low level. The surplus absorption by the industrial sector has, therefore, a limit given by the investment needs of the agricultural sector, which itself constitutes the basis for that surplus. There is no explanation of what determines the level or changes in the terms of trade, unless reliance is on exogeneous variables. Since the total agricultural surplus in one period is dissected into

$$S_t^A = S_s^A + S_i^A, \tag{6a}$$

where s designates the self-invested surplus and i the surplus transferred (or transferable) to the industrial sector, the contribution agriculture can make to industrial development is

$$S_i^A = S_t^A - S_s^A. \tag{6b}$$

The growth of the advanced-industrial sector is thus defined as

$$\Delta O^I = (S^I + S_i^A)1/k. \tag{2e}$$

The second major role the agricultural sector has to play in the production-function-focused model is to supply additional labour for the expanding industrial sector. In an early phase, labour is amply available from the pool of unemployed, and ΔO may be expressed as a function of I. In the second phase, labour becomes an equally scarce production factor and must be expressed explicitly; say in a Cobb-Douglas function. The growth rate of output equals

$$r_o = r_o^k + {}^{rI}_{o}, \tag{7}$$

where k and l denote the contribution K and L make to r_o. While r_o^k depends mainly on the advanced-industrial sector (particularly in the initial phases), r_0^l depends solely on the agricultural-backward sector (as far as the factor supply is concerned). If we write for the allocation of the total labour force

$$L^T = L^I + L^A \tag{8}$$

and for the production function of the agricultural sector

$$O^A = \lambda^A \cdot L^A, \tag{9}$$

then L^A is given by

$$L^A = O^A/\lambda^A \tag{10}$$

and the labour surplus by

$$L^S = P^A - (O_L^A/\lambda^A), \tag{11}$$

where P^A stands for the agricultural population of working age willing and able to work. Both population growth and labour productivity of the agricultural sector determine the size of the labour pool available for the expansion of the industrial sector.

The argument may be summarised by referring to equation (7). Here, r_o^k depends on generating an agricultural surplus which must equal the decrease in the profit rate (due to increasing wages) if r_o^k is to remain constant. r_o^l depends on the agricultural labour surplus which depends (*ceteris paribus* constant propensities to consume) on the marginal productivity and population growth of the agricultural sector. Labour supply due to population growth is, in the classical model, treated exogenously. In the neoclassical model it is endogenously determined by the neomalthusian assumption that population growth depends only on output growth.

II. VALIDITY OF COGNITIVE STEPS AND RESULTING HYPOTHESES

The relevance of classical-neoclassical theory for contemporary Asia depends on its successfully passing a fourfold verification test. Let us first make explicit the cognitive procedure which underlies the formulation and application of classical and neoclassical theory. By definition, the term 'classical' implies that the theory is a generalisation of 18th- and 19th-century European experience. This is the starting point in Fig. 14.1, indicated by the arrow 1 to 2. The theory proceeds with the assertion that an application to contemporary Asia is feasible: step 2 to 3. Once the feasibility is assumed, the normative assertion is made that the premises and outcomes are desirable: step 3 to 4.

The verification applies to all steps: (i) the verification whether classical and neoclassical theory is a valid generalisation of European experience; (ii) verification whether classical and neoclassical theory can be applied to the conditions prevailing in contemporary Asia; (iii) verification whether classical and neoclassical theories are desirable in terms of the value premises underlying Asiatic social conditions and traditions; and (iv) verification of classical and neoclassical theories in terms of actual outcomes.

1. Compatibility with Historical Experience of Western Countries

It clearly goes beyond the scope of this analysis to subject European history to empirical scrutiny. However, it will suffice to highlight a few

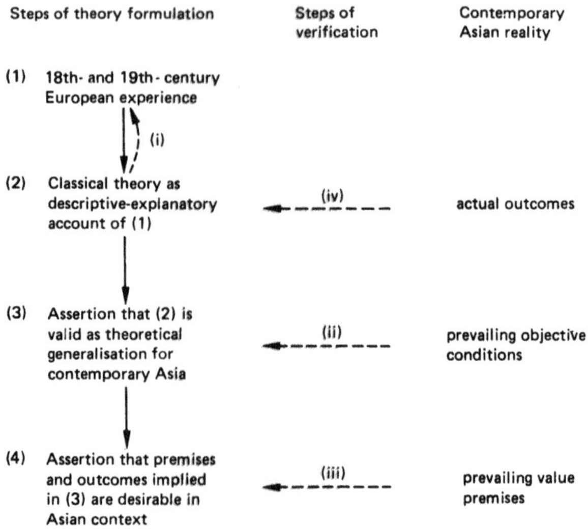

FIG. 14.1 *Framework of cognitive steps*

empirical instances which may serve as relevant for the verification of the preceding theoretical statements. The empirical argument pertaining to the values of the behaviour of π/w and S/π, we find neatly summarised in a statement by Keynes:[5]

> The immense accumulations of fixed capital which, to the great benefit of mankind, were built up during the half century before the war, could never have come about in a Society where wealth was divided equitably. The railways of the world, which that age built as a monument to posterity, were, not less than the Pyramids of Egypt, the work of labour which was not free to consume in immediate enjoyment the full equivalent of its efforts.
>
> Thus this remarkable system depended for its growth on a double bluff or deception. On the one hand the labouring classes accepted from ignorance or powerlessness, or were compelled, persuaded, or cajoled by custom, convention, authority, and the well-established order of Society into accepting, a situation in which they could call their own very little of the cake, that they and Nature and the capitalists were co-operating to produce. And on the other hand the capitalist classes were allowed to call the best part of the cake theirs and were theoretically free to consume it, on the tacit underlying condition that they consumed very little of it in practice. The duty of

TABLE 14.1 *Long-term changes in Pareto coefficients in England and Germany (Prussia), 1850–1960*

Year	England	Germany (Prussia)
1850	1·47	1·89
1880	1·41	1·58
1913	1·31	1·56
1930	1·61	1·78
1960	2·11	2·00

Source: Colin Clark, *The Conditions of Economic Progress* (London: Macmillan, 1957), pp. 538–9.

> 'saving' became nine-tenths of virtue and the growth of the cake the object of true religion. There grew round the non-consumption of the cake all those instincts of puritanism which in other ages has withdrawn itself from the world and has neglected the arts of production as well as those of enjoyment. And so the cake increased. . . .

The statistical data confirm Keynes's statement. Income equality shows a decreasing trend in the initial phases of development, while it increases as development proceeds (Table 14.1). The empirical phenomenon has been generally referred to as the inverted-U-income pattern. A similar verification is suggested by the data on labour absorption of the advanced-industrial sector. Agricultural labour decreased (or remained constant) in absolute terms while the additional population was absorbed by the advanced-industrial sector (Tables 7.6 and 14.2). In some countries the agricultural sector played a predominant role in financing development. In Japan, the state accounted for about 30 percent of the total gross domestic fixed-capital formation during the years after the Meiji Restoration, an amount which rose to about 40 per cent between 1887 and 1936. A substantial part of the governmental capital formation was siphoned off by the state from the farmers.[6] In France in the 1860s, about 15 per cent came from taxes on the land. Russia established a new tax system about 1880 through which the state absorbed the increased agricultural surplus, enabling it to finance investment activities in the industrial sector.[7] Without pretending that our conclusions have much rigour, we may say that the European experience of the 18th and 19th centuries does by and large confirm the body of hypotheses propounded by classical and neoclassical theory.

TABLE 14.2 *Absolute number of workers in agriculture in Great Britain and France, 1831–1931*

Year	Britain* (in millions)	France (in millions)
1831	1·8	4·8
1841	1·9	5·0
1851	2·1	5·3
1861	2·0	5·34
1871	1·8	5·28
1881	1·7	5·47
1891	1·6	5·04
1901	1·5	5·52
1911	1·6	5·33
1921	1·4	4·99
1931	1·3	4·45

* Forestry and fishing included

Sources: P. Deane and W. A. Cole, *British Economic Growth, 1688–1959* (London: Cambridge University Press, 1962) p. 143; J. C. Toutain, *Le Produit de l'agriculture de 1700 à 1958* (Paris, 1961) pp. 200–1.

2. *Feasibility and Desirability of Repeating Western Experience in Contemporary Asia*

Next, the question arises whether the conditions prevailing in contemporary Asia allow conclusions *per analogiam*. The discussion on the M^{aa}-level has provided evidence that the ecosystem and the population system have significantly different features in terms of levels and rates of their variables. The unique historicity of any sequence of M^{aa}-variables constitutes what has earlier been called the 'macro-determinacy' of the total-system. Furthermore, the 'rules' of accumulation are better understood today as compared to previous periods; expectations and ideals have changed; the capacity to conduct policies scientifically has increased; technological progress has been having far-reaching implications on socio-economic processes and institutions. This compounded experience of Western development is available to contemporary Asian countries. The emerging development will be of the simultaneous-sequence type, rather than of the ordinary successive-sequence type. The assertions implied in that notion are that Western experience is not repeatable as far as the 'conditional'-historical context is concerned.

Next, verification (iii). If we act as 'if' (ii) were in conformity with the requirements made by the theory, the question would still arise whether the value premises on which that theory is based are desirable in the Asian cultural context. Suffice it to state that various Asian value premises are inconsistent with those in the West. As the awareness of the limitations due to (ii) increases, the basic value premises which underlie the current socio-economic development will very likely be reassessed in the light of the values of the Asiatic societies. This itself will constitute a forceful critique of the present development, and hence of the theory which postulates and intends to explain it.

3. Predictive Capacity for Contemporary Asia

The ultimate test to which most testing has been directed thus far is the verification of those hypotheses proper which claim validity within the framework of the postulated premises. Assuming (ii) and (iii) were not at variance with the predictive capacity of the theory, the testing pertains to specific statements about the behaviour of economic variables.

The assumption of unity of I/S, first of all, hardly seems warranted. A comparison of Tables 14.3 and 14.4 demonstrates the tendency of investment to exceed domestic savings. At least to some extent, the investment surplus may be quoted in favour of the theory. It may indicate the willingness and ability of entrepreneurs to invest the available savings fund. It contradicts somewhat the thesis that a lack of investment opportunities is the major hindrance to development. Equally, the small supply of entrepreneurs does not appear as the foremost bottleneck in the process of capital accumulation.

The conclusion receives some revision when we disaggregate the two determinants of the ratio. Theoretically, for the early phase of development, we should have a situation close to

$$\pi'/S = 1{\cdot}0$$

and

$$I'/I = 1{\cdot}0,$$

and for the entire S/I ratio subject to the above conditions of unity,

$$\frac{\pi'/S}{I'/I} = 1{\cdot}0,$$

TABLE 14.3 *Gross domestic saving as % of GNP, selected Asian countries (at current market prices)*

Country	1960	1965	1969	1970	1971
India	13·8	16·1	13·4	13·3	13·2
Korea, Republic of	9·9	15·1	22·7	20·5	16·7
Malaysia	—	17·8	20·4	18·1	—
Pakistan	—	11·4	11·2	11·6	—
Philippines	13·9	20·7	17·9	20·4	—
Sri Lanka	11·0	12·8	12·4	16·1	15·2
Thailand	15·5	16·3	22·7	21·6	—

Sources: *Economic Survey of Asia and the Far East*, Part 1 (United Nations: Tokyo, 1973):
INDIA: *Fourth Plan Mid-Term Appraisal and Economic Survey, 1971/72;*
INDONESIA: *United Nations Statistical Yearbook, 1969;* the figure for 1970 is from national sources.
KOREA, REPUBLIC OF: *Economic Statistics Yearbook, 1972;*
MALAYSIA: *Second Malaysia Plan, 1971–75;*
PAKISTAN: *Fourth Five-Year Plan, 1970–75* and *Annual Plan, 1970/71;*
PHILIPPINES: *Four-Year Development Plan, 1971–74* and *The Statistical Reporter*, vol. 15, no. 2, Apr.–June 1971;
SRI LANKA: *Central Bank, Annual Report*, 1970 and 1971;
THAILAND: *National Income of Thailand, 1968/69* and *Central Bank, Annual Report.*

TABLE 14.4 *Gross investment as percentage of GNP, selected Asian countries (at current market prices)*

Country	1960	1965	1969	1970	1971
India	16·3	17·8	16·1	14·2	14·2
Indonesia	7·9	8·4	10·6	13·0	—
Korea, Republic of	10·9	14·9	30·4	28·1	26·1
Malaysia	—	16·3	14·2	16·3	—
Pakistan	—	18·3	14·8	15·7	—
Philippines	13·0	20·2	21·0	20·8	—
Sri Lanka	14·5	12·5	19·7	19·7	17·5
Thailand	15·7	20·2	26·8	25·7	23·1

Sources: see Table 14.3 above.

where the prime indicates the portion of the industrial-advanced sector of total π and I respectively. That is to say, all investment is done by the industrial-advanced sector, which also provides the total savings fund.

As the savings gap itself indicates, the above relationship does not hold empirically. Specifically, both the π'/S and I'/I ratios are far from being at unity. In institutional terms this means that a significant share of saving and investment is done by the governmental and foreign sectors. Indeed, the total government sector accounts for about one-third in the Asian developing countries. The relative share of public-consumption expenditures out of total public expenditures varies among Asian countries, but in all of them the share of public investment still appears significant. For instance, in Malaysia the public sector's share accounted for M$7,250 million out of an investment total of M$14,350 million. From this portion, M$6,000 million fall under the heading 'public development expenditures'. It is a most significant feature for the general development pattern of all Asian developing countries that a substantial share of the total public savings is used not for the creation of public physical capital assets but for financing private capital formation. In Malaysia this share amounts to M$742 million, or about 10 per cent of private investment.[8] In the Republic of Korea, the total investment in 1970 amounted to 26·9 per cent of the GNP, out of which 9·2 per cent was financed by the foreign sector and 16·9 per cent by domestic savings. Approximately 40 per cent (or 6·8 per cent of the GNP) of the total domestic savings available for investment purposes was provided by the government.[9] In Thailand, the share of public capital formation amounts to over 30 per cent of the total gross fixed-capital formation. In the construction sector, which accounts for 49 per cent of the total gross capital formation, the public sector contributes 20·1 per cent of the total capital formation, or about 40 per cent of the investment in that sector.[10] The Philippines provides an indication of how small a portion of total saving really comes from the 'capitalist's' savings. The domestic corporate savings contributed only 13·5 per cent to the total of private investment in 1972. If non-institutional private savings are added, the total amounts to about 40 per cent of the total savings fund. In comparison, foreign savings (mostly direct investment) accounted for over a quarter of total savings in 1972 and it is estimated will increase to 35·3 per cent in 1977.[11]

The discrepancy between theoretical statement and facts paradoxically supports rather than refutes the theory. The logic to explain this is straightforward. *Ex hypothesi*, a small advanced-industrial sector determines the rate of capital accumulation to be small. This is the core of the theory. Yet Tables 14.3 and 14.4 do not indicate that the savings and investment rates are correspondingly small; quite the contrary. Thus, there is no explanatory variable to account for this difference, unless the government and the foreign sectors step in. Once we keep in mind that the classical economists intended to make theoretical statements about England—not about the latecomer countries (the rest of the world)—it is easy to understand why classical economists failed to include the two sectors. The duties of the English government in the 18th and 19th centuries were reduced to mere night-watchman functions. Consider, for instance, an increase in the budget from £6 million to £16 million from 1740 to 1790 due to an increase in expenditure for wars against the French. Once the wars against the French were over, government expenditure decreased to £12 million in 1850 and to £9 million in 1870.[12] A government in its function as 'developmental agent' which would lend support to infant industries or even substitute for private activities was virtually absent. More than that, investment that nowadays is typically viewed as public, such as roads, bridges, etc., was executed by the emerging entrepreneurial class.[13] As an example, in 1760 Bridgwater and his inventor Bundley constructed the first canal in England in order to ship coal cheaply from Worsley to Manchester. On a larger scale, private enterprise created its own external (dis-)economies and made profits by doing so. This was the experience on which the classical theory was built.

When the continental European countries took their first steps in industrialisation, their intention was to develop rapidly and to reduce the English lead. The fast spurt could be accomplished only with governmental support and heavy reliance on foreign countries. The significant contribution the government made to capital accumulation has already been mentioned. We should add that a new type of investment bank or 'development bank' was created in most of the continental European countries.[14] All European countries drew heavily on foreign capital during the first decades of industrial development. France sold a third to a half of its railway shares in Great Britain. French, Belgian, and Swiss capital financed the bulk of the non-ferrous-metal and textile industries of Germany.[15] Much as in the Asian countries today, continental European industrialisation owes a significant debt to governmental and foreign support. The indirect inference to be drawn from classical and neoclassical theory—that a small domestic industrial sector is consistent with a high rate of capital accumulation only in the context of supporting sectors—fits well with broad historical experience.

Until this juncture, our analysis is a historical-empirical account of the Harrod-Domar aspect of classical and neoclassical theory. The savings and investment rates are high, and, given a low capital-output coefficient, the growth rates of the GNP (Table 14.5) will be high. Such a statement is, of course, tautological, as indeed much of modern

TABLE 14.5 *Annual growth rates of real GNP, selected Asian countries, 1950–80*

	GNP annual growth rates 1950–60	Annual rates 1960–70	Compound (%) 1965–70	GDP projected growth rate 1970–80
India[1]	3·5	3·8	4·4	5·5– 6·5
Indonesia	3·3	3·3	4·7	—
Korea, Rep. of[2]	5·2	9·2	12·0	8·0–10·0
Malaysia, West[3]	4·0	6·3	6·9	6·5– 6·5
Pakistan	2·5	5·4	5·5	6·0– 7·0
Philippines	4·0	5·7	6·3	6·0– 7·0
Sri Lanka	3·0	4·5	5·1	4·5– 5·5
Thailand[4]	6·4	7·9	8·5	8·0– 8·5

[1] For 1950–60 NDP at factor cost
[2] 1953–60
[3] 1955–60
[4] 1951–60

Source: *Economic Survey of Asia and the Far East, 1971*, table II-1-2. The projections are contained in two ESCAP documents, *Feasible Growth and Trade Gap Projections in the Developing ESCAP Region*, Developing Programming Techniques, Series no. 7, and *Sectoral Output and Employment Projections for the Second Development Decade*, Development Programming Technique Series no. 8, all three United Nations publications.

growth theory is. It is a simple identity unless *I* and *S* are historically-empirically explained. From the above growth relationship nothing can be said about the future behaviour of the determining variables unless additional variables are introduced.

Predictions based on high growth rates will suggest that the Asian countries rapidly approach the 'turning point' where all agricultural labour surplus is absorbed and the wage rate rises according to marginal labour productivity. In a way, this is reminiscent of neoclassical models for advanced countries where Keynesian thought is nonchalantly bypassed and full employment (which should be explained)

TABLE 14.6 *Total labour force and unemployment, selected Asian countries*

Country	Period	Total labour force (thousands)	Total number of unemployed (thousands)	Rate of unemployment (%) Total	Rural	Urban
India	July 1960–June 1961[a]	—	—	—	3·9	2·4
	June 1964–June 1965[a]	—	—	—	—	2·0
	July 1964–June 1965[b]	—	—	—	4·4	3·5
	July 1966–June 1967[b]	—	—	—	2·7	1·6
Indonesia	1961	—	—	—	—	8·5
	Nov. 1964–Feb. 1965	36543	845	2·3	2·0	5·1
	Sept.–Oct. 1967[c]	23734	195	0·8	0·6	2·5
Korea, Rep. of	1963	8653	706	8·1	2·9[d]	16·4[e]
	1965	—	—	—	3·1	12·7
	1970	10020	446	4·5	1·6	7·5[e]
Malaysia	1962[f]	2453	148	6·0	5·0	8·9[g]
	1967–1968[f]	2598	177	6·8	5·4	9·9[g]
	1967–1968[h]	—	—	8·9	—	—
	1971[h]	—	—	7·1	—	—
Philippines	Oct. 1958	8976	647	7·2	—	—
	Oct. 1963	10233	469	4·6	—	—
	1967	—	—	—	6·9	13·1
	Oct. 1968	11371	900	7·9	7·4	9·0
	Nov. 1971	13233	699	5·3	—	—
Singapore	1966	577	53	9·1	—	—
	1971	—	—	4·8	—	—
Sri Lanka	1968–69	4150	476	11·5	11·9 6·4[i]	15·6
	1969–70	4081	546	13·3	13·9 7·5[i]	17·3
Thailand	1966	—	—	—	—	2·8
	July–Sept. 1969	17196	39	0·2	0·1	1·2[j]

[a] National sample survey
[b] Integrated household schedule
[c] Java and Madura
[d] Farm households
[e] Non-farm households
[f] 'Active unemployment'
[g] Average of metropolitan and other urban areas
[h] Includes 'passive unemployment'
[i] Estates (tea, rubber, coconut, and other plantations)
[j] Average of Bangkok–Thonburi and other municipal areas.

Sources: V. R. U. Tilak, *Unemployment in Asian Countries and Problems of Measurement*, July 1972; for Sri Lanka, India, the Republic of Korea, Malaysia, and the Philippines, national official publications and information in the ILO and United Nations; and David Turnham and Ingles Jaeger, *The Employment Problem in Less-Developed Countries: A Review of Evidence* (Paris: OECD Development Centre, 1970) p. 57.

enters as an assumption with seemingly *a priori* plausibility. Asian experience strikingly demonstrates that high output-growth rates or investment rates are not a sufficient condition for absorbing an ever-increasing labour force.

A statistical-descriptive account of employment trends must remain, though, highly tentative. Few countries report even fewer statistics about employment to the ILO (International Labour Organisation). The differences and deficiencies in the data collection and nomenclature are considerable. Table 14.6 must be viewed in the light of these restrictions; the actual unemployment rates must be assumed to be generally higher. Consider merely the fact that in various countries, such as the Republic of Korea, the Philippines, and India, laws exist which forbid settlement in urban slum areas. The estimates of total population living in the slum areas will therefore be underestimated. Nevertheless, Table 14.7 reckons about 30 per cent of the urban population as slum inhabitants. A large portion of them must be considered to be underemployed or unemployed.[16] Equally, rural unemployment—against the neoclassical premise—is rampant. Rural unemployment is often less apparent, since the agricultural labour surplus migrates to the cities and alleviates the pressure on the rural areas. The increasing urban slums are to a large extent a result of rural population growth and inadequate agricultural employment opportunities—given the

TABLE 14.7 *Urban slums and uncontrolled settlements, selected Asian countries*

City	Year	Urban population (thousands)	Population in slums and uncontrolled settlements: Total (thousands)	Population in slums and uncontrolled settlements: % of urban population
Calcutta, India	1961	6700	2200	33
Colombo, Sri Lanka	1963	69·5*	30·5*	44
Djakarta, Indonesia	1961	2906	725	25
Karachi, Pakistan	1968	2700	600	27
Kuala Lumpur, Malaysia	1961	400	100	25
Manila, Philippines	1968	3000	1100	35
Seoul, Rep. of Korea	1970	440*	136·6*	30
Singapore	1966	1870	280	15

* Dwelling units

Sources: United Nations, *Housing, Building and Planning*, Document A/8037, p. 55; *Economic Survey of Asia and the Far East*, part 1 (United Nations: Tokyo, 1973) p. 141.

labour-absorptive capacity of the urban sector. The situation resembles communicating tubs where the liquid increases on one side as soon as the liquid decreases on the other. The 'pressure coefficient' is determined by the rate of migration and the urban-rural fertility differentials. The previously mentioned estimates suggest a 'pressure coefficient' above unity (which would indicate an equal increase in both sectors). Urban population growth and thus the section of the population seeking employment is rising in Asian countries at about 4 per cent per annum up to the year 2000, increasing its relative share of total population from 25 per cent to 43·5 per cent (Table 7.5).

Projections of employment or unemployment tend to be even more biased than the estimates presented in Table 14.8. To be valid a projection must be based on a theory. If the projections are based on the assumptions that the increasing advanced-industrial sector will absorb the agricultural labour surplus at a rate proportionate to the rate of capital accumulation—an assumption possibly underlying many protections—the labour absorption rates and the employment figures will clearly be biased upwards. Discounting these biases, the data presented in Table 14.8 still show a considerable increase in the unemployment rates in some areas of Asia within one decade. There is little use attempting or quoting projections beyond a decade on the basis of the present body of theoretical assumptions and hypotheses. The general hypothesis will suffice—that unemployment will increase in the future if the current path continues. In the subsequent sections, we shall have to explain why this is likely to be the case.

To continue the descriptive account, the second test has to be passed by classical-neoclassical theory with regard to income distribution. The empirical picture of European development has been stated to describe an inverted U-curve. This experience has been completed and a description of that trend would, in principle, be feasible without relying on a theory. A theory may facilitate the formulation of plausible hypotheses to be tested and direct the empirical research into proper channels; but it does not constitute a necessary condition for the description of the empirical trend. Although often, and with justification, criticised, the 'facts without theory' have a validity of their own. The case is entirely different when we attempt, not a historical description, but a theory which should allow predictions. The plausibility and consistency of the theory will determine the validity of the predictions. Assessing income distribution in Asia, we have available historical experience for the first part of the inverted U-curve. Figure 14.2 shows the Gini ratios related to various levels of *per capita*

TABLE 14.8 *Estimated levels of unemployment by region in Asia, 1970 and 1980*

Region	1970 (in thousands)			1980 (in thousands)			Unemployed as % of economically active population		
	Economically active population	Employed population	Unemployed	Economically active population	Employed population	Unemployed	1960	1970	1980
East Asia excl. mainland China	20257	18907	1350	27404	23235	4169	5·7	6·7	15·2
Middle South Asia	283088	272968	10120	344290	331878	12412	7·4	3·5	3·6
South-East Asia	110108	102510	7598	140975	128645	12330	5·6	6·9	8·7
South-West Asia	26586	24600	1986	34908	33123	1785	6·0	7·5	5·1

Source: Yves Sabolo, 'Sectoral Employment Growth: The Outlook for 1980', *International Labour Review*, vol. 3, no. 5, Nov. 1969, pp. 464 and 465.

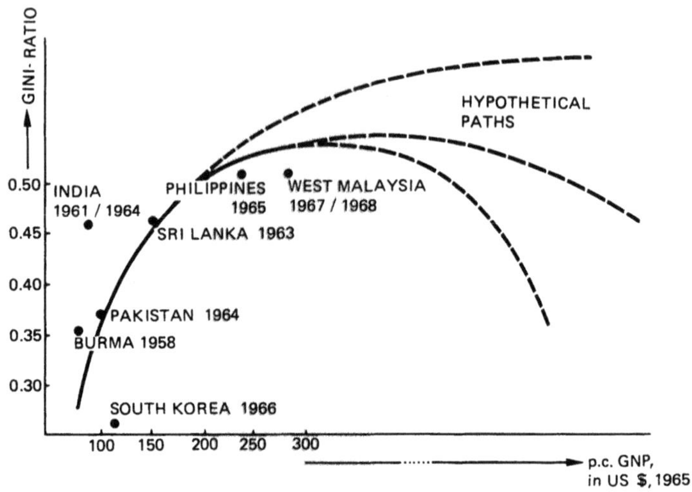

FIG. 14.2 *Gini ratios against GNP per capita, in selected Asian countries, 1965*

Sources: Mahar Mangahas, 'Income Inequality in the Philippines: A Decomposition Analysis', in *Income Distribution, Employment and Economic Development in South-East and East Asia*, Papers and Proceedings of the Seminar, sponsored jointly by the Japan Economic Research Center and The Council for Asian Manpower Studies, 16–20 December, 1974, vol. 1 (Tokyo/Manila, 1975) p. 332; figures for GNP (1965) from Felix Paukert, 'Income Distribution at Different Levels of Development: a Survey of Evidence', *International Labour Review*, no. 108, 2–3, 1973, pp. 97–125; for Gini ratios see Felix Paukert, *ibid*, David Soo, *Income Distribution in the ADE Region* (Manila: Asian Development Bank, May 1974) and Warnasana Rasaputram, 'Changes in the Pattern of Income Inequality in Ceylon', *Marga*, 1 : 4, 1972, pp. 60–91. From the available Gini ratios those closest to the year 1965 were taken.

GNP of selected Asian countries. Beyond the value of about $300 plotted on the horizontal axis, the paths are open to conjecture. 'The facts have not spoken.' A prediction is needed; the question arises—on the basis of what theory? It is plausible to start with classical-neoclassical theory, since the first part of the curve seems to support that theory. However, the empirical statement is on a level of generalisation that allows various theoretical explanations, of which the classical-neoclassical theory is only one. Hence, the test has to be not only in terms of empirical verification but also in terms of plausibility and consistency of the theory. Consistency is required on the 'horizontal' plane—with regard to the partial hypotheses referring to the first part of the curve, and with regard to the intertemporal scope combining the hypotheses of various phases in the entire development sequence. If 'horizontal' consistency exists, the validity in the 'vertical' may be expected. A preliminary test of the 'horizontal' consistency has been provided by contrasting the conditions of Asia with European conditions. The propositions of a 'relative marco-determinacy' and a 'simultaneous-sequence'-type development have attempted to refute the hypotheses of the feasibility of telescoping that conditional setting into contemporary Asia. Thus, the first part of the inverted U-curve is—although a proper empirical description of the predictions based on classical-neoclassical theory—not a meaningful test, since the explanation provided does not fulfil the criteria of plausibility and consistency. A choice among the hypothetical paths as depicted by the three broken lines in Fig. 14.2 is hence not feasible on the basis of classical-neoclassical theory. It will predict a decrease in the Gini ratios as development proceeds, along either the lower or intermediate path, or any path with a declining shape. In contrast, the theoretical framework to be elaborated will suggest the upper broken line to be the most likely outcome if the current trends continue. An alternative theoretical explanation is necessary, since the explanation of the first part of the curve is at variance with the actual forces at work. The inconsistency is apparent not only with regard to the previously mentioned unemployment figures in the light of high output and investment growth rates, but also with regard to the trends in real wages.

Empirically, we have downward trends in real wages in various Asian countries within the past decade or two. An empirical indication is provided by the figures on real wages in urban manufacturing industry (Table 14.9). Real wages in the rural sector are more difficult to ascertain empirically, since much of the income is in kind; but at least the average real consumption in the rural areas has declined in various Asian countries in the last decade or two. For instance, in India average real consumption in the rural areas had declined by about 16 per cent from 1960/61 to 1967/68.[17] In terms of classical theory, a decrease in real wages is not conceivable since the institutional wage rate is from the outset at a subsistence level (and a decrease would incur loss of human life). If the wage rate was above the institutional wage rate, it is from the outset in contradiction to that theory. In terms of neoclassical theory, the decrease in real wages would presume (under the condition of a constant employment rate) a decline in the average labour productivity in the manufacturing sector, which is at variance with the high savings, investment, and output-growth rates in that sector.

TABLE 14.9 *Increase in money and real wages in manufacturing industry, 1963–66 and 1966–69, selected Asian countries (% for 3-year period)*

Country	Pay period	Increase 1963–66 (%) Money wages	Increase 1963–66 (%) Real wages	Increase 1966–69 (%) Money wages	Increase 1966–69 (%) Real wages
India	monthly	27·2	−7·4	21·4	−4·9
Korea, Rep. of	monthly	70·4	4·1	108·0	50·7
Pakistan	monthly	21·5	3·0	1·4*	−5·3*
Philippines	monthly	15·5	−13·5	11·1	0·7
Singapore	hourly	−1·1	−4·8	5·5	1·7
Sri Lanka	daily	9·3	5·9	12·2	−3·5
Thailand	hourly	−6·3	−12·3	20·2	10·8

* Increase 1966–68.

Source: International Labour Organisation, *Yearbook* (Geneva, 1971).

The inconsistency of classical and neoclassical theory comes into clear focus when positing the empirical statement of decreasing wages to that of increasing unemployment. Following that theoretical understanding, decreasing wages will reflect either a decreasing marginal labour productivity or an increase in employment, or both. Positing the first assumption against the high output-growth rates, an increase in employment must be assumed. According to the neoclassical rationale, entrepreneurs are not willing nor forced to pay more for the input-factor labour than the marginal labour productivity. Since a decreasing shape of the curve of marginal labour productivity is assumed, any drop in the wage rate reflects a lower intersection point on the marginal labour productivity curve, and accordingly a higher level of labour employed. Given decreasing wages, neoclassical theory will predict a tendency of total employment to increase. In reality, employment opportunities are relatively decreasing. In the classical framework, the wages cannot drop below subsistence minimum (which is assumed under conditions of labour surplus) in the first place. There is consequently no explanation for a downward trend in the wage level in the second place.

The discrepancy between theoretical prediction and actual trends may be summarised in Fig. 14.3. On the vertical axis, the marginal labour productivity *MLP* is depicted; on the horizontal axis the total (unskilled) labour force *L*, employed and unemployed. By assumption,

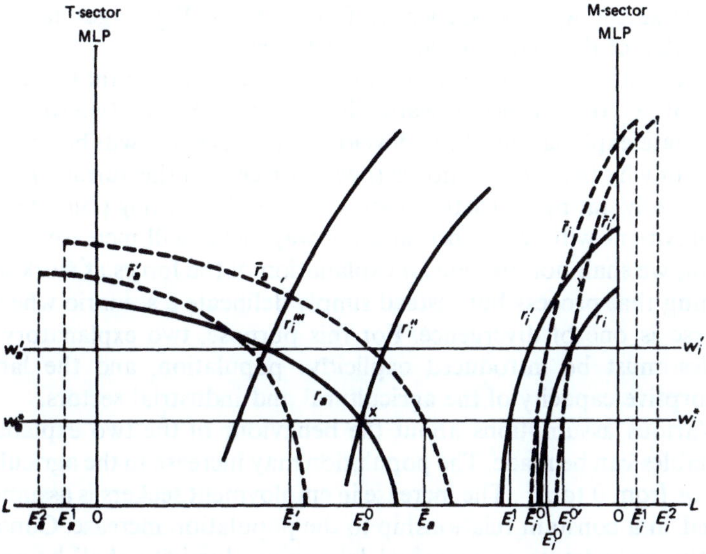

FIG. 14.3 ***Wage and employment levels given various assumptions about population growth and increasing productivity differentials***

the marginal labour productivity decreases as additional people are employed. The left-hand triangle represents the backward-agricultural sector, *T*-sector; the right-hand side the advanced-industrial sector, *M*-sector. The wage rate is in the former sector at w_a^*, in the latter at w_i^*, both of which may stand for a subsistence minimum wage rate. For the sake of simplicity we take in Fig. 14.3 w_a^* and w_i^* as equal. In the *T*-sector the employment at the wage rate w_a^* and a marginal labour productivity r_a is at E_a^0. In the *M*-sector at a wage rate w_i^* and a marginal labour productivity r_i, people are employed up to E_i^0. Neoclassical theory assumes that no significant (agricultural) unemployment exists in the pre-transition phase, while classical theory allows for unemployment. The common assumption of both is that r_i shifts westwards. Let us consider three intersection points. At r_i' the people employed in the advanced-industrial sector increase from E_i^0 to E_i^1. Unemployment still exists at a level E_a^0 to E_i^1. At r_i'', the marginal labour productivity of the fully employed *M*-sector equals the subsistence wage of the *T*-sector. Unemployment ceases to exist. From that intersection point on, the neoclassical world begins. As the marginal labour productivity shifts to r_i''', the wage level stands at w' for both *T*-

and M-sector, $w'_a = w'_i$. Generally, from x on (at E_a^0), wages increase at the value of the marginal labour productivity.

The course of actual events, however, does not warrant the hypothesis of a convergence toward the 'turning point'. Indeed, for an adequate explanation of the development process it will be crucial to explain why the process moves toward or against the 'turning point'—not merely stating that 'if the process reaches the turning point, then full employment will be reached and the wage level will increase'. At this point, we shall not provide an explanation of the forces at work determining that process but instead simply delineate a scenario where the course is one of divergence. For this purpose, two explanatory variables must be introduced explicitly: population, and the labour-absorptive capacity of the agricultural and industrial sectors.

Various assumptions about the behaviour of the two explanatory variables can be made. The population may increase in the agricultural sector from 0 to E_a^1. The increase in employment seekers is assumed to stand in a constant relationship to the population increase. Concomitantly, an increase in marginal labour productivity shall be accomplished. By a first assumption, the employment absorption effect of the latter exceeds the unemployment effect of population growth. The broken line $\bar{r}_a$ designates the path. At the ongoing wage rate w_a^* the employment increases from E_a^0 to $\bar{E}_a^0$, plus additions from 0 to E_a^1. By a second assumption, let the population growth be larger, exceeding the compensating increases in marginal labour productivity. The population increase from 0 to E_a^2 offsets the increase in the marginal labour productivity from r_a to $\bar{r}'_a$. At the same wage rate w_a^*, the 'unemployment effect' of the increasing population is 0 to E_a^2. The total of people employed in the agricultural sector is from E_a^2 to $\bar{E}'_a$. Assuming a population and MLP in the M-sector of r_i, the total unemployment will increase from $\bar{E}'_a$ to E_i^0. Unless the M-sector does not increase its marginal labour productivity at an equivalent rate, unemployment will occur. A race occurs beteween urban population growth (natural growth plus migration) and the labour-absorptive capacity of the advanced-industrial sector.

In actuality, the low labour absorption by the M-sector largely prevents a gradual integration of the additional labour force into the production process. Since the growth rates in that sector are relatively large, the explanation lies in production functions of that sector which favour capital over labour inputs. The substitution process may be expressed by a gradual transformation of the marginal labour productivity as described, e.g. by $\bar{r}_i$. The employment effect of the shift from r_i to

$\bar{r}_i$ is an insignificant increase from E_i^0 to $\bar{E}_i^0$. This modest result is accomplished under the assumption of a low increase in the urban population from 0 to $\bar{E}_i^1$. It can easily be concluded from the curvature of the marginal labour productivity slope of the industrial sector that a further shift, say up to E_i^2, will cause an increase in unemployment in the urban-industrial sector. Against the initial unemployment situation designated by the difference between E_a^0 and E_i^0, the new unemployment stands at a magnitude denoted by the difference between E_a^0 and $\bar{E}_i^{0'}$. Unemployment increases from E_i^0 to $\bar{E}_i^{0'}$. Both the counterforces of rapid population growth and the limited absorptive capacity of the advanced-industrial sector (due to its small initial size and changes in the production functions) explain a persistent or increasing unemployment rate, even in the presence of high output-growth rates. What needs further explanation are the two explanatory variables themselves.

Our analysis does not suggest that classical and neoclassical theory would not explain anything at all. It is only the second part of the story which fails. The investment and savings rates correspond neatly with the output performance. In its aggregate terms the nucleus of the model is intact. Beyond the initial point, however, the model may hardly serve as a basis for rational and successful policy-making. By no means should partial hypotheses be taken out of the overall context of the theory and serve as a rationale for policy-making. In particular, increases in income inequality cannot serve as a panacea to produce a higher savings rate. Positive effects in terms of a higher labour absorptive capacity of the advanced-industrial sector could not be expected. Inadequate labour absorption itself being a major cause of increasing income inequality, increasing income inequality cannot be a remedy for the former.

A novel approach is needed. It must head in two directions. First, relevant explanatory variables must be included as endogenous variables. They cannot be treated as undetermined exogeneous variables nor as *ceteris paribus* assumptions. Second, the explanation of the socio-economic process must include plausible hypotheses for the second part of the development story: the trend toward increasing productivity, asset, and income differentials. It is clear from the immanent logic of the development process that the first and the second part are closely interrelated. To the extent that this is the case, the first part will also need revision.

15 Against the Current

I. BIRD'S-EYE VIEW

Let us first delineate the basic theoretical relationships. Figure 15.1 embraces all variables relevant for developing a set of hypotheses about the development process. A distinction between the agricultural and industrial sectors is not made in this general context, but will be introduced later on in the discussion. The economic-resource flows constitute the core of the model delineated. The variables of the explicitly stated economic system S_e are related to the systems S_t, S_c, and S_n. The behavioural aspects are excluded at this stage of the analysis; they will be introduced in Chapter 17.

In describing the development process we may start anywhere. There is mutual causation, and an initial change in any of the variables will affect other variables, or the entire composite of systems. Let us start with the distribution of assets. We assume a dual structure with a classification according to size of the establishments. We have 'modern' enterprises $\bar{F}^m$ and 'traditional' enterprises $\bar{F}^t$. They may vary in size from $\bar{F}_1, \ldots, \bar{F}_n$. The relationship between the two criteria may be assumed to be one of two linearly related sequences

$$\bar{F}^t, \ldots, \bar{F}^m$$

$$\bar{F}_1, \ldots, \bar{F}_n.$$

This assumption simplifies the theoretical discussion. It will be sufficient to focus on only one of the two criteria. We choose in the following the scale size of firms as the criterion for stating the differentials. Certainly, there will be deviations; but as a rule it is plausible to assume that small enterprises will be of the traditional type while large enterprises will be modern. In any case, the null-hypothesis and the opposite hypothesis may claim little plausibility.

The distribution of the scale size of the firms determines the type of production functions applied

$$F_1, \ldots, F_n.$$

In explicit form the set of production functions may be written as

$$\{O_1, \ldots, O_n\} = \mathbf{f}\{X_1, \ldots, X_n\},$$

where O_i designates the output, and X_i the input vector of the firm group F_i, and $\mathbf{f}$ a vector-valued function. Since we must expect the differences in the production functions to be large, it cannot be meaningful to start with the concept of an aggregate production function. Both O_i and X_i are assumed to differ significantly; hence the relevance and validity of aggregate output and aggregate factor combination concepts are questionable. The micro-production function of $\bar{F}_i$ may be stated in explicit form

$$O_i = f(X_i) = \mathbf{g}(K_i, L_i, S_{n_i}, S_{c_i}, S_{t_i}),$$

where K_i stands for both accumulated capital stock and investment, L_i for the labour force employed, S_{t_i} for technology applied or possible access to the range of available technology (financial and informational), and S_{n_i} and S_{c_i} for the impact of population and the ecosystem respectively on producing the output O_i.

The income is defined as $y_i = \pi_i + w_i$; $w_i = L_i \cdot \bar{w}_i$, where $\bar{w}_i$ designates the average wage level of $\bar{F}_i$. In Fig. 15.1, a bimodal world is for simplicity assumed. The input-factor mixes are split into one for small and one for large enterprises, X_1 and X_n respectively. The 'micro'-distribution, as defined by the profit-wage-ratio π_i/w_i, is determined by the average factor mix of each firm group $\bar{F}_i$—an aggregation 'in the small'. Specifically, the share of the wages fund w_i is determined by the size of L_i in relation to K_i, K_i/L_i-ratio, and the average real-wage level prevailing in $\bar{F}_i$. The share of profits π_i is determined by the initial

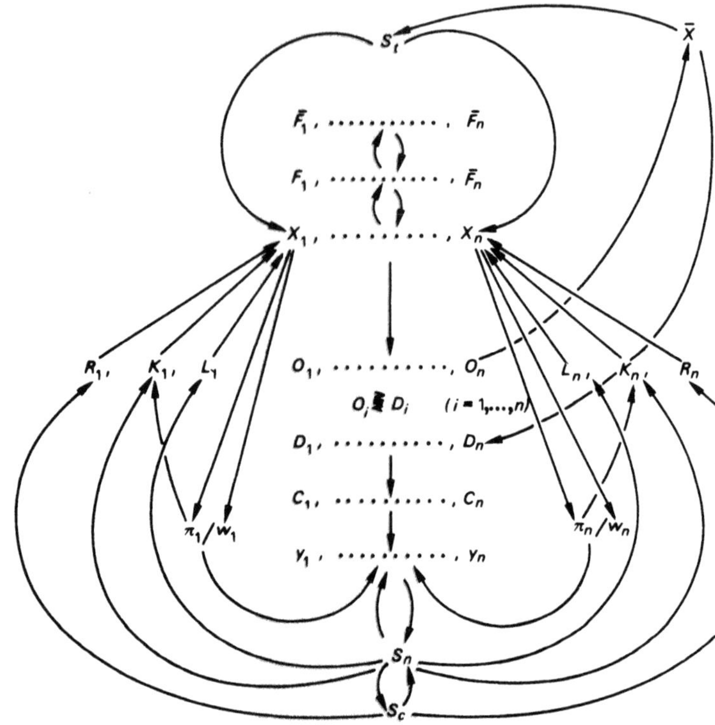

FIG. 15.1 *Basic causal links of socio-economic variables within a multi-systems context*

$\bar{F}_i$ = Set of enterprises of Group i; where for this and all subsequent variables $i = 1, \ldots, n$; for $\bar{F}$ the subscript i indicates the scale size; small (large) numbers denote small (large) scale size
F_i = Production function of Group i
O_i = Output of Group i:
X_i = Set of input factors of Group i
  R_i = Natural resources used in Group i
  K_i = Capital stock, investment (rate) in Group i
  L_i = Level and structure of employment (rate)
  S_t = Techno-system, factors related to capital-output ratio, labour productivity
Y_i = Total income of Group i:
  $\sum Y_i = Y$ = total income of all groups
  w_i = wages fund of Group i
  π_i = profits earned by Group i
C_i = Consumption propensity of Group i

capital stock and investment rate K_i, the returns from sales of output O_i, and the forces underlying the determination of w_i.

The overall income distribution $y_1, \ldots, y_n$ is given by (1) the overall profit distribution, (2) the overall wage distribution, and (3) the overall ratio π/w—all three categories determined by the scale-size distribution $\bar{F}_1, \ldots, \bar{F}_n$. In addition (4), income level and differentials are determined by the population size and distribution, and the population-growth differentials. Saving is assumed to be done in the model outlined by capitalists only (link from π_i to K). The total income is

$$Y = \sum_{i=1}^{n} y_i,$$

an aggregation of the group incomes according to the above scale-size pattern. If π is subtracted from Y, the income (depicted on the last line) is used up for consumption only. Aggregate consumption C is obtained by multiplying Y with the average propensity to consume,[1] the consumption structure, by multiplying the incomes of each group by the propensities to consume of each group. In an analogous way, aggregate demand and structure of demand are obtained by allowing for the respective elasticities of demand, where the additional link to foreign demand $\bar{X}$ should be noted. The locus where a specific level of aggregate demand and demand structure meets with a specific level of aggregate output and output structure is—the central focus of market-equilibrium theory—the 'market place'. Market equilibrium exists if the aggregate levels and structural patterns of the two sets of variables, supply and demand, conform, say if

$$D_i - O_i = 0, \qquad i = 1, \ldots, n.$$

The above condition, clearly, is static. Little can be gained in actual progress or analytical understanding if, for a historical instance, the equilibrium condition is fulfilled. The crucial question is whether or not the forces at work in the two sets of variables, demand and supply,

---

D_i = Demand (aggregate, average, elasticities) of Group i
S_n = Population system
S_e = Ecosystem
S_t = Techno-system
$\bar{X}$ = Foreign demand (exports) and foreign supply (imports)

can move along a path where the two sets of variables converge and are mutually consistent. There is no immanent law which would force the aggregate levels and structural traits of the variables into congruence. The following discussion will demonstrate this, and show, too, why Asia is a case in point.

II. ASSET DIFFERENTIALS AND CONCENTRATION TRENDS

As stated earlier, the analytical entrance into the complex of causal interactions is possible at any point. We start from the asset distribution. Our basic hypothesis is that—in the context of the development patterns prevailing in Asia—the asset differentials are rapidly increasing. In putting forth this hypothesis we revert for a brief theoretical outline to the proposition of a 'simultaneous-sequence' type of development. This, first of all, again brings into focus the sectoral distinction between agriculture and industry. The distinction implies that scale size and degree of 'advancedness' are not intrinsically linked to the type of productive activity. Although the agricultural sector may, indeed, be more 'backward' than the industrial sector, the emphasis given to development differentials in both sectors adds a crucial criterion for explaining the development processes.

Starting with the industrial sector (see Fig. 13.1), the range of 'advancedness', or (in the widest sense) of technologies, has been assumed to be, in period 2,

$$\bar{B}^{a'}, \ldots, \bar{B}^{m'}.$$

The two values constitute the hypothetical range of feasible development paths. The development path will show an extreme form of dualism if the two partial paths move along the outer boundary lines.

Pertaining to the empirical situation of Asia, the 'technology' applied appears to follow very much a dualistic pattern whose outer boundaries are, indeed, near $B^{\bar{a}'}$ and $B^{\bar{m}'}$. The large value in the development differential of various sectors of contemporary Asian countries is a specific feature pertaining only to contemporary Asia and not, for instance, to 19th-century Europe or Japan. In European latecomer countries and Japan, the entrance into the historical sequence was much earlier and the dualistic differential not so large.

A second hypothesis refers to the change in the dualistic differential.

Clearly, $\bar{B}^{m'}$ follows contemporary technological progress of the advanced Western countries. The rate of change in the dualistic differential is therefore very high. Assuming a 'stagnation path' for the traditional sector in both contemporary Asia and 19th-century Europe, the differential between the two sectors will increase more rapidly in contemporary Asia, since the rate of technological progress is faster in the advanced sector in contemporary Asia than it was in 19th-century Europe. Both the initial value of the dualistic differential and the rate of increase in that differential are higher in contemporary Asia. As a consequence, the nature of the two unevenly structured segments and their interrelationships are different in contemporary Asia from the now-industrialised countries. For instance, in Japan (where considerable differentials in the economic structure continue to exist), the traditional, usually small-scale enterprises had the function of supplying intermediate products to the emerging modern, large-scale industrial complex. Today a close dependency still exists between a large number of enterprises of a smaller scale and a few huge industrial conglomerates.[2] No such 'natural' companionship is usually found in the developing Asian countries today. It is bound to become even more impossible if the development process continues in the current pattern.

A close causal nexus between technology and capital accumulation exists. As a consequence, differentials in the degree of 'advancedness' or 'modernity' of the technology will, first of all, be reflected in increasing differentials between production functions of the labour-intensive and the capital-intensive types. Furthermore, out of a given capital stock, an increasing relative share will be devoted to production in modern enterprises. The relative decrease in the capital supply for the smaller traditional enterprises constitutes an increasing bottleneck for new investment and investment which enhances labour productivity.

Increasing differentials in capital accumulation lead to increasing productivity differentials. Thus, profits increase relatively faster in the modern large-enterprise sector as compared to the traditional small-scale sector, which increases the differentials in the capacity to accumulate capital. Increasing economic power of the 'elite' enterprises corresponds to an increasing power in the body politic. Most directly, governmental investment loans (from the domestic budget or international agencies) are secured for developmental projects of the modern-industrial complex. The know-how for entering financial markets necessary to secure financing is not available for the bulk of small producers. Indirectly, the infrastructural investment is directed in such a way that complementarities and economies of scale for the modern enterprises are sufficiently available, increased, or newly created. Acess to education is concentrated in urban areas and biased toward 'modernity'. Private capital accumulation concentrates rapidly in a relatively small modern sector and creates at a similar rate the logistic support it needs to sustain and accelerate the cumulative process. The traditional small-scale enterprises are not only kept down by their small capital basis but also by an infrastructural setting which becomes increasingly hostile to them.

Similar concentration processes occur in the agricultural sector—in classical and neoclassical theory, by definition the 'backward' sector. There are various causes for the initial unequal distribution of land and productive assets. Inequality in the productive capacity will be largest in countries where landlord systems and/or foreign occupation of land and physical assets dominate the distribution pattern. Irrespective of the causes which lead to the present distributional pattern, the pattern itself constitutes a determinant of the present and future processes in the agricultural sector.

As in the industrial sector, we may divide the farms according to their size into large, medium, small, and marginal farms. These types have distinct features in the institutional arrangements and production functions, the largest distinctions being between the large and the marginal farms. Large farms are usually owned by landlords. In India 12 per cent of all farmers own half of the total agricultural land. The medium farms are close to the big farms in the type of production function used, but are often not based on landlord institutions but rely instead on self-employed and non-family labour. The small farmer either owns a small plot of land or rents land from the landlord. He employs family labour to cultivate his plot. The production function is of a traditional type; in contrast to the big and medium farms, it is not capital- but highly labour-intensive.

Given the initial distribution of assets, institutional arrangements, and changes in agricultural land densities, there is a strong tendency in the socio-economic process emerging from this constellation to increase the existing differentials in the asset ownership and outputs accruing to farms. The 'green revolution' dramatically accelerated this process, although it would have occurred even without the drastic changes the 'revolution' implied. On top of unequal distribution of assets to start with, those who own vast amounts of land—large and medium farmers—have access to modern inputs such as mechanisation, chemical fertilisers, etc. The modest starting point of the small and marginal farmers precludes the use of similar input combinations. As a consequence, output differentials reflecting the differentials in the changes of the input size and quality are increasing. The output-growth rates (not only the absolute output) increase faster in the large farms than in those without the advanced inputs.

The increasing differentials in the agricultural surplus explain the increasing capital concentration which is—in a cumulatively reinforcing cycle—the basis for increased surplus generation in subsequent periods. The landlords have little inclination to pay to landless labourers wages higher than the subsistence minimum, and they increase the rent for the land let to tenants.

In both cases the surplus is absorbed by the landlords in the classical fashion (in Fig. 14.3 the area depicted by marginal labour productivity and subsistence wage line w_a^*). The concentrated capital is used further to consolidate the asset basis. In particular, landlords, but also medium farmers, view it as advisable either to release the small tenants and operate large-scale farms with labourers (some of the farmer tenants will constitute that labour force) or to purchase new land from small landowners. As the productivity per hectare increases, the price for land increases adding to the problems caused by an increasing agricultural density).

Increased returns for those who own most of the land already, together with higher relative prices for land, make a gradual land expropriation an almost deterministic event. Both capital accumulation and land concentration constitute the economic basis for the large farmers to consolidate and extend the existing asset distribution. The linkages to the technical system accelerate the concentration process and increase the disparities in the distribution of asset ownership. The analogous hypotheses of a large divergence between the two boundary values on the simultaneous-sequence scale apply, *mutatis mutandis*, to the agricultural sector. Although not explicitly stated in Fig. 13.1, the argument may be extended to the agricultural sector, say

$$\bar{A}^{k'}, \ldots, \bar{A}^{q'},$$

and we may relate the corresponding scale sizes and production functions of the farmers to the above set of states in the agricultural sector

$$\bar{F}^{t'}, \ldots, \bar{F}^{m'}$$

$$F'_1, \ldots, F'_h.$$

As stated, there is a positive correlation between the values of the sequence of $\bar{A}$, $\bar{F}$, and F. The width between $\bar{A}^{k'}$ and $\bar{A}^{q'}$ becomes a constituent determinant of the disparity-increasing process in the agricultural sector. The larger the initial disparity, the larger the acceleration of the change towards more disparity. In most Asian developing countries, land reforms are implemented in one form or another. The degree of success in implementing these reforms, however, correlates positively to a significant extent with the degree of initial equality of land distribution. The higher the levels and/or changes in the asset disparities, the more difficult it appears to be to implement the reforms. First, the economic mechanism works towards concentration. Second, political power is closely linked with economic power. Political reforms—their formulation and implementation—are a product of political forces. The rural elite (though usually weaker than the urban) has sufficient political power to influence if not to shape laws according to their own interests. If ideological phraseology or well-intended policies bring about substantial progress in laws referring to institutional changes, the intended changes usually fail in the phase of their execution.[3] Indeed, most Asian countries have well-formulated land-reform plans; but the fact that the inequality in the distribution of productive assets and land remains unmitigated and is in various regions increasing drastically proves that the paper plan is not implemented. There are various legal and illegal ways to circumvent governmental decrees. Blatant bribes to government officials are one way. The registering of land (if size limits on land holdings per person are introduced) in the names of relatives is another. In both circumvention manoeuvres, age-old traditions may give social approval to law-circumventing behaviour. Given the trend toward increasing capital concentration, there is an eminent tendency to concentrate additional land in order to further increase or at least to sustain the current rates of capital formation and output.

Under this regime, the small farmers have little chance to improve their lot. If they do not sell part of their plot, the present politico-socio-economic setting makes it difficult to improve the assets. The capital surplus of the large farmers is insufficiently redirected to farmers' banks (which are still grossly lacking, insufficiently advertised and administered, or subject to the suspicion of the tradition-oriented farmers). While in Meiji Japan and in the period of early European industrialisation, a substantial agricultural surplus could be channelled into the industrial sector (see p. 129), in contemporary Asia this surplus is hardly used for a redistribution within the agricultural sector itself.[4]

Irrespective of the fact that the agricultural sector is a debtor to the industrial sector, a redistribution at least of the increases in the differentials would constitute the minimum requirement to initiate growth on a broad front in the agricultural sector.

III. INCREASING INCOME DIFFERENTIALS

The concentration trends have a strong bearing on major variables determining income distribution. Urban unemployment increases due to the shift in the micro-production functions towards labour-saving combinations and the relative shift from small enterprises to enterprises using basically capital-intensive production functions. As a consequence, the income (including transfer-income) differentials increase between wage earners and urban underemployed or unemployed.

Within the two major income classes, capital has a tendency to increase relative to labour. Theoretically, the increase in the total profits over the wages fund may be explained by fast-increasing profits with wages remaining approximately constant. The increasing profits are explained by the rise in profits of the larger firms, with profits of the smaller firms remaining unchanged at a low level. The rise of the π/w ratio is therefore explained by the rate at which the profit differentials increase (assuming no drastic absolute decrease in profits of the small firms). The empirical data to support this hypothesis are scanty, but broad observation will already suggest the hypothesis to be valid in the empirical context of Asia. The hypothesis receives some specific support from a recent study which reckons the ratios of profits to wages per employee according to firm size in the Greater Bangkok area (in which most of Thailand's industry is located).[5] Table 15.1 shows a clear tendency for the π/w ratio to increase as the size of the firms increases. The differentials in the π/w ratio are almost entirely due to the differentials in π. While the range in average profits is 53·8 (7·6–61·4), the range in average wages is only 8·3 (6·8–15·1); or, in other words, the deviations from the mean appear to be insignificant in average wages against the deviations from the mean in average profits.

The large profits of the larger firms allow large investment rates which—leading to the expansion of production and 'capital deepening'—induce profit increases in subsequent periods. The increase in the differentials of π is thus propelled by the imminent forces underlying the differential capital-accumulation process. The income

TABLE 15.1 *Average profits and wages per person employed by size of industrial firms in Greater Bangkok area**

Size of firms (no. of persons employed)	Average profit per employee per year (฿'000)†	Average wages per employee per year (฿'000)	Ratio of profits to wages per employee
1–5	11·3	7·6	1·50
6–9	7·6	7·8	0·98
10–49	9·9	6·9	1·45
50–99	34·1	12·1	2·83
100–249	31·8	13·4	2·37
250–500	61·4	15·1	4·06
501–1000	19·7	9·1	2·18
Over 1000	46·3	9·7	4·79
Average for all sizes	38·5	10·3	3·74

* Survey taken in summer of 1972.
† 1 ฿ = 1 Thai *Baht* (20 ฿ = $1 US).

Source: N. K. S. Sarkar, *Industrial Structure of Greater Bangkok* (Bangkok: United Nations Asian Institute for Economic Development and Planning, 1974), p. 31.

effect is a dual one. First, it expands the gap between small and large firms. And, second, it expands the gap between the social classes of profit- and wage-earners (in the F_n-sector, and in the total average).

Increasing inequalities in asset distribution have a similar impact on income distribution of the agricultural sector. A principal determinant is, again, increasing unemployment, which deteriorates the ratio of wage-earners to non-wage-earners (transfer receivers, dissavers). Changes in the production functions may be, in principle, land-saving and labour-saving. Since the technology that accounts for the two changes in the production functions are closely interrelated, a response to increasing land density often does not increase the labour employed but instead leaves the unemployment rate constant or increasing. This phenomenon applies in general to all farms. The forces working against employment are, of course, stronger in the large-scale farming sector. Production is capital-intensive, and due to the dual substitution effect, the additional capital invested not only augments output per hectare but also largely saves labour. Small farms, on the contrary, have not the funds to introduce labour-saving machinery such as combine harvesters, etc.; they employ labour instead. The small-scale production functions remain basically 'stable' at a traditional sector mix.

Though not unambiguous, there is empirical evidence that the number of people employed per hectare decreases as the farm size increases.[6] The effect on employment by technology is a dual one. First, the production functions of the large farms change towards the labour-saving, capital-intensive type. Second, the concentration process, in terms of size, capital accumulation, access to modern inputs, and political influence, increases the relative share belonging to farms using capital-intensive production functions. The concentration process is closely linked with the ability to substitute capital for labour. The latter, in turn, is necessary to sustain the concentration process. The causality clearly is mutually reinforcing. Both the feasibility of implementing technology along the outer boundary on the simultaneous sequence, and the institutional and economic conditions enabling the concentration process, determine the rates of agricultural (un-) employment.

The persistently high rate of rural unemployment will suggest that wages remain at a low (basically subsistence) level while the difference between the increase in productivity and wage rate is appropriated as additional profit by the landlords. The large farms will pay higher wages in some areas where labour becomes scarce (particularly during the harvest season). However, the persistent population growth does not suggest a long-run scenario where full employment constitutes the major premise in a model of wage determination—a question that will be taken up in more detail in section IX, 'Impact of Population Growth on Socio-Economic Processes' (see, in particular, Table 15.3 and Figure 15.5). The empirical indication is that the average real-wage level remained basically at a low level or even decreased. It seems that, on mere logical grounds, the wage differentials of the landless labourers cannot change significantly. Being at subsistence level, drastic decreases in the lower-income brackets seem to be infeasible—which would be necessary to offset the larger incomes of the more successful members or groups of the labour force. The principal determinant of the increasing income inequality among the rural poor is increasing unemployment rather than increasing disparities in wages. Since income in rural areas is typically shared in a family, the decrease in the average family income is more or less proportionate to the number of people (un-) employed per family. These phenomena probably explains better than any explanation by the wage rate, the large number of people living under the 'poverty line'—a topic which will constitute a main theme in Chapter 16, 'New Normative Directions of Socio-Economic Processes' (in particular, Section III, 'Poverty Line and Minimum Income,' pp. 204–211).

IV. EFFECT OF INCREASING INCOME INEQUALITY ON SAVING AND CONSUMPTION BEHAVIOUR

Increasing income disparities have an impact on the aggregate level and structure of both saving and consumption. Let us start with an asset or scale distribution among enterprises

$$\bar{F}_1, \bar{F}_2, \ldots, \bar{F}_n.$$

For ease of developing the argument, we neglect at this point the sectoral distinction into industry and agriculture. The propensities to save and invest from assets (for the sake of simplicity taken as equal) shall be $\alpha_1, \ldots, \alpha_n$, so that we have

$$\bar{F}_1 \cdot \alpha_1. \bar{F} \cdot \alpha_2, \ldots, \bar{F} \cdot \alpha_n.$$

$1, \ldots, n$ again designate the direction of the increases in the asset concentration and size of enterprises. The empirical picture of increasing capital concentration lends support to two hypotheses. First, the propensities to accumulate capital α positively correlate with the scale size

$$\alpha_1 < \alpha_2 < \cdots < \alpha_n.$$

Second, the savings differentials and the political factors mentioned earlier allow the rates of increase in the capital accumulation to increase absolutely and relatively faster in the large-scale than in the small-scale enterprises. We may give a micro-economic interpretation to the classical hypothesis that only the modern sectors save, and suggest that only or mainly the larger enterprises save and, moreover, that they increase their share as development proceeds. In this context, a shift from small-scale to large-scale enterprises increases the overall propensity to save and decreases the overall propensity to consume. According to classical doctrine, this will increase the productive capacity of the economy, generate income growth, and eventually lead to a self-sustained development process. The assumption implied is that the newly created income generates sufficient demand to sustain production at large. As will become apparent in the following section, demand does not come forth 'automatically', but may prompt constraints to that process.

For the disaggregated consumption functions of individual entrepreneurs, we have the reflected image of disaggregated savings functions

$$\bar{F}_1 \cdot \beta_1, \bar{F} \cdot \beta_2, \ldots, \bar{F} \cdot \beta_n,$$

where $\beta_1, \ldots, \beta_n$ denote the individual propensities to consume, assumed to decrease with increasing asset size. We have a pattern of income distribution

$$\bar{y}_1, \bar{y}_2, \ldots, \bar{y}_n,$$

which is explained by the above asset distribution; $\bar{y}_i$ is defined as average income of $\bar{F}_i$. Total income for the groups and for the whole economy is

$$\bar{F}'_1 \cdot \bar{y}_1, \bar{F}'_2 \cdot \bar{y}_2, \ldots, \bar{F}'_n \cdot \bar{y}_n$$

or

$$\sum_{i=1}^{k=n} \bar{F}'_i \cdot \bar{y}_i = \sum_{i=1}^{k=n} y_i,$$

where y_i stands for the total group income of the ith group, and $\bar{F}'_i$ for people employed in the ith sector. Population growth and changes in population-growth differentials (which would change in the long-run $\bar{F}'_i$) are at this point excluded. As is known from our earlier discussion (see Ch. II, I and p. 317 n. 2), the population-growth rate determines total as well as *per capita* income growth. However, introducing population does not vitiate the argument; it rather reinforces it. For instance, persistently high population-growth rates in the low-income groups and decreasing population-growth rates in the upper strata as experienced in contemporary Asia will increase the income differentials between the two income groups, or, more generally, along $\bar{y}_1, \ldots, \bar{y}_n$. We shall return to the differential behaviour of population in the next section. Here, assuming constancy, the change in the income distribution for the whole group may be expressed as

$$\frac{\Delta y_1}{y_1} \leqslant \frac{\Delta y_2}{y_2} \leqslant \cdots \leqslant \frac{\Delta y_n}{y_n};$$

for instance

$$\frac{\Delta y_1}{y_1} = \frac{\Delta y_2}{y_2} = 0 < \cdots < \frac{\Delta y_n}{y_n}.$$

As stated, increases in y_i are due only to increases in $\bar{y}_i$ but not to changes in the distribution of the members pertaining to each income group. The distribution in the increase of consumption due to the income increase in the various sub-groups is, using the above pattern of distribution change, for example,

$$\frac{\Delta y_1}{y_1} \cdot \beta_1 = \frac{\Delta y_2}{y_2} \cdot \beta_2 = 0 < \cdots < \frac{\Delta y_n}{y_n} \cdot \beta_n.$$

Although small-scale enterprises have high propensities to consume, the levels and increases of consumption are nevertheless low, since the levels and increases of income are low. For instance, consumption increases in sub-groups 1 and 2 are zero because the income increases are zero. The propensity, and thus the potential, of consumption increases is high but the income to realise the potential is lacking. In the upper sub-groups, say n, the propensities to consume are relatively low and will decrease as the income of that group increases. The increases of consumption may nevertheless be comparatively large (assuming a marginal propensity to consume above zero) since Δy_n is large.

The pattern of income distribution determines both the aggregates of savings and consumption as well as the structures of the two aggregates. Using the assumed distributional pattern of income increase and keeping the propensities constant, ΔC and ΔS are determined by

$$\begin{aligned} \Delta C = \Delta Y\beta &= \Delta y_1\beta_1 + \Delta y_2\beta_2 + \cdots + \Delta y_n\beta_n \\ +\Delta S = \Delta Y\alpha &= \Delta y_1\alpha_1 + \Delta y_2\alpha_2 + \cdots + \Delta y_n\alpha_n \\ \hline \Delta Y = \Delta Y(\alpha + \beta) &= \Delta y_1(\alpha_1 + \beta_1) + \Delta y_2(\alpha_2 + \beta_2) + \cdots + \Delta y_n(\alpha_n + \beta_n) \end{aligned}$$

As income grows in the described distributional fashion, the structures of both total savings and consumption change. The small units have both low or zero increases in savings and low or zero increases in consumption. The large-scale units have both high increases in savings and high increases in consumption (as compared to the small-scale units).

V. DEMAND AS AN EXPLANATORY VARIABLE

The level and structure of demand are *ceteris paribus* determined by income distribution. Usually income distribution is kept constant as a *ceteris paribus* assumption—as in the Keynesian income approach and the income-growth approach. Given the features of highly distinct income-growth differentials, it is theoretically more adequate to keep those determinants as the *ceteris paribus* assumptions and to introduce the income-distribution variable as the principal determinant. The distributional traits have been assumed to constitute the principal determinants of the changes in the levels and structure of aggregate savings and consequently of the entire process of capital accumulation. It can be shown that the distributional features have a similar crucial impact on the behaviour of demand.

The level and distribution of effective demand depends on (1) the level of income, (2) the propensities to consume, and (3) the income elasticities of demand, each according to the distribution $\bar{F}_1, \ldots, \bar{F}_n$. In assessing demand we carry over from the preceding discussion the assumption that (a) the income differentials are increasing and (b) the propensities to consume decrease the higher we move up the income strata. Additional assumptions about the income elasticity of demand must be introduced. It is theoretically plausible, and ever since Engels empirically supported, that lower-income groups, as the group $\bar{F}_1$, respond to income increases strongly with an increase in the consumption of food and of basic necessities, while luxuries or consumer durables are not demanded. There are notable exceptions as, for instance, funerals in some Indonesian islands whose costs equal the relative costs for a car in Western countries. Higher-income groups, say $\bar{F}_n$, will have low income elasticities of demand for foodstuffs and basic necessities (particularly of inferior goods) and high income elasticities of demand for any consumption beyond the necessities that typically constitute the lion's share of the low-income-strata demands. We thus get four basic types of elasticity behaviour. We designate them as ε_1^h, ε_n^h,

ε_1^l, ε_n^l, where the subscripts stand for income class, and h and l for commodities with high and low elasticities respectively. A change in the level and structure of aggregate demand may be described as

$$dD = dD_1^h + dD_1^l + dD_n^h + dD_n^l$$
$$= \varepsilon_1^h \frac{D_1^h}{y_1} dy_1 + \varepsilon_1^l \frac{D_1^l}{y_1} dy_1 + \cdots +$$

where

$$\varepsilon_k^n = \frac{dD_k^n y_k}{dy_k D_k^n}, \quad \text{and the terms} \quad \frac{D_1^h}{y_1}, \quad \frac{D_1^l}{y_1}$$

are average propensities to consume group h goods and group l goods respectively.

The discussion is (following the dualistic outline) reduced to the outer boundary sets $\bar{F}_1$ and $\bar{F}_n$. ε_i^j expresses the change in demand in relation to the income change dy_i. The upper line designates the demand for commodities from the small-scale sector $\bar{F}_1$, the lower line the demand for commodities from the large-scale sector $\bar{F}_n$. The behaviour of demand will depend on the behaviour of the determining variables y, β, and ε.

By assumption, the income increases in $\bar{F}_1$ will be zero (excluding still the effect from dP). The effect on demand over ε_1^h will thus be nil. The income increase accruing to $\bar{F}_n$ will be high. The propensity to consume decreases and damps that effect. In addition, the overall effect of dy_n may be relatively small, since the relative size of $\bar{F}_n$ within the total economy is still small. Irrespective of the actual income increases and propensities to consume, the demand for commodities from the traditional small-scale sector $\bar{F}_1$ will be small, since we have ε_n^l for commodities from $\bar{F}_1$. The total demand for commodities from the $\bar{F}_1$-sector is, in total, depressed by the low income level and zero income increases of the $\bar{F}_1$-sector, and the low elasticities of demand for commodities of the $\bar{F}_1$-sector that prevail in the modern $\bar{F}_n$-sector.

The same rationale applies *mutatis mutandis* to the large-scale $\bar{F}_n$-sector. The first two terms of the above demand equation drop out since dy_1 and ε_1^l are zero or low. The demand for commodities from the $\bar{F}_n$-sector increases, since ε_n^h becomes effective because dy_n is high.

It will be remembered that both savings and consumption increase faster in $\bar{F}_n$ in relation to the lower strata. The relationship may be expressed as

$$dy_1(\alpha_1 + \beta_1) \overline{<} 0$$
$$dy_n(\alpha_n + \beta_n) > 0.$$

In this relationship, the increases in the savings and the consumption differentials are due to the increases in the income differentials. However, the marginal propensities may also be expected to change. The marginal propensity to save (consume) is likely to be higher (lower) in the F_n-sector than in the F_1-sector, as the earlier analysis on rapidly increasing asset differentials (of which the savings differentials are a necessary pendant) suggests. The cumulative changes in the savings and consumption differentials, on the one hand, and the conditions of the demand elasticities, on the other hand, generate increasing inconsistencies in the basic structure of demand and supply—a process which ultimately brings to bear its own constraints.

Consider first the advanced $\bar{F}_n$-sector. The demand increases; but due to the falling propensities to consume and the lack of demand from the $\bar{F}_1$-sector, the production potential will tend to exceed that demand. The more production tends to rely on the demand from consumption of the $\bar{F}_n$-sector, the larger the gap becomes between aggregate demand and supply. The supply (in terms of output) may not be actually forthcoming; but increasing idle capacities have similar economic effects (only the variable costs do not accrue in the latter alternative while the fixed costs do). The assumption of profit 'hangovers' in the F_n-sector in connection with the lack of effective demand for products from that sector provide some plausible explanations for the frequently encountered phenomenon of idle capacities in South and South-East Asian economies. Furthermore, much demand from the $\bar{F}_n$-income class will be satisfied only from modern Western-style goods. It is likely that the higher the income of the $\bar{F}_n$-group the larger will be the need for imported goods. Both decreasing propensities to consume and a likely unfitness of the advanced $\bar{F}_n$-sector to satisfy the demand of the $\bar{F}_n$-sector lead to increasing demand constraints for that sector. It is conceivable that the modern industrial sector approaches an absolute limit of expansion unless foreign demand is opened up to that sector. Exports are, thus, a necessity of a less-developed country with a rapidly expanding modern sector and high income and assets differentials. As development proceeds, the expansion and size of the modern sector become more and more a function of foreign demand. Clearly, there are limits to that demand, as the political dispute about a new economic world order documents. The pressure of a highly competitive world economy and the relatively high consumption standards of the industrialised countries will force the developing countries that rely on a modern-sector-focused development pattern to switch to an increasing extent to capital-intensive techniques, large-scale size, and modern products. To the extent that the modern sector is successful, it will become dependent in its operation on foreign demand. The argument goes that investment goods are required from industrialised markets. The volume and type of investment goods imported, however, is itself a function of the size and structure of the modern sector, and not of the traditional sector.

In an analogous way, the traditional sector is self-contained and isolated from the modern sector. Because of the above-mentioned set of determinants, aggregate demand remains depressed. The shift in the income elasticities of demand in the modern sector has led to the emergence of a production- and commodity-supply structure which decreasingly fills the needs of the traditional sector. The investment industry of the modern sector is either non-existent (hence the large dependence on imports) or unfitted for the needs of the traditional sector. We shall return to the aspects of 'adjustedness' after having analysed in more detail the intersectoral relationships.

VI. 'SUBSISTENCE SURPLUS', INTERSECTORAL TERMS OF TRADE, AND RESPONSIVENESS OF SUPPLY

Let us revert at this juncture to the classical–neoclassical surplus aspects. The basic hypothesis may be re-stated (see Ch. 14.I) that sustained development depends on the generation of an agricultural surplus

$$S^a = O^a - C^a$$
$$\doteq ((\lambda^a \cdot L^a/P^a) - c^a)P^a.$$

S^a depends, for a given level of O^a, on the 'innovation intensity' in the agricultural sector. The 'innovation intensity' depends on the terms of trade as they are determined in the intersectoral commodity markets. Terms of trade favourable for the agricultural sector will initiate new cultivation practices and provide the financial basis for productivity-enhancing-factor inputs from the industrial sector. The agricultural surplus S^a may be defined in terms of agricultural commodities to be exchanged for industrial commodities, of capital surplus (investment, taxes), and of labour surplus. An increase in all three sub-categories will allow the sustained expansion of the advanced industrial sector. The rate of expansion (growth of manufacturing output) will depend on the growth rates of the 'surplus input factors', the rate of industrial capital accumulation, and the rate of technological progress. Generally, development depends on the adequate intersectoral reallocation of the production factors at certain 'technological-intensity' or 'technological-progress' rates.

At no phase of the socio-economic development process, according to the classical-neoclassical theory, do productivity, asset, and income differentials affect the intersectoral reallocation of the production factors; this is hardly surprising, since they do not play any role in determining the intrasectoral processes. Similarly, aggregate demand is not integrated as an explanatory variable. Consequently, constraints set by inadequate aggregate demand or by changes in the demand structure do not constitute a determining factor in development. Demand is assumed to follow automatically. This is a surprising fact. The entire theory of intersectoral factor reallocation receives its economic rationale only if broad shifts in the sectoral demand are assumed. But the preoccupation with the supply factors has been so strong that demand is hardly ever mentioned as an explanatory variable.

The agricultural surplus S^a will have an impact on agricultural production and productivity over the long run only if adequate demand for that surplus from the industrial sector D^{ia} is forthcoming. In static terms, the equilibrium situation required is

$$S^a - D^{ia} = 0.$$

In turn, a surplus in the industrial sector S^i will be generated when

$$\begin{aligned} S^i &= O^i - C^i \\ &= ((\lambda^i \cdot L^i/P^i) - c^i)P^i. \end{aligned}$$

The industrial surplus (output not used for self-consumption) can be exchanged for agricultural commodities only if demand for that surplus from the agricultural sector D^{ai} exists. We have again the static equilibrium condition

$$S^i - D^{ai} = 0.$$

We may express the entire developmental process in terms of intersectoral equilibria

$$S^a = D^{ia} = S^i = D^{ai}.$$

The development process will describe a dynamic equilibrium path if all variables grow at the same rates

$$s^{a*} = d^{ia*} = s^{i*} = d^{ai*}.$$

The determinants of the growth rates are not the same for the supply and demand variables. The supply capacity is determined by the productive capacity of all enterprises which are distributed as $\bar{F}_1, \ldots, \bar{F}_n$. The effective demand is determined by the income distributed according to $\bar{F}_1, \ldots, \bar{F}_n$, as well as the specific consumption propensities and income elasticities of demand of the sub-groups. According to level and distribution of the assets and activities in an economy, the supply capacity and effective demand of the sectors may show different features. The above-delineated equilibrium path must, therefore, be understood as a coincidental path. The path may not be in balance at all: the *structural* causes underlying the behaviour of d and s may constitute a tendency for the growth rates to diverge.

Analysing the sectoral-exchange relationships, we shall start with the demand for industrial goods of the agricultural sector D^{ai}. We may write for the total demand

$$D^{ai} = y_1^a(\beta_1^{ai} + \alpha_1^{ai}) + y_n^a(\beta_n^{ai} + \alpha_n^{ai}).$$

The scale sizes and institutional settings are again reduced to two groups, $\bar{F}_1$ and $\bar{F}_n$. Here, β_j^{ai} may be given the meaning of demand of the agricultural sector for industrial consumer goods, while α_j^{ai} constitutes the demand for investment goods used in the agricultural sector. A savings-investment gap is for the sake of simplicity ruled out. The income of the self-employed marginal or subsistence farmers is represented primarily by y_1^a. We introduce the further assumption that there exists a subsistence minimum in the consumption of industrial goods. We denote this average minimum as $\bar{s}^{ai}$. Total output growth in the

$\bar{F}_1$-sector is determined by population growth (which, after a time-lag of one or one-and-a-half decades, becomes effective as growth in employment ΔL or r_L). The $\bar{F}_n$-sector is assumed to save and to purchase modern inputs from the industrial $\bar{F}_n$-sector. The exchange transactions of the $\bar{F}_1$-sector are, therefore, mainly or only over the exchange of consumer goods; those of the $\bar{F}_n$-sector over the exchange of both consumer and investment goods. D^{ai} may be written in an explicit form, dissected according to the determinants population and $\bar{y}$, and according to income categories $\bar{\pi}$ and $\bar{w}$. Thus

$$D^{ai} = (\bar{y}_1)P_1^a + (\bar{w})P_w^a + (\pi)P_\pi^a,$$

where the subscripts w and π stand for labourers and landlords in the $\bar{F}_n$-sector. We assume that $\bar{y}_1$ and $\bar{w}$ just cover the subsistence level for the consumption of industrial commodities, $\bar{s}^{ai}$. This assumption reflects reality for a large part of the farming populations in Asia. The total demand dissected according to categories of commodities is

$$D^{ai} = \bar{s}^{ai}(P_1^a + P_w^a) + (\bar{I}^{ai} \cdot P_\pi^a).$$

$\bar{I}^{ai}$ designates the average demand for investment goods. From this relationship we see that the demand for industrial consumer goods from the $\bar{F}_1^a$-sector is largely determined by the population of the $\bar{F}_1^a$-sector and the landless labourers of the $\bar{F}_n^a$-sector. Average income increases are insignificant as determinants for the effective demand, since the population-growth rate usually equals and sometimes exceeds the total output-growth rate of that group. In turn, the demand for intermediate inputs from the industrial sector by the $\bar{F}_n^a$-sector is almost entirely determined by π. Changes in the population size of the profit-earners is an insignificant determinant of the demand for total investment. The demand for industrial consumer goods is similarly not crucially affected by P_π^a; for the sake of simplicity, it is excluded from the above relationship. Changes in total investment of the $\bar{F}_n^a$-sector are linearly related to changes in the π/w ratio.

The question arises whether the subsistence demand for industrial and agricultural commodities encounters the corresponding supply responses from the respective sectors. In the conventional model, this is seen as a problem of appropriate supply responsiveness of the industrial entrepreneurs and farmers, concomitant with capital accumulation and technological progress. The supply-responsiveness function as determinant of output behaviour seems, however, to be overemphasised in a situation where, as in the $\bar{F}_1$-sectors, the producers have a subsistence income. Instead, the motivation or initiation to supply is given by the necessity to produce a surplus which will enable the producers to cover the subsistence minimum. At a level where the productivity and real incomes in the $\bar{F}_1$-sectors cover only the subsistence minimum, the intersectoral exchange must be viewed as exchange of subsistence commodities. Hence, we may write for the exchange transaction

$$\bar{s}_1^{ai} \cdot p_1^i = \bar{s}_1^{ia} \cdot p_1^a,$$

where p_1^i designates the price level at which the industrial subsistence surplus is bought by the $\bar{F}_1^a$-sector, and p_1^a the price level at which the agricultural subsistence surplus is bought by the $\bar{F}_1^i$-sector. The intersectoral terms of trade are thus determined by the sectoral surplus quantities needed to cover the subsistence minima in both sectors. The relative price, for instance, for agricultural commodities in exchange for industrial commodities is

$$p_1^a = \left(\frac{\bar{s}_1^{ai}}{\bar{s}_1^{ia}}\right) p_1^i.$$

In an early development phase, agricultural commodities will be a large share of total consumption; $\bar{s}_1^{ia}$ will constitute a larger share of the average income than $\bar{s}_1^{ai}$. Assuming identical populations in both sectors, the total agricultural surplus can be sold only if the prices for agricultural commodities p_1^a are correspondingly low. The assumption of subsistence exchange quantities in $\bar{F}_1$ for both sectors provides a first explanation of why the agricultural terms of trade tend to be unfavourable for agriculture in an early development phase. This explanation is consistent with actual terms of trade in Asia, which are unfavourable for agriculture.

We have been keeping the population variable neutral by assuming identical populations in both sectors. Clearly, the agricultural population P^a is larger than the urban-industrial population P^i. The populations may be explicitly expressed as

$$(\bar{s}_1^{ai} \cdot p_1^i)P^a = (\bar{s}_1^{ia} \cdot p_1^a)P^i.$$

The larger agricultural population P^a will partly offset the larger fraction of $\bar{s}_1^{ia}$ in the average income $\bar{y}_1^i$. The actual impact of both determinants will depend (1) on the propensities for agricultural and industrial commodities to be consumed, or on what are considered to be the respective subsistence minima, and (2) on the distribution of the population among sectors. The above relationship demonstrates the crucial impact that urban migration has on the deterioration of the terms of trade for the agricultural sector. If we assume $\bar{s}_1^{ai}$ and $\bar{s}_1^{ia}$ to remain unchanged and to be the only commodities exchanged in the $\bar{F}_1$-sector—a picture which accurately reflects the increasing urban slums and the impoverished agricultural-rural population—the rate of migration, that is, the change in the sectoral population differentials, becomes the sole determinant of the terms of trade. We have

$$\frac{\bar{s}_1^{ai}}{\bar{s}_1^{ia}} \cdot \tau = \frac{P^i}{P^a},$$

where $\tau = p_1^i/p_1^a$. Since $\bar{s}_1^{ai}/\bar{s}_1^{ia}$ is a constant, the behaviour of the terms of trade is well approximated by the linear relationship

$$\tau = \theta\left(\frac{P^i}{P^a}\right),$$

where θ is a proportionality factor. For an assessment of the empirical behaviour of P_1^i and P_1^a we may refer to Table 17.5. From this table we learn that the urban population growth rates (including migration) are considerably higher than the rural population growth rates. In addition, as the urban population becomes a relatively larger section of the total population, the relative rates of change apply to higher absolute values. While in the initial phase when P^a is very large the high relative rates may be offset, P^i will grow faster once it reaches a certain threshold level. With urban populations generally in the neighbourhood of 30 per cent and rates of growth for the urban population between 4 and 5 per cent, this threshold level is reached at present in most Asian countries. Thus, urban migration, under the present socio-economic conditions of impoverished populations in both sectors, has an unfavourable effect on the terms of trade for the agricultural sector. The result is inconsistent with classical-neoclassical reasoning. But it is in accordance with the actual behaviour of the terms of trade in Asian countries.

Figure 15.2 combines the two hypotheses of (1) a negative correlation between the $\tilde{p} = P^i/P^a$ ratio and the terms of trade $\tau = p_1^a/p_1^i$,

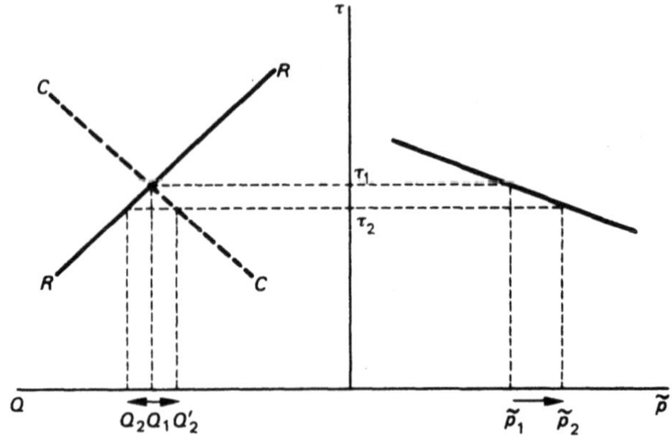

FIG. 15.2 *Sectoral terms of trade under conditions of rural-urban migration and subsistence consumption*

and (2) the supply responsiveness under conditions of subsistence consumption. (1) is depicted on the two axes of the right-hand quadrant and (2) on the left-hand quadrant. Assuming an increase in $\tilde{p}$ from $\tilde{p}_1$ to $\tilde{p}_2$, the terms of trade will fall from τ_1 to τ_2. Given assumption (2), as depicted by the R-curve, the quantity of agricultural commodities supplied will increase from Q_1 to Q_2. Given classical-neoclassical assumptions, the agricultural surplus will decrease from Q_1 to Q_2. However, a decrease would be inconsistent with the conditions of subsistence consumption in both sectors given an increasing population P^i.

In the context of the relationships delineated, the agricultural subsistence sector finances the expansion of the urban slums. Historically, this is reminiscent of the role which agriculture has played: the agricultural surplus finances development. However, development stands, by definition, for a rise in the average magnitudes of the socio-economic variables. In the present context only shifts in the total magnitudes are accomplished without concomitant increase in the average level of the socio-economic variables.

The question arises as to what role the advanced $\bar{F}_n$-sectors could play to alleviate the depressed situation in the $\bar{F}_1$-sectors. As we may assume, the agricultural $\bar{F}_n$-sector will exhibit little inclination to produce for a domestic market with depressed prices (if the production structure is adjusted to the domestic needs at all). In a similar vein, the industrial $\bar{F}_n$-sector has little inclination to engage in exchange activities with the agricultural subsistence sector. The question brings into focus again the intersectoral relationships, which shall now be more fully described.

VII. STAGNATION AND CRASH-MODERNISATION TRANSITIONS

The intersectoral relationships or transitions from agriculture to industry depend on the specific intrasectoral 'mechanisms' at work in both sectors. By the same token, the intersectoral relationships reinforce the intrasectoral development. It is useful to revert here to the idea of the 'simultaneous-sequence' type of development. In Figure 15.3, an explicit statement of the nature of a 'dualistic transitional

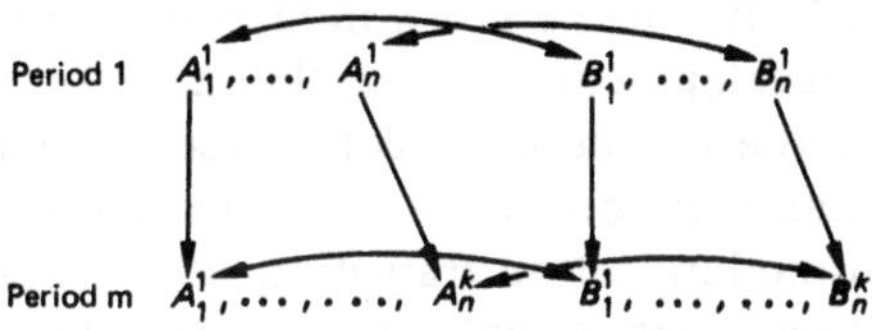

FIG. 15.3 *Nature of a 'dualistic transitional process'*

process' is attempted. It should be recalled that the dualism is not only between the agricultural and industrial sectors as in classical-neoclassical theory, but includes the dualism as expressed by $\bar{F}_1$ and $\bar{F}_n$. We start in period 1 with a developmental state for $\bar{F}_1$ and $\bar{F}_n$ in the agricultural sector A_1^1 and A_n^1. The superscript denotes an index for development; 1·0 represents the base value. The subscript denotes the 'degree of advancedness' as, for instance, stated in $\bar{F}_1^a$ and $\bar{F}_n^a$. In analogous terms, the industrial sector is subdivided into B_1^1 and B_n^1. As development proceeds from period 1 to m, little progress is realised in the traditional agricultural sector. The developmental state is denoted by A_1^1 in period m. The development path of the $\bar{F}_1^a$-sector is typically one of stagnation. Analogously, the $\bar{F}_1^i$-sector does not develop, and equally describes a stagnation path. The intersectoral relationships between A_1 and B_1 from period 1 to m are basically at the same average levels of exchange. The commodity structure of the exchanged tradables is also basically the same. Investment (e.g. repair and extension of irrigation) is done in the agricultural sector by using the unemployed—rarely by importing productivity-enhancing inputs from the industrial sector. In the industrial $\bar{F}_1^i$-sector, the mix of subsistence commodities will be fairly constant. Not only do both sectors A_1 and B_1 describe—in intrasectoral terms—stagnation paths but also the intersectoral relationships reinforce the stagnation path and constitute a 'stagnation transition'.

In contrast, the intersectoral relationships of the $\bar{F}_n$-sectors are of a more dynamic type. We start with high development levels at A_n and B_n. Given an index of, say, 1·0 in the first period, the developmental states of A_n and B_n increase to k. A crash-modernisation path is actualised in both sectors. The rate of change is determined by the initial developmental levels A_n^1 and B_n^1 and the feasibility of exchanges between the sectors. The intensity of the intersectoral relationships depend on the 'correspondence' of the two sectors and the possibility of switching over to the foreign sector. A crash-modernisation path of the B_n-sector is necessary if the A_n-sector follows a crash-modernisation path. In turn, a crash-modernisation path in terms of forced industrial development will stimulate the use of more modern industrial inputs in the advanced agricultural sector. The two modernisation paths mutually reinforce each other, and constitute what could be called a 'crash-modernisation transition'. Only if either or both of A_n and B_n constitute export-oriented enclave sectors will a correspondence of the structures in rates of change of the two sectors be unnecessary for their development. Their rates of change will (independent of the degree of intersectoral correspondence) be determined by the demand and technological progress in the foreign sectors.

In Asian reality, mixed types of domestic intersectoral and foreign-exchange relations prevail. From the point of view of supply, exchange transactions with the foreign sector accelerate the rate of change of the respective domestic sector. High rates of capital accumulation in the $\bar{F}_n$-sectors will allow the import of the latest technology, and the rates of change in those sectors will be nearly proportional to the exponential rates of change of technological progress of the advanced industrialised countries. For instance, a development path relying primarily on domestic exchange relationships may be from A_n^1 to A_n^k. A development path with strong reliance on the modern sector may describe an accelerated path from A_n^1 to, say, A_n^p, which would be to the right of A_n^k. The relatedness of one sector, for instance A_n, with the foreign sector will have repercussions on the other sector via intersectoral relationships. The intersectoral relationships will tend to be from A_n^p to, say, B_n^p, and not from A_n^p to B_n^k (the developmental level as in the transition relying only on primarily domestic exchange relations given by A_n^k).

There will be a strong tendency to enhance the foreign-exchange relationships on the side of both $\bar{F}_n$-sectors because of the demand constraints faced by both sectors. As the connectedness with the modern sector accelerates, the development of the $\bar{F}_n$-sectors accelerates and the demand constraints for the two sectors will increase. The rate of intersectoral relationships between the $\bar{F}_n^a$- and $\bar{F}_n^i$-sectors may therefore decrease as development proceeds. The isolation of the advanced industrial and agricultural sectors may thus exist not only in relation to the backward part of the two sectors but also in relation to the intersectoral relationships between the advanced sectors themselves. While in the $\bar{F}_1$-sectors the intersectoral relationships are kept low due to a lack of productivity-enhancing inputs and effective demand, the intersectoral relationships in the $\bar{F}_n$-sectors face constraints primarily due to the lack of effective demand—be it from foreign markets or the domestic F_1-sectors.

VIII. IMPACT OF SOCIO-ECONOMIC PROCESSES ON POPULATION BEHAVIOUR

Up to this point, the population variable has not been analysed in its causal implications. The subsistence equilibrium condition may be simply stated as

$$r_o - r_p = 0,$$

where r_o stands for total income growth and r_p for population growth—given an initial average income at subsistence level. The algebraic relationship, however, conceals the facts that the socio-economic processes determine r_p, and that r_p determines the socio-economic processes. There is reciprocal causation between both sets of variables, which generates cumulative effects on the interrelated process.

Analysing the two lines of causation, we first take up the impact that level, rates, and the nature of the socio-economic processes have on the variation of population growth. The level of average economic activities or average income is generally assumed to be negatively correlated to population growth. As stated earlier (Part Two, Chapter 11,II), an identical level of total individual (family) utility may be derived from a smaller number of children at a high socio-economic level when compared to a low socio-economic level; and improved availability of contraceptive devices makes the implementation of individual welfare considerations feasible.[7] Though the mortality rates decrease concomitantly (improved medical care, relative increase of number of doctors, hospital beds, etc.), the decrease in the fertility rates as development proceeds outweighs the decrease in the mortality rates, leading to a decline in r_p.

To conclude our earlier discussion, we must face large income differentials. Consequently, the welfare 'weights' and socio-economic factors closely connected to the average income variable will be correspondingly unequally distributed. Hence, there will be fertility (and to a lesser extent mortality) differentials. Assuming an initial pattern of income distribution

$$\bar{y}_1 <, \ldots, < \bar{y}_n$$

and an initial pattern of differential fertility expressed by differentials in population growth

$$r_{p_1} >, \ldots, > r_{p_n},$$

a shift from $\bar{y}_n$ to $\bar{y}_1$ will tend to decrease the fertility rate. Alternatively, any increase in average income may have little or no effect on the decline of the fertility rate if the income-distribution pattern deteriorates.

Figure 15.4 shows the population growth behaviour as a function of the level of average income given various assumptions about income distribution. The vertical axis represents the population growth rate r_p, the horizontal axis the level of average income $\bar{y}$. At subsistence income $\bar{y}_*$ the population growth is assumed to be at r^*_{p0}. Depending on the capacity to generate an increase in total income, the population growth rate will stand at different levels. Two extreme situations may be envisaged. One is the Malthusian state where both r_p and r_o are zero; the other a maximum population growth rate of 3–4 per cent under conditions of an economy growing at the same rate. The pattern of income distribution is relevant only insofar as the income must not fall below the subsistence minimum in any income class. If that constraint is not set to changes in the income distribution, a worsening of distributional inequality (even in the presence of increasing average income growth) may lead to an increase in the mortality and thus away from the maximum population growth rate. This implies, alternatively, that an increase in income of the upper classes and thus of the average income, for instance, from $\bar{y}_*$ to $\bar{y}_1$ will not significantly affect the population growth rate r^*_{p0}. According to the income distribution pattern Z_i, different levels of $\bar{y}_i$ are required to induce a decrease in r_p.

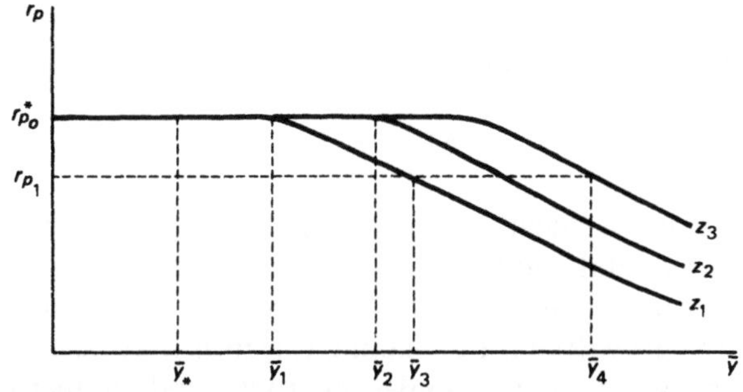

FIG. 15.4 *Population growth as function of average income level given various assumptions about income distribution*

Given a distribution pattern Z_1, r_{p0}^* will start declining from $\bar{y}_1$ on. Assuming Z_2, a large average income $\bar{y}_2$ is required for setting in motion a process of a declining r_p at the level r_{p0}^*. Similarly, to realise a population growth rate of r_{p_1}, an average income of $\bar{y}_3$ is required at a distributional pattern Z_1; but an average income about 50 per cent as large is required to attain the same population growth rate if the distribution pattern Z_3 prevails. Given the fact that various income distribution patterns will yield different population growth rates, any change in the income distribution pattern will affect the population growth rate. The condition for distributional changes to affect population behaviour is that the distributional change be 'downwards' and not 'upwards'. As stated above, a relative income change in terms of additional income accruing to the small upper-income segment of the population will not affect population behaviour. Similarly, an improvement in income equality achieved by making the upper strata less rich but leaving the lower strata at the same level of poverty will not reduce the population growth rate. Only a change in the average income of the low-income strata will affect the population growth rate, since that sector comprises a large share of the total population, and the elasticity of fertility reduction with regard to changes in income is high.

IX. IMPACT OF POPULATION GROWTH ON SOCIO-ECONOMIC PROCESSES

Population is not only determined by, but also crucially determines, the socio-economic processes. If we define V as a set of economic variables which determine the total output, and assume linearity for the changes in all variables, the growth in V may be written as

$$\Delta V = r_o(V).$$

Any increase in V is linearly related then to the output growth rate. We know that the total output growth rate may be dissected into the population growth rate and the average output growth rate. Accordingly, the growth of the economic variables may be dissected into a component pertaining to population growth and another to average income growth

$$r_o(V) = (r_p + r_i)V.$$

The component $V \cdot r_p$ may be called the demographic component. It defines the value for economic variables used up for sustaining the additional population $P \cdot r_p$. If $r_o = r_p$, all economic resources are devoted to the support of the additional population, leaving no net-value $V \cdot r_i$ which could generate an increase in the *per capita* output in the subsequent period.

The aggregate picture may be given a specific interpretation by substituting the production-factors capital K and labour L for V. If we write $\dot{I}$ for the investment rate (I/O) and k for the capital output coefficient, the growth rates may be written in explicit form

$$\frac{\dot{I}_o}{k} = \frac{\dot{I}_p}{k} + \frac{\dot{I}_i}{k},$$

where the subscripts o, p, and i designate the components pertaining to the total, demographic, and net investments per person. The rationale applying to the general applies also to the specific. $\dot{I}_p/k$ denotes at a given level of k the investment rate needed to sustain a population growing at r_p. It constitutes the minimum investment rate if the average output is not to decline. Anything above $\dot{I}_p/k$ constitutes net investment which allows an increase in average income.

Table 15.2 provides some empirical indication of the burden population exerts on investment in the Asian countries. The investment rate needed to sustain the additional population ranges from 6·5 per cent in Indonesia to 12·5 per cent in Thailand. Demographic investment constitutes about 50 per cent of the total gross investment in all Asian developing countries (except the Republic of Korea). Although the

TABLE 15.2 *Rates and shares of demographic investment in selected Asian countries, 1970*

	Rate of population growth (1)	Gross investment rate (2)	Growth rate of total GNP (3)	Capital output coefficient (4)	Demographic investment rate (5)	Demographic investment as % of total investment (6)
India	2·7	14·2	5·3	2·7	7·3	51
Indonesia	3·1	13·0	6·3	2·1	6·5	50
Korea, Rep. of	2·4	28·1	8·9	3·2	7·7	27
Malaysia	2·9	16·3	6·1	2·7	7·8	48
Pakistan	3·5	15·7	6·6	2·4	8·4	53
Philippines	3·5	20·8	6·2	3·4	11·9	57
Sri Lanka	2·4	19·7	4·1	4·8	11·5	58
Thailand	3·3	25·7	6·7	3·8	12·5	49

Sources: Figures for col. 1 see *Economic Survey of Asia and the Far East*, part 1 (United Nations: Tokyo, 1973), p. 34; for col. 2 see table 14.4 col. 4; for col. 3 see *Economic Survey*, op. cit., p. 31; col. 4 is obtained by dividing col. 2 by col. 3; col. 5 by multiplying col. 1 by col. 4; col. 6 is obtained by dividing col. 5 by col. 2, multiplied by 100.

figures will be subject to statistical errors, the small deviation from the mean gives them some significance. The constancy is partly due to the fact that the investment rates shown in Table 14.4 negatively correlate with the capital-output coefficients. This may be a coincidence. The capital-output coefficient is subject to considerable fluctuations within a short time interval. Even from one year to another, *k* may vary within a range of −50 per cent to +100 per cent.[8] However, even if we allow for reductions in *k* within those limits, the rate of demographic investment will still be substantial in all countries mentioned.

Population growth affects not only the rate, but also the structure of investment. Demographic investment is used for a widening of the productive capacity of the economy. It aims at constancy of the K/L ratio, and therefore is basically not productivity-enhancing.[9] Net investment, in turn, may be used for a change of the K/L ratio, which either creates new employment opportunities, or increases the labour productivity, or both. As a consequence, *k* pertaining to demographic investment must be assumed to differ from *k* pertaining to net investment. The aggregate value for *k* does not show this structural effect of an increasing population on investment. Our hypothesis is that the higher the ratio between demographic investment over total investment, the higher the overall capital-output coefficient. A country with a high rate of population growth is confronted not only with a relatively lower net-investment rate but also with a relatively higher capital-output coefficient. Statistically, the elements determining *k* are not easy to disentangle. Countries with the lowest income usually have the largest share of their activities in agriculture, and consequently a low capital-output coefficient. In statistical terms, a low capital-output coefficient may even correlate with a high rate of population growth. This, however, cannot discount the hypothesis that a decline in population growth would change the existing investment structure towards a more productive one, although its satisfactory measurement may be infeasible.

Productivity differentials between demographic and net investment exist not only for private but also for public investment. Public health services, housing, education, nutritional programmes, and infrastructural investment are shared by a larger number of people at unchanged or insignificantly enhanced productivity levels. For instance, capital must be directed to primary education, slighting secondary education. Nutritional programmes must be directed towards sustaining minimum nutritional intakes for a larger number of people, leaving a large share of the population undernourished. There is a close complementarity between the effects stemming from productivity of private and public investment. Low nutritional and educational standards detrimentally affect labour productivity, adding to the effect of the low productivity of private investment. Low productivity of private investment precludes a taxation of that sector sufficient to finance productivity-enhancing public investment, consumption, or transfers.

The second instance where population growth impinges on socio-economic development is employment. Assuming constancy in the average K/L ratio, additional capital must be used at a rate linear to the increase in L (job-seeking labour) if the (un-) employment rate is to remain constant. The equilibrium path of (sustained but not increased) unemployment under conditions of population growth is

$$\frac{dK}{dt} = \theta \frac{dP}{dt},$$

where θ is a proportionality factor which includes both (1), the relationship between P and L (where L is assumed to be proportionately related to P, with a time-lag of 1–2 decades), and (2) the average capital requirements for creating new employment opportunities. If we have the inequality

$$\frac{dK}{dt} - \theta \frac{dP}{dt} = K' > 0,$$

there exists the capacity to enhance labour productivity at the magnitude K', which is the analogue of the (non-demographic) net investment. The above relationship suggests that the employment problem depends on the growth of P, the growth of the capital stock K, and the capacity to generate additional jobs per unit of K as stated by θ (once a rapid change in the L/P ratio is ruled out). Our previous discussion has revealed that the growth of the capital stock does not necessarily imply constancy in the K/L ratio but rather that its increase (due to increasing asset, productivity, and income differentials) must be expected. Under these conditions the employment problem could be alleviated only if the growth of P and, concomitantly, the employment-seeking labour-force growth would slow down at a rate proportionate to the employment-eroding effects of the differential development process. However, this is not what must be expected.

We learn from Table 15.3 that in Asia as a whole (including developed Japan) the labour-force growth increases from 1·84 per cent p.a. in 1960–65 to 2·05 per cent p.a. in 1980–85. In South-East and South-West Asia the additional employment opportunities must grow at a rate of 2·67 per cent and 2·75 per cent respectively if unemployment is not to increase. Although a decline in the labour-force growth may be expected from the 1990s on (if the targeted decline in the population growth can be accomplished; see section on population, p. 51 ff), the absolute additions to the population remain a cause of concern, as we see from the second part of Table 15.3.

TABLE 15.3 *Growth rates of labour force (%) and net additions to the labour force, Asia, 1965–85 (in millions)*

	1960–65	1965–70	1970–75	1975–80	1980–85
Overall growth rates					
1. Asia	1·84	1·87	1·92	1·91	2·05
2. Mainland Region	1·70	1·62	1·61	1·44	1·50
3. Japan	1·94	1·59	1·13	0·76	0·74
4. Other East Asia	2·50	2·56	2·90	2·71	2·51
5. Middle South Asia	1·86	1·99	2·12	2·28	2·50
6. South-East Asia	2·04	2·26	2·43	2·52	2·67
7. South-West Asia	1·94	2·30	2·39	2·56	2·75
*Net additions to the labour force**					
1. Asia	68·1	75·9	85·5	93·4	110·3
2. Mainland Region	26·5	27·5	29·3	28·6	31·7
3. Japan	4·4	3·9	3·0	2·1	2·3
4. Other East Asia	2·2	2·4	3·4	3·7	3·7
5. Middle South Asia	22·9	27·0	31·7	38·0	46·9
6. South-East Asia	9·8	12·0	14·6	16·6	20·5
7. South-West Asia	2·2	2·9	3·4	4·2	5·1

* Figures may not add up because of rounding.

Source: *Manpower Growth and Labour Absorption in Developing Asia* (Tokyo: International Labour Organisation, 1972), mimeo, p. 46.

In sectoral terms, over two-thirds of the labour force in Asia is engaged in agriculture and less than one-third in manufacturing, services, and the informal sectors. The contribution the non-farm sectors can make to the absorption of the additional labour force is, therefore, limited by the absolute size of that sector. Figure 15.5 reproduces a few scenarios with various assumptions about the rates of labour absorption of the non-farm sectors.[10] Those scenarios most adequately depicting Asian reality are chosen. The hypothetical paths are

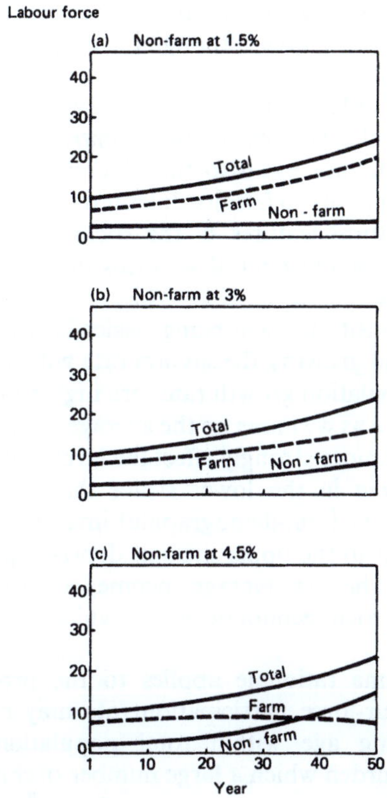

FIG. 15.5 *Hypothetical total and sectoral growth-path assumptions; growth of total labour force 2%; initial labour force in agriculture 80%*

Source: Bruce F. Johnston, *Agriculture and Economic Development: the Relevance of the Japanese Experience*, Food Research Institute Studies, vol. 4, no. 3 (Stanford University, 1966), pp. 251 ff.

self-explanatory. It must be added merely that the rates of labour-force growth are in two major regions 20–30 per cent above the hypothetical growth rate of 2 per cent; thus the hypothetical predictions underestimate the actual development in at least the first two decades. In addition, the assumption of a 4·5 per cent growth rate of the labour-absorptive capacity of the non-farm sector must appear overly optimistic in the light of recent findings. For the developing countries as a group and for Asian developing countries in particular, the data reveal that manufacturing industry has been absorbing only a tiny part of the additional labour force, although the output growth rates in that sector were high.[11]

Both level and differentials in the distribution of average income determine the population growth rate. *E contrario*, not only the overall population growth rate but also the differentials in the population growth rates (due mainly to fertility differentials) determine the rates of change and structural features of the socio-economic process. The argument becomes self-evident, if we focus on the micro-aspect of the production factors.

First, the propensity to save being basically a function of average income $\bar{y}$ (level and growth), the savings rate will be higher, the higher $\bar{y}$ is. Since the population growth rates are higher in the lower-income strata and decrease as we move up the average-income scale, the population growth will more strongly affect the levels and rates of change of the average income in the lower strata than in the higher. As a consequence, the net (non-demographic) investment in the $\bar{F}_1$-group will be lower than in the upper groups, depressing the growth of the average income. The low average income, in turn, keeps down the provision of those socio-economic factors which would allow a fertility reduction.

Second, the same rationale applies to the production factor of labour. The labour-force participation rate may be defined as total labour of working age within total population.[12] In a micro-perspective, the burden which a large number of children exerts on the working population increases as we move from $\bar{F}_n$ to $\bar{F}_1$. Not only the income but also the population differentials are in favour of the upper groups. That is, the number of children entering the labour force will be larger as we descend the income scale. If we assume, for instance, available employment opportunities for each family to be the same, say three children, the unemployment rate for a family with three children entering the labour force will be zero per cent, those for a family with six children of new entrants 50 per cent. Since the asset, income, and educational differentials are crucial determinants of the capacity to obtain a job, the average number of family members unemployed is *ceteris paribus* likely to be higher the lower we are on the socio-economic scale. As the result both of low skills and the larger number of children per family or economic unit, unemployment tends to be concentrated in the low-income sectors.

Though data on differential employment rates are lacking, an empirical indication is provided by the fact that in most urban areas of developing Asia, rural reproduction rates prevail—while, in contrast, the demographic-transition theory will suggest that urbanisation is a major explanatory variable of a fertility decrease. It will suffice to refer to Table 14.7, which shows that over 30 per cent of urban populations are living in slums. The hypothesis that fertility behaviour and poverty are closely mutually reinforcing variables is empirically supported not only on the aggregate level of trans-national comparisons but also by the respective differentials within single countries.

X. ECOSYSTEM, DEVELOPMENT DIFFERENTIALS, AND SOCIAL CHOICE

The preceding discussion sheds some light on various aggregate as well as differential facets of the socio-economic development process. The related set of variables pertaining to the M^{aa}-level has not been integrated within that analysis in an explicit way. However, as may be concluded from Part 2, the ecosystem critically determines the pace and quality of the development process. The conclusions of the earlier discussion may be recalled by referring to Figs. A5.1 and A5.2.

The following analysis highlights some of the complex causal interactions between population growth, eco-ratios and socio-economic development. Figure 15.6 combines two hypotheses: first, income level and income differentials determine the population growth rate, and, second, the population growth rate and population growth differen-

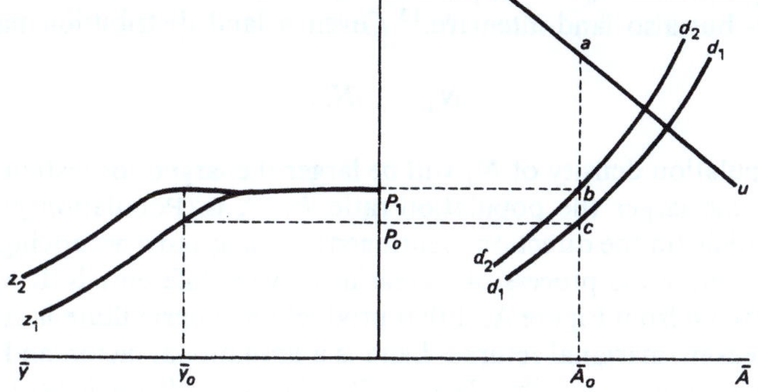

FIG. 15.6 *Income and population growth differentials as determinants of net social welfare*

tials determine social welfare according to the specific historical conditions of the ecosystem.

Given the level of average activities $\bar{A}_0$, an absolute population size of P_0 will incur welfare losses—in terms of marginal social disutilities d, due to a detrimental impact on eco-ratios—at a magnitude depicted by d_1. The population growth rate r_{p_0}, which caused P_0, is determined by the level of average income $\bar{y}_0$ and the income distribution Z_1. At the same level of $\bar{y}$, the population will stand at P_1 if an income distribution pattern Z_2 prevails. As a consequence, the effect the additional population exerts on the ecosystem and thus on the social welfare at a level of average activities $\bar{A}_0$ will increase to d_2. Assuming the marginal social utility schedule to be u, the loss in net welfare due to differences in the income-differential patterns may be measured by the distance $a - c$ minus $a - b$; or, directly, by the distance $b - c$ times $\overline{O\bar{A}_0}$.

Some reflections on the nature of the production functions in the various groups $\bar{F}_1, \ldots, \bar{F}_n$ suggest that the eco-coefficient k (see Part 2, Chapter 10) is not a constant. Thus, population determines not only a shift in the d-curve but also a change in the eco-coefficient k due to various patterns of asset distribution. The indirect effect of asset differentials via the determination of population differentials as expressed by various d-curves is compounded by the direct effect that asset differentials exert on the k-pattern. Clearly, the two are intrinsically causally interlinked and analytically not easy to disentangle. The causation nexus is of importance in the agricultural and industrial sectors as well.

We shall confine the subsequent discussion to the agricultural sector; but it is readily apparent that the differentials in the industrial sector will have a similar bearing on the ecosystem and eco-coefficient. The agricultural $\bar{F}_n$-sector, particularly if export-oriented, is not only capital- but also land-intensive.[13] Given a land distribution pattern

$$N_1, \ldots, N_n,$$

the population density of N_1 will be larger the larger, for instance, N_n is, and the larger the population ratio P_1/P_n is. Population growth differentials (in the direction mentioned) in the groups occupying land will accelerate the process of increasing density differentials. It will be remembered from Figure A3.1 that production in agriculture is subject to decreasing marginal returns. Land is a limitational factor, and agricultural output is crucially related to P/N (number of people per unit of arable land). Any 'upwards' shift in the above land distribution will affect the output of the subsistence sector, first, by decreasing the available arable land, and, second, by supporting the factors making for high population growth. Assuming no change in land distribution, the population growth differentials still induce a faster increase of the P/N ratio in the subsistence sector as compared to the sectors above the subsistence level.

A well-implemented land reform which would redistribute arable land more equally would slow down the process of increasing differentials in the man-land ratio. The result of such policy measures would be felt most strongly in countries with both a large $\bar{F}_n^a$-sector (e.g., the export enclave sector) and a large overall man-land ratio. By inspection of the empirical cases, it appears that those Asian countries have a large agricultural $\bar{F}_n$-sector which still have available relatively large land reserves.[14] Countries where land is critically scarce already have a larger relative share of the land occupied by the subsistence population of the $\bar{F}_1$-sector (small and marginal farmers), or already have the production of the $\bar{F}_n$-sector oriented towards subsistence crops. Even if the land is very unevenly distributed, a policy of land redistribution would face severe limitations due to the large overall population size. A case in point is India.[15] A hypothetical land reform which would include the radical transfer of over 40 million acres from the landlords to the landless would reduce the number of people living at subsistence level by 20–25 million. The proportion of farmers living in absolute poverty would be reduced from two-fifths to about one-third—still leaving 80–100 million people landless, dependent, and poor.

Assessing the shifts in the d-curve in terms of social costs resulting from increasing land densities, the persistent population growth must figure as a major explanatory variable. The detrimental impact of asset-land differentials and the removing of these differentials by land reforms may in some cases—but not in the most severe cases—have a significant impact on d. However, as is evident from the preceding discussion, population-growth differentials are themselves a function of asset-differentials. A land reform is, therefore, likely to have a dual impact on the man-land ratio and output (as far as related to the man-land ratio). First, the available land to be cultivated will increase, and, second, as a conceivable repercussion of the concomitant output increase, population may decrease, affecting the denominator of that ratio—the reverse of the Malthusian threat. The logic of this causation nexus will apply more successfully as N is higher and/or P lower. A land reform in terms merely of land redistribution will have the weakest impact in those countries (such as India, Indonesia, and the Philippines) where the man-land ratios are highest and, usually in concomitance, agricultural average incomes are lowest.

The stronger the limitations to an extension of production by extensive cultivation, the stronger the pressure to substitute intermediate inputs for the unavailable production factor of extra land. Intermediate inputs, however, are themselves highly dependent on the availability of non-renewable resources and on the carrying capacity of the ecosystem. Here there exists an overall optimum distribution of the resource-use in intertemporal and spatial terms.

First, considering the intertemporal aspects, energy comes into focus as a major intermediate input. Its use is closely functionally interlinked with the use of other intermediate inputs such as chemical fertilisers, pesticides, and herbicides. Theoretical and political problems arise to govern the use of an absolutely scarce input factor like fuel in an optimal way over time. Generally, we have to depart from the earlier stated hypothesis that capital intensity of the production functions increases as we move up the scale of size. Assuming the energy inputs per unit of output to be larger the larger the K/L ratio, any increase of K/L and/or increase in the differentials of K/L will induce an increase in the energy-per-output ratio. Although economies of scale may slow down the increase in the energy-per-output ratios in the largest firms, the fact that the energy-per-output ratios in the industrialised countries are a multiple of those in the less-developed countries is empirical indication enough to support the general hypothesis that developmental differentials increase the total energy consumption. Modern cultivation methods, such as the 'green revolution', require a minimum package encompassing the intermediate inputs mentioned. The hypothesis may be put forth here that the energy-use in Asian countries extends over that minimum determined by the complementarity of the intermediate input factors (labour is replaced by energy using real capital without being a necessary condition for the given output performance). The extent of the deviation from the optimum path must be assumed, rather, to be proportionate to the degree of inequality in the distribution of assets and land.

This suggests, in turn, that the optimum with regard to the use of energy as intermediate input lies not in an energy-free agriculture but in one where energy allows the realisation of food-production increases despite the increases in the man-land densities. The assumption implied in this assertion is that population responds favourably to an increase in agricultural production and food consumption, and that a smaller population itself constitutes a favourable momentum in the relief of the pressure on energy reserves.

A precise delineation of the optimal energy distribution is not feasible in mere positive-analytical terms, since it entails normative premises pertaining to the discount factor (when assessing the welfare of the present over future generations; see Part Two, Chapter 11,III). On an objective plane, a redistribution of assets and the related change in the scale size, as well as the production functions, may in the long run bring an increase in the rates of average output and a decrease in the average energy consumption per output unit. Both suggest an egalitarian policy on the grounds of economic rationality—although this contradicts the common notion (ingrained from the classical economists on) that redistributional policies always bear a cost. Once the costs are not obvious but, indeed, can be turned into their opposite, the proposition that any distributional policy requires a value judgment becomes meaningless, or is, equally, turned into its opposite.

The second criterion for an optimal non-renewable-resource-distribution policy pertains to the spatial aspect. The ecosystem constitutes a composite of variables which are not only functionally but also spatially interrelated in cause and effect. Given a confined (e.g., national) territory, effects of socio-economic processes may extend from one area which is singled out for specific activities to another area which is not. This 'spill-over' effect clearly will be stronger the more pollution-intensive are the types of production functions used. Given a finite carrying capacity of the total ecosystem, the over-proportionate demand on the ecosystem by some sectors may rob other sectors of the possibility of applying similar production functions and/or of facing increased costs in terms of a degraded environment. The connection springs immediately to mind in the extreme case of large-scale clearing of tropical rain forests, which frequently also erodes the land, impinging on the soil used for cultivation (for a discussion on ecological problems see Part Two, Chapter 10). In many cases, the land cleared is basically lost for subsistence agriculture in the future since tropical rains wash out the organic and mineral compounds, making cultivation infeasible or highly costly (previous reforestation). The same rationale, in terms of a distributional optimum of the negative effects, applies also at this point. The hypothesis, hence, may be put forth that agricultural activities emerging from the present asset and land distribution are beyond the point where the impact on the ecosystem is spatially distributed in an optimal way. In a dynamic view, the *d*-curve shifts upwards as the asset and land differentials continue to increase.

16 New Normative Directions of Socio-Economic Processes

I. GENERAL POLICY INFERENCE: NARROWING THE DEVELOPMENT DIFFERENTIALS

Until this juncture, our analysis has brought into focus some of the major resource relationships. The account has been descriptive-explanatory, not normative. However, any descriptive-explanatory account also has normative implications. For instance, the theoretical insights revealed by classical-neoclassical theory—an emphasis on the process of capital formation with a concomitant transitional process in a two-sectors context—lends corresponding support to a development strategy which is directed toward increased capital formation in the sectors assumed to be relevant for development, viz. the modern sectors. The theoretical account presented here differs quite significantly from the classical-neoclassical theory. Development differentials have been conceived as a major determinant of the current development processes in Asia. The capital-focused view was abandoned in favour of a comprehensive view integrating the relevant variables of the demand side. Beyond this, the socio-economic processes were viewed in a multi-systems context allowing for complex causal interactions among all (not only socio-economic) variables. Consequently, socio-economic differentials were viewed as having an impact on the population behaviour, which, in turn, has an impact on the socio-economic differentials. The population, as well as the socio-economic systems, similarly, affect the ecosystem—which, turn, is bound to have its impact on the socio-economic process.

Clearly, departing from this theoretical framework, policy inferences are necessarily different from the ones suggested on the basis of classical-neoclassical theory. If development differentials (such as income inequality) are not considered a prerequisite for rapid capital formation but rather a hindrance to development, the strategic emphasis will necessarily lie on the avoidance of those differentials and will suggest a redirection of the processes supporting them. Furthermore, a multi-systems context logically contradicts a strategy composed of an unrelated set of partial policies. There can be no population policy unrelated to socio-economic policies, nor a socio-economic policy unrelated to a natural-resource or environmental policy, and so forth. A development strategy necessarily must constitute an integrated set of related partial policies. Each of the partial policies must prove its rationality in the context of an overall strategy. Each partial policy, therefore, must establish its consistency not only within its own confines—e.g. a population policy consistent over a number of periods of time—but also within the context of the total-system.

Admittedly, we do not have a precise idea of how the total-system operates. This is true in theoretical as well as empirical terms. Hence, there are numerous shortcomings to be expected from a development strategy based on the theoretical framework proposed. However, it is better to be approximately right than precisely wrong. Any reduction in the analytical scope does more than limit the validity of the theoretical statements and subsequent policy inferences; it is likely to invalidate them entirely. In the past, development strategies have often yielded results that were unwelcome, or even entirely unexpected. The reasons for this were directly linked to the narrow delineation of the theoretical framework, the limitation to a reduced set of explanatory variables, and the consequent impossibility of drawing theoretical conclusions from a context which allowed for the complex causal interactions. Theoretical refining and empirical testing have usually been directed to the existing set of variables and the limited hypotheses it allowed. This study has assumed that the step beyond that of reasoning within given theoretical confines to be a necessary step toward a valid and relevant development theory. Inasmuch as a theory along this line may serve as a basis for a development strategy, it also improves the validity and relevance of a development strategy.

II. THE BARE BONES OF A NORMATIVE MODEL

1. An Outline

The general strategy inference for changing the current development processes leaves open the possibility of alternative development paths. The proposition of finality precludes the emergence of but one single development path. The negation of the current development path does not automatically yield the new direction, nor does it lay the precise normative foundations on which an adequate strategy could be formulated. The negation of the existing path yields the broad contours: the range of desirable paths other than the existing path.

A first objection could be made by proving that the range is undesirable in normative terms. But this does not reflect a real case. The new directions resulting from a negation of the processes delineated in our descriptive-explanatory account do not contradict but, rather, are in accordance with the normative ideals held by various people or groups in Asian countries. For instance, the objectives of narrowing the development differentials, redistributing the income, closing the productivity gaps, etc., are all held as desiderata in contemporary Asian countries among politicians, bureaucrats, technocrats, the academic community, as well as the bulk of the population.

The intricacy of the problem reveals itself in the next step: specifying the new direction of the development process. The range of paths is given, but not the choice among them. The problem is to find the 'better' ones (perhaps the best or optimal one) among the 'good' ones. Further rational criteria are required to make a choice among various feasible 'good' paths.

Our analysis proceeds by, first, stating a set of desiderata which indicates the new direction. This will first include the integration of the descriptive resource stratum (see Fig. 15.1) with a welfare or normative stratum (see Fig. 16.9). Second, we analyse the effects of the implementation of the new desiderata on the long-run behaviour of the total-system, i.e. the effect of a specific set of desiderata on the productivity of the input factors (labor, etc.) and subsequently the possibility of reaching the initially stated desiderata at a later period of time (say, through an infinite time horizon as far as minimum desiderata are concerned).

There are two directions in which we shall not attempt an analysis. First, we shall not focus on the set of policy tools required to implement the set of desiderata.[1] However, the description and explanation of development processes may themselves suggest the choice of some tools while it may discriminate against the choice of others.

Second, we shall not compute the quantity of inputs needed in order to attain a specific desiderata set—for instance, what inputs are needed in order to attain the minimum-caloric intakes for a population now or in a specific future period. There exist some scenarios for the developing countries, including the Asian countries;[2] we do not attempt to add more. The crucial problem lies on the theoretical and empirical level. Theoretically, various hypothetical production functions reflect not only variations in the computations but may well be responsible for major and yet theoretically little-understood changes in the entire development process. Empirically, data are least adequate for just those phenomena which are the major determinants of the (new) models. Further progress in strategy formulation crucially depends on further theoretical insights and an improved data basis.

Figure 16.1 distinguishes between three strata; the social-welfare, the productivity and the provisional stratum. Social welfare depends on the provision of welfare components from the market and the non-market contexts; these two contexts constitute substrata. The provisional stratum is introduced because social welfare is not directly dependent upon productivity but upon actual provision of welfare entities. They depend (i) on the possibility of using an efficient allocational scheme, such as the market or government, and, hence on the possibility of making supply and demand consistent, and (ii) on the extent to which social welfare cannot be related to the productivity stratum (which constitutes part of the economic system) at all but must rather depend on contributions from other sub-systems, such as the ecosystem S_c and the population system S_n. For simplicity, in Fig. 16.1 the techno-system is assumed to be implied in the productivity stratum, viz. in $K_1, \ldots, K_n$ and $L_1, \ldots, L_n$. Similarly, the foreign sector X/M is dropped for analytical simplicity.

A specific position assumes the political system S_p. We have divided the political system (see Part One, Chapter 4,VI) into S_p^{α}, which stands for a set of political institutions and behavioral rules (the 'structure' of the political system), and S_p^B, which stands for the decisions and actions of the members operating within this structural entity (the policy or strategy proper). In Fig. 16.1 only the policy or strategy aspect is considered, while the 'structure' of the political system will be analysed in Chapter 18,I–V. The policy may pertain to (a) the formulation of the social-welfare function S'_p, or (b) the implementation of the social-welfare function S_p. The superscript B is in both cases deleted for notational simplicity.

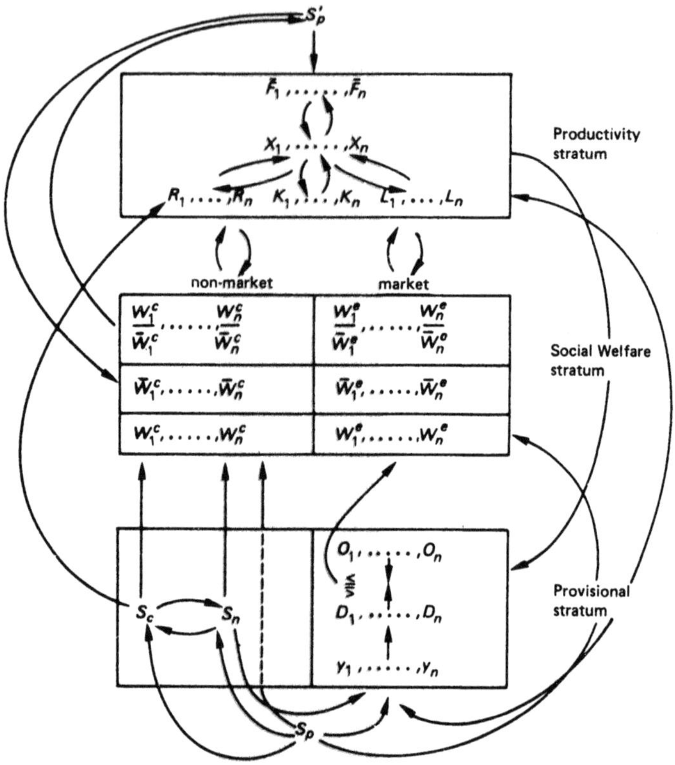

FIG. 16.1 *Social welfare in multi-systems context—with policy linkages*

For explanation of terms used in the productivity and provisional strata see Fig. 15.1.

W_i^j = Welfare actually attained by Group *i*, generated by components *j*

$\bar{W}_i^j$ = Desired welfare, with regard to *i* and *j*, social welfare function

$W_i^j/\bar{W}_i^j$ = Welfare deficit (<1; or surplus ≥ 1) in group *i* with regard to provision of component *j*

$j = e$ or c

e = derived from market contexts

c = derived from non-market contexts

S'_p = Policy related to formulation of social-welfare function

S_p = Policy related to implementation of social-welfare function

The welfare stratum is composed of three levels which are of strategic relevance. Through all three levels the initially introduced distinction between market and non-market contexts will be applied. The first level is the actually attained welfare $W_1^c, \ldots, W_n^c, W_1^e, \ldots, W_n^e$, where the superscripts stand either for welfare generated by the provision of market entities *e*, or the provision of non-market entities *c*, and the subscripts $1, \ldots, n$ designate the social groups. The second level consists of the desired welfare or the social-welfare function, conceived again in the context of various social groups. The third level represents the 'trade-off' or deviational level. It is composed of the ratios of the social-welfare norm ($\bar{W}_i$) and the actually attained social-welfare (W_i), viz. $W_i/\bar{W}_i$.

Irrespective of what the content of welfare actually is, Fig. 16.1 reveals that welfare will be impaired by (1) an inadequate level of actually attained welfare, and as such on (a) the behaviour of the productivity stratum and (b) the non-market and market provisional strata—for instance, welfare losses occur if the production functions are inoptimal in terms of factor prices or are poorly adjusted to ecological conditions, if productivity potential is inadequately utilised, etc., or if the market which provides the welfare entities is unfitted to meet the demand and creates inconsistencies in the demand-supply conditions as described. If (2) a strategy is pursued which explicitly states a social-welfare function, such as $W_1^e, \ldots, W_n^e, W_1^c, \ldots, W_n^c$, the formulation of the social-welfare function may be non-optimal. It is possible that (a) the distributional judgement is false. For instance, the inegalitarian postulate of classical-neoclassical theory in expectation of later gains in investment and productivity is objectively false (at least, if the theoretical foundations on which that postulate rests are considered to be false). It is also possible that (b) the formulation of a set of welfare entities to be provided to the people is ill-composed—for instance, the average calorie intake may be objectively wrongly computed. The lopsidedness of the welfare function may also pertain to the broader scale of market and non-market entities, such as imbalance between private and public consumption.

More intricate problems are posed by the welfare assessment in a dynamic view (over a finite or infinite time horizon). As stated, the desiderata themselves affect productivity or, more generally, the possibility of satisfying the (same or different) desiderata in a future period of time. In a later section various hypotheses pertaining to the relationships between the welfare and the productivity strata shall be formulated.

At this point, a rational basis for formulating a set of welfare desiderata should first be found. This includes (i) the choice of relevant welfare components, (ii) the assessment of the welfare generated by a specific level of welfare components, or the assignment of levels for the components in order to attain a specific level of welfare, and (iii) a distributional statement.

2. *Classification of Welfare Components*

In Fig. 16.1 various arrows arrive at the welfare stratum. Traditionally, economics has considered but one arrow as relevant for describing the generation of welfare: the arrow from the economic system. This, furthermore, was reduced to the market substratum, excluding welfare components of non-market contexts. All non-economic (including economic non-market) contexts were conceived as 'instrumentals' for the economic process which alone generated welfare.

However, all systems mentioned have not only an instrumental character but have themselves an intrinsic normative quality. This follows from our basic approach—which is holistic. It would be inconsistent with the reasoning in this study to single out a specific system, say the economic system, and assume a normative quality only for that system. The assessment of the normative quality of all systems is a concomitant of a descriptive analysis which includes all systems. Hence, the inclusion of a non-market context in the welfare stratum (expressed in Fig. 16.1 as $W_1^c, \ldots, W_n^c$) goes far beyond the conventional consideration of public consumption as a welfare component. The latter constitutes a sub-set of the economic system which constitutes a sub-set of the M^a-level which constitutes a sub-set of the total-system. The former includes the large entity of (often) intangible values which nevertheless are of paramount importance in determining the level and change in welfare.

In pursuit of a classification of welfare components, we shall follow the previously introduced classification into system levels (see Part One, Chapter 4,VI). This yields the classification of welfare components into

M^{aa} – welfare components
M^a — welfare components
M^i — welfare components.

A further sub-classification is derived by relating the various system levels to each other. For instance, the M^{aa}-components may be formulated in terms of the entire M^{aa}-level only; say in terms of the intrinsic value of the environment, with no direct relation being established to the welfare components of the socio-economic system (M^{a}-level) and/or individual well-being (M^{i}-level). The M^{aa}-components may also, in turn, be formulated in terms of their combined effect, e.g. ecological balance in its implication for the existence, correct functioning etc. of the socio-economic system, and the well-being of the individual.

For the entire sub-classification we have respectively the

M^{aa} — welfare components
M^{aa}/M^{a} — welfare components
M^{aa}/M^{i} — welfare components
M^{a} — welfare components
M^{a}/M^{i} — welfare components
M^{i} — welfare components.

There is no priority of one level over the other (no normative hierarchy; see Part One, Chapter 4,VI); the term M^{a}/M^{i}, say, could be as well be written in its inverted form M^{i}/M^{a}. The classification suggested must be conceived so as to serve as a basis for policy-making. We have considered that the major socio-economic processes should be 'redirected'. This implies not only that we specify the 'new normative directions' by dissecting the welfare components into classes and into groups according to their common traits (denoted by capital letters and arabic numerals, i.e. A-1, etc.) but also that we make the concept 'operational'. This means that, first, further criteria must be introduced which indicate how the welfare components contribute to welfare, and that, second, the indicators must be made quantifiable and appropriate methods of measurement be indicated. Taking into consideration the two additional requirements for making the concept 'operational', the list presented will be trisected into respectively

(i) welfare components
(ii) welfare indicators
(iii) types of measurement.

Combined with the previous classification, we get a matrix where the welfare components, welfare indicators, and types of measurement constitute the rows and the system levels and respective sub-groups the columns.

The content of the classification draws on the literature on the subject.[3] Extensions are made where gaps in the literature used suggest the necessity of so doing. The broad approach chosen provides a basis for locating the gaps and for integrating the various aspects into a consistent framework.

As for (ii), the indicators may be expressed in positive or negative terms. In positive terms, the 'number of classes of species' as stated in A-2/(ii) would, for instance, 'indicate' how the welfare component 'species diversity' as stated in A-2/(i) may be expressed; or, the 'calorie intake' would indicate how the welfare component 'nutrition' may be expressed. In negative terms, the 'land ecologically destroyed', may express the state or change of the 'ecological equilibrium'; or the 'length of working time' could serve as an indicator for the welfare component of the 'process of working'.

As for (iii), the types of measurement will vary according to the type of indicator envisaged. Basically, we have a cardinal and ordinal scale of measurement. Cardinal scales usually provide more and better information, and, therefore, should be used if possible. For instance, the protein intake may be measured in grams per day per person. A reduction to, say, a first, second, and third group, neglecting the information provided by the cardinal scale, would be uneconomical. If measurement on a cardinal scale is difficult or impossible, the ordinal type of measurement (denoted in the classification by 'ord.') may be used. The ordinal ordering, i.e. first, second, ..., *n*th, may be given various concrete expressions, such as 'intolerable', 'inadequate', 'adequate', 'affluent'. Various quantities, i.e. percentages, may be assigned to levels of satisfaction. The group 'intolerable' may be expressed as, say up to 50 per cent of a given norm, the group 'inadequate' 80 per cent, and so forth. We shall not assign numerical values in the list presented. They will depend in each country on the specific social preferences, climatic factors, etc. If our intention were to extend the discussion on the relevance of social indicators for policy-making, development-planning, etc., a specific assessment of the factors mentioned would be of central importance. However, our analytical aim is to give a broad outline of the 'new normative directions', and consequently the focus will be on providing criteria which allow us to indicate and assess that direction. In doing so, criteria for the assessment of needs will be considered which themselves are not without considerable significance when numerical values are assigned to the welfare indicators.

The term 'structural' (denoted by 'struct.') indicates that significant causal interactions exist between a designated variable and other variables on the list. An analytical account of these 'welfare repercussions' will be given in a subsequent section (see Chapter 16,III).

Distributional judgements are not introduced into the list, the simple reason for this being the desire to avoid a continuous repetition of a specific distributional judgement. As mentioned, our distributional judgement will be egalitarian and, as a matter of consistency, an egalitarian proposition would have to apply to the distribution of all welfare components referred to. The discussion on distributional judgements will be further extended (see Chapter 16,II.3).

CLASSIFICATION OF WELFARE COMPONENTS, INDICATORS AND TYPES OF MEASUREMENT

Components	Indicators	Measurement
M^{aa}-level welfare components		
A-1 ECOLOGICAL EQUILIBRIUM	Land ecologically destroyed (preserved) Contaminants in air water (lakes, rivers, ocean) land	(Struct.) Ratio of land area destroyed to overall land area Ratios for ecologically classified environments tropical rain forests soil regions, etc. Levels of contaminants as proportion of maximum norms, for all categories mentioned Degree of laterisation and podzolisation
A-2 SPECIES DIVERSITY	Number of classes of species Number of species in each class	(Struct.) Number of classes of species extinct relative to total number of classes (initial or ecologically 'optimal' number of classes) Number of species extinct in each class relative to total number of species of that class
A-3 RECREATIONAL SPACE	Quality of natural environment Population density Population dispersion	(Struct.) Density ratios sub-ratios (see Part 1, Chap. 7,I

Components	Indicators	Measurement
M^{aa}/M^{a}		
B-1 PROVISION OF NATURAL RESOURCES AS INPUTS	Availability of natural resources Quality of natural resources Price of natural resources	(Struct.) Reserves, related to initial stock annual consumption requirements synthetic substitutes Grade of ores, oil, etc., extracted Marginal costs of resource recovery (technology available, grade of ores, etc.; see Part 2, Chapt. 9)
B-2 SPACE FOR SOCIO-ECONOMIC ACTIVITIES	Congestion	Density and dispersion ratios Hours lost due to congestion
M^{aa}/M^{i}		
C-1 ENVIRONMENTAL AESTHETICS	Enjoyment of environment	(Struct., Ord.) Aesthetic evaluations Symptoms of alienation attributable to bad ecological conditions
C-2 PHYSICAL AND MENTAL WELL-BEING DUE TO A LIFE IN ACCORDANCE WITH ECOLOGICAL LAWS	Contaminants harmful and/or unpleasant for humans in food air water (drinking, other use) land	(Struct.) Level of pollution compared to maximum values for categories mentioned (contaminants accumulated in human body, etc.) Deficiencies (i.e. oxygen, etc.) ratio of actual and standard values Medical expenses for physical and mental diseases caused by pollution
M^{a}		
D-1 INTRINSIC VALUES OF SYSTEM PREMISES (INSTITUTIONS, ETC.)	Stability of M^{a}-level as integrated whole of socio-economic system of political system Dynamic adjustment to change and generation of	(Struct., Ord.) Strikes, lockouts, riots, hours lost compared to potential working hours per year, etc. Political oppression

Components	Indicators	Measurement
	change required to solve emerging problems Cultural and ethnic development Social differentiation and integration Defence of national unity and cultural-ethnic integrity Self-sufficiency	Level of mass communication, media Literacy rate Linguistic homogeneity Military strength, compared to strength of potential aggressors Participation in political and economic associations (ASEAN, etc.) Extent of self-reliance with regard to resources decision-making (heteronomy) import/export dependency ratios see E-1
M^a/M^i		
E-1 PARTICIPATION IN SOCIO-ECONOMIC AND POLITICAL SYSTEMS	Role in decision-making and implementation in systems mentioned Employment Representation in political structure Social mobility, social esteem, etc.	(Struct.) Representation of groups in decision-making and implementation in systems mentioned (Un-)employment rate Extent of discrimination and hindrances when attempting to change social stratum ascribed social norms, habits, roles, etc. religious taboos administrative, by law Regional mobility Strength of dominant political groups (of opposition) Extent of (de-)centralisation of political power Position of disadvantaged groups
E-2 PROTECTION AND SECURITY	Effective protection from violence and harassment Confidence in the administration of justice and other	(Struct., Ord.) Rate of crimes involving persons property

Components	Indicators	Measurement
	executive organs (i.e. police, etc.) Protection against economic hazards	Rate of crimes solved pertaining to both sub-groups Quality of executive organs, extent and effectiveness of control over executives Insurance for predictable and unpredictable income losses (unemployment, accident, death, etc.), provided by family extended family system, including other secondary groups (neighbourhood, etc.) governmental agencies
F-1 PROCESS OF LEARNING	Acquisition of basic knowledge, skills, values necessary for individual development	(Struct., Ord.) Quality of family life Ratio of illiterates within population and groups School enrolment ratios combined primary, secondary, and vocational enrolment rate according to age groups (5–14, 15–19) people with higher education as proportion of total population, according to school types, social (income) groups Pupil-teacher ratios in educational institutions mentioned Quality of education (teachers, textbooks, other teaching material) Extent of integration of physically and mentally handicapped Enrolment of females, according to educational levels Cases of repression by teachers Number of children requir-

Components	Indicators	Measurement
		ing medical care due to physical and mental stress from school attendance Newspaper circulation, per 1000 inhabitants Radio and TV receivers, per 1000 inhabitants Telephones, per 1000 inhabitants Access to information via other channels Level of objectivity of information number of (independent) newspapers number of radio and TV stations quality of media
F-2 PROCESS OF WORKING	Length of working time Satisfaction with work, satisfaction with profession practised job	(Struct., Ord.) Average working hours per week Possibility of initially choosing and later changing profession and job Professional and job challenge Supervision and autonomy (see E-1 participation, etc.) Career prospects Fair treatment with regard to promotion Working conditions number and quality of factors and institutions which contribute to self-realisation, improvement of social relations, etc. rate of accidents at work
F-3 LEISURE	Length of leisure time Satisfaction from leisure	(Struct., Ord.) Average leisure time, as proportion of total time available and working time Leisure time used for recovery from working stress Flexibility in choice of leisure (working) time (daily

Components	Indicators	Measurement
		schedule, holidays) Access to and quality of leisure-time opportunities via market provision of public services number of cinemas, theatres number of libraries number of other cultural institutions see G-3, G-4, and H-1 Availability and quality of surroundings relevant for enjoying leisure time environmental, see A-3 primary (family and secondary groups societal, see E-1
G-1 NUTRITION	Calorie intake Protein intake Other nutritional intakes	Total average daily calorie intake compared to (minimum, optimum) requirements Calorie intake derived from cereals and starchy roots as proportion of total calorie intake Total average daily protein intake compared to (minimum, optimum) requirements Protein intake derived from animal protein as proportion of total protein intake Level of other nutritional intakes vitamins minerals others Balance (composition) and quality of nutritional intake items
G-2 CLOTHING	Availability and adequacy of clothing and footwear	(Ord.) Average quantity of cloth and footwear available

Components	Indicators	Measurement
		Appropriateness in terms of specific needs climatic professional, age groups, sex aesthetic (colours, design, etc.)
G-3 HOUSING	Services of dwellings Density of occupancy Quality	(Ord.) Average number of persons per room Dwellings with piped water as proportion of all dwellings Dwellings with electricity as proportion of all dwellings Quality of architecture appropriate to needs climatic cultural (social, economic)
G-4 HEALTH	Possibility of living a healthy life (absence of sickness and diseases) Length of lifespan	(Struct., ord.) Infant mortality rate Proportion of deaths (not) due to infection parasitic diseases Life expectancy at birth Inhabitants per physician in '000's Quality of medical care in terms of restoring functional capabilities reducing pain See M^{aa}/M^{i} (particularly G-1) and M^{i}
G-5 COMMAND OVER GOODS AND SERVICES NOT INCLUDED IN G-1–G-4	quality of and range of choice of goods and services	(Struct.) Number of commodity classes and number of commodity items within class Quality of commodities (improvements over time) New products introduced to above categories in specific period of time

	Components	Indicators	Measurement
H-1	PHYSICAL ENVIRONMENT (PUBLIC SERVICES)	Cleanliness Public amenities	(Struct., ord.) Extent and quality of public services for amenities and for keeping habitat clean Extent and quality of urban planning Urbanisation rate Number, size, and dispersion of parks in populated areas
M^i			
I-1	SELF-REALISATION	Possibility of reaching full human potential in pursuing an activity non-activity, e.g. meditation	(Struct., ord.) See M^{aa}/M^i and M^a/M^i Partly incommensurable and unmeasurable Measurement of distance-from-happiness (Levy/Guttmann, op. cit., p. 382 ff.)

3. Poverty Line and Minimum Income

Up to this point, we have elaborated a set of welfare components supplemented by its corresponding indicators and types of measurement, and we have suggested a specific judgement to be applied to the distribution of these welfare components. The subsequent discussion will bring into clearer focus the relationship between welfare, provision of welfare components, income, and their distribution according to needs. In setting out the analytical frame, only the market context will, for the sake of simplicity, be considered. This gives the discussion some concreteness. It can easily be seen that the arguments could be extended to the entire set of welfare components mentioned.

On a formal level, the welfare W of a social group i is seen to be dependent on the provision of commodities j; whence W_i^j. The total welfare obtained by all social groups from commodity j may be written as

$$W = W_1^j + \cdots + W_n^j.$$

The total welfare received by all social groups from the provision of all commodities is

$$W = (1, \ldots, 1) \begin{Vmatrix} W_1^1, \ldots, W_n^1 \\ W_1^m, \ldots, W_n^m \end{Vmatrix} \begin{pmatrix} 1 \\ \vdots \\ 1 \end{pmatrix}$$

$$\equiv \sum_{j=1}^{m} \sum_{i=1}^{n} W_i^j.$$

The provision of commodities can be measured by the quantity of commodities provided and their price

$$C = c \cdot p,$$

where C designates the monetary value, c the quantity in physical terms (kg, cal.) and p its unit price. By substituting the terms, the matrix can be written as

$$C = \begin{Vmatrix} c_1^1 p_1^1, \ldots, c_n^1 p_n^1 \\ \cdots\cdots\cdots\cdots \\ c_1^m p_1^m, \ldots, c_n^m p_n^m \end{Vmatrix}.$$

Relating both matrices to each other, the implicit form of a 'welfare generation function' (in terms of welfare components provided, excluding productivity aspects) may be expressed as

$$W = W(C),$$

where W is a real valued function of an $n \times m$ matrix.

The provision of welfare components such as C is made possible by (a) providing income y, or (b) providing welfare components in kind. According to the extent a monetary economy is introduced, the proportion of monetary income required to buy the commodities will accordingly vary. For ease of developing the argument, we assume that all provision of commodities is via income. Then we may write, for the income which buys the commodities,

$$y_i = c_i' p_i',$$

where c_i' and p_i' are respectively the average consumption of all commodities and the structure of relative prices (weighted price level) for social group i. If multiplied with the portion of the population constituting the social group, the total consumption of all commodities in that group is

$$(c_i' p_i')P_i$$

and for the income required to buy $(c_i' p_i')P_i$ accordingly

$$y_i P_i.$$

For all social groups, the required income is

$$y_1 P_1, \ldots, y_n P_n$$
$$= Y_1, \ldots, Y_n.$$

With the existing pattern, say the above pattern, a desired distribution may be contrasted. The normative distribution,

$$Y_1^*, \ldots, Y_n^*,$$

where

$$y_1^* = \cdots = y_n^*$$

is an absolute condition up to the point at which the minimum desiderata are reached (there may be differences in y_i^* due to differences in the population structure, which will be allowed for subsequently).

The differential pattern for all groups is

$$\frac{Y_1}{Y_1^*}, \ldots, \frac{Y_n}{Y_n^*},$$

and for the 'average' individual according to groups

$$\frac{y_1}{y_1^*}, \ldots, \frac{y_n}{y_n^*}.$$

Since we are interested in the magnitude of the poverty problem, it is appropriate first to determine an income level representing the poverty line, and then to ask how many people reach that level. The proportion of the population in an income group P_i is then seen as the dependent variable of the desired average income y^*, and of the actually obtained income y. Since at any given instance of time y^* will be a given constant, the level and variation in P_i will depend on the level and variations in y^*.

Table 16.1 provides two scenarios with y^* set at $50 and $75 respectively (in 1971 prices). Although the minimum income levels assumed are rather arbitrary, this gives a first rough idea of the order of magnitude of the poverty problem in Asia.[4] The figures indicate that there is a negative correlation between average income and the portion of the population living below the poverty line. This must be directly attributed to the possibility of raising the average income at the pace of development, not only in the upper but also in the lower-income strata. However, it is difficult to single out the effects arising out of the level of development from those resulting from the pattern of income distribution. The income distribution is itself dependent on the level of development. *Ex hypothesi* (see discussion on inverted U-pattern of changes in income distribution, pp. 138–41), the income distribution deteriorates in a first phase of development while it may or may not tend to become more equal in a later phase. Therefore, an increase in the total income growth will lead to an improvement in the income situation of the poverty strata; but this improvement will be slowed down due to the built-in tendency towards more inequality in an early phase of development.

In the global context, Asia ranks lowest in the provision of minimum incomes. In table 16.2, 88 per cent of the Asian population tanks as 'poor', 71 per cent as even 'seriously poor'. Latin America is, in terms of absolute poverty, comparatively better off than Asia. However, it also provides an instance where the detrimental impact of a more unequal distribution on the attainment of minimum income levels becomes apparent. Although the average income is considerably higher, its more unequal distribution still destines a section as large as 27 per cent of the total population to belong to the 'destitute'. A further aspect brought to mind by the above table is the significance of the absolute size of the population in the Asian region. Latin America's population is 274 million, compared to Asia's 1,196 million (without mainland regions). Both the large proportion of Asian population living below the poverty line and Asia's large proportion of the total world population indicate where the critical development problems of the future lie—if viewed from a global perspective.

From the degree of income disparity according to social groups, policy inferences may be drawn. The trade-offs according to social

TABLE 16.1 *Estimates of population below poverty lines*

Country	1969 GNP per capita (U.S. $)	1969 population (millions)	Population below $50		Population below $75	
			millions	% of total population	millions	% of total population
Asia						
Burma	72	27·0	14·5	53·6	19·2	71·0
Sri Lanka	95	12·2	4·0	33·0	7·8	63·5
India	100	537·0	239·0	44·5	359·3	66·9
Pakistan (E. & W.)	100	111·8	36·3	32·5	64·7	57·9
Thailand	173	34·7	9·3	26·8	15·4	44·3
Korea	224	13·3	0·7	5·5	2·3	17·0
Philippines	233	37·2	4·8	13·0	11·2	30·0
Taiwan	317	13·8	1·5	10·7	2·0	14·3
Malaysia	323	10·6	1·2	11·0	1·6	15·5
Total*	132	872·0	320·0	36·7	499·1	57·2
Latin America						
Total	545	244·5	26·6	10·8	42·5	17·4
Africa						
Total	303	83·8	23·8	28·4	36·6	43·6
Grand Total	228	1200·3	370·4	30·9	578·2	48·2

* The total for the selected Asian countries includes also Turkey, Iraq, Iran, and Lebanon, not shown in the table.

Note: the figures may sometimes be misleading; e.g. $50 in Burma will buy a different range of goods from $50 in Taiwan.

Source: *Redistribution with Growth*, by Hollis Chenery *et al.* (eds.), op.cit. p. 12; the figures are selected.

TABLE 16.2 *Poor, seriously poor, destitute, and total population by region, 1972*

	(%)			Population[1] (millions)			
	Poor	Seriously poor	Destitute	Poor	Seriously poor	Destitute	Total
Asia	88	71	42	1048	853	499	1196
Africa	86	69	39	296	239	134	345
Latin America[2]	65	43	27	274	118	73	274
Main regions[3]	84	67	39	1523	1210	706	1815

[1] Excludes socialist countries
[2] Including Caribbean
[3] Excludes developing countries of Europe and Oceania

Source: Peter Richards, 'Poverty, Unemployment and Underemployment'; in *Tripartite World Conference on Employment, Income Distribution and Social Progress and the International Division of Labour*, vol. 1, (Geneva: International Labour Office, 1976) p. 3; computations are based on figures mentioned in Table 16.1 above.

groups are

$$1 - \frac{Y_1}{Y_1^*}, \ldots, 1 - \frac{Y_n}{Y_n^*}.$$

The above pattern will serve as a distributional criterion up to zero, i.e. where $Y_1/Y_1^* = 1$.

The absolute income to be distributed to an individual in a specific period of time will be

$$\left(1 - \frac{y_i}{y_i^*}\right)y_i^*$$

and for the group

$$\left(1 - \frac{y_i}{y_i^*}\right)y_i^* P_i.$$

The presentation makes clear that the problem of alleviating poverty depends on both the average difference between the actual income and the minimum income, and the size of population to which that income deficit applies—a general reiteration of the above empirical statement.

A major redistributional question is whether

$$1 > \frac{Y_1}{Y_1^*}, \cdots \frac{Y_n}{Y_n^*} > 1$$

is an acceptable distributional pattern; that is, whether an income above the minimum level should be allowed at all as long as the income of other social groups does not meet the minimum requirements.

Generally, it will be considerably easier to implement redistributional policies in a growing economy than in a stagnant or even declining economy (as was the case in the Indonesian economy during the late Sukarno era). Since Asia has been experiencing an average income growth (see Table 14.5), the scenario of a growing economy will serve as a point of departure for further redistributional considerations. A first postulate will be to redistribute the additional income according to the trade-offs

$$1 - \frac{Y_i}{Y_i^*}$$

in the various groups. Any additional income accruing to groups which are above the minimum income level is redistributed to groups below the minimum level. Political acceptance of this plan may be easier to attain, since no social group will suffer an absolute decline in income.

A more flexible and differentiated policy would be required if an absolute decline in the income of any social group were considered (this decline must not necessarily fall to a point where the minimum income level is reached). Here, not only will vested interests resist the redistributional policy; it will also stand to reason that a massive absolute decline in the income of the upper strata may in the short run affect the productive capacity of the economy, lead to an outflow of capital, tax evasion, and generally to a deterioration of the economic climate. Although our preceding descriptive-explanatory account suggests that an egalitarian policy of this type is likely to have favourable effects on the socio-economic process in the long run, the immediate effects may be undesirable in terms of further increases in the poverty of the masses. The transitional process—the turn from a socio-economic system which produces increasing differentials to a socio-economic system which narrows those differentials—may be too costly in terms of the immediate welfare impact if the effects of redistributional policies on productivity are not appropriately allowed for. We shall return to the effects of a redistributional policy on the productivity of the socio-economic system in the following section. In anticipation of those results, we may state that a well-implemented redistributional strategy will have positive effects on productivity.

4. *Welfare and Needs*

For ease of developing the argument, we have been equating welfare with the provision of welfare components. This leaves open various interpretations as to the quantity of welfare components needed to attain a specific level of welfare. To bring the issue into proper perspective, the broad causal nexus will be stated explicitly. We have

$$\begin{array}{ccccccccccc} W_i & \leftarrow & U_i & \leftarrow & \dfrac{C_i}{N_i} & \leftarrow & C_i & \leftarrow & Y_i & \leftarrow & O_i \\ & & & & \uparrow & & & & & & \downarrow \\ & & & & X(N_i) & & & & & & S_i \end{array}$$

where

W_i = welfare,
U_i = utility,
C_i = level (and quality) of welfare components provided
N_i = needs
$X(N_i)$ = factors determining needs
Y_i = income
O_i = production, productivity
i = social group

The welfare level depends on the provision of welfare components. However, there are various intermediate factors which determine the effect which a specific level of welfare components has on welfare. We may start on the right-hand side of the causal chain. As is intuitively clear, different people have different needs. Trivial as it may sound, much is at stake for welfare theory when this complex is discussed. It is more than a subtle methodological nuance to make a distinction between needs and utilities. The 'new welfare economics' has propounded that utilities are not interpersonally comparable. If utility is directly linked to the provision of welfare components or even to the aggregate concept of income, indeed, little can be said about what level of utility these 'instrumentals' are capable of generating. The proposition will appear even more meaningful, if utility is understood as a concept which applies only to the realm of psychology, i.e. the psychic state, taste, etc. However, if the category of needs is introduced, an objectivity (at least, almost unanimous agreement) is called forth which necessarily substantiates the concept of utility and suggests the non-comparability proposition as being overly restrictive.

The crucial question, then, really is: are there any criteria for formulating an objective need structure? If so, an objective distribution of income, welfare components, utilities and, finally, welfare may be attained.

It would not have been worthwhile to introduce the concept of needs if it were not conceivable to make the concept operable. An obvious piece of evidence is the age structure, which can easily be seen to be relevant for the determination of the needs of a population. A baby does not need the same daily calorie intake as an adult. The ratio may be, for example, 300 : 1800. If the two humans are to attain the same level of utility (in terms of need satisfaction), the distribution of welfare components, namely, calories per day, will be in the ratio of 1 : 6.

Applied to the welfare component mentioned, the age structure of a population provides an objective criterion to ascertain approximately the needs of a population. Further criteria such as the sex composition and occupational structure must be introduced. Combined, they will reflect more or less faithfully (less if the empirical basis is inadequate) the needs of a population. For minimum desiderata (where the satisfaction of physical needs is of major importance), the above criteria help to determine objectively a significant part of the total needs.

A simplified picture (which nevertheless indicates major problems) is presented in Fig. 16.2. The distributional scheme is reduced to the needs for a single welfare component, the daily calorie intake c as plotted on the vertical axis, and a single factor determining those needs, the age groups of the population A, plotted on the horizontal axis. The hypothetical distribution of minimum calorie intakes is designated by the m-curve, the hypothetical distribution of actually attained calorie intakes by the a-curve. An optimum distribution according to the needs with regard to the age structure would be established when the a-area completely covers the m-area. The conditions to be met for the optimum are that (1) the overall provision of calories be sufficient, and (2) the distribution of the total calories accord with the needs of the age groups. The optimum pattern would be

$$\frac{c_1^{\text{act}}}{c_1^*} = \cdots = \frac{c_k^{\text{act}}}{c_k^*} = 1,$$

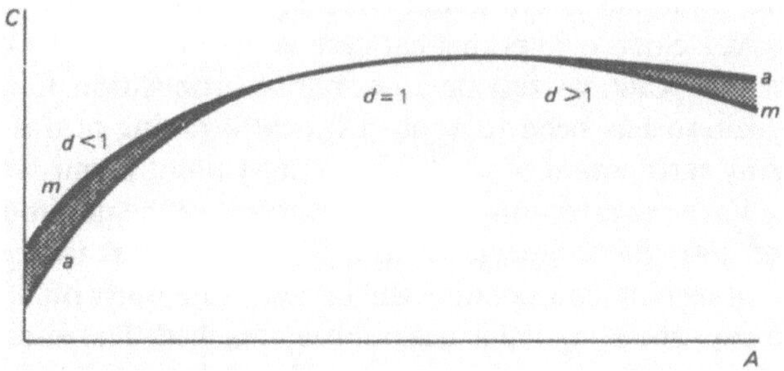

FIG. 16·2 *Needs and actual provision of calories according to age groups: deviations from the optimum distribution*

c = daily calorie intake
A = age groups
m = minimum calorie intake
a = actual calorie intake
$d = a/m$

where the superscripts 'act' and * indicate the actual and minimum intake levels respectively, and $l, \ldots, k$ are various age groups. Deviations from the optimum (minimum) occur if either (1) and/or (2) deviate from the optimum (minimum) conditions. In Fig. 16.2 the shaded area covering the calorie intake in the younger age brackets is a case in point. A deficit in the daily calorie consumption occurs which deviates from the minimum norm with

$$1 - \frac{c^{\text{act}}}{c^*} > 0$$

where the optimum condition (in terms of the overall distribution)

$$1 - \frac{c^{\text{act}}}{c^*} = 0$$

is not reached. By way of another example, the middle age group is assumed to have satisfied the minimum requirements. The ratio is at unity.

Less unambiguous are distributional statements pertaining to a situation where

$$\frac{c^{\text{act}}}{c^*} > 1,$$

and where trade-offs occur simultaneously in another age group (as stated above). Such a hypothetical case is assumed for the older age group. At this point, we rely on a normative proposition. Our normative proposition has been to apply a lexical ordering in this realm of welfare. Any satisfaction of needs above unity is not permissible unless all people have reached unity in the satisfaction of the minimum needs. Translated into the language of utility, the marginal utility for any provision of welfare components will be zero from unity on, if in any of the age groups the unity value has not been reached. The total utility in a society facing differences between actual and desired outcomes in the form

$$-d_1, -d_2, \ldots, +d_{k-1}, d_k,$$

would be

$$1 - \sum_{i=1}^{m} -d_i < 1,$$

which implies that

$$\sum_{i=1}^{m} (-d_i) \leq 0,$$

where 1. represents here the satisfaction of all subsistence needs, $-d_i$ the calorie deficit of age group i (weighted by the members of that group), and m the number of age groups suffering from a calorie deficit. Since the total subsistence utility cannot lie above unity, the total utility reached is determined solely by the total deficit.

A difficult evaluation problem emerges in situations where (a) all age groups suffer from (the same or different) trade-offs and (b) where all age groups have a satisfaction level above unity. Excluding (b) as irrelevant for the contemporary Asian countries, the distributional problem pertains to the optimal apportioning of the nutritional intakes to the various age groups. The distribution problem may be (theoretically) more easily settled where large differences among age groups in the calorie deficit occur. If all age groups suffer from comparably severe calorie deficits, complex evaluation problems are posed. On the one hand, the welfare loss of a single intake unit during the life cycle must be assessed. Calorie deficits for babies may have a lasting impact on the health over the entire life span. Any later calorie intake will be discounted by a coefficient which is determined by the initial calorie intake. In the middle age groups which constitute the labour force, a calorie deficit will depress the labour productivity (see subsequent section) and detrimentally affect the provision of calories. On the other hand, calories constitute but one factor in the diet. There is a subtle balance among all intakes which allow the human body and mind to develop optimally. We yet know little about how the various nutritional intakes affect human well-being. Only a complex biological model would allow meaningful results. The default of such model may explain why biologists have revised their data on nutritional minimum intakes drastically over the years. As an example, in 1950 for protein intake a value of 2·5 (gm/kg body-weight/day) was suggested for adults and a value of 3·5 for an 18-month-old child. The values were revised in 1973 to 0·5 and 1·5 respectively.[5]

The following data must be viewed in the light of eventual shortcomings with respect to the scientific basis biology provides. Little empirical research has been conducted at all on this topic. As a piece of scarce empirical evidence, we refer to an Indian survey taken for the Calcutta area in the early 1970s. All nutritional groups and age groups (except

TABLE 16.3 *Calcutta: mean intake of nutrients (as a fraction of requirements, in the poorest one-third of the families)*

Age groups	Calories	Proteins	Calcium	Vitamin A
2–4 years	0·55	1·05	0·70	0·75
12–16 years	0·56	0·85	0·69	0·65
22–56 years	0·59	0·95	0·94	0·69

Source: *Food Habits in Calcutta* (Calcutta: Hindustan Thompson Associates, 1972).

the 2–4 years age group in the protein intake) show large deficits. The deficits are larger in the calorie intake (compared to other nutritional items) and generally larger in the age brackets of children and youths.

The restrained validity of average magnitudes and, equally, the importance of need differentials are relevant also in the micro-context. The age groups run not only through the total population but also through families. The average income of a family may be sufficient to provide for the average calorie intake. But the micro-distribution may be inoptimal, due to a wrong diet, etc. More important, however, is the case where the family income is too small to provide for sufficient nutritional intake.

Table 16.4 shows that the average daily calorie intake decreases as

TABLE 16.4 *Household size and nutritional intakes compared, Philippines survey*

Number of household members	Daily *per capita* intake: Calories (no.)	Proteins (g)
1–3	2180	66
4–6	1750	51
7–9	1620	45
10–12	1600	44
Over 12	1500	43

Source: E. Quiogue *et al.*, 'Nutrition Survey of Eight Regions in the Philippines-Dietary Phase', *Philippine Journal of Nutrition*, vol. 22, 1969, quoted in *Population Aspects of Social Development*, Asian Population Studies Series, no. 11, (Bangkok: United Nations, 1972), p. 76.

TABLE 16.5 *Food supplies: calories and proteins* per capita *compared with respective requirements*

Regions	Calories				Proteins				Animal Proteins		
	Supplies			Require-ments	Supplies			Require-ments	Supplies		
	1962	1965	1970		1962	1965	1970		1962	1965	1970
Less-developed regions	2080	2120	2190	2280	55·2	54·7	56·4	29·0	10·4	11·0	11·4
Asia and Far East (excluding China)	1990	1980	2080	2220	51·2	49·4	51·7	28·0	6·9	7·6	7·9
Near East	2160	2310	2380	2460	65·4	65·9	66·8	35·0	14·3	13·1	13·4
Africa	2120	2150	2180	2340	58·0	58·2	58·6	32·0	9·2	9·3	9·5
Latin America	2350	2470	2520	2380	61·4	63·7	64·9	29·0	22·4	23·7	24·7
Developed regions*	3010	3090	3150	2560	86·4	90·7	92·2	30·0	43·1	46·9	50·9

* Including USSR and Eastern Europe and excluding other developed countries.

Source: P. V. Sukhatme, 'Human Calorie and Protein Needs and How Far They Are Satisfied Today'; in Bernard Benjamin *et al.* (eds.), *Resources and Population*, op. cit., p. 30; data are taken from the food balance sheets for the countries prepared by FAO and WHO.

the number of household members increases. On the one hand, this reflects the different needs of families composed of members of different age groups. On the other hand, as the Indian survey suggests, the higher deficits in the age brackets of the younger may also increase the average deficits of the families as their number of members increases. Irrespective of the distributional aspects, it is clear that a large number of family members will induce a comparatively low average family income, and provide for a smaller *per capita* basis when the calories are purchased.

The following data show the orders of magnitude on a comparative scale. In Table 16.5 the major world regions are included. The actual supply and requirements for various nutritional intakes are shown on a *per capita* basis. The table is self-explanatory. One fact perhaps deserves particular attention: Asia is the only region which experienced a fall in the calorie and protein-supply in the period 1962–65. The reversal of this trend in the period 1965–70 must be largely attributed to the 'green revolution'. The supply of animal protein appears, in statistical terms, 'normal'. Nevertheless, this reflects the fundamental trend of increasing income inequalities, which allow an increase in the animal-protein consumption (for the upper-income

TABLE 16.6 *Alternative projections of calorie deficits, affected population*

	*Population with daily calorie deficits, 1980**				
	More than 200 calories		*Less than 200 calories*		Total daily calorie deficit
Region	Numbers (millions)	Average deficit	Numbers (millions)	Average deficit	
Asia & Far East	608	289	496	88	220
Latin America	39	445	80	150	29
Near East	—	—	62	170	10
Africa	170	277	139	64	56
Total	817		777		315

* Estimated total population is 2,300·694 million. Estimates for Latin America include extrapolations of calorie deficits for Brazil on the basis of data provided by *Food Consumption in Brazil: Family Budget Survey in Early 1960s* (Getulio Vargas Foundation, Nov. 1970).

Source: Shlomo Reutlinger and Marcelo Selowsky, *Undernutrition and Poverty*, IBRD Staff Working Paper no. 202 (Washington DC, 1975) p. 31; medium projections have been taken.

groups) concomitant with a decrease in the average calorie and vegetable-protein intakes (affecting the lower-income strata).

Alternative projections of calorie deficits by the year 1980 are presented in Table 16.6. A medium projection is chosen. The table is revealing since it again brings the population problem into focus. Over 600 million people will suffer from a daily calorie deficit of over 200 calories in the Asian region by 1980. This is 15 times more than the comparable figure for Latin America. If the better-nourished groups with a daily calorie deficit of less than 200 are included, the figure adds up to over 1,000 million people suffering from a calorie deficit in Asia. Over two-thirds of the world calorie deficit in 1980 will be located in Asia.

III. PRODUCTIVITY EFFECTS OF REDISTRIBUTIONAL POLICIES

1. Composite Productivity Effects: a Model

Our policy suggestions have been (1) to narrow the socio-economic differentials, and (2) to implement a social-welfare function which satisfies the minimum needs of the masses. The question arises whether the realisation of a policy pertaining to (1) and (2) incurs a cost in some distant future. We shall call the effects stemming from the implementation of (1) and (2) 'productivity effects' and, accordingly, distinguish between productivity effects pertaining to the socio-economic variables, and productivity effects pertaining to the welfare variables. The effects may in both instances be (a) positive, (b) negative, and (c) neutral.

Since the implementation of (1) and (2) is desirable *per se*, i.e. from the point of view of the egalitarian postulate, (a) and (c) would justify the implementation of (1) and (2) while (b) would either still justify the implementation or lead to a reassessment of the social-welfare function and the policies devised.

The implementation of (1) and (2) may be via a change (A) in the socio-economic variables, (B) in the welfare variables, or (C) in the variables of the related systems (S_n, S_s). There are, by definition, mutual causal links between the three sets of variables. For instance, level and changes in the socio-economic variables determine level and changes in the welfare variables (direct productivity effect), and the level and changes in the latter exert productivity effects on the former (indirect productivity effect).

Policies relating to (A) include changes in (a) asset distribution, and (b) income distribution. The term 'asset' should here be given a broad meaning including all production factors, such as land, financial assets, access to technology, education, and information, etc. An improved income distribution may be achieved by directly redistributing income using progressive tax schemes, subsides, etc.—this being the meaning of (b). However, income generation must also be—and primarily—conceived of in the context of distributional policies relating to (a), viz. as a result of policies bringing about a redistribution of assets.

Policies relating to (B) include a direct redistribution of welfare components. As far as the set of welfare components is composed of market commodities, a direct link exists between the provision of income and the possibility of claiming from a given set of market commodities. Our list of welfare components has made evident that the total set of welfare components includes a large number of non-market components. In particular, we have the governmental provision of welfare components such as education, infrastructure, etc., and welfare components related to the intrinsic value of politico-socio-economic institutions and to the processes occurring in the institutions.

Policies relating to (C) include (a) policies bringing about institutional change, (S_s), and (b) population policies (S_n). As indicated in (B), these systems constitute, themselves, desiderata included in W. In turn, the systems mentioned have instrumental character by contributing to changes in W.

Figure 16.3 gives an overall view of the major policy links and the three sets of productivity effects. While the policy links are denoted by arrows from the political system (S_p) to the asset ($\bar{F}_i$), income (Y_i), commodity (C_i) and welfare (W_i) variables, the productivity effects originating from that policy set are further broken down by stating the production function in explicit form. The break-down follows that introduced in Figure 15.1. The technical system is explicitly allowed for in the form of the capital coefficient k and the labour productivity, λ, and in implied form, the K/O ratio. The subscript i again denotes the type of group.

The direct productivity effects of redistributional policies, whether related to (A), (B), or (C), may be stated in terms of: the output growth effect, the employment effect, and the capital formation effect; while the indirect productivity effect, viz. the productivity effect of welfare,

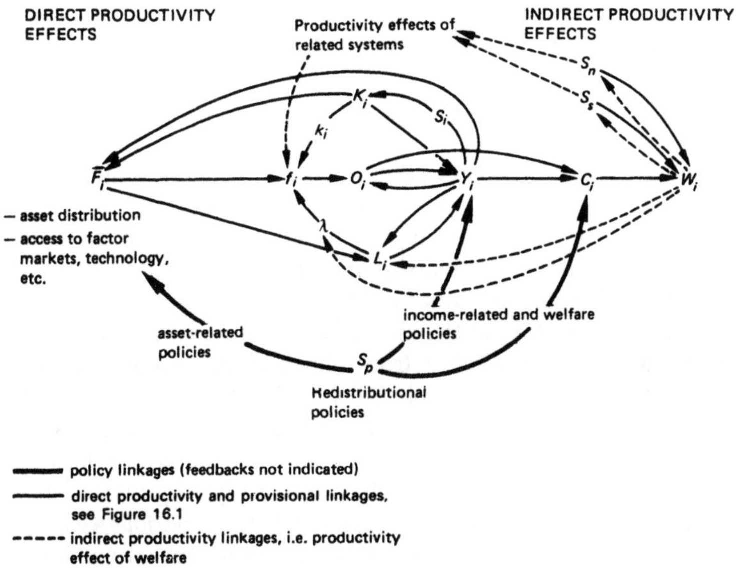

FIG. 16.3 *Causal model combining direct and indirect productivity effects*

——— policy linkages (feedbacks not indicated)
——— direct productivity and provisional linkages, see Fig. 16.1
- - - - indirect productivity linkages, i.e. productivity effect of welfare

C = Set of commodities provided by market O and purchased with income y
W = Welfare generated by C
i = by assumption for (traditional) $\bar{F}_1$-sectors

For explanation of terms constituting the production function, viz. K, O, L, and of S_n, S_s, and S_p, see Figure 15.1 and discussion in Chapter 15.1.

may be stated in terms of the employment effect, the labour productivity effect, and the effect on related systems S_s and S_n. Clearly, there are dependencies between the productivity effects such as the employment and output growth effects, or the labor productivity and employment effects, and so forth. This is clear from our earlier discussion (see the discussion on the relationship between employment and labour productivity, etc.). Consequently, direct and indirect productivity effects are usually combined effects reinforcing or offsetting each other.

From the distributional side, it is important to note that the productivity effects pertain to a specific social group $\bar{F}_i$ and are thus not 'aggregate' effects. Departing from an egalitarian postulate, we must assess whether the positive effects in the $\bar{F}_1$-sectors exceed the negative effects in the $\bar{F}_n$-sectors, in terms of output, employment, productivity, etc.

2. *Direct Productivity Effects*

An assessment of the productivity effects of redistributional policies may rely more on a single-sector or decomposition analysis, as attempted in the 'sources-of-growth analysis'; or more on a 'holistic' assessment of the entire socio-economic process, focusing on the complex causal interactions among the relevant variables.

Within the context of the single-factor approach, capital formation has been the *cause célèbre* from the classical economists on. The hypothesis is that rich people have a higher propensity to save and therefore any egalitarian shift will decrease the savings rate. While this may be true under the condition of a number of *ceteris paribus* assumptions, those assumptions themselves are hardly insignificant enough to warrant being treated as such. A principal *ceteris paribus* assumption is that the capital-output ratio k remain constant. Once we no longer rely on this restrictive assumption, the assessment of redistributional policies in terms of their effect on capital formation and output growth may show more favourable results. First of all, we may assume that the differentials in k are in favour of the (traditional) $\bar{F}_1$-sectors, leaving the (modern) $\bar{F}_n$-sectors with a higher capital-output ratio. An initial shift in the income distribution towards the $\bar{F}_1$-sectors may, indeed, decrease overall savings, since the propensity to save may be lower than in the $\bar{F}_n$-sectors. If this shift, however, is accompanied by a shift in the differentials of k, we have counteracting forces. Only if the decrease in the overall propensity to save and of total savings exceeds the (positive) effects of the decreasing capital-output ratio, may the output growth be smaller after the redistribution. However, it may well be that the effects of the falling savings propensity are compensated or overcompensated by the fall in k. If overcompensated, the positive effects will be on both capital formulation and output growth: increased output growth in the $\bar{F}_1$-sectors will lead to an increased propensity to save multiplied by increased income available for savings. Keeping k constant, the output growth will increase in the $\bar{F}_1$-sectors and, subsequently, further contribute to the capital formation in that sector. Thus, it is quite conceivable that an egalitarian policy initially impairs the overall savings rate but later improves the productivity of the capital stock, due to a decline in k, and increases the savings propensity and rate (due to higher output growth rates).

Next, the employment effect may be singled out. Analytically simplified, employment will depend on marginal labour and capital productivity ('technical intensity'). Following classical-neoclassical reasoning, any additional employment will contribute to output growth since only labour with positive marginal productivity is employed. Classical writers introduced, in addition, an institutional or subsistence wage, which set a limit to additional employment at a point where the marginal productivity equals the institutional wage. If differentials in the production functions are introduced, the employment effects of redistributional policies may differ significantly from those conjectured by classical-neoclassical writers. Generally, the K/L ratio or capital intensity will be higher in the $\bar{F}_n$-sectors than in the $\bar{F}_1$-sectors. Therefore, a marginal contribution to the capital stock of the $\bar{F}_1$-sectors, at the expense of an equal marginal loss for the capital stock of the $\bar{F}_n$-sector, will increase overall employment. In a growing economy, any output growth in the $\bar{F}_1$-sectors will induce a larger marginal employment effect than the equivalent in the $\bar{F}_n$-sectors.

The question is whether the increased wages fund will induce a fall in capital formation. A redistributional policy has been assumed to increase the capital stock of the traditional sectors because of the favourable impact on the capital output coefficient, propensity to save, and the income growth used up for additional savings. In a static context, additional wages would decrease the π/w ratio and eventually affect the savings propensity and capital formation. In a dynamic context, demand generated by an increasing wages fund will play a crucial role in the subsequent process. Additional employment will generate additional output which satisfies the additional demand created by additional employment. The process would be impaired only if a relative shift in output in favour of the $\bar{F}_1$-sectors led to a fall in overall capital productivity. However, the assumptions of differentials in k (in favour of the $\bar{F}_1$-sectors) would not support that hypothesis.

The discussion of single productivity effects demonstrates that the relevant variables are difficult to separate analytically. The variables and effects interact in complex ways. Since differentials exist in all variables, non-linearity in the change of the variables must frequently be expected. Complexity in the causal interactions, and non-linearity in the change of the variables, both develop a dynamic which carries the initial cause far beyond levels expected from simple mono-causal and basically linear relationships. The subsequent empirical assessment of some single direct-productivity effects must be seen in the light of these considerations.

Empirical data for differential aspects of development are scarce. Theory and empiry were preoccupied with aggregates. Only a broad indication of the orders of magnitude may be given. First, there is empirical evidence that k is lower in the $\bar{F}_1$- than in the $\bar{F}_n$-sectors. Data for foreign and domestic industrial firms (which may be taken as a specification of the general dualistic scheme used) compiled for Thailand show a higher capital productivity (measured in the ratio of output to fixed assets) for domestic firms (Table 16.7).

TABLE 16.7 *Ratios of output and profits to fixed assets of foreign and domestic firms in Greater Bangkok area, 1972*

	Foreign firms	Domestic firms	All firms
Ratios of output (valued-added) to fixed assets	0·4111	0·6717	0·6023
Ratios of profits to fixed assets	0·2875	0·4957	0·4403

Source: N. K. S. Sarkar, *Industrial Structure of Greater Bangkok*, op.cit., p. 61.

Data for India support the findings from Thailand. Capital productivity is higher in 'traditional' industrial sectors such as cotton-weaving than in 'modern' industrial sectors such as the flying-shuttle hand loom and (even more so) the automatic power loom.[6] However, empirical findings for the agricultural sector partly contradict the results of favourable productivity effects to be expected from a shift to the $\bar{F}_1$-sectors.[7]

Some further insights into the orders of magnitudes may be gained from a simulation model.[8] Its weakness is that it necessarily relies on gross assumptions about empirical relationships and excludes relevant variables because of difficulties in including more variables which are 'operational' from the viewpoint of model building. The advantage lies in the possibility of quantifying the (hypothetical) changes in the variables included. Table 16.8 includes the variables k, net savings rate, and change in capital stock, and envisages changes in these variables in the time span of 50 years (dissected into five decades). The simulation results show that the rate of capital formation accelerates in the course of time and increases from 0·023 to 0·041 p.a.

TABLE 16.8 *Capital-output ratio, net savings rates, and annual rates of capital formation—simulation results*

Period	Capital-output ratio	Period	Net savings rates (%)	dK/K (%)
1	1·9	1–10	6·6	2·3
10	1·8	10–20	7·2	3·1
20	1·7	20–30	7·8	3·5
30	1·7	30–40	8·2	3·8
40	1·7	40–50	8·5	4·1
50	1·7			

Source: Allen C. Kelly and Jeffrey G. Williamson, 'Sources of Growth Methodology in Low-Income Countries: A Critique', *Quarterly Journal of Economics*, vol. 87, no. 1, 1973, p. 145.

Of this increase, approximately two-thirds is attributable to the declining k, while the remainder is due to increased savings rates. Since the model operates with the theoretical assumption of a rising non-labour share and a concomitant fall in the total capital-output ratio, the simulation results may claim even more validity in a theoretical context where k is assumed to fall, given the conditions of a constant or even falling K/L ratio (not increasing the non-labour share of primarily the modern sectors).

Furthermore, there is the employment effect of redistributional policy. The empirical findings do not unambiguously support our theoretical assumption of increasing employment due to the narrowing developmental differentials. The pessimistic result may be due to the fact that basically the effects of income redistributional policies only were considered, and not those of asset redistributional policies. Additionally, statistical shortcomings such as the use of a two-digit classification when assessing the employment effects in industries may account for the pessimistic findings.[9] For instance, it is conceivable that the production of simple transistors or pocket calculators has a significantly lower K/L ratio (i.e. higher labour intensity) than the production of modern computers, sophisticated electronical equipment, and even software. Similarly, traditional and modern agriculture cannot be put in the same statistical bracket merely because they produce (possibly) homogenous goods. Besides the potential 'gains' from a statistical reclassification, some empirical data indicate that the employment effect is positive. A survey made in Pakistan shows that rural households consume a more labour-intensive basket of commodities than urban households, and that the same is true for the low- and high-income strata respectively.[10]

If at least a neutral effect on employment could be attained, the redistributional postulate would not be in conflict with the employment desideratum. The redistributional postulate having a value in itself, redistributional policy would improve welfare. The same conclusions may, *mutatis mutandis*, be drawn with regard to the effects on output growth and capital formation. Since theoretical considerations and empirical findings indicate the possibility of arriving at positive effects, the assumption of neutrality in those effects with regard to redistributional policies would be justified. Analogously, the fact that conflicts fail to appear between the two desiderata would justify pursuing a redistributional policy from the point of view both of the normative propositions and the potential productivity effects.

A conclusive assessment of the output growth, employment, and capital formation effects is conceivable only on the basis of a consistent overall development theory. To some extent the single variables were related to each other in the preceding discussion. The earlier descriptive-explanatory account (Chapter 15, 'Against the Current') has provided a more comprehensive picture. Although the theory presented cannot claim to be a definitive account of the development problems in contemporary Asia, it is important to note that the inferences drawn from that body of hypotheses does not contradict the empirical findings stated. The 'holistic' assessment of the current developmental processes has shown that critical developmental variables tend to interact in such a way that major developmental outcomes are detrimentally affected. The differentials—in asset and income distribution, production functions, and the K/L and K/O ratios—tend to increase, and reinforce fundamental (structural) inconsistencies in the supply and demand conditions. Increasing differentials aggravate social inequalities, social disharmony, and social imbalances. They increasingly and effectively keep the large majority of the population far removed from political decision-making and decision-implementation. They perpetuate high population growth rates or, at least, slow down the favourable impact of a potentially effective antinatalist policy.

In conclusion, the present state of theory and empirical findings does not seem to allow us to ascertain in a definite way the productivity effects of redistributional policies, i.e. in a multi-causal context, or to formulate more precise hypotheses about the causal impact of the variables. Yet, there is enough evidence from the preceding discussion to indicate that the positive effects of a redistributional policy are likely to exceed its negative effects. This is so, at least, if the social-welfare function is directed towards the set of desiderata suggested—which sharply contrast with the normative outcomes actually attained and run counter to vested interests and outdated theories.

3. *Productivity Effects of Welfare*

The productivity effect of welfare depends on the level as well as the distribution of welfare W. The level and distribution of welfare depends on the level and distribution of welfare components C, and the utility derived from the consumption or possession of these welfare components, u. Since we have grouped C according to social groups i and according to types of welfare components j, we may obtain a matrix,

$$[C_i^j] \qquad \text{where} \quad j = 1, \ldots, m \quad i = 1, \ldots, n.$$

Accordingly, we have a matrix of utility coefficients

$$[u_i^j].$$

In matrix form we have for the total welfare

$$W_i^j = C_i^j u_i^j .$$

The row vectors denote the welfare generated by a specific welfare component and utility coefficient as distributed over various groups, and the column vectors the total welfare received by a specific group.

W has been assumed to have an impact on employment, labour productivity, and the related systems S_n and S_s. Therefore, the productivity effect of welfare may be classified according to social groups and types of welfare components *vis-à-vis* the various productivity effects. The welfare matrix may be related to sets of coefficients φ_i which express the productivity effects of the social groups and the welfare components. The sets of the three mentioned productivity effects of welfare may be written as

$$W\phi_1 = L$$
$$W\phi_2 = \lambda$$
$$W\phi_3 = S_{n,s}.$$

All variables mentioned constitute matrices. The sets of coefficients could be seen as sets of 'productivity functions' which express the impact of W on L, λ, $S_{s,n}$.

The analytical presentation does not include a statement about the causal interactions among the variables of each matrix. It merely states that a specific change in welfare causes productivity to change according to the productivity function. Clearly, there are complex causal interactions which determine the values in the rows and columns of the matrices. Furthermore, the sets of coefficients must not be expected to remain constant but to change with time. This itself is explained by the causal interactions among the variables of each matrix as well as the complex causal interactions among various matrices. We shall, therefore, first outline the salient structural features of a causal model which shows the productivity effects of welfare, and, second, discuss the changes in the value of the variables and coefficients assigned to them.

Let us proceed to the first step. Figure 16.4 includes various sets of welfare components, utility indicators, and productivity variables effected by changes in welfare. The set of welfare components includes four basic welfare components, viz. housing, H, education, E, nutrition, N, and medical care, M. To all welfare components are assigned the respective utilities, u_h, u_e, u_n, u_m. The sets of productivity coefficients are distinguished according to the welfare components, ϕ_h, ϕ_e, ϕ_n, ϕ_m. A further decomposition of the productivity effects according to the productivity variables affected, viz. L, λ, $S_{s,n}$, is for simplicity not introduced in the causal structure delineated. The combined productivity effects Π feed back to the real income Y and the provision of welfare components. Alternatively, we may start from Y, assuming that a redistributional policy is pursued. The model may then be applied to the $\bar{F}_1$-sector only. The assumption would be that Y is increased in order to increase the provision of welfare components. The question is, how the increased welfare generated by the improved provision of welfare components determines productivity, and, in a subsequent period, determines the provision of income and hence, again, the level of welfare components. When assessing the productivity effect of welfare on an entire society, the productivity effects of welfare of the $\bar{F}_n$-sector (besides

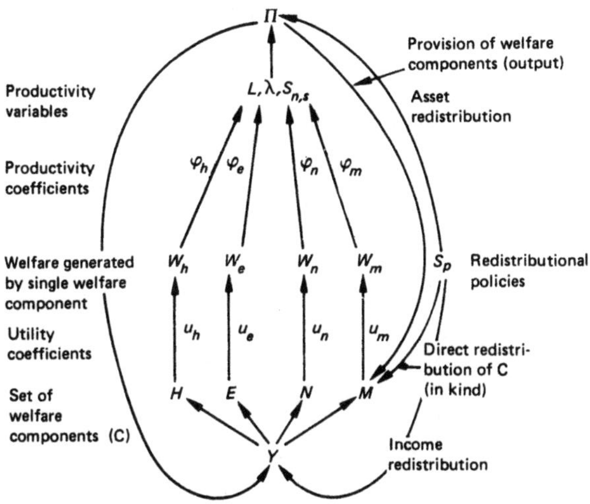

FIG. 16.4 *Productivity effect of welfare—causal model with policy linkages*

Π = production function, combined productivity effect
H = housing
E = education
N = nutrition
M = health care
λ = labour productivity
S_s = social system
S_p = political system
Y, L, S_n are explained in Fig. 15.1

all others) must also be taken into account. However, the productivity effects of welfare are likely to be insignificant from a specific level of income on. The marginal utility of additional basic welfare components will be small or zero, since at that level the basic needs are usually fully satisfied. Accordingly, income will not be expended on those welfare components and, consequently no additional productivity effect may be expected from those. Analogously, few effects may be expected if the income of the $\bar{F}_n$-sectors is diminished by redistributional policies. The liquidation of savings reserves and the curtailment of luxurious consumption will precede any reduction in the consumption of welfare components constituting basic necessities. Additionally, the number of people constituting the upper-income strata is insignificant when contrasted with the bulk of population living in poverty. The small marginal productivity effects to be expected and the insignificant proportion of the total population that they constitute justify neglecting

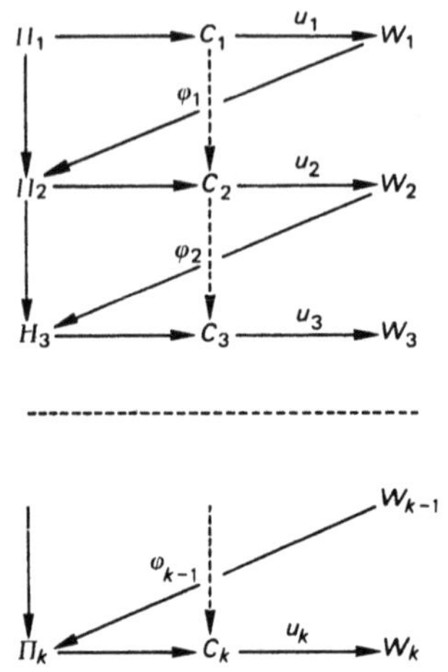

FIG. 16.5 *Productivity effects of welfare over* k *periods*

Π_j = total set of productivity effects
C_j = total set of welfare components
u_j = utility coefficient
W_j = total welfare generated by C_j, given a utility coefficient u_j
ϕ_j = productivity coefficient
j = number of periods, $j = k$

potential productivity effects of welfare of the $\bar{F}_n$-sectors or the upper-income strata. The reduction of the model to the traditional sectors much simplifies the theoretical exposition (Figure 16.4). Changes in the values of the coefficients pertain, in the context of the analytical reduction suggested, only to levels that are below, at, or modestly above the minimum norm, while insignificant changes in the productivity effects (lying above those values) can be neglected.

Proceeding to the second step—assessing the changes in the values of the variables and coefficients—the dynamic character of the problem stated must first be made explicit. In Figure 16.5 the model presented is dynamised by introducing various periods in which the model operates. Π, *W*, and *C* represent matrices composed of column and row vectors as previously mentioned. The subscripts denote specific periods. In reality, the periods may stand for planning periods (i.e. short-, medium-, or long-term planning), parliamentary sessions relevant for policy implementation, convenience when devising theoretical models, empirically relevant time spans in which changes in the variables become meaningful and can be measured, etc. Conceiving the relationships as simple difference equations enables one to bypass non-linear equations which—when defined as a system of equations—become insoluble. Π constitutes a composite variable set embracing all single productivity variables, L, λ, $S_{s,n}$. The utility and productivity coefficients are denoted by u_t and ϕ_t respectively, where the total of periods t envisaged is k. The productivity effect of welfare is denoted by the arrows connecting the welfare stratum W of period t with the productivity stratum Π of period $t + 1$. The vertical arrows from Π_t to Π_{t+1} indicate that the productive capacity of the previous period determines—together with the productivity effect of welfare of that period—the present productive performance, provision of welfare components, and level of welfare. A rationale for the vertical arrows from C_t to C_{t+1} is provided by the fact that some welfare components such as housing or education can be accumulated, and to some extent a stock concept be applied. Some welfare components, however, are consumed and, therefore, their being effective over the entire sequence relies on a continuous flow of welfare components—justifying, rather, the application of a flow concept when assessing or measuring this relationship. The dualistic stock-flow characteristics of the welfare components and the welfare to be derived therefrom suggest that the intertemporal relationships between the welfare components (i.e. from C_1 to C_k) should be indicated in the figure with broken (rather than solid) arrows. The welfare in the period k (by our initial assumption only for the $\bar{F}_1$-sectors) is, generally, given by

$$W_k = C_k u_k .$$

For instance, the welfare in period 1 is

$$W_1 = C_1 u_1 .$$

The productivity effect of welfare in period k is, generally, given by

$$\Pi_k = W_{k-1} \phi_{k-1}$$

and, accordingly, for the first period

$$\Pi_1 = W_0 \phi_0 .$$

At any period the value of the sets of variables C, Π, and W will be different, since the two sets of coefficients lead to their change over time. The coefficients are not assumed to be constants. The marginal value for u is assumed to decrease as C increases above the minimum level (assumption of decreasing marginal utility). The marginal values for ϕ are assumed to be negative, that is, the (positive) coefficient ϕ is assumed to decline as W increases; it keeps declining until the zero-point is reached, leaving open the possibility of negative productivity coefficients thereafter.

The structural features of the model may be refined in two ways: first, the causal links—welfare components → welfare → productivity effect—may be further specified, and second, the causal interactions within the various strata—such as the strata of welfare components, welfare, and productivity—will be made explicit. We will not embark on a discussion of the specific causal interactions of the various strata and variables, but merely provide a more comprehensive idea of the basic causal links, i.e. the causal 'structure' of the welfare and productivity variables involved.

The further assessment of the causal links of the model requires that we distinguish between

A. Productivity effects on L, λ, $S_{s,n}$ arising from changes in the level of welfare components due to changes in income: the 'induced productivity effects' (see Figure 16.4)

B. Productivity effects resulting from changes in the level of the welfare components due to causal interactions within the stratum of welfare components themselves: the 'autonomous productivity effects of the welfare stratum'

C. Productivity effects due to causal interactions within the stratum of productivity variables L, λ, $S_{s,n}$, without causal impact from the welfare components: the 'autonomous productivity effects of the productivity stratum'.

It goes without saying that the productivity effect proper—the productivity resulting from an initial input in K, L, ϕ—also has a significant impact on the determination of the level and structure of welfare components, this being indicated in Figure 16.5 by the sequence of arrows connecting Π_t and Π_{t+1}. At this point, however, only the 'additional' impact on productivity not included in the initial inputs will be analysed.

A diagrammatic presentation of the model would provide a somewhat confusing picture, since an immense number of arrows would depart and arrive at any of the variables mentioned. We shall, therefore, provide an overall view of the causal links in the form of a matrix-table instead. The following table is dissected according to the categories introduced.

Impact of welfare change on productivity variables—induced productivity effects

A.	Employment	Labour productivity	Population system	Social system
Housing	Improved housing location → increased job availability → increased employment; improved housing conditions → less absenteeism at work	Improved housing → increased satisfaction → higher efficiency at work; improved housing location → less travelling time → more recreation, less fatigue at working place due to long travelling-times → increased labour productivity	Improved housing → decrease in mortality; → shift to other consumer items related to housing → increase of opportunity costs of having children → decrease in fertility	Improved housing → improved neighbourhood → decrease of social tensions; → improved social contacts and communication → possible increase in social harmony
Education	Higher educational level → extension of labour supply; improved educational structure → more adequate supply of labour for all types of work, reduction of 'educated unemployed'	Higher educational levels and improved structure of education (school enrolment, etc.) → increase in labour productivity; job satisfaction → increase in labour productivity	Improved education → better knowledge about effective contraceptives → reduction of fertility; → change in opinion about desired ('ideal') family size → reduction in fertility; → improved knowledge about human body, diseases, possibilities of using medical care (doctors, hospitals, family-planning centres) → reduction in mortality, reduction in fertility	Improved educational opportunities → decrease in social tensions; → increased open-mindedness towards institutional change, improved capability to implement effectively decisions pertaining to institutional change

Nutrition	Improved nutritional intake → fewer absentees, due to better physical and mental state of workers	Improved nutritional intake → better physical health → increase in labour productivity; → improved mental health → more satisfaction from work → increase in labour productivity	Improved nutritional intake → more surviving children → lowering of fertility rate; → reduction in mortality	Improved nutritional intake → less aggression due to malfunctioning of metabolism → improved social harmony; → decrease of lethargy → improved social commitment; → open-mindedness towards institutional change; → reduction of social inequalities among men, women, and children when distributing food (male priority etc.)
Health care	Improved medical care → improved health → fewer absentees;	Improved medical care → improved physical health → increased physical strength, resistance, endurance → increase in labour productivity; improved mental health → improved satisfaction → improved labour productivity; → improved mental health → better use of leisure time → improved restoring of physical and mental capabilities; → increased intellectual capacity → improved control over working process, faster understanding of functions of working process, etc.	Improved medical care → increased number of surviving children → reduction of fertility rate; → improved access to effective contraceptives → reduction in fertility rate; → improved effectiveness of contraceptives used due to better knowledge and improved standards of hygiene; → increase in life span → decrease in mortality rate	Improved medical care → better physical and mental state of people → decrease in aggression → decrease in social tensions; decrease in apathy → increase in social commitment, improved social harmony; → increased time available for social activities not related to the care of sick people

Self-reinforcing productivity effects in welfare stratum—autonomous productivity effects

B.	Housing	Education	Nutrition	Health care
Housing		Improved housing → improved learning environment; → improved rest → increased concentration; → increased school attendance and attainment	Improved housing → improved storage and preparation of food; → improved housing location → better availability of food (infrastructure, markets)	Improved housing → improved hygiene sanitation, etc.) → decrease of susceptibility to infectious disease → improved health; → improved psychic well-being → improved health
Education	Improved education → improved knowledge pertaining to acquisition and use of housing facilities; → improved information about adequate location of housing		Improved education → increased knowledge (particularly of mothers) about adequate diet	Improved education → better knowledge about life style in accordance with biological requirements → improved health; decrease in illness, disease; → improved knowledge about bodily functions → improved restoring of malfunctioning in cases of illness; → less fear of consulting doctor → increased frequency of visits to doctor → possibly improved health

Nutrition		Improved nutritional intake → improved development of brain and of vital organs in early childhood → improved basis for human development; → improved physical condition, resistance, etc.; → improved learning efficiency; → improved mental state → increased satisfaction from learning → improved learning efficiency		Improved nutritional intake → improved development of brain and other vital organs in early childhood → improved resistance to illness and diseases; → quicker restoration of disordered bodily functions (shorter recovery periods): → improved mental state
Health care	Improved medical care → improved hygiene → improved quality of life at home	Improved medical care → less illness → longer time for learning; → less illness and better health → improved school attendance and attainment; → improved state of health → improved learning efficiency	Improved medical care → improved functioning of metabolism → improved (optimal) utilisation of nutritional intakes; → improved resistance to harmful intakes; → improved efficiency of nutritional intake not optimally adjusted	

Self-reinforcing productivity effects in welfare stratum—autonomous productivity effects

C.	Employment	Labour productivity	Population system	Social system
Employment		Increased employment → increasing or decreasing marginal labour productivity depending on educational level of additionally employed; → improved employment structure → increase in labour productivity; → increased attendance at work → increased labour productivity	Increase in female labour force → decrease in fertility	Increased employment → decrease of competition on labour market → reduction of social tensions; → increased self-esteem, increased self-dependence and -reliance of individual, family, groups, etc. → possible increase in social harmony
Labour productivity	Improved labour productivity → increase or decrease in labour force depending on the level and structure of demand for labour and level and structure of education		Improved labour productivity → improved productivity, efficiency, rationality also in pursuing of activities not related to work → improved efficiency in use of contraceptives (visits to family-planning centres, etc.) → decrease in fertility rate; → reduction in child labour required to sustain regular production processes (particularly in agricultural sector and urban slums) → decrease in fertility rate	Improved labour productivity → increased income, self-dependence and -reliance → decrease in need to strike, riot, etc. → decrease in social tensions

Population system	decrease (increase) in fertility → decrease (increase) in labour force, decrease (increase) in unemployment (under prevailing conditions of persistent unemployment)	Decrease (increase) in fertility → 'better- (worse-) quality' children (with regard to educational opportunities, etc.) → higher labour productivity		Decrease in fertility → perhaps fewer problems due to too many children in family → improved social commitment; → improvements in social institutions
Social system	Improved social institutions → improved social relations → increased willingness to work → increased supply of labour; → decrease in social tensions (strikes, riots, etc.) → increased supply of labour; → improved information → improved job selection	Improved social institutions → increased efficiency and satisfaction derived from work	Improved social institutions → improved communication and information pertaining to family size, medical care, contraceptives, etc. → reduction in fertility; → increased social harmony → increase in life span → reduction in mortality	

17 Behavioural Stratum

I. M^i-UNIT CHARACTERISTICS, BEHAVIOURAL SEQUENCE, AND CLASSIFICATION OF ACTIVITIES

Economists are used to thinking in patterns of resource flows or stocks. Indeed, we have been doing so up to this point. However, underlying those flows or changes in the stocks is human behaviour. There is little which 'flows' or changes unless people behave in a specific way. Thus, to each resource variable—say savings, investment, consumption, etc.—a behavioural variable must be assigned. If we view the resource variables in aggregate terms, a change in the resource variables appears as the specific behaviour of the people constituting that resource context, for instance, an economy. We may say that the level of savings is determined by the savings behaviour of a population. However, we cannot say that an economy 'behaves' in a certain way, as individuals do. We may say that the values of the resources 'behave' or rather change in a certain way; but if 'behaviour' is used in its correct sense, it is only individuals who behave. Hence, the explicit analytical reference to the micro- or M^i-level is required. Up to this point, our behavioural premises have been implicit. If this has entailed the tacit assumption that resource relationships determine human behaviour or even only that they are sufficient to describe the development process, it has been an unavoidable side-effect of the analytical distinction—neither intended nor warranted.

When classifying the M^i-level, a first result may be obtained by falling back upon the classification of the entity of which it constitutes the logical pendant: the resource relationships. In Figure 15.1 we have delineated the salient features of a resource model. With some modifications (omission of sectoral distinctions and of differentials in the variables used) in Figure 17.1 the behavioural pendant is constructed on the basis of the resource model presented. An additional link to the M^{aa}-level is established. The behavioural stratum surrounds the resource circle, with each resource variable linked to the corresponding behavioural variable by bold lines. The inter-resource relationships and the inter-behavioural relationships are designated by broken lines. For diagrammatic clarity, only the links to the neighbouring variables in the behavioural stratum (e.g. from S^b to C^b, or from S^b to d^b, etc.) are depicted. Governmental policy, as an exogenous variable, is viewed as affecting both the resource and the behavioural strata. That is to say, developmental outcomes may be influenced by influencing the resource transfers, or the behaviour of the agents involved in resource transfers, or both. Feedback loops from the two sets of variables to the governmental policy (e.g. performance control) are, for simplicity, excluded in the figure. As is evident from the previous discussion, the resource variables are closely interlinked and reinforce each other in complex ways. To the extent that resource relationships require consistency, it must be expected that the behavioural variables will also require consistency. This may be contrasted with the consistency among the variables which determine the behaviour of the agents: for instance, the consistency of a historically grown social system or the traditional outlook of the people involved in specific activities. One of the problems of a development strategy consists in keeping down the costs which accrue due to breaking up or not conforming to the consistency of either of the composite of variables, given a level of benefits which results from that strategy.

Next, the single M^i-unit of which the M^i-level is composed and the major variables determining the M^i-unit shall be brought into focus. In Figure 17.2 the rectangle represents a single M^i-unit. An M^i-unit is composed of either one or more individuals or agents. If more than one agent constitutes the M^i-unit, a 'rule' which relates the agents to each other (for instance, an organisation) in order to achieve the objective of the M^i-unit is needed. The objectives of the M^i-unit are not necessarily the objectives which the individual agents have in mind.[1] The potential trade-off may positively correlate with the number of agents combined in a M^i-unit. If the M^i-unit is composed of a single individual, the objectives necessarily coincide. If the M^i-unit is a large firm, there will be a trade-off in the magnitude of the average difference

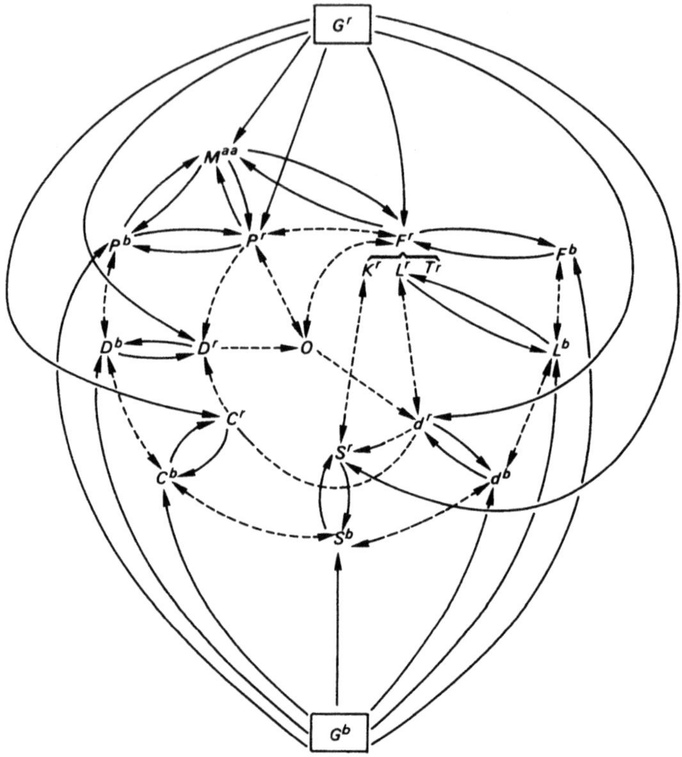

FIG. 17.1 *Interactions between resource and behavioural variables with policy linkages*

P^r	additions to population, structure of population
P^b	population behaviour (fertility, mortality, migration)
F^r	production function
F^b	entrepreneurial functions (capacity to coordinate, organise, decide, bear risks, and innovate)
D^r	aggregate demand, structure of demand; private and public demand
D^b	demand behaviour; private and public agents; elasticities of demand, budgetary policy
C^r	aggregate consumption, structure of consumption; private and public
C^b	consumption behaviour; private and public agents; propensities to consume, budgetary policy
S^r	aggregate savings, structure of savings; private and public
S^b	savings behaviour; private (households, entrepreneurs) and public; propensities to save, tax system

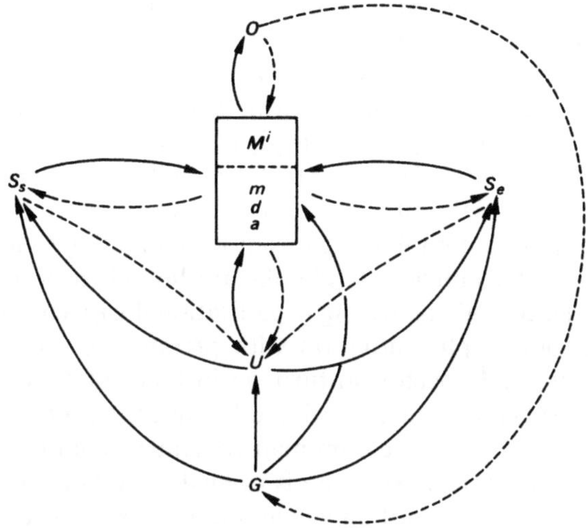

FIG. 17.2 *Determinants of micro-behaviour*

S_e = resource availability, for individual M^i-units or groups of M^i-units
S_s = social structure, social norms
U = socio-economic institutions
G = governmental policies
m = motivations
d = decisions
a = actions
O = outcomes

---

d^r	π/w ratio; sectoral distribution; $\bar{F}$-differentials; wage differentials
d^b	capacity to obtain share from social product by single individuals or groups of individuals; distributional policies
L^r	overall participation ratio; occupational structure; labour productivity
L^b	attitude toward work; work-leisure preferences
K^r	capital stock; investment rate; capital-output coefficient
K^b	investment behaviour (included also in F^b)
T^r	level and rate of technological progress
T^b	capacity to apply specific technologies (included also in F^b)
G^r	governmental policies related to resource transfers and redistribution
G^b	governmental policies related to behaviour of economic agents

between individual and M^i-unit objectives multiplied by the number of (subordinate) agents employed in that M^i-unit, or firm. The average difference between individual and M^i-unit objectives will depend on the type of organisation of the firm (e.g. type of supervision), the prevailing mentality (e.g. solidarity), the inter- and intra-firm wage differentials, etc. In the Asian context, we are faced with large differentials between the M^i-units in the productive sphere. M^i-units in the $\bar{F}_n$-sector require a complex organisation resembling that of the firms of industrialised countries. Trade-offs are bound to occur frequently due to the large and increasing organisational capacity needed, even under a labour-surplus situation with pressure on the labour force employed. In the $\bar{F}_1$-sector, in turn, an instance of M^i-units in which the single agents are identical with the M^i-unit itself, a trade-off usually cannot occur in view of the imminent coincidence of the objectives. In the $\bar{F}_1$-sector analytical extension is needed, in a way, in the opposite direction. The M^i-units not only combine agent and M^i-unit in a single entity but also combine activities typically divided in the larger M^i-units—such as production and consumption—in the same M^i-unit. Particularly in rural areas—but also in urban areas, notably if the establishments of the 'slum economies' are considered—the households and 'firms' are part of the same M^i-unit.

The total of activities in the M^i-unit is defined by the total of motivations, decisions and actions occurring in that M^i-unit during a specific period of time. The elements of motivation, decision, and action usually constitute a sequence immanent in the logic of human behaviour. However, as is readily apparent, people may sometimes decide to act or simply act without being motivated, or may be motivated without deciding to act or actually acting. The M^i-behavioural unit is determined, as indicated by the various lines with arrows in Figure 17.2, by resource availability and by the social system, which is subdivided into social norms and social institutions. The policy link is again viewed as exogenous. The governmental impact may reach directly to the M^i-unit in the form of stimulation of human behaviour, for instance by ideological slogans calling for mass participation, or, indirectly, through the elements which in turn are determinants of the M^i-units, viz. social norms, institutions, and resource availability. The activities thus determined produce outcomes which are assessed (or not) by the governmental authorities. The assessment may have implications both on the entire developmental system and the strategy pursued (through feedbacks indicated by broken lines from O to M^i, and O to G).

The key to conducting a successful strategy is to bring about activities of (1) the proper nature (savings, investment, consumption, etc.), (2) placed in the right location within the developmental system ($\bar{F}_1, \ldots, \bar{F}_n$), (3) at adequate levels in terms of quantity (e.g. man-hours worked, effort per unit) and quality (e.g. skills, educational level, etc.). The complex of activities defined by the three criteria may be succinctly expressed by a matrix. Let the column vector of matrix B designate the classification referring to (1) and the row vector designate the classification according to (2): then a_{ij} stands for the number of activities of type i occurring in a group or sector j—for instance, savings occurring in the agricultural $\bar{F}_1$-sector. The level of the activities in each type of activity is defined as the average number of activities multiplied by the number of agents in each group at a given level of 'intensity' or productivity of the activities pursued. Let, furthermore, the coefficients $\alpha_1, \ldots, \alpha_n$ denote the elements of the single column vector of matrix C expressing the characteristics pertaining to (3). Then we have the total activities A, obtained by multiplying matrix B by C. The matrix in explicit form is

$$B = \left\| \begin{matrix} a_{11} & a_{12} & \cdots & a_{1n} \\ a_{21} & a_{22} & \cdots & a_{2n} \\ \cdots & \cdots & \cdots & \cdots \\ a_{m1} & a_{m2} & \cdots & a_{mn} \end{matrix} \right\|, \quad C \equiv \left\| \begin{matrix} \alpha_1 \\ \alpha_2 \\ \vdots \\ \alpha_n \end{matrix} \right\|$$

or more compactly,

$$B = [a_{ij}] \qquad \begin{matrix} i = 1, \ldots, m \\ j = 1, \ldots, n \end{matrix}$$

$$C = [\alpha_i] \qquad i = 1, \ldots, n,$$

and for the total activities of the developmental system described,

$$A = BC.$$

An assessment of A or the search for a formula initiating, sustaining, and optimally distributing the activities, combined in A, must refer to all the vectors. The column vectors of matrix B refer to the specific resource relationships. The resource relationships necessary have been described in the chapters on resources. If additional stress is needed, we may reiterate that activities that enhance labour productivity, increase investment, and save resources are of importance. In addition, reducing fertility is a crucial concomitant of any resource policy. Such a policy inference is modest, but when starting with an approach which neither takes into account the distinction between groups, sectors, etc., nor allows for changes in the differentials of these (typically the one- and two-sector development models), a less obvious result cannot be obtained. However, the overtness of the result should not lead to underestimating its relevance for achieving developmental progress.

An approach more useful as a policy device, however, must include statements about a distribution of activities according to their 'place' in the socio-economic system. A positive statement again has to rely on the conclusions from an analysis of the resource relationships. The prevailing socio-economic processes have been stated to result in increasing differentials of the relevant socio-economic variables and outcomes which are undesirable in terms of the desiderata of both the M^{aa}- and M^{a}-levels. The logical conclusion with regard to the redistribution of activities will be to support activities in the sectors on the lower rank of the distributional scale—typically the bulk of $\bar{F}_1$-sector activities. As a formalised statement, the postulate will be that

$$\frac{\Delta a_{i1}}{a_{i1}} > \cdots > \frac{\Delta a_{in}}{a_{in}}$$

where the subscript i designates the type of activity which is itself a policy variable, viz. the redistribution of activities within a group, say relative increase of savings against consumption, as described by the column vector of matrix B.

The above postulate may be interpreted as (1) increasing the supply of agents in the $\bar{F}_1$-group, or (2) increasing the number of average activities of the $\bar{F}_1$-group, or (3) both. The choice among the strategy options will depend on the specific activities to which it applies.

Primary attention in development economics has, naturally, been given to activities related to production—in Figure 16.1 depicted by the link to the production functions. Discussing the supply and quality of production-related activities, the emphasis has traditionally been on category (1): the supply of entrepreneurs. The scarcity in entrepreneurial supply has been assumed to constitute, aside from capital, the developmental bottleneck *par excellence*. This view is perfectly valid if development is defined as a gradual increase of the modern industrial sector of an economy. Agents who conduct modern production-related activities are in this context a necessary prerequisite. But the hypotheses have little meaning if the increase in the relative share of the modern industrial sector is not viewed as the panacea for development. The 'switch' is then not from the M^i-unit of the $\bar{F}_1$-sectors to the $\bar{F}_n$-sectors; hence, the behavioural attributes needed to accomplish the switch to new activities are not required. Neither the capacity to enter new occupations—for instance, to change from trade to industrial activities—nor the capacity to fulfil the new functions in the new M^i-unit constitutes a scarce factor once the increase of the $\bar{F}_n$-sectors is not postulated. In fact, an increase in the supply of agents for the $\bar{F}_n$-sector may not be required at all, unless a decline in the K/L ratio in that sector is acceptable—i.e. a shift in the production functions substituting labour for capital. Such a shift will be a postulate in view of its favourable effects on employment and overall income generated, but it is not what must be actually expected from the current trends. Hence, the need for agents, including those with entrepreneurial attributes, may be smaller in the $\bar{F}_n$-sectors in terms of numbers, while it may be increasing in terms of qualifications assigned to the functions to be accomplished: a fierce competition due to inadequate demand, increased knowledge necessary to choose from an increasingly more sophisticated technology, and more inventiveness in the political justification and legitimation of the increasingly obvious failure of their own existence. Neither the current differential trends nor the postulates of a development strategy shows the supply of entrepreneurs, in the conventional sense of innovators, to be a strategic factor of development or, even, whose scarcity would cause the development process to fail.

There is, evidently, no scarcity in the supply of agents in the $\bar{F}_1$-sector—say in small farmers, or rural artisans or self-employed in urban slums. Nor is the number of M^i-units critically scarce—whether identical with a single agent or five to ten or more people combined in a productive unit. The scarce factor is the 'supply of opportunities' for the M^i-units—the utilisation of the existing potential of activities. The postulate, thus, must be to increase the average activities of the M^i-units, be it to use fully the under-utilised capacity or to increase the existing capacity of opportunities in the M^i-unit of that sector.

The second requirement to elevate the M^i-units of the $\bar{F}_1$-sector on a development path is—often taken to be synonymous with development—the increase in the average labour, capital, or land productivity (depending on which is the 'limitational' factor) of the $\bar{F}_1$-sector unit. In terms of our formal statement (applying column vector C), the postulate may be expressed as

$$\frac{\Delta\alpha_1}{\alpha_1} > \cdots > \frac{\Delta\alpha_n}{\alpha_n},$$

which states that the productivity should increase faster in the M^i-units of the lower strata than in those of the upper strata, reducing the development differentials and thus avoiding the inconsistencies to be expected from the current trends. Methodologically, it would be feasible to view the problem of the productivity increase in terms of category (1). That is to say, productivity is kept down because not enough agents with sufficient 'drive', skills, or 'activity potential' are appearing. Hence, there is again a bottleneck in the supply of agents. This view would obscure the fact that development as a process of productivity-enhancing activities on a broad scale will constitute an evolutionary process, and not one of 'shifts', as the emergence of a 'modern' entrepreneurial or political elite which fulfils its unique historical duty.

We arrive at the strategic problem of how to increase the number of activities and the average productivity in the $\bar{F}_1$-sector. The first part of the problem refers to category (2) stated in row vector of matrix B, the second to column vector of matrix C. If we designate the average activities of activity type i as $\bar{a}_i$, the policy postulate for inducing a change in $\bar{a}_i$ according to the scale size groups may be stated as

$$\left\| \bar{a}_{i1} \quad \bar{a}_{i2} \quad \cdots \quad \bar{a}_{in} \right\| \left\| \begin{matrix} \alpha_1 \\ \alpha_2 \\ \vdots \\ \alpha_n \end{matrix} \right\|$$

subject to the conditions

$$\frac{\Delta\bar{a}_{i1}}{\bar{a}_{i1}} > \frac{\Delta\bar{a}_{i2}}{\bar{a}_{i2}} > \cdots > \frac{\Delta\bar{a}_{in}}{\bar{a}_{in}}$$

and

$$\frac{\Delta\alpha_1}{\alpha_1} > \frac{\Delta\alpha_2}{\alpha_2} > \cdots > \frac{\Delta\alpha_n}{\alpha_n}.$$

The difference Δ may refer to any time unit; the equation system has a solution for each time period once we know the empirical values for the change in the distribution of the number of activities and the average 'intensity' or productivity level of the activities.

Assessing the potential of increasing the number and productivity of activities in the $\bar{F}_1$-sectors, the determinants again come into focus. We have been suggesting a classification of the activities into (a) motivations, (b) decisions, and (c) actions. All three elements are combined in a behavioural sequence of the M^i-unit. The M^i-unit itself—that is, the three behavioural elements—is determined by (1) social norms, (2) institutions, and (3) resource availability. In total, there are nine combinations of determinants of developmental outcomes—for instance, motivation as determined by resource availability, or decisions determined by social norms, and so forth.

There is interdependency between both the variables (a), (b), and (c), and the variables (1), (2), and (3)—besides the latter variable set being the determinant of the first variable set and the repercussions extending from the first variable set to the latter. The interdependency between the variables (a), (b), and (c) is not on the line of one-way causality. This includes not only, as stated, the possibility of a non-causality between two variables, say action without motivation, but also the reversal of the sequence and causal nexus. Hence, we may have a sequence

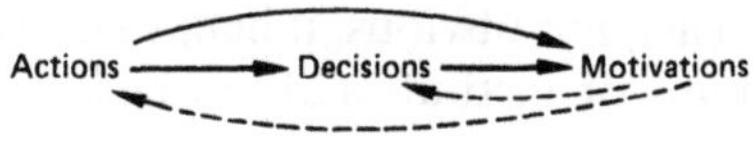

In this sequence, the actions are the primary cause affecting decisions and motivations, and the latter constitute feedbacks leading to actions and developmental outcomes. In any specific instance, the line of causality will be different, and it may be merely a question of taste whether to regard actions, for instance, as the determined or the determining variables. Clearly, motivations and decisions are also determinants, and not merely determined. 'Mutually reinforcing causality' comes closest to being a valid generalisation of behaviour relevant for development—if such generalisation is at all desirable.

Interdependency exists also between the variables (1), (2), and (3). For instance, land resource availability is closely linked to the type of land tenure. The institution of land tenure is closely linked to the norms prevailing in a social system. The social norms, again, are linked to the resource availability. The interactions are among all determinants, and not only between two, or only in a unidirectional way. There have been theoretical attempts to establish a monocausal relationship between the variables—for instance, the Marxist approach of establishing the deterministic sequence of resource relationships → institutions → social norms. While this link is important, it is not the only one, and in many historical instances does not even rank as the most critical one. The monistic approach is theoretically futile, and denies the possibility of shaping events by policies which change social norms and institutions autonomously (although not separated from the resource relationships). A redistribution of the resources supports institutional and social change, but is not the only policy link and in most cases is insufficient to bring about changes in the developmental system and outcomes. Such simplistic determinism is, of course, abandoned by those actually 'in charge' of development, even in Marxist societies—as the case of the People's Republic of China proves. One may note, with some surprise, that the modern version of the classical school and the neoclassicists follow a quite deterministic line by treating the behavioural premises as unalterable in space and time.[2] Self-interest serves as a proper vehicle for development whenever the resource framework is appropriate. Hence, analytical emphasis on the resource relationships will solve the development problem. Deviations from the behavioural premises are not conceivable and certainly not subject to empirical scrutiny and theoretical modification. The limitations, at least, are obvious, if behaviour is set in a context of different social systems or institutional settings.

Besides the interdependency within the two sets of variables, there is, by definition, causal interdependency between the two sets of variables. The complex process combining the behavioural sequence of the M^i-units and the determinants is depicted in Figure 17.3. It contains on the three vertical axes the elements of the behavioural sequence—motivation, decision, action. The scale is thought of as having some quantitative meaning, although perhaps not easily measurable. The determinants are symbolised by the arrows from the rectangle which combines the set of determinants—social norms, institutions, resource availability. We may start the process with the assumption of increased resource availability causing an increased motivational level in M^i-units of the $\bar{F}_1$-sector. The value in the scale of the motivational level may increase from an initial value (not plotted) to a value m_1. The motivational level m_1 will lead to decisions of a level d_1. In the diagram, d_1 is lower than m_1, indicating a coefficient defining the 'transformation' of motivations into proper decisions below unity. The actual actions are assumed in the diagram to lie above the level of

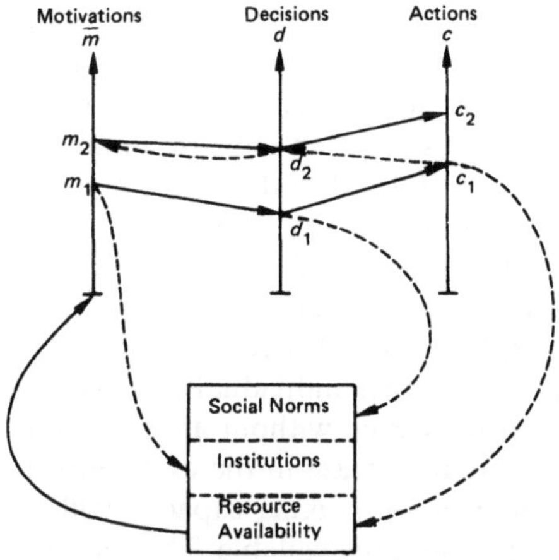

FIG 17.3 *Impact of determinants on type and level of behavioural components—examples of feasible linkages*

decisions at c_1. That is, the coefficient defining the 'transformation' of the motivations-decisions component into the actions is above unity.

From the level of combined activities (m_1, d_1, c_1) various feedbacks go back to the initial determinant(s). The broken lines show some of the feedbacks. One of the feedbacks reaches from the actions to resource availability, another from the decision-making level to the social norms, and a third one from the motivational level to the institutions. There are, in total, nine feedbacks; analogously there are nine determining links.

The process becomes more complex if we introduce feedbacks within the two sets of variables. For simplicity only feedbacks in the behavioural sequence have been introduced. The feedback from c_1 is assumed to increase the coefficient of both the *m*- and *d*-components. In a subsequent period, the transformation from motivations to decisions to actions takes place at higher rates than in the previous period. The feedbacks are, for simplicity, depicted directly to the values of the *m*- and *d*-axes, which represent the values for *c*, *m*, and *d* of period 2 and not those of the coefficients themselves. The path of period 2 is depicted by m_2 and d_2, and a new value for c_2. The feedbacks start anew affecting the determinants and the behavioural elements.

Discussing some of the behavioural sequences and 'intra-feedbacks', a special case is made in the feedback within a single component of the behavioural sequence. For instance, we may have an initial level of action c_m, where, by assumption, c_m stands for an increase in c. The very existence of c_m or the increase in c, or both, may lead then to further actions in subsequent periods. This is readily apparent in a resource context. For instance, an increase in investment may stimulate further investment. Related to the higher resource flow is a correspondingly higher level of activity. The same intra-feedback may be effective in the motivation- and decision-sphere. Higher motivations may accumulate over a period of time, for which the psychologists will provide various explanations. Above all, an increase in the motivational level may 'affect' other individuals, as yet little motivated, increasing the overall level even without an increase in the level of the individuals whose initial increase in the motivational level caused the 'effect'. Equally, the decision-making capacity will increase as the results of previous decisions are available. The 'learning-by-doing' effect will be particularly strong in the realm of decision-making. Again, it may work in an internalised way for each individual and have an effect on social interactions. In summary, even without a continuous energetic flow from the determinants, an initial cause may initiate various processes within the context of the behavioural sequence which accumulate via 'internal' feedbacks.

II. MULTIPLE NATURE AND IMPACT OF BEHAVIOURAL DETERMINANTS ON DEVELOPMENT AGENTS

Given the confines in which activities take place (locus and type as stated in matrix B), the focus is on the level and quality of the activities—how specific activities are initiated, increased, and sustained, be it in the context of 'self-regulating' developmental 'laws' or of a development strategy. The comprehensive scope of our approach suggests that a multiplicity of determinants, rather than one, cause specific activities to come about. Analogously, the behavioural composite is not confined to a single behavioural component which would constitute the principal behavioural *causa movens* of development, but rather combines a number of behavioural traits which all act upon development according to the specific instances to which they apply. This comprehensive approach provides not only a fair chance of arriving at plausible hypotheses about the behavioural aspects of development, but also a theoretical background against which the prevailing single-focused theories may be contrasted. The reduction in the approach occurs both as a reduction of the total set of determinants to a single determinant and as emphasis on a single behavioural element of the total behavioural sequence of the M^i-unit. Since determining and determined variables are closely linked, logically and causally, the choice of a variable in either of the two variable sets will determine the scope of the subsequent theory formulation which pertains to the other variable set.

A case in point is the emphasis on the behavioural element of motivation. The hypothesis is stated that people in LDCs are not sufficiently motivated. A potential of proper decisions and their implementation into proper actions awaits fulfillment by motivation-related determinants. The choice of determinants is thus delineated. Emphasis is on social norms and institutions, while resource availability is viewed merely as a determinant but not as a determining variable of activities. In contrast, we state the hypothesis that, first, motivations are heavily overemphasised as compared to decision-making and actions, and, second, that changes in social norms and institutions are ill-conceived when treating them generally as 'prerequisites' and precluding resource conditions as a generating force for the initiation and sustainment of behavioural functions and activities. This, at least, seems to be valid when reference is made to the empirical context of contemporary South and South-East Asia. Departing from a comprehensive approach, it is clear that the emphasis on the latter variables does not constitute a primacy within the set of explanatory variables. It is a convenient device to bring the overemphasised issues into proper perspective.

1. 'External' and 'Internal' Determinants of Social Change

The notion of social norms may be given a dual meaning. First, on an objective plane, social norms stand for a generally agreed or enforced 'code' of behaviour (laws, customs, religion, etc.). They constitute a set of 'rules' which combine primary norms ('You ought to do X!') and secondary norms ('If you do not do X, you will be punished by Y'; or 'If you do X', you will receive rewards R"). There is an objectively intelligible social pattern of behavioural postulates and of rewards and punishments. Second, the social norms are 'internalised' in the individuals who constitute the society to which the norms apply; they determine the psychic state of the individual. Clearly, both elements of the social norms are in close interaction.

Theories of the first type underlie historical approaches which work with 'grand designs'. Generally, they may be combined under the heading 'traditional versus modern': traditional social norms inhibit 'rational' behaviour, e.g., profit maximisation or cost minimisation, drive for material well-being in renunication of non-material values, etc. And there are manifold political-ideological vehicles that are assumed to work against development-inhibiting traditional norms. Reference is sometimes made to European history, where nationalism played its role as 'nation-builder', catalyst of industrialisation, and prime mover for 'modernisation'. Communism is another variant of a society-wide concept of a blueprint for a social norm which advocates a 'new' principle of organisation and social morality. As nationalism, it has its roots in Europen history and thinking. Finally, religion, as in Weber's analysis of early capitalism, constitutes the great transforming power and bringer of a new ethics of rationalism and frugality. All the determining variables mentioned have played their role once in history, and are likely to play it to various degrees again in the future. Nevertheless, the strength of these theoretical approaches lies less in the descriptive-explanatory capacity, than in their serving to legitimise the usurpation and maintenance of power—in the name of those whose ostensible or actual interest is served. As such, they gain in theoretical relevance and validity to the extent to which they are used and abused. As strategic instruments, they are usually ineffective when applied in isolation unless they resort to force. The 'grand designs' can generate activities only if coordinated with other determinants. Comprehensive and appropriate resource policies—including institutional changes as far as they pertain to resource redistribution—may bring to effectiveness some of the postulates of the 'grand designs'. Cases in point are the military regimes prevailing in contemporary Asia, which appear to be less stable than their communist counterparts, since their stress is on nationalism without proof of their capacity to supplement their slogans and promises with policies that could bring about the desired changes on a broad front. Neither the 'Good Thai Society' nor the 'Pride of Being a Filipino', nor Pakistan's 'New Islamic Society' is necessarily an ill-conceived concept for nation-building or for transforming society, but the failure properly to relate these concepts to an adequate socio-economic policy deprives them of their meaning and actual effectiveness.

While the first approach attempts to implement a policy pertaining to the social system, its underlying behavioural rules, and ideological blueprints 'from above', the second approach views the problem of change of the behaviour-guiding norms 'from within'. The direction of the change is the same: toward 'modernisation', 'rationalisation', the 'industrial man' with his creative, innovating, and dynamic attributes. The emphasis within the analytical subject and the strategic inferences drawn from it differ. However, it is readily apparent that the two aspects, being only different sides of the same coin, will be intrinsically related to each other. Hence, the change of the psychic state of an individual can hardly be attempted in isolation from its surrounding social context. In this respect, the 'internalist' theories supplement the theories which operate with 'grand designs' from above, rather than constituting their own and autonomous nuclei of development. The psychic state and properties of the individual are determined by the specific traits of the 'traditional society' that, in turn, constitute the basic 'obstacles' to changing the 'traditionalism' of the society. Specifically, they find themselves to be arbitrarily thrown into their societies with little possibility to analyse, control, or change their state or their social context. Thus a type of man is created who is 'uncreative', obedient to proscriptions which regulate interpersonal relations, and who exerts authority within the confines of that social context, himself oppressing the creativeness of others. The 'traditional' attitude is passed on from father to son by specific modes of child-rearing and educational training.[3] Only the withdrawal of status (of the father or of a whole social group) breaks the mutually reinforcing process between social norms and the psychic state of individuals, releasing the creative-innovating potential of individuals. The emerging individuals are typically seen as 'social deviants' who, destroying the traditional system of social proscription and coercion, are the pace-setters for a new society. The psychic attributes of these 'deviant' individuals are a high 'need for achievement' (*n*-achievement),[4] the drive to innovate, to organise, and to change an environment so far believed to be unchangeable.

The validity of the hypotheses expounded in the 'internalist' approach depends on the individual being the dynamic, innovating, and creative agent in a specific historical context. In addition, granted that a developmental agent with those attributes is required, the question is whether such an individual can be formed only by incisive changes in the social system, by breaking up the social fabric and complex web of social norms. As for the first condition, the requirements for dynamic agents with an innovating capacity, high *n*-achievement, etc., depend on the type of activities required to be pursued. Given the postulates from matrix *B*—activities related to the increase of labour productivity in the sectors of traditional argriculture, small-scale manufacturing, and services; the concomitant application of intermediate technology, etc.; and the fertility reduction in the social groups constituting these sectors—a developmental agent as a rigorous innovator and destroyer of the past does not emerge as a central precondition or prerequisite for development. Agricultural productivity has been increasing over many decades in all Asian countries, keeping pace with an increasing population even under conditions of a rapidly decreasing land-man ratio and the threat of decreases in the marginal output it induces. If the term 'inventiveness' needs any explanation, some references to the artistically built terraces in Java and the Philippines, the introduction of new cultivation methods and cropping systems, the gradual improvement in the tools used for planting and harvesting, and the adaptation to new forms of inputs whenever available, will suffice to give it substance in the Asian context. This inventiveness differs from the type which these theories have in mind, however—that of the modernising creator with his inventive capacity and achievement drive. In fact, such theories clearly mis-state the role of 'pace-setter for development' in the context of Asia—not because innovative capacity is either irrelevant or over-applied, but rather because of the lack of true innovation involved in uncritically taking over foreign technology, standards of execution, business morals etc. The imitation of modes successful in other developmental contexts, their uninventive transference to basically ill-prepared indigenous contexts, is the act not of an innovator, although it would qualify as such on the basis of the aforementioned theories and will appear as social deviance *par excellence*, but of an imitator who has lost the cultural ground which would allow him to select, refuse, and accept with a reasonable degree of autonomy. The true innovative-creative man is an innovator by virtue of the choices he makes. He carefully selects among alternatives, paying due consideration to the environmental-historical constraints he faces. He will be needed or found in both private and governmental sectors. Governmental agents face the dual task of choosing the overall development path from a set of alternatives within the simultaneous-sequence type of development (and subsequently providing the private agents with the information which allows them to forecast the outcomes and rationally compare their results), as well as redirecting the resource flows in such a way that the broad masses may participate in the development process.

It follows that the 'great transformation' from 'traditional' to 'modern' is a rather metaphysical concept if posited as a necessary historical process to which all societies must submit on their way to socio-economic progress. In actual application, it may be definitely harmful when it serves to support socio-economic processes which work in a direction undesirable from the point of view of the large majority of people of that society. There is no historical instance where mere imitation of cultural (techno-socio-economic) patterns has brought sustained progress. Americans responded to their new environment in a distinctively different way from Europeans; and the same is true for the Japanese when compared to Western experience. South Asian development is very likely to fail in terms of sustained progress unless the specific indigenous way is found. The prerequisites are high inventiveness and creativeness, including the capacity to combine the old with the new—a capacity clearly far beyond mere 'imitation'.

This brings into focus decision-making and actions, on the one hand, and socio-economic institutions and resource conditions as their principal determinants, on the other. The hypotheses are that (1) motivations (required for the tasks delineated) will emerge once the decision-making capacity and the feasibility to engage in actions is made available to individuals, and that (2) a change in institutions is necessary mainly to the extent to which these institutions impose constraints on resource availability for the masses at large; furthermore, the institutional change must be supplemented by well-coordinated resource redistributional policies of the non-institutional type if it is to be effective.

2. *'Holistic' and 'Particularistic' Aspects of Institutional Change*

The resource-oriented view of institutional change encounters a forceful doctrine which propounds, first, that institutions constitute a consistent entity which cannot be split up easily, and second, that their being 'traditional' constitutes an 'obstacle' to development. Hence, unless the total institutional structure is changed, it is inconceivable that the obstacles to development can be removed, and consequently there can be no development. Since a radical institutional transformation is usually difficult to bring about, and, at the least, often accompanied by terror and suffering for the masses at large (as the case of Kampuchea tragically exemplifies), the status quo is allowed to persist—theoretically and actually. This approach is not only impracticable in policy terms, but also cognitively unwarranted. There is theoretical plausibility as well as empirical evidence that some institutions are impaired by dynamic change, while others are not.

A case where institutional change is not necessary for increasing agricultural productivity—a foremost objective and theoretical touchstone—is the extended-family system. The arguments may obtain their rationale from the previously discussed authoritarian rule of the family heads who are repressive, conservative, and averse to introducing change. However, the fact that relatively high and sustained increases in agricultural productivity could be accomplished over decades places the theory at variance with the facts. Not only that; what could be swept under the carpet by reference to other determining variables is difficult to ignore in a case where the extended-family system has proved to be more innovative and to produce higher average agricultural productivity or yields than small-family units. That is to say, there are empirical instances which suggest a comparative advantage of the traditional family system.[5] What could be theoretically maintained, at best, in view of the empirical evidence is the hypothesis that other determinants are much more important than the institution of the family system and that the type of family system applied does not significantly influence the productive performance at all. The argument will gain in substance by the introduction of other performance criteria, particularly a fertility decline (although the theories mentioned usually do not have this behavioural component in mind). A rationale similar to productive behaviour may apply to fertility behaviour. Lacking well-founded empirical knowledge, we are forced to rely on conjecture. We are nevertheless quite safe in assuming that the biological maximum supply capacity of a female is subject to social and economic constraints within the extended-family system—constraints just as severe as those in the nuclear-family system. Precisely because the fathers are authoritarian (although it is difficult to see how a Thai or Filipino father is more authoritarian than, say, a German father), they will impose constraints on the behaviour of the members of the family. The problem really lies in the type of decision; and it tends to be pro-natalist in view of favourable net-welfare effects still to be expected under the socio-economic conditions which face the bulk of the Asian populations. Similarly, the extended-family system is often seen as a primary cause of rural-urban migration. The rural extended-family system provides a security cushion which any family member who looks for an urban job enjoys. But one could ask whether a small family could and would not also support its family members. Even if it would not, the jobless member would still have the choice between the rural and urban labour market. His decision will basically depend on his assessment of the probability of finding a job, coupled with consideration of rural-urban wage differentials. If we assume that it is easier to enter the rural labour force, the extended-family system may indeed contribute to the rural-urban migration more than does the small-family unit. But as our earlier discussion revealed, there is little reason to assume that the landless labourers more easily find long-term jobs in the overpopulated rural areas than in the urban slums. The causes for migration, as those for fertility decisions, lie deeper, in the roots of economic misery, the misguided expectations, and other characteristics of the differential socio-economic process.

Objecting to an approach that views institutions as a 'whole' that must be changed does not imply a bias in favour of traditional institutions. The objections necessarily include as their pendant a statement about those institutions which impede desirable development processes. They are, as stated, those institutions which preclude use of resources on the broad social scale required to eliminate mass poverty and to induce a sustained development process. Two institutional reforms must be pushed vigorously if any further progress is to be accomplished. First, the land must be redistributed. As stated earlier, lofty promises have been made and laws passed in most of the Asian countries; but the implementation has proved to be difficult. In addition, land redistribution finds its natural constraints (given the size and growth rates of population) in the size of the land mass and the ratio of arable land to total land. India, Indonesia (Java), Sri Lanka, Pakistan, and the Philippines are instances of high-density countries (see Table 7.2, and Chapter 15,VIII) with low redistributional potential and no virgin land reserves left once land is redistributed. Although not the solution for all problems, land reforms will increase the activity level (number of people involved in activities times activities per M^i-unit) and its quality ('learning by doing', spread of information, etc.). It would in various cases allow the integration of a considerable part of the unused labour-force potential or of the tenants as yet vegetating on the edges of society.

The second institutional change required to bring about broad-based activities is the abolition of rigid discriminations resulting from the caste system—a system confined to India. That this is a protracted process has been well understood. The South-East and East Asian countries may be definitely better off in terms of the resource constraints imposed by rigidities of the social system. In some of these countries, egalitarian ideals have existed throughout society for centuries, in complete contrast to the hierarchical-inegalitarian Indian caste system. However, even in the case of the caste system, total and immediate abolition (which is probably infeasible and certainly will not succeed by decree alone) does not seem a prerequisite for development if viewed in a context of activity increases in the $\bar{F}_1$-sectors. If unable to assure inter-caste mobility, governmental policy must give its support directly to the lower castes (against the opposition of the members of the upper castes who have a vested interest in the system). The policy is a specific application of a 'direct attack' on mass poverty under aggravated social conditions.

3. Resource Availability as Determinant of Behavioural Change

We have been stating that constraints to developmental activities result from an incapacity to make and implement decisions rather than a lack of motivation precluding engaging in any activity at all. This has brought the resource aspects into focus as determinants of developmental behaviour. Social rules and institutions are an obstacle to the extent that they preclude the redistribution of resources in the direction stated earlier

$$\Delta\bar{F}_1 > \cdots > \Delta\bar{F}_n.$$

This may be accomplished in relative or absolute terms, leaving the $\bar{F}_1$-sectors better off in the growth rates or decreasing the absolute share of the $\bar{F}_n$-sectors. The same distributional postulate applies to the redistribution of resources. Although the statement is self-evident, it should be noted that the opposite hypothesis has also been propounded[6]—with some plausibility.

The hypothesis states that resource shortage, rather than resource availability, will constitute the basic force for generating activities. Resource shortages will exert pressure on people to act. If this pressure is small they will rely on the existing modes of behaviour; if it critically threatens the people's existence it will force them to act. Development is seen as a sequence of bottlenecks paired with subsequent responses that successfully solve them. The development path appears as a sequence of step functions which are composed of rather distinctively different regimes. Clearly, this theory is motivation-focused. As such it is limited to the historical cases where the supply of that behavioural component is scarce. For contemporary Asia the theory does not provide a plausible explanation. There is certainly enough resource shortage to keep the people motivated and to make them interested in finding new modes of doing things. For instance, the large man-land ratios in most Asian countries constitute a permanent challenge which provides sufficient stimulus to policy-makers as well as to the large majority of the farming population. If used as a descriptive-explanatory account, the 'pressure theory' may perhaps be given the interpretation that the successive increases in average agricultural productivity are due to the pressure from land. But on this general plane, many statements are consistent with the facts. The impact of the theory certainly would be disastrous if applied as policy guidance. To postulate a decrease in the resource supply or increase in the population growth as a means for increasing the motivation of the people would result in a frustrating experience for the policy-makers and certainly would constitute a fatal blow to the cause of development.

This brings our attention again to the postulate along the lines suggested. A general account has been given in Ch. 16 on policy inferences—themselves a conclusion of the more elaborate preceding chapters on development differentials. The direct link between resource availability and actions is readily apparent. Financing institutions, loans, and taxation policies adjusted to the needs of the $\bar{F}_1$-sectors (still largely biased in favour of the $\bar{F}_n$-sectors), and transport facilities to link the hinterland with the market centres, spring immediately to mind as necessary conditions for the expansion of the activities of the $\bar{F}_1$-sectors. Equally important is the access to information. This includes, particularly, the opening of education to people of the $\bar{F}_1$-sectors. A flattening of the hierarchical structure of the educational system will in many countries (for instance, India) bring a more adequate skill structure and a higher level and quality of activities under equal budgetary costs (once the initial costs for the change are met). Higher educational levels on a broader front will increase the average labour productivity and the decision-making capacity in the M^i-units of the $\bar{F}_1$-sectors (those already existing and those yet to emerge).

Information must not be confined to the educational system in the narrow sense of a school system, although it will be of primary importance. Information is closely linked to the social norms and social ideals, as previously discussed. The substance of the message given to the people in most Asian countries is composed of a mixture of nationalism and modernism. A 'wind of change' in the basic informational policy will be required if the decision-making capacity at large is to be enhanced. What is basically required is an 'intermediate' message encompassing all social spheres; specifically, messages pertaining to intermediate production methods, intermediate types of commodities, and intermediate levels of technology, fine arts, architecture, medicine, socio-economic institutions, and life-styles. The intermediate message would necessarily be a dynamic concept and not attempt a once-and-for-all statement about the state and pace of the societies. It would imply a continuous creative process. The creativeness in the early Western development consisted in creating the new along a successive sequence (see Part 3, Ch. 13). It was less a problem of choices on a simultaneous-horizontal range of options. However, the large range of choices faced by contemporary Asian countries entails similarly complicated problems in terms of the assessment of the conditions under which alternatives apply. The options are subject to more constraints and are usually conceived under the immediate pressure to make decisions to fend off the subsistence threat. Clearly, both formulating the choice problem and combining the elements chosen from the range of alternatives require a high degree of creativity and not merely imitation. The present differential development precludes this creativity in two ways. It leaves the $\bar{F}_1$-sectors in 'traditionalism' and forces the $\bar{F}_n$-sectors to follow a path of modernisation at a rate similar to that of the now-industrialised countries. Both are inadequate responses to meet the challenges faced by contemporary Asian societies. The complex composite of intermediate messages will have to relate to a resource policy aimed at reducing the socio-economic differentials. Both are mutually reinforcing, and seem indispensable for developmental progress.

18 Political Structure: Deterministic Forces and the Exogenously Determined 'Energy for Change'

I. OUTLINE OF POLITICAL STRUCTURES

Theories are intellectual constructs. As such they must satisfy criteria such as objectivity and analytical rigour. However, when applied to social reality they may become politically relevant. Social reality then constitutes not only the relevant context for, say, empirical testing, but also a specific 'matrix of interests' into which the theory, more or less faithfully, fits well. In political terms, a theory will be appropriate or adequate if it is in accord with the requirements of the specific interest matrix, for instance if it explains, justifies and helps in effectively pursuing those interests.

Generally, theories may either (A) favour the *status quo* or (B) favour a change in the *status quo*. We shall designate strategies based on theory type A as *A*-strategies, and those based on type B as *B*-strategies. The application of a theory—in terms of the respective strategy—must take place in the context of a political structure, denoted by S_P^A (see Part 1, Ch. 4,VI).

The application of a strategy presupposes the assessment of the political structure within which the application of the strategy is feasible. This entails a dual discussion. First, under what conditions is a change in the political structure (e.g. in order to enable the pursuit of a *B*-strategy) justified? Second, how, assuming it to be desirable, could a change in the political structure be achieved? We will start with the first set of questions: does the present context of the Asian developing countries call for a change in the political structure? More specifically, is a change justifiable in terms of its conceivable impact on welfare and productivity? If, and only if, well-reasoned arguments suggest a change in the political structure, will the further questions arise: first, what is the *modus operandi* of the prevailing political structure? and, second, how can the *status-quo* structure be changed to provide a context in which the pursuit of a *B*-strategy is feasible?

The implementation of a *B*-strategy is justified if (1) the implementation of the *B*-strategy is superior to the *A*-strategy in terms of welfare and productivity, and if (2) changes in the political structure do not entail welfare and productivity losses which exceed the welfare and productivity gains resulting from the implementation of the *B*-strategy. We call a political structure appropriate to the implementation of the *A*-strategy an α-structure and that appropriate to the implementation of the *B*-strategy a β-structure. In reality, they may be identical. But, theoretically, we must distinguish between them beoause they might be—and, as will be shown, they actually are—different from each other.

II. WELFARE AND PRODUCTIVITY IMPLICATIONS OF CHANGES IN POLITICAL STRUCTURE

The assumption that the *B*-strategy—a strategy changing the *status quo* in terms of narrowing development differentials, pursuing an egalitarian distribution, and alleviating mass poverty—is desirable in terms of increases both in welfare and productivity does not need any further elaboration. The entire study has been devoted to that issue, and has provided some rationale and substance for the acceptance of the *B*-strategy outlined. Once accepted, the question arises whether the change from an α-structure to a β-structure will favourably affect the welfare and productivity of a society subjected to that change, i.e. whether the welfare losses possibly incurred by the new political structure will not exceed the welfare and productivity gains generated by that political structure. A brief analytical outline will demonstrate with sufficient plausibility that the existing political structure is neither productive in terms of implementing an alternative strategy of the type *B*, nor shows much concern for welfare in terms of representation and participation in the political process.

Advancing the analytical exposition, we will, first, delineate a causal model. In so doing, we shall depict the relationships between changes in the political structure and the productivity and welfare effects. In a second step, the causal impact which the two types of political

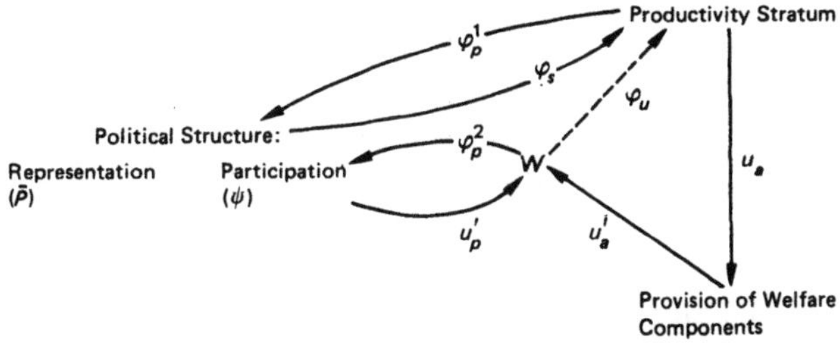

FIG. 18.1 *Welfare and productivity implications of political structure—basic causal links within a multi-systems context*

u'_p = coefficient expressing the utility derived from the type of the political structure, i.e. $\bar{P}$ and ψ, e.g. from participating in political processes

ϕ^1_p, ϕ^2_p = direct and indirect (welfare) productivity effects determining levels of political representation and participation

ϕ_u = productivity effect of welfare (not including productivity effect related to political representation and participation, i.e. ϕ^2_p); see Ch. 16,III/3

ϕ_s = productivity effect of political structure related to the pursuit of a specific strategy, e.g. *B*-strategy

u_a = coefficients expressing contribution of productivity stratum to welfare, e.g. production function: see Ch. 16,II, Fig. 16.1

u'_a = coefficient expressing the utility derived from the welfare components provided; see Ch. 16,II,4

structures—the prevailing and the alternative—exert on productivity and welfare will be assessed. Delineating the causal structure, in Fig. 18.1, the starting point is the political structure, which includes the type of representation and participation of various groups and individuals. Representation is explicitly distinguished from participation. Representation is defined by the ratio between the people actually engaged in the pursuit of a specific activity and the number of people required adequately to pursue that activity—for instance, the type and extent of actual representation of a social group *vis-à-vis* the representation required to articulate and pursue the interests of that social group. We denote the representation ratio with $\bar{P}$. Participation is defined as the ratio of actual involvement over involvement required to pursue effectively specific activities, given a specific extent of representation for the group concerned. We denote the participation-ratio as ψ.[1] The 'composite efficiency' of a given representation and participation Φ thus depends on the values for $\bar{P}$ and ψ,

$$\Phi = f(\bar{P}, \psi).$$

The efficiency function of the political structure is, consequently, related to the variables of the productivity and the welfare strata. Productivity stands here for efficiency in the realisation of a specific strategy ϕ_s, welfare stands for the welfare derived from the provision of welfare components due to the implementation of that strategy, u_a and u'_a, and for the welfare generated *sui generis* by the political process, i.e. the type and extent of representation and participation of the population in the political process, u'_p. There are two productivity feedbacks affecting the productivity of the variables representation and participation; one reaching from the productivity stratum ϕ_p^1, another from the welfare stratum ϕ_p^2 to the political structure. Furthermore, the productivity effect of welfare as discussed in the previous chapters is indicated by broken arrows from W to the productivity stratum.

As for the empirical assessment of the causal links, it may be difficult to apply a cardinal type of measurement. Ideally, we should have empirically ascertained coefficients expressing the levels of change of the productivity and welfare variables in response to a change in the political structure. However, for a first evaluation of the two competing political structures, it will suffice to apply a crude ordinal scale. The question will be to what extent, or merely in what direction, a change in the political structure will affect the three 'efficiency' variables in the above function. The evaluation may be given a straightforward appraisal. The alternative political structure (β-) is assumed to increase the representation and the participation as compared to the prevailing political structure (α-).[2] Hence, by assumption, we have

$$\bar{P}_\alpha < \bar{P}_\beta,$$

$$\psi_\alpha < \psi_\beta.$$

Since a positive association between the levels of 'input factors' and the corresponding levels of output (i.e. welfare) may be assumed, the political structure of the β-type is generally preferable to the α-type. However, we should not be particularly enthusiastic about this conclusion.

A conclusive statement about the welfare impact of different political structures can never dispense with value judgements. Since the representation and participation of some groups may decline as the levels of representation and participation of other groups increase, we are confronted with the dilemma of weighing the welfare gains and losses against one another. We may perhaps, operate with the assumption of decreasing marginal utilities, as is usually done in economics. Then, up to a level where all marginal utilities are equal, any decrease in the representation and participation of, say, and $\bar{F}_n$-group enjoying a large share of those welfare components would incur a welfare loss smaller than the welfare increase generated by the additional representation and participation of, say, the underprivileged $\bar{F}_1$-groups. However, for the evaluation procedure to be valid, we must assign equal utility weights to all members of the society considered. If we apply a different scheme of utility weighting (which would not include an egalitarian but another value judgement), we would run into the problem of weighting the individual utilities against another. On a mere theoretical plane, the discussion leaves us with but formal statements. To increase the relevance of the structural model, we would have to apply empirical coefficients which naturally would imply value judgements. The major significance of introducing the welfare components 'political representation and participation' into the analysis may consist in drawing attention to the fact that representation and participation in political life have themselves a value which must be considered when pursuing a welfare-oriented strategy.

When assessing the productivity effect of political representation and participation ϕ_s, two aspects must be distinguished, one being the adequacy of the political structure in terms of the interests articulated in the strategy pursued, the other being the 'efficiency' of the political structure, e.g. the informational efficiency, administrative capacity, etc. Generally, when structural changes in the body politic are actually considered, both factors will play a significant role in the assessment of an alternative political structure. Countries with a well-functioning political structure, supported by an efficiently operating administration, will be more likely to consider a change in the development strategy by changing the prevailing political structure only modestly in order to retain the efficiency in the implementation of the strategy.

III. RESOURCE DISTRIBUTION AND INSTITUTIONAL FACTORS AS DETERMINANTS OF POLITICAL STRUCTURE

The existence of and the changes in the political structure are determined by two principal factors: first, the distribution of resources and, second, the institutions in which the processes related to the first factor take place. Both composite determining factors pertain to socio-economic and to political realms. Socio-economic resources include income, the control of the means of production, economic power, social prestige, social acceptance, social esteem, social status, social power, etc. Political resources include the disposition of and control over information, education, legitimacy, force, and power.[3] Socio-economic and political institutions combine the total set of organisational and behavioural rules encompassing the prevailing social order (i.e. caste system, place of minorities, etc.), land-tenure systems, the organisation of factor and commodity markets, family systems, as well as the apportioning of political decision-making powers and the role of governmental executives (i.e. prime minister, ministers, military leaders, and key bureaucrats), parties, unions, and interest groups.

There are reciprocal causal interactions between the institutions and the resource distribution in the socio-economic and the political realms. The prevailing institutional setting determines the distribution of resources, and the latter determines the sustainment of the institutions that support the prevailing distribution of resources.[4] And there are close reciprocal causal interactions between the socio-economic and political realms. Socio-economic power enables political power to be maintained; and political power is, in turn, necessary to protect the socio-economic interests, the wealth distribution, and supporting institutions.

A causal model encompassing the relationships highlighted is depicted in Fig. 18.2. Along the horizontal axis the distinction between resource strata and institutional strata is made. Along the vertical axis the classification is into the socio-economic and political realms. We thus arrive at a matrix with four variable sets which are all interlinked, with arrows indicating the causal interactions. The variables determined by this matrix of determining variables are the political structure, i.e. the variables of representation and participation, and, consequently, the formulation and implementation of a specific type of development strategy. In the context of this causal model the type of resource relationships, distribution of assets, access to factors, etc., and the prevailing institutions in the socio-economic and political systems, determine the existence of a specific type of political representation and participation. The latter, in turn, determines the execution of a specific type of strategy. The strategy not only refers to socio-economic processes but implies activities which relate to the change of the type of political representation and participation and thus to the structural basis of the strategy itself. A change in the entire institutional setting underlying the strategy is a most critical and intricate problem, because

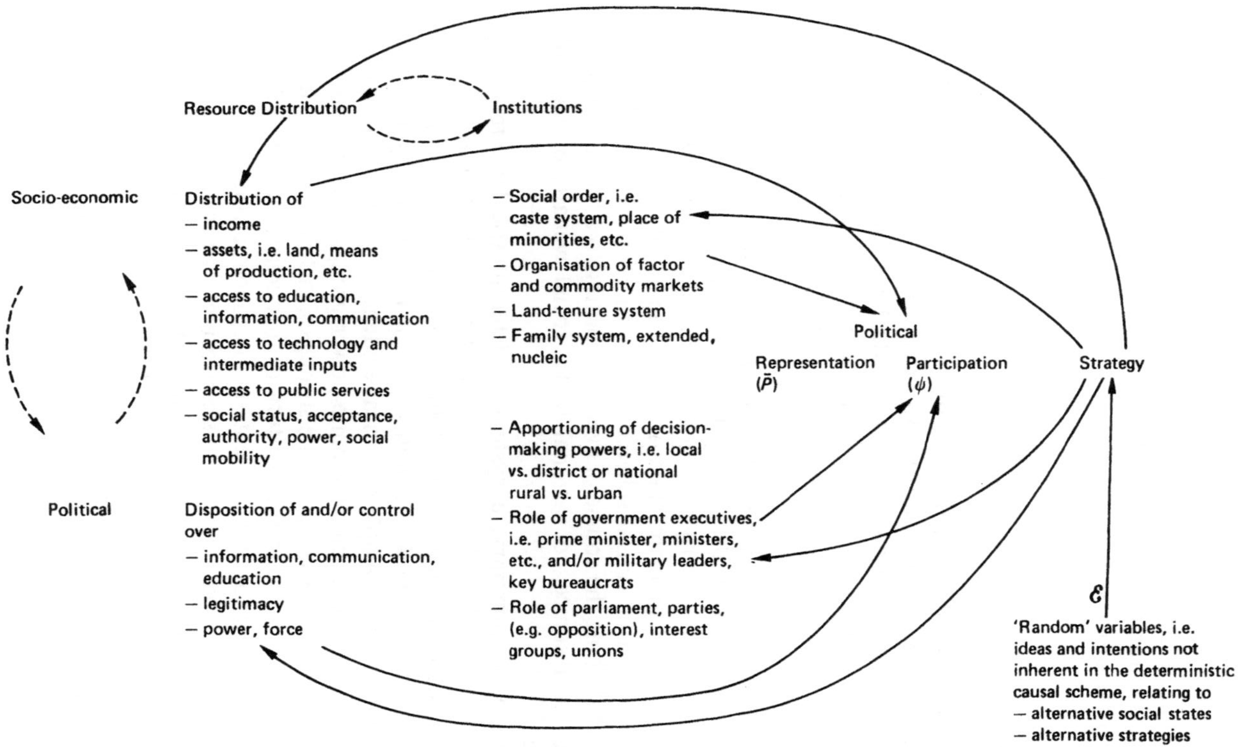

FIG. 18·2 *Resource distribution and institutions as determinants of political structure and development strategy —basic causal linkages in multi-systems context*

the realisation of such a stragety itself assumes an adequate institutional framework, which is yet to result from this strategy. If we are not to fall victim to a fatalistic attitude, we necessarily must abandon the deterministic framework of causal interactions that has evolved from our foregoing discussion. Reference, therefore, must now be made to a set of exogenous factors.

IV. IDEAS AS AUTONOMOUS FACTORS

The exogenous variable set, denoted by $\mathscr{E}$ in Fig. 18.2, does not constitute some sort of *deus ex machina.* It is justified by our basic assumption of finality (in the teleological sense), which plausibly demonstrates that human beings, as agents in social contexts, are not entirely determined by a complex of 'objective conditions' but face choices, which brings in probability, and thus accidental outcomes as a constituent element: they have a drive to change and are apt to adjust to changes, adhere to ideals, are capable of altruism and self-sacrifices (which contradicts any rigid form of 'interest-determinism'), respond to challenges, and so forth. There are ideas and intentions not inherent in the deterministic causal scheme constituting autonomous factors capable of shaping the course of events according to a 'higher insight', relating, for instance, to national unity, social welfare, or cultural heritage.

We have, in summary, a system of deterministically interacting endogenous variables. The coefficients all work in the same 'direction', leading to the sustainment of the *status quo* or even to a cumulation of the causes strengthening the *status quo*—if not altered by political intervention. There is ample empirical evidence for the contemporary Asian countries that socio-economic power groups have a considerable influence on the shaping of the strategies, including those parts of them which are related to the institutions that constitute the legitimation of, and basis for, the present socio-economic processes. More power in the socio-economic realms constitutes, basically, more power in the political realm. The cycle is self-reinforcing and self-sustaining.

However, the emergence of exogenous forces has been assumed to be a possibility which breaks into the deterministic cycle, allowing for change in the strategy. The crucial question is how these exogenous forces, on which, for developmental change, much depends, are generated.

In analytical terms, the set of exogenous factors constitutes random variables, and random variables are not explained but accepted as they are; for this reason they are random variables. Unfortunately—or perhaps not—this theoretical consideration reflects a real factor in human history. Much of what happens in the realms of politics depends on mere chance. The chancellor of Sweden during the 30 Years' War expressed this succinctly: *Nescis, mi fili, quantilla ratione mundus regatur*—you don't know, my dear boy, with what little reason the world is governed.

However, not all accidents are equally accidental. There are good reasons to assume that the exogenous-variable set is itself not totally independent of the system that we have assumed to be basically deterministic. The exogenous-variable set is, at least in part, quasi-deterministic and, thus, the variables are quasi-exogenous. This additional assumption suggests that one should classify the set of exogenous variables into a set of (1) quasi-deterministic random variables and (2) a set of genuinely un-deterministic, genuinely random variables in terms of the system outlined.

As an intermediate conclusion, historical change depends, on the one hand, on the extent of determinism in the system, the mode of distribution of resources, the prevailing institutions, political representation, and participation, and, on the other hand, the exogenous variables as they determine the system by quasi-determined, not easily predictable, random variables, and random variables entirely dependent on historical chance.

The assessment and the actual implementation of strategic changes require, first, that we have a conception about the social structure prevailing in a specific political context and about the impact that strategy changes brought about by 'exogenous' pressures have on this social structure, i.e. the responses and reactions emanating from the ruling elites; and, second, that we have an idea about the forces that determine the quasi-deterministic element of the exogenous-variable set.

V. 'ENERGY FOR CHANGE' VS. DETERMINISTIC OPERATION OF SYSTEM

Starting with the latter question, we are drawn to the problem of how the 'developmental energy' stemming from the exogenous-variable set may be generated. The set of exogenous variables may be given a more precise meaning by defining them as the social groups supporting new ideas, and alternative intentions and actions. The emergence of new elites, 'social deviants', and 'outsiders' will depend on the entire politico-socio-economic system. It is here that a quasi-deterministic link between the exogenous-variable set and the deterministic endogenous-variable set exists. Some politico-socio-economic systems may favour the emergence of 'new elites', others not. There are specific variables determining the emergence of new social groups, and thus the strength of the potential impact of that group on new forms and contents of alternative political structures. There are, basically, three variable sets: social mobility, education, and information. All three composite variables are closely related to one another causally, and, in many instances, the existence of one is a prerequisite for another. There is little social mobility without information, little information without adequate education, little education without social mobility, little social mobility without education, and so forth. When assessing the combined effects of these variables in contemporary Asian countries, we may start with the hypothesis that the social dynamics brought about by the interactions of these three composite variables are sufficiently large to support the emergence of alternative social groups. A school system increasingly opened up to the masses in various countries of contemporary Asia and improvements in the information systems (the provision of which often seems over-proportionate to improvements in the basic necessities of life) provide the logistic infrastructure and basis for adequately articulating the interests and accordingly organising these interests within social groups.

Assuming that the social dynamics sufficiently increase the proliferation of alternative groups, the question is to what extent these groups will exert pressure towards change. Analytically, we may write for the social groups initiating change, P_h, and relate it to the total population P,

$$\frac{P_h}{P},$$

for the extent of pressure initiating change σ, and write the total political pressure bringing about change, H, as

$$H = \frac{P_h}{P}\sigma.$$

The level of H will depend on the level of both determinants. P_h/P may become relatively smaller if the level of σ accordingly compensates for the decline in P_h/P, in order to achieve the same level of H. In other words, small elites may bring about change if the political pressure is sufficiently large; or, large masses may induce political change even if the pressure is not as large as in the former case. We may find various reasons why P_h/P and σ are mutually causally dependent. A small group may find it necessary, just because it is a small group, to exert its strength to the utmost extent. Given a large group, the value of σ may increase, since cumulative effects, say 'social infection', lead to an increase in the pressure for change, political participation, and political claims. In large groups, however, decreasing returns on additional popular participation may occur, possibly even weakening the political group (for example, if the 'marginal pressure' is negative, i.e. the additional participants do not have the 'right' information, attitude, etc.).

Given the level of alternative groups, 'political deviants', and 'outsiders', the crucial variable is σ, viz. the extent of (average) pressure exerted on the existing socio-economic and political elites. σ will depend on two principal variable sets: the expectation of having satisfied certain interests or realised certain ideals and normative concepts, I_e, and the actual satisfaction of these interests, ideas, and concepts, I_a,

$$\sigma = \frac{I_a}{I_e}.$$

The interests or conceptions may relate to a specific social group—for instance, to the group articulating its own interests—or they may refer to the whole of society, that is, covering also the interests of other groups. The latter intention would include a logically consistent idea of a 'good society' and call for virtues such as self-sacrifice. It constitutes that part of the exogenous variables that we have called the 'genuine random variables'. In reality, both will often be mixed—if only for tactical reasons to pursue their own interests more efficiently.

Indicators for I_a and I_e will refer both to the socio-economic and political realms. A classification of indicators and relevant types of measurement has been given in Ch. 16,II.2 (pp. 197–204). We may recall some of the major socio-economic indicators, such as provision of basic necessities—i.e. nutrition, clothing, housing, health, and education—and political indicators, such as representation and participation in political life.[5]

The empirical assessment of the *status quo*, I_a, appears straightforward by reference to the empirical data and statistics available. The statistics available, however, do not always portray current social problems with sufficient accuracy and often conceal rather than stress existing or emerging problems. The new political groupings will, therefore, often have a different interpretation of I_a when compared with that of the ruling elites. The re-formulation or reinterpretation of theories will constitute a first step in clearing the way for increasing the relevance of the statistics available, improving the respective taxonomies and gathering appropriate data.

The specific elaboration of a concept of an 'ideal' society and, combined with it, the level of expectation I_e, will rely on a multiplicity of factors—the two major ones being education and information. The level of education not only determines the assessment of the *status quo* but also the type of ideas about the alternative social state and the strategy required to implement it. Education may (it is hoped positively) correlate with the extent of realism with which the alternative social blueprints are formulated and articulated in political life. Information depends on education; but it is also causally interrelated to a number of factors not directly related to education, such as the level of the provision of informational means (i.e. radios, TV, etc.) and the type of channels of social communication. The content and articulation of I_e will thus depend on a complex composite set of variables which are theoretically difficult to disentangle in their multiple reciprocal causal interactions.

Figure 18.3 provides an integrating idea of the causal interactions of the major variables. The average pressure for change I_a/I_e is considered to be determined by the variables of information and education, whereas linkages to both I_a and I_e are allowed for separately. The two determinants will lead to a reinterpretation or new formulation of the *status quo* and will determine the alternative ideas and expectations. The total pressure exerted to bring about change is a result of the coefficient of average pressure for change I_a/I_e and the size of the group intent upon change P_h/P.

The strength of the total pressure for change is dependent on the strength of the power of the existing elites. Hence, the total pressure to change must be related to that counteracting force R,

$$\frac{\frac{P_h}{P}\sigma}{R}.$$

The variable R depends on the deterministic processes occurring in the

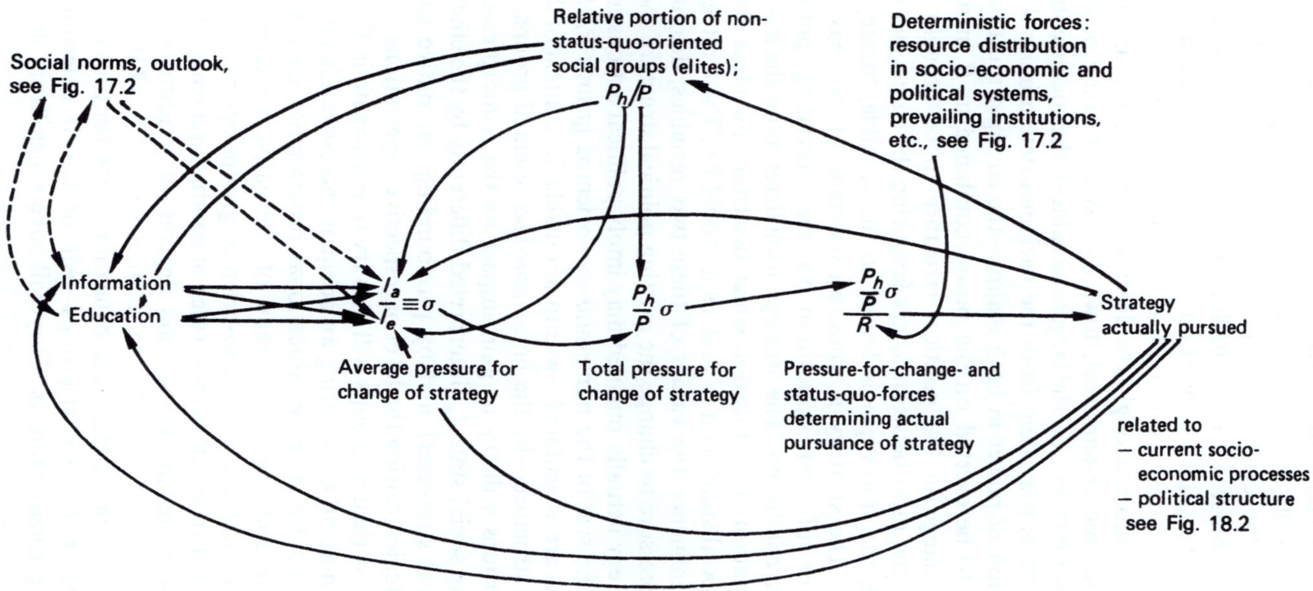

FIG. 18.3 *'Energy' for strategy change*

politico-socio-economic system (see Fig. 18.2). If the socio-economic power allows the smooth implementation of adequate strategies which consolidate the existing socio-economic power, R will have a high value as compared to a situation where either the socio-economic power is not similarly concentrated and/or the political forces shaping political decisions are more autonomous from the socio-economic realms. The more strongly the deterministic processes in the politico-socio-economic system work towards a strengthening of the existing power distribution—i.e. the larger the value in the coefficients cumulating the effects that stem from the variables determining the unequal distribution of power in both realms—the stronger must be the total pressure to be exerted on the power combined in R in order for a specific change in the political structure to be brought about. In Fig. 18.3 the ratio between forces favouring the *status quo* and forces opposing the *status quo* is linked to the variable, 'strategy actually pursued'. The strategy is, thus, an outcome of two basic forces of acceptance of and opposition to the prevailing politico-socio-economic conditions. The strategy itself determines the level and type of information and education which determine the ideas about I_a and I_e, the social state 'as it is' and 'as it should be'. The strategy will also directly influence the values of these two variables, determining the level of pressure to change the existing political structure and strategy. The strategy actually pursued may imply political actions intended to control the size of the non-*status-quo*-oriented groups P_h/P. In turn, new ideas are articulated—within or outside the context of the existing political structure—by the non-*status-quo*-oriented groups. The alternative groups will try to gain impact on the reinterpretation of the prevailing social state I_a (interpreted differently by the elites pursuing the official strategies), and by propounding alternative social states and strategies, raising the level of respective expectations I_e. The non-*status-quo*-oriented groups will also try to participate in the process of opinion-making by securing an adequate access to channels of information and by shaping educational programmes conducive to the emergence and eventual pursuit of alternative strategies. Both the *status-quo*- and non-*status-quo*-oriented groups operate within a complex context of social norms, rules of conduct, schemes of social rewards and punishments, specific degrees of 'traditionalism' and of 'modernisation of outlook', etc., as discussed in Ch. 17.II. The contents and forms of information and education—whether provided by *status-quo* or alternative social groups—will be largely determined by the prevailing social contexts. They will have a significant impact on the perception, articulation, and formulation of the ideas about prevailing and alternative social states and strategies. The links allowing for these complex causal interactions are indicated by broken arrows in Fig. 18.3.

The relationships delineated appear deterministic. However, the causal chain is dynamic in terms of changes in the coefficients. Say improved education for a large part of the population and improved information generate to an increasing extent the capacity and ability to articulate—with more or less vigour and accuracy—ideas about alternative social states and strategies. The system is not bound to operate within the confines of a deterministically constrained set of variables. It develops, in its current dynamics, quasi-random variables leaving open the possibility for structural change in the politico-socio-economic realms. In any (historical) event, there is the genuine random variable of human action which may change the Asian societies to an extent comparable with the now more developed countries—though, perhaps, in a quite different direction.

Conclusion

Of all conclusions, none is less ambiguous than the one that the developing countries must 'go their own way'. The conditions contemporary Asian developing countries face differ in essential aspects from those of the Western countries at a comparable period of their development. Specifically, the population dynamics constitute much more of a threat to subsistence and a sustained development process than was the case in the Western countries. The absolute scarcities in the non-renewable-resource availability, the arable-land/man ratio, and the carrying capacity of the ecosystem are felt in terms both of decreasing marginal net welfare as we move up on the scale of average development indicators, and of ultimate constraints to the further expansion of total productive and consumptive activities. Theoretically, the phenomena become self-evident only within a framework which treats time in its historical properties—not as a formal ahistorical concept. This cognitive-epistemological premise brought into perspective the specific historical 'epoch' of contemporary Asia. It leads to the proposition of 'relative macro-determinacy' of any development process: the specific historicity of the M^{aa}-variables which constitute the 'objective-historical' confines to which the socio-economic processes have to adapt and the 'finality' of human action finds its constraints. The value and choice problem we are confronted with is of a historical dimension. It is not, primarily, the choice within a set of commodities, but among long-run variables which determine the domain of this set, that constitutes the major choice problem of the long-run development process.

Within the historical confines of the thus-delineated M^{aa}-framework, the socio-economic processes must take place. Again, the recognition of the historicity is critical for the understanding of the socio-economic processes. The fact that a 'simultaneous set'—composed of alternatives which needed over 200 years to develop in a 'successive sequence'—is available to contemporary Asian countries has crucial implications on the choice and actual outcome of their development path. Applying mere logical-theoretical reasoning, the broad range of alternatives would suggest that the possible differentials resulting from the choice will be large. Beyond logical inferences and conjectures, the empirical evidence of the developing countries of Asia sufficiently demonstrates that the differential processes constitute a real pendant to the predictions based on that theory. The salient feature of that process has been that, following its own logic, it creates inconsistencies between the major socio-economic variables—particularly demand, income distribution, and output—and ultimately produces its own constraints, impeding a desired sustained development process. The socio-economic differentials are reinforced by differentials of the population growth and the resulting eco-ratios, which are themselves a result of the socio-economic differentials. Given the unfavourable effects of that development pattern, the policy inference seems self-evident: correction of the differentials and embarking upon a strategy which attacks the state of 'underdevelopment' in the agricultural and non-agricultural $\bar{F}_1$-sectors directly and on a broad front.

The behavioural requirements to be met for that resource policy are not the 'new way of doing things' isolated from compounded historical experience, and not the uncritical transfer of patterns which have been applied with success in the now-industrialised countries—rather the genuine choice from a set of existing alternatives in due consideration of and subsequent adjustment to the specific historical-cultural-geographical conditions. It is a new type of creativity which emerges as a necessary condition for the redirection of the socio-economic process. The major tasks of governments appear to consist in the sharpening of that awareness and the provision of information about the set of feasible alternatives—'in the large' among the long-run variables, and 'in the small' among the socio-economic variables. The scarcest factor in development is the knowledge about feasible choices, and about their probability of success and failure when applied in a specific historical context.

Appendixes

APPENDIX 1
Relative Determinacy of Historical Processes: The Case of Simultaneous Sequence Development in LDCs

The idea of relative determinacy of the total-system, or *relative macro-determinacy*, may be elucidated by showing the salient features of the 'simultaneous-sequence' type of development. In Fig. A1.1 the horizontal and vertical axes X and Y represent sets or pairs of development variables, and the curves $a, \ldots, d$ represent various combinations of these sets or pairs at various levels of development.

Substitutability for the members of pairs is assumed. We write t_i for a specific period of time in which the development process takes place. The bold lines indicate the range of alternatives in development paths for Asia or less-developed countries; the broken lines those for Western countries. We may start with the small range of development alternatives for the Western countries at t_1. No 'external' factors exist that significantly widen or narrow the range of alternatives for the less-developed countries. As development of the developed countries proceeds to b, the repercussions from the developed countries (for instance, due to persisting colonial patterns, transfer of know-how, 'rising expectations', external economic relations, etc.) change the range of alternative development paths for less-developed countries still at a, this being indicated by broken lines with arrows. In a similar fashion, the process proceeds from a to d. Given the assumption of a 'simultaneous-sequence' type of development for the Asian countries,

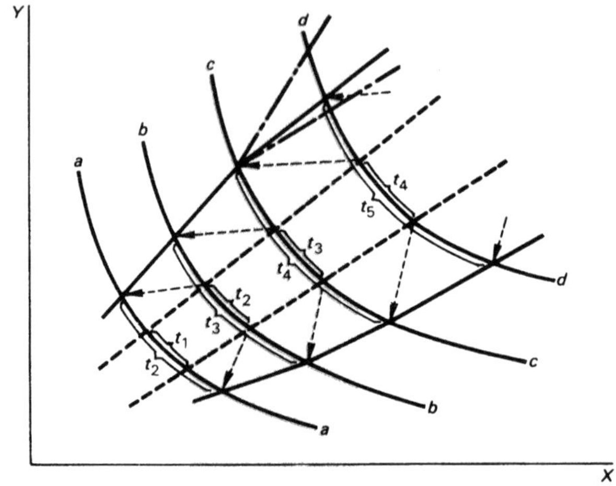

FIG. A1.1 *Impact of development of industrialised countries on development of Asian countries (hypothetical paths)*

the range where bold and broken lines overlap on the curve of alternatives (indicating the repetition of the development patterns) is not feasible for Asian countries. However, *X* and *Y* constitute composites of variables. The infeasibility exists only for the whole set of pairs of variables, not for single variables depicted on *X* and *Y*. The configurations of the variables may be different, and new variables may appear in the Asian context. The hypotheses of whether the preceding development of advanced countries widens or narrows the range of feasible development paths for Asian countries (broken lines with arrows) will depend entirely on empirical assessment. At each time curve, the historical repercussions will be different, and because of the changes in the system of the less-developed countries, will alter the impact on these systems.

APPENDIX 2
Finality, Equifinality, and Historically Feasible Paths

Both the past behaviour and the anticipated behaviour of the system determine the actual events. This hypothesis shall now be reduced to its general form[1]. The entire time interval in which the development process occurs can be written as

$$t_{-1} \leq t' \leq t_0 \leq t'' \leq t_1$$

where t_{-1} indicates the initial point in the past, t_0 the present point (or initial point with regard to the future), and t_1 the terminal point. The state of the system, $\mathbf{S}(t)$, is defined at any time t' in the past (from t_{-1} to t_0) and at any time t'' in the future (from t_0 to t_1) by $\mathbf{S}(t')$ and $\mathbf{S}(t'')$ respectively. The behaviour of the system is determined by both the initial state $\mathbf{S}(t_0)$ and the final state $\mathbf{S}(t_1)$. The past path (from t_{-1} to t_0) can be written as

$$\{\mathbf{S}(t')\} = \{\mathbf{S}(t') \in E^n \,|\, t_{-1} \leq t' \leq t_0\}$$

The future path of the system (from t_0 to t_1) can be written as

$$\{\mathbf{S}(t'')\} = \{\mathbf{S}(t'') \in E^n \,|\, t_0 \leq t'' \leq t_1\}$$

where n designates the number of sub-systems $\mathbf{S}_e$, $\mathbf{S}_s$, $\mathbf{S}_p$ etc. (it could as well denote the larger total set of sub-system variables). Hence, $\mathbf{S}(t')$ and $\mathbf{S}(t'')$ are to be understood as vectors

$$\mathbf{S}(t') = (S_1(t'), S_2(t'), \ldots, S_n(t'))$$
$$\mathbf{S}(t'') = (S_1(t''), S_2(t''), \ldots, S_n(t'')).$$

Since we have six systems that constitute the total-system, we have $n = 6$. The behaviour of the total-system from its present state $\mathbf{S}(t_0)$ to its final state $\mathbf{S}(t_1)$ as defined by

$$\{\mathbf{S}(t'')\} = \{\mathbf{S}(t'') \in E^6 \mid t_0 \leq t'' \leq t_1\}$$

is determined by

$$\{\mathbf{S}(t'')\} = f\{\mathbf{S}(t'), \mathbf{S}(t_1)\}$$

where $\mathbf{S}(t')$ describes the past behaviour of the system as it resulted in a new initial state at t_0, and $\mathbf{S}(t_1)$ designates the specific final state chosen among a set of alternative final states.

In Fig. A.2.1 the horizontal axis includes the interval from t_{-1} to t_1, bisected by t_0 into two sub-intervals which represent time past and time future. On the vertical axis a variable set, Y, representing the states of the system is plotted.

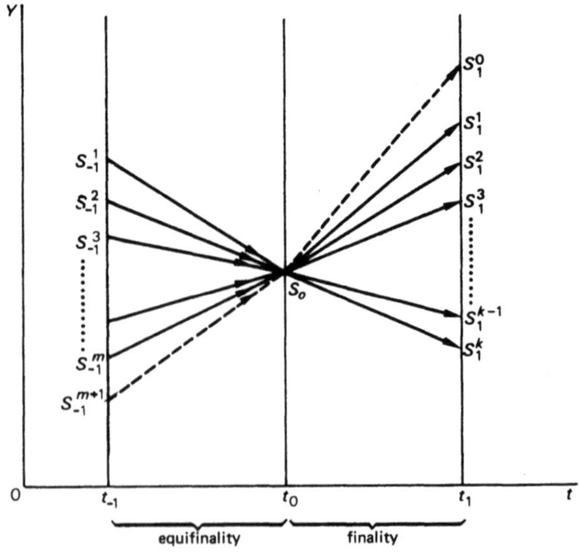

FIG. A2.1 *Finality and equifinality*

Finality means that the system S at t_0—in simplified notation, S_0—may move either to the (hypothetical) state of $S_1^1, S_1^2, \ldots, S_1^k$, where the superscript stands for the ith alternative and k for the total number of alternatives. Within the range of initial points in the past period, $S_{-1}^1, \ldots, S_{-1}^k$, the range of future alternatives, $S_1^1, \ldots, S_1^k$, is not restricted. That is to say, any of the n alternatives is feasible. This does not imply that the past behaviour of the system would not determine the future path of the system, but merely that it is not limiting the choice within the range indicated. In contrast, the broken line from S_0 to S_1^0 indicates a shift of the whole range of future possibilities caused by a different behaviour of the system in the past, indicated also by the broken line from S_{-1}^{m+1} to S_0. A rationale for this case is provided, for example, by the observation that an accelerating process in the past carries its dynamic momentum also into the future and allows higher rates of change than a system with lower (positive) rates of change in the past could reach.

The past behaviour of the system cannot be expressed in terms of finality. However, although the question of hypothetical alternatives cannot be asked with regard to the final states, it can be asked with regard to a set of initial states *vis-à-vis* a uniquely determined final state. Say the range of possible initial states is given by $S_{-1}^1, \ldots, S_{-1}^{m+1}$. From any of these initial states, S_0 can be reached. This allows for the important fact that countries starting from different levels of development can reach an identical level of development in a specific future period whenever the rates of change in the relevant developmental variables are sufficiently large or small. The property of reaching a certain terminal state of a system from different initial states is sometimes referred to as *equifinality*.[2] This property of systems' behaviour is shown in the domain from t_{-1} to t_0.

The question remains how the total-system behaves over a relevant time span, e.g. fifty years. A finite range of alternative terminal states within partial or single intervals implies that some terminal states in those intervals are not possible and therefore are excluded. It logically follows that not all development paths can be possible over the entire time span suggested. The overall path is composed of the partial paths; consequently, the overall path must be expected to be found within the range of the options stated in those partial paths. For instance, in Fig. A2.2 the set of final states starting from the initial state S_0^* is given by $S_1^1, \ldots, S_1^n$. Depending on which final state is actually reached at t_1, a new set of final states will be approached at t_2. Starting from S_1^k, the new set of final states at t_2 is $S_2^1, \ldots, S_2^m$. Analogously, from the state

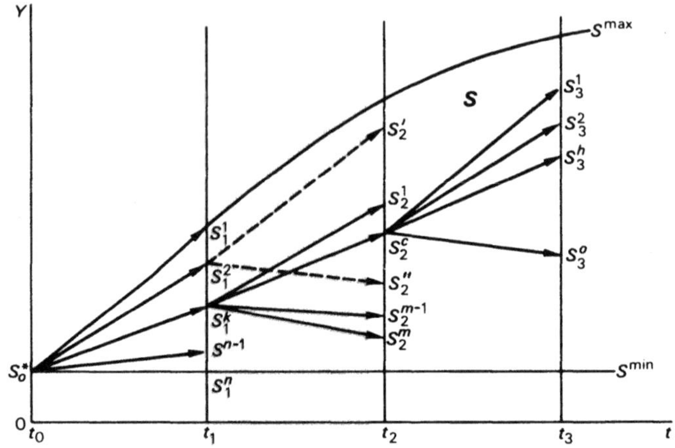

FIG. A2.2 *Ranges of Single Paths within Total Area of Possible Paths*

actually reached at t_2, a new set of final states, e.g. $S_3^1, \ldots, S_3^j$, will result. Thus the process proceeds over the entire time space envisaged.

There are various feasible paths which depend at a time t_k on a past initial state S_{k-1} (which includes the compounded historical experience) and on the choice of the future final state S_{k+1}. The feasibility of the paths is thus determined by the past as given by a 'simultaneous-' or 'successive-sequence' type of development and by their anticipated future states given by specific 'historical' choices.

The *feasible* paths must be distinguished from the range of (hypothetically) *possible* paths. The range of possible paths is given by the area $\mathcal{S}$, which is defined by the two boundaries $S_{\max}$ and $S_{\min}$. Therefore, all feasible paths are possible paths but not all possible paths are feasible paths,

$$\mathcal{F} \subset \mathcal{P} \,|\, \mathcal{P} \equiv \text{entire area of } \mathcal{S}$$

where $\mathcal{F}$ designates the (sub-) set of all feasible and $\mathcal{P}$ the set of all possible paths: $\mathcal{P}$ is the universal set of all feasible and all infeasible paths ($\bar{\mathcal{F}}$), i.e., $\mathcal{P} \equiv \mathcal{F} \cup \bar{\mathcal{F}}$. For instance, a path from S_0^* to S_2' is possible; but it is feasible only if a sufficient performance of the system is accomplished already from S_0^* to S_1. For instance, from S_0^* to S_1^2, resulting in a range from S_2' to S_2''. If, however, the system moves, say from S_0^* to S_1^k, S_2' may not be a feasible state of the system at t_2 (though it would have been possible). Both the limited range of future alternatives at any initial point of the system and the constraints set by minima and maxima for the entire range indicate that the behaviour of the system obeys certain regularities or 'laws'. The idea of constraints imposed on the development of the total-system is immediately clear if we consider that the system is realised in the context of time and space and hence is subject to the laws which govern entities in the context of these categories. For instance, it is easy to see that there must be a maximum rate of capital accumulation as a result of maximum rates of technical innovation, the initial capital stock, the capacity to bring about behavioural change, etc. Say S'_2 is the maximum path feasible from an initial point S_1^2. Analogously, a maximum path is given for the entire path, i.e. along S^{max}. Ecological constraints may account for a long-run maximum rate. Similar constraints prevent the system from falling below certain minimum values. The daily minimum food intake (i.e. S^{min} line) must be reached if a population is to survive and the collapse of the system is to be avoided from that side. The minimum value for present consumption is itself a crucial determinant of the feasible maximum value for the rate of capital accumulation.

APPENDIX 3
Shifting Production Functions under Finite Resource Constraints

The pressure of increasing population has traditionally been most critically felt on food production. The classical economists propounded as one of their principal hypotheses that land may not be sufficient to sustain additional populations in the long run. Malthus contrasted the geometrical progression of population increase with the arithmetical progression of food production. Ricardo stressed the necessity of cultivating less-fertile land as population increase led to increased demand for food. Smith viewed the development process as a race between population growth and technological advances which the latter possibly was bound to lose because of the constancy of the production factor, land, and the law of decreasing marginal returns it implies. Whatever the economic consequences and the theoretical underpinnings that describe and explain them, the main conclusion is fairly clear: an ultimate stalemate at the state where food resources are critically scarce and the existence of the human race is constantly threatened. The discussion on the equilibrium state ε_1 and the human sufferings it entailed (Ch. 6,II) indicated why the political economists of the 18th and 19th centuries were not prepared to view the future optimistically. In the sequel, European history took another turn. The population growth rate decreased and has been reaching the equilibrium position ε_4. Technology increased at an unprecedented rate, leaving behind the Malthusian link between food shortage and fertility adjustment.

When assessing whether Asian countries may follow a path similar to that of the Western countries, it must first of all be recognised that it is not the law of decreasing marginal returns that has been refuted by European experience, but the specific hypothesis pertaining to the historical situation in Europe: that her development would ultimately end in an equilibrium position which precludes any further development. The relevant question for Asia, therefore, is whether its empirical conditions can be located at similar points on the long-run return curve.

Let us, first of all, generalise the long-run agricultural-production function. In an early phase where the population per agricultural land unit D is small, the growth of total agricultural output O with respect to growth of population (which we assume for the ease of developing the argument as being linearly correlated to labour employed in agriculture) starts to increase linearly, e.g. $f'' = 0$. Additional land can be taken under the plough, and the method of cultivation is typically extensive. In addition, adjustments in social organisation and improvements in technology within the context of a specific mode of production T (defined here as a complex of social institutions in which a specific technology is applied) have been observed in most historical societies, leading to $f'' > 0$ for O, resulting in a concave upward curve. As population grows, the fertility of additional land taken under cultivation will, following the Ricardian hypothesis, decrease. The marginal benefits from the application of additional technology and social adjustments under a given T_i will decrease, although the pressure from land may stimulate the inventiveness of the people, compensating for some of the losses. For the time being we assume that the production function $F\ (O : D)$ is not shifted upwards by introducing a new T. The phase expounds the characteristics of a slackening downward growth, where $f'' < 0$. As population continues to grow, a maximum output that land at T_i can sustain is ultimately reached. At this point the rate of growth is zero, or the first derivative $f' = 0$. Finally, the sustained population pressure on land will lead to a decrease in the total output.

We are confronted with a new situation when a new T is introduced. Theoretically, we may assume a sequence $T_1, \ldots, T_n$ which leads to a sequence of production functions $F_1, \ldots, F_n$. In Fig. A3.1 the production functions are $F_1, \ldots, F_5$, corresponding to the sequence $T_1, \ldots, T_5$. At a point of density D_i we get five outputs $O_1^i, \ldots, O_5^i$, depending on the T or F applied. Along D, for a given production function F_k, we get various outputs $O_k^1, \ldots, O_k^n$. All theoretically feasible output points can be written as

$$\begin{array}{c} O_1^1, \ldots, O_1^n \\ \cdots\cdots\cdots\cdots \\ O_5^1, \ldots, O_5^n . \end{array}$$

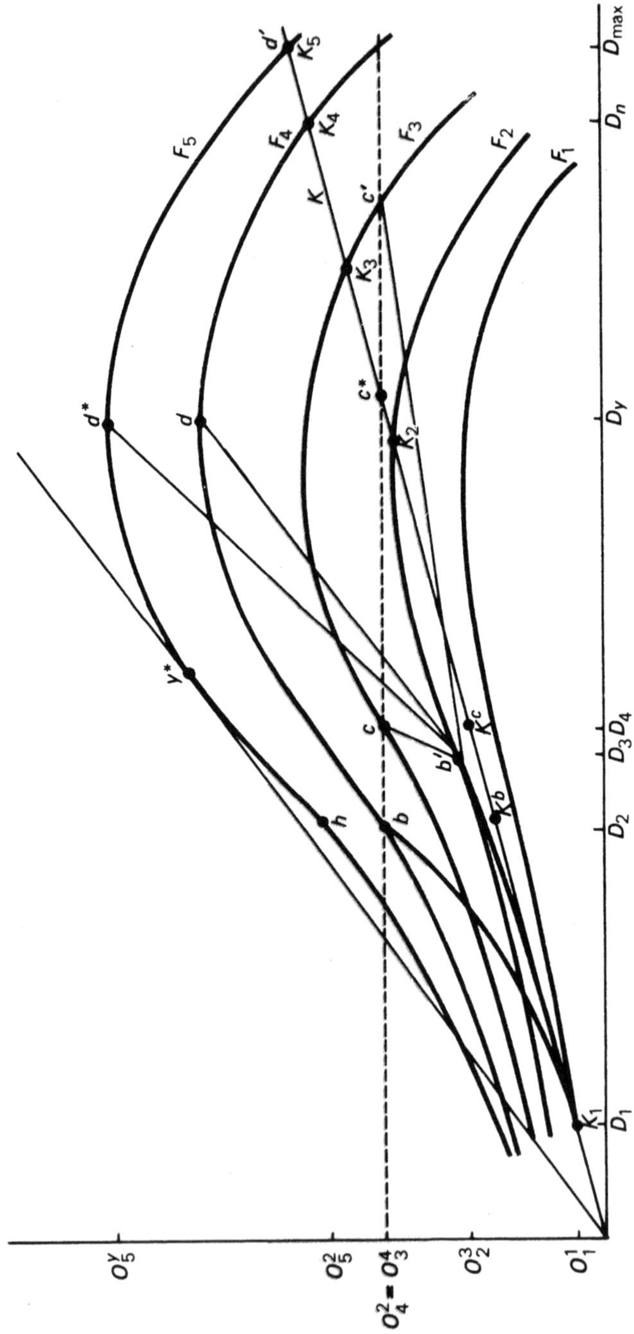

FIG. A3.1 *Shifting agricultural production functions and arable land densities in comparative view*

Empirically, we assume that Asia and Europe were located at similar points on the production functions around the year 1750 and the period before. The point is denoted as k_1 with corresponding values O_1^1 and D_1, implying that T_1 (which is at this point the only mode of production, e.g. technology, available) is applied. (The scale for O will differ, owing to differences in size of total land and population.) As development proceeds and population grows, Europe shifts successively from the lower production functions to the higher ones, viz. as D_1 increases to D_2, production functions shift from F_1 to F_4. If we plot labour employed in agriculture on the horizontal axis L/N, we get a steep O-curve and generally even a backward-bending O-curve (due to shifts in F_i) for most of the Western countries. At density D_2, say in 1950, a population P_2 is sustained at a *per capita* agricultural consumption O_4^2/P_2. In contrast, Asia proceeded in the period 1750–1950 to D_3, a higher density level than the Western countries, along a lower production function F_2 reaching output O_2^3. It does not interfere with the substance of the argument if we express the historical advances in those 200 years with a single shift from F_1 to F_2 rather than by more shifts (e.g. for various types of technology, biological innovations, land reforms, opening of markets, etc.). Clearly, agricultural growth relies on a continuous process, and any shift as expounded in different Fs combines many complex processes.

Reverting to the initial problem of whether Asia will follow a path similar the Western countries, we may set O_4^2 as a 'performance standard', indicated by the broken line *b*, *c*, *c*′. Starting from *b*′, all output points on F_2 lie below that performance standard; thus, the level of O_4^2 cannot be reached unless a shift from F_2 to F_3 is accomplished. The shortest path to that level would be from *b*′ to *c*, resulting in O_3^4, and the slowest or least efficient path would be from *b*′ to *c*′. The range of feasible paths would be given by triangle b'_c, *c*, *c**, constrained by the total subsistence consumption line *k* (average subsistence consumption times population). Whether reserves from the extensive cultivation assumed in further increases in O when moving from D_3 to D_4 of F_2 and F_3 can be expected is an entirely empirical question. The discussion in Ch. 8 suggests that the assumption may be overly optimistic. Following the optimistic assumption of output reserves in the production function and the capacity to shift rapidly from F_2 to F_3, the average output (O/P) still would compare unfavourably with that of the Western countries, since the population stands at D_4 as compared to the populations of the Western countries at D_2, while the total output is the same in both regions, $O_4^2 = O_3^4$. Lines for various values for the average output could easily be further introduced, showing that the increasing D requires a shift not only to F_3 but to F_4 or F_5 in order to offset the large populations and to obtain the same *per capita* output-levels as in the Western countries with their smaller populations.

If we develop the argument further along this line, we may next take k as performance standard. The performance indicator could be defined as the ratio between k and O, where k = output would mean that $O_1^1, \ldots, O_5^{D_{max}}$ is produced along $k_1, \ldots, k_5$, or simply that the outputs always equal the subsistence consumption levels. Anything above the value 1·0 of O/k will be total agricultural surplus, which contributes to the present welfare by increasing consumption above subsistence and/or, in a dynamic view, by the provision of surplus for financing non-agricultural development. Anything below 1·0 constitutes a food deficit. It can first of all be recognised that, as either D or the population increases, frequent shifts of F are required in order to maintain the population at a subsistence level, that is, to produce along $k_1, \ldots, k_5$. Any increase in D beyond k_2 appears to be particularly critical, since the density intervals in which the shifts to k_3, k_4, k_5 must be accomplished are short. Various paths for O can be assumed. The path from b' to c, as assumed above, would result in a surplus $O_3^4 - k^c$ at c, still lower than the surplus of the Western countries at D_2, $O_4^2 - k^b$. A less-rapid development path would be from b' to d^*, which represents the absolute maximum point for O. From there on, any increase in D will decrease the surplus and finally develop into a food deficit after k_5 is reached. The point k_5 can be called the ultimate Malthusian trap around which the population 'fluctuates'. Another path would be from b' to d. The total output and surplus would be at density D_y, below that of d^*. The critical point at which the population is threatened in its subsistence would be reached at k_4 instead of k_5 and would result in a smaller maximum population D_n capable of being sustained and of surviving.

All possible paths for Asia will theoretically fall into the range from k^b to k_5 as the lower boundary (assuming that the population cannot increase in the long run when O is below subsistence consumption) and F_5 from h to k_5 as the upper boundary (where h or O_5^2 represents a hypothetical 'total technology transfer' which would instantly raise F_2 to F_5). The actual path will depend, first, on the feasibility of shifting up the production functions F—that is, of implementing new types of technology, of transforming institutions, setting a system of prices conducive to change, etc.—and, second, of controlling the population growth, slowing down the increase in D. The danger is real that O will move along $k^b, \ldots, k_5$, not allowing any surplus, and ultimately stagnate at k_5. Any definite assessment of the set of feasible paths will depend on the assessment of factors which pertain to the M^a-level, such as the social, economic and political systems.

There are, however, preliminary conclusions which can be derived from the constellation of the M^{aa}-variables, leaving open the specific outcomes to the complex interactions of both the sets of M^{aa}- and M^a-variables. First, the efforts needed to sustain an increasing population at a subsistence level and/or to produce an agricultural surplus for non-agricultural activities must increase as D increases. Contemporary Asia being located on higher densities than 18th- and 19th-century Europe, the input (labour, T)-output ratio will be less favourable in Asia. Second, the speed with which a density change ΔD is accomplished accelerates the higher the density level. The statement is immediately clear if we recall that the absolute change in population can be expressed by the differential notion

$$dP = cP\, dt.$$

If we write P^A for the population of Asia and P^E for the Western countries,[1] we can then write

$$cP^E\, dt_E = cP^A\, dt_A$$

$$\therefore \quad dt_A = \frac{P^E}{P^A}\, dt_E.$$

Third, it is conceivable that the population approaches a level where on the locus of a 'maximum' production function, say F_5, must be produced and decreasing returns will set in; this is indicated by any point beyond d^*. To what extent this constellation will be real will depend on the specific empirical location of contemporary Asia on the D-axis, the possibility of utilising virgin lands and fertility reserves along established production functions, of shifting the F-curves upward, and, closely causally related to it, the ability to use the agricultural surplus efficiently.

APPENDIX 4
Major Causal Linkages Between Ecosystems and Related Systems

In Fig. A4.1, let $A_1, \ldots, A_k$ (Col. 2) denote a set of activities which generate pollutants $\pi_1, \ldots, \pi_n$ (Col. 3) which affect (i) the activity set $A_1, \ldots, A_k$, (ii) the ecosystem as a composite of eco-variables $C_1, \ldots, C_m$ (Col. 4), and (iii) the physical and mental state of men as members of a social group or class (Col. 5). The total of activities is a product of average activities (Col. 1; S_e) and population (Col. 1; S_n). The total activity set shall be composed of agricultural activities A_1, industrial (including service) activities A_2, and transport activities A_3. Each A_i constitutes inputs $a^i_\alpha, \ldots, a^i_\gamma$ and outputs $b^i_\alpha, \ldots, b^i_\gamma$. The inputs include labour, capital, land, energy, renewable and non-renewable resources, intermediate goods, and 'free' goods such as air. The outputs encompass (a) a set of commodities O and (b) externalities from production (consumption externalities derived from (a) are excluded). Pollutants $\pi_1, \ldots, \pi_n$ (CO, SO_2, etc.) constitute negative externalities. To each input factor a^i_i, a pollution coefficient may be assigned. Each pollutant π_i combines the multiple effects of several activities (e.g. toxic emissions from energy-use in agriculture, industry, etc.). The overall pollution level Π depends on (1) the overall level of activities as determined by the average economic activities and population; (2) the composition of activities, for instance, the relation of the ratios between single activities and overall activities, A_j/A, $A = \sum_j A_j = \rho_j$, and $j = 1, 2, 3$, where $\sum_j \rho = 1$; (3) the average input-factor mix of A_j; and (4) the pollution coefficients assigned to each factor.

Given Π and the pollution 'structure' $\pi_1, \ldots, \pi_n$, various areas as denoted by the categories (i), (ii), and (iii) are affected. Category (i)

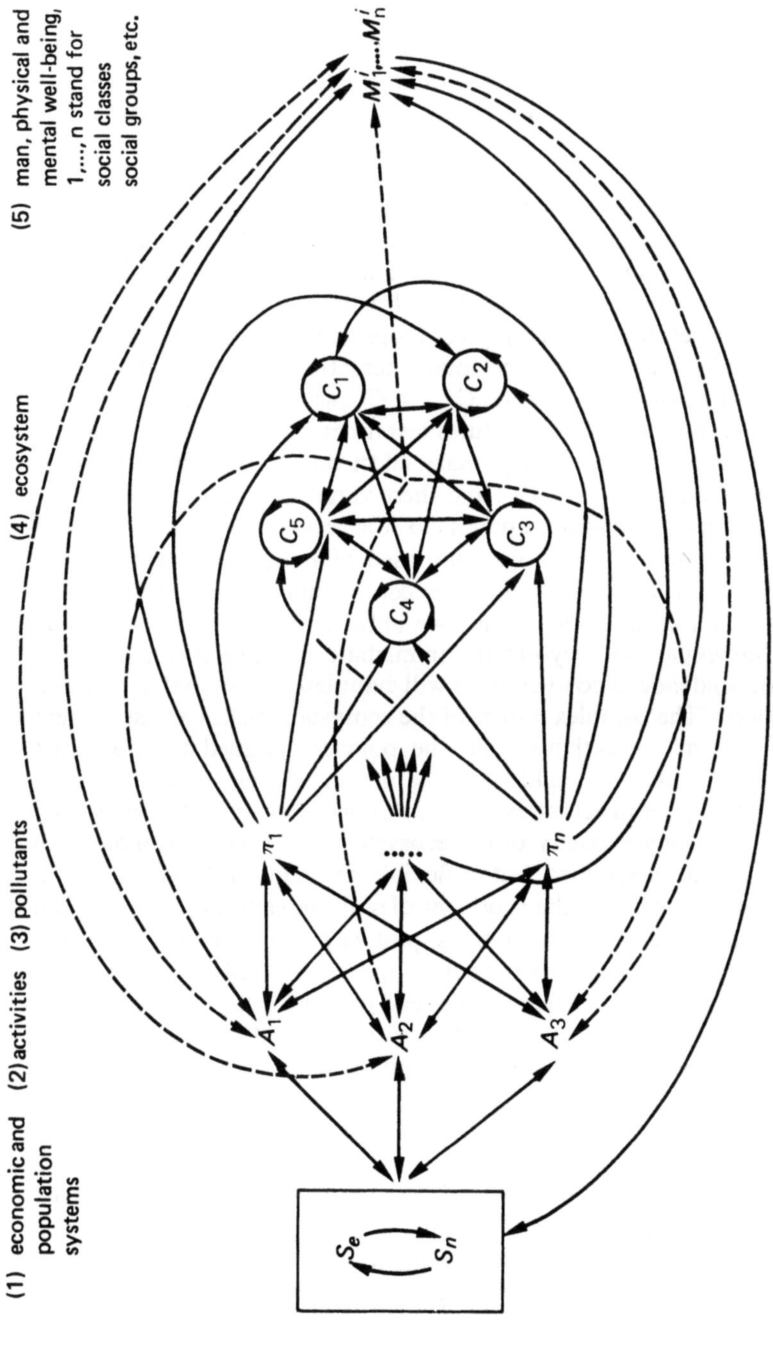

FIG. A4.1 *Causal impact model of pollution in multi-systems context*

constitutes a direct feedback loop from $\pi_1, \ldots, \pi_n$ to $A_1, \ldots, A_3$. Multiple causation applies also to feedback processes, not only to the primary cause of π-generating activities; for instance, commodities derived from A_1 may be affected by π_1 and π_2, or the input-factor mix of activity A_2 and A_3 may have to be changed or adjusted because of π_1 and π_4. The possibilities of multiple causation and multiple effects are depicted by the web of arrows connecting all πs with all As.

A more complex interrelationship exists in (ii), between the pollutants $\pi_1, \ldots, \pi_n$ and the ecosystem S_c. The characteristics of S_c lie in the complex causal interrelatedness of all variables constituting S_c. The various cycles designated by small loops composed of arrows (Col. 4) are causally interrelated. The total interactions are represented by a graph connecting the variables $C_1, \ldots, C_5$, where the Cs designate soil, air, water, flora and fauna, natural resources, etc. In generalized form, a pollutant π_i will have a primary effect on C_g. C_g will affect other variables, say C_1, C_2 and C_5, and these variables will feed back to C_g. The multiple causation applies to the eco-variables representing specific circular flows (loops composed of arrows) and to the interrelatedness of the circular flows encompassing the entire ecosystem (graph connecting eco-variables). An initial cause of a pollutant π_i will have an impact far beyond the immediate primary effect, since the interdependency of eco-variables will cumulate causes and compound the effects. The complex nature of the ecosystem makes an assessment of the impact of activities and the policies designed to counteract undesirable effects a highly delicate matter. Generally speaking, the effects of any set of activities $A_1, \ldots, A_n$ may be assumed to depend on: (a) the carrying capacity of the ecosystem, the level or standards of which can be ascertained, but at flexible and adjustable values due to the complex nature of the processes of multiple causation; (b) the level of accumulated pollution from the past, say up to time period t_i; and (c) the pollution flow in time period t_i as a result of $A_1, \ldots, A_n$ in t_i. The assessment of all three will depend on (1) whether the effects of π on S_c are reversible or irreversible (e.g. eutrophication of lakes, extinction of species), and (2) whether the effects are confined to a territory of regional or national boundaries or extend over the globe.

Finally, π may affect human health and well-being, category (iii). The effects will, first, stem from direct interferences of pollutants with the health or well-being of people of specific groups or classes. Consumption (particularly of food) may contain toxic elements, and production conditions may cause psychic stress and ill-health. Possibilities of this kind are indicated by the arrows from $\pi_1, \ldots, \pi_n$ connecting

Col. 5. The second linkage is indirect, affecting human health and well-being *via* damages to the ecosystem, The impact of a degraded ecosystem on human well-being is on the quality of the ecosystem *qua* recreational space and environmental integrity (which will include aesthetic values). In addition, the environmental degradation may feed back to the input and output levels and compositions of $A_1, \ldots, A_n$ and interfere with human well-being, compounding the initial effects of a pollutant. The ecosystem constitutes unalterable input factors for some activities, particularly for A_1. Any breaking-up of the cyclic processes will interfere with the 'laws' whose functioning is instrumental for the 'renewability' of the natural resources.

APPENDIX 5 Social Welfare in a Finite World A Formal Presentation

In Figs. A5.1 and A5.2 the vertical axes depict the marginal social utility, $du/d\bar{A}$ and the marginal social disutility $dd/d\bar{A}$, and the horizontal axes the developmental levels $\bar{A}$; we first consider the assumption of 'minima' and 'maxima' of social utility and disutility. For the sake of simplicity, linearity in the change of $f'(\bar{A})$ and $g'(\bar{A})$ is assumed. The minima and maxima are defined by $du/dA = \infty$ and by $(\bar{A} \cdot P/S_c)\,k = 1$, designated as $\bar{A}_{min}$ and $\bar{A}_{max}$ on the horizontal axis. If $\bar{A}$ falls below $\bar{A}_{min}$, minimum nutritional intakes and other subsistence consumption cannot be satisfied; a part of the population will starve to death. A_{min} signifies the Malthusian locus around which the population fluctuates, and, eventually, depending on the causal strength of the interactions between P and $\bar{A}$, will face extinction. Any 'survival population' finds itself typically in an ε_1-equilibrium situation (see chapter on population, pp. 41–44). Any development beyond $\bar{A}_{max}$ will lead to ecological disaster and lethal consequences for humans. The intersection point at $\bar{A}_x$ and $du/d\bar{A} = dd/d\bar{A}$ constitutes the developmental 'optimum'. To the left of $\bar{A}_x$, marginal social utility derived from development exceeds the marginal social disutility, and an unused welfare potential exists. Conversely, any development $\bar{A}_i$ over the intersection point $\bar{A}_i > \bar{A}_x$ will yield net marginal social disutility, since $f'(\bar{A}) - g'(\bar{A}) < 0$. We may call this situation 'overdevelopment'. The path of overdevelopment is defined by the range from $\bar{A}_x$ to $\bar{A}_{max}$.

Next we may scale the marginal social utilities and disutilities to give $f'(u)$ and $g'(d)$ ordinal or cardinal significance. We may choose an

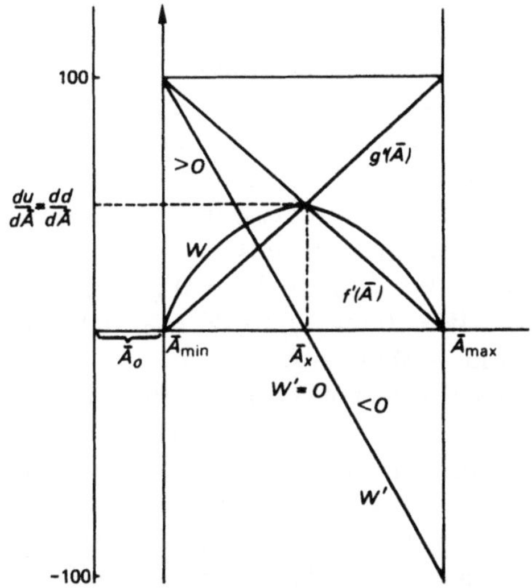

FIG. A5.1 *Social welfare at various levels of activities given finite resource constraints and constant population.*

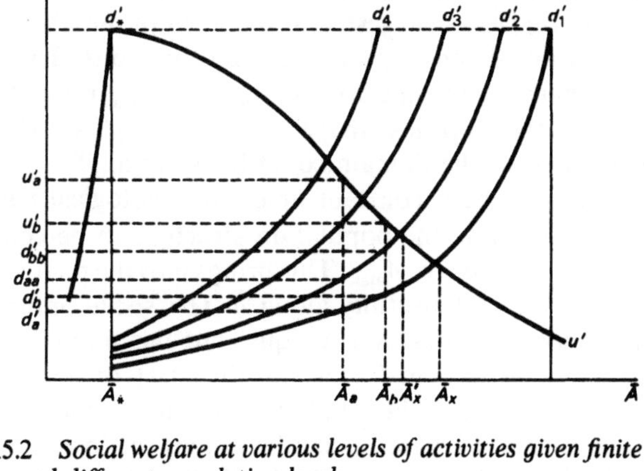

FIG. A5.2 *Social welfare at various levels of activities given finite resource constraints and different population levels.*

index from 1 to 100. The whole range may be applied assigning the value 100 to the value closest to substitence, $du/d\bar{A} = \infty$, and the value 1 to the value closest to infinite disutility, $dd/d\bar{A} = \infty$. A specification may be made by introducing sub-scales dissecting the domain into $\bar{A}_{min}$ and $\bar{A}_x$, and $\bar{A}_x$ and $\bar{A}_{max}$. The former index measures net marginal social utility. The second measures net marginal social disutility and represents an 'index of overdevelopment'. All marginal net values are designated by the W'-line, where $W' = f'(\bar{A}) - g'(\bar{A})$. The marginal welfare index is from $W' = 100$ to $W' = 0$ (at A_x). The overdevelopment index is from $W' = 0$ (at $\bar{A}_x$) to $W' = -100$. Any value beyond the range $+100$ and -100 is $+\infty$ or $-\infty$.

Given the marginal values it is routine to construct a *total* social-welfare index. The path has the domain $\bar{A}_{min}$ and $\bar{A}_{max}$, and an optimum where $du/d\bar{A} = dd/d\bar{A}$, or $du/d\bar{A} - dd/d\bar{A} = 0$ at $\bar{A}_x$. Analogously, we may apply a welfare index, say a scale from 1 to 100. (It goes without saying that the validity of the statement is not dependent on the measuring scale.) The departing point of W at A_{min} (and not at zero) brings out the central theme in an explicit way: total social welfare derived from a given level of average income or equivalent set of physical commodities consists, first, of subsistence utility derived from the income $\bar{A}_{min}$, and, second, of supplementary utility which increases from the origin of $\bar{A}_{min}$ at a decreasing pace up to a maximum net welfare.

Figure A5.2 introduces the second assumption, that is, more plausible empirical functions for $f'(\bar{A})$ and $g'(\bar{A})$. Comparing Figs. A5.1 and A5.2, it appears that the intersection point $\bar{A}_x$ (the optimum) does not drastically shift given the above assumptions about the empirical shape of $f'(\bar{A})$ and $g'(\bar{A})$ as suggested in the form of initially flat and later steeply downward- and upward-moving functions. The social-welfare path is determined by the domain $\bar{A}_{min}$ and $\bar{A}_{max}$ rather than by great variations in the empirical shape of $f'(\bar{A})$ and $g'(\bar{A})$. Thus, the critical question is how the domain could be widened. The value for $\bar{A}_{min}$ naturally must remain constant unless the biological nature of man is changed (assuming the population structure to be constant). The focus, therefore, will be on $\bar{A}_{max}$. This brings into the picture P and k, as they determine social disutility along $\bar{A}$. The 'social optimum' at the intersection point is, thus, not 'unique' but has many historical configurations. Any increase in P will shift the $g'(\bar{A})$- or (in simplified notation) d'-curve upwards. The whole development process will be accompanied by higher marginal social disutilities (or lower net marginal social utility) as well as a lower value for the optimum point $\bar{A}_x$ and the maximum development point $\bar{A}_{max}$.[1]

In Fig. A5.2 a sequence of shifts in the d'-curve is depicted by $d'_*, \ldots, d'_1$. The intersection point $d'_* = du/d\bar{A}$ at $\bar{A}_*$ constitutes the absolute Malthusian trap. Any shift in A westward or eastward of A_* will threaten the survival of the population. In a dynamic context, population growth may either increase both social utility and social disutility or only increase social disutility without increasing or even decreasing social utility. The statement is immediately clear if we keep in mind that the percentage change in $\bar{A}$, specified, for example, as the percentage change in average income r_y, is approximated by the difference between the percentage change of the total income r_o and the percentage change of population r_p,[2]

$$r_y = r_o - r_p.$$

If $r_o > r_p$, or $r_y > 0$, the total social utility will increase (though at decreasing rates) and, simultaneously, the total social disutility will increase (at increasing rates). The higher levels of $\bar{A}$ partly offset the welfare loss due to increasing total social disutility by increasing total social utility. If $r_o \leq r_p$, or $r_y \leq 0$, only additional social disutilities accrue, without compensation by higher social utility. In Fig. A5.2, $\bar{A}_a$ remaining constant, the shift from d'_1 to d'_2 will increase the social disutility from d^*_a to d'_{aa} but leave social utility at u'_a. As an increase in $\bar{A}$ from $\bar{A}_a$ to $\bar{A}_b$ (due to a total income growth rate higher than the population growth rate) is accomplished, the difference in marginal social disutility will be higher, viz. from d'_b to d'_{bb}; but the utility increase due to $\bar{A}_b - \bar{A}_a$ compensates for this welfare loss, although at a rate falling from u'_a to u'_b. Although the second alternative is better in terms of the 'welfare flow' accomplished in the period needed to increase $\bar{A}$ from $\bar{A}_a$ to $\bar{A}_b$, the ultimate constraints set to $\bar{A}$ by worsening M^{aa}-ratios shift $\bar{A}_x$ from the initial value $\bar{A}_x$ to $\bar{A}'_x$. The relationship

$$r_o = r_y + r_p$$

says nothing about social disutility since it relies entirely on the economic and population systems, ignoring the ecosystem. Granted, for instance, that the 'minimum' level for r_y (assumed to initiate and sustain a developmental 'take-off') is reached, the development process will still impose higher social disutilities and may run into an impasse earlier, because of absolute constraints when P is increasing and establised at a high level. A rapidly increasing r_y becomes relevant, however, considering the empirically established negative correlation between r_p and the level of $\bar{A}$—a relationship discussed more fully in Ch. 15,VIII–IX.

Notes

Chapter 3

1. J. C. Smuts, *Holism and Evolution* (New York: Greenwood, 1961); J. W. Bews, *Human Ecology* (New York: Russell, 1935).
2. Webster's New International Dictionary, 2nd ed.
3. Ludwig von Bertalanffy, *General System Theory: Foundations, Development, Applications* (New York: Braziller, 1975) p. 38; George J. Klir, *An Approach to General Systems Theory* (New York: Van Nostrand, 1969). See pp. 50–1 for a list of 13 definitions of systems according to principal system traits; John P. van Gigch, *Applied General Systems Theory* (New York: Harper, 1974) p. 2 ff.
4. See, for instance, Kenneth E. Boulding, *Economic Development as an Evolutionary System*, Fifth World Congress of the International Economic Association, Tokyo, Aug.–Sept. 1977, mimeo.
5. The suggestion of conceiving a system in the form of simultaneous differential equations has been made by Bertalanffy, op. cit., p. 56 ff.
6. The system may be even said to be ahistorical. For instance, if $\alpha, \beta, \ldots, \mu$ are read as $\alpha_t, \beta_t, \ldots, \mu_t$, it does not matter what value, e.g. $\mu_{t-\Omega}$ assumed. Further discussion in Chapters 4,I and 4,II.

Chapter 4

1. For the major original contributions see Karl Marx, *Zur Kritik der Politischen Oekonomie* and *Das Kapital* (particularly first volume); Walt W. Rostow, *The Stages of Economic Growth: A Non-Communist Manifesto* (London: Cambridge University Press, 1960).
2. Gustav Ranis and John C. H. Fei, 'Agrarianism, Dualism and Economic Development', in Irma Adelman and Eric Thorbecke (eds), *The Theory and Design of Economic Development*, (Baltimore: Johns Hopkins University

Press, 1966) pp. 3–43. The authors conclude that 'what is ultimately needed is a new deterministic transition theory' (p. 40). For further discussion of this approach see Ch. 18,III.

3. Gerhard Tintner, J. K. Sengupta and E. J. Thomas, 'Applications of the Theory of Stochastic Processes to Economic Development', in *The Theory and Design*, op. cit., pp. 99–110.
4. On this point see, for instance, F. A. Hayek, 'The Theory of Complex Phenomena', in *Studies in Philosophy, Politics and Economics* (London: Routledge & Kegan Paul, 1967) pp. 22–42.
5. See, for instance, D. V. McGranahan, C. Richard-Proust, N. V. Sovani and M. Subramanian, *Contents and Measurement of Socio-Economic Development: An Empirical Enquiry* (Geneva: United Nations Research Institute for Social Development, 1970); R. Diaz, 'Myrdal's Mechanism of Underdevelopment and Development', UN Asian Institute for Economic Development and Planning, *Occasional Papers*, vol. 1, no. 2, (Bangkok: Dec. 1969) pp. 27–57.
6. The composite variable V_i implies a statement about the relative importance of the variables combined in V_i. Analogously, the minimum desiderata values m^* require that we have a scale based upon which the various composite variable sets can be measured, assessed, compared and added. A formal exposition of the evaluation problem will be given in the subsequent discussion of this chapter. A specific discussion of the evaluation of various variables (i.e. indicators) and of the relative importance of various variables against another will be given in part 2, ch. 11, and in part 3, Chapter 16. However, we may note, in anticipation of that discussion, that the evaluation problems are far from being solved in a satisfactory way and that theoretical constructs allowing a rational choice procedure await to be further developed.
7. Other terms have been suggested such as 'first floor' and 'second floor' desiderata or needs. For further discussion and for related literature see Chapter 16,II.
8. For further discussion see John Rawls, *A Theory of Justice* (London: Oxford University Press, 1971) p. 42.
9. We might argue that the survival of the total-system (human, ecological, etc., sub-systems) is a desideratum to be further discussed. However, instead of embarking on a philosophical discourse, we abbreviate the analytical procedure by simply explicitly stating our value premises which assume the desirability of the survival of the total-system.
10. For international comparisons of the development performance see *Contents and Measurements of Socio-Economic Development*, op. cit. (73 indicators); Hollis Chenery, *Targets for Development*, Economic Development Report no. 153, Cambridge, Mass., March 1970; Hiroshi Takamori and Shoichi Yamashita, 'Measuring Socio-Economic Development: Indicators, Development Paths and International Comparisons', in *The Developing Economies*, Vol. 11, no. 2 (Tokyo, June 1973) pp. 111–145.
11. As is apparent, a system may be a member of more than one level; the rationale will become clear as the study proceeds, i.e. as the single variables are related to another.
12. For instance, R. G. Wilkinson, *Poverty and Progress: an ecological model*

of economic development (London: Methuen, 1973); Albert Sasson, *Développement et environnement: Faits et perspectives dans les pays industrialisés et en voie de développement*, (The Hague, 1975); Urs Meier, *Oekologie und Entwicklungsländer* (Winterhur: Schellenberg, 1975).

13. For instance, Gunnar Myrdal, 'What is Development?' Paper for the volume in honour of the late Professor Ayres, n.d. mimeo; 'By development I mean the *movement upward of the entire social system* . . .'. (Orig. ital.) Dudley Seers, 'The Meaning of Development', *International Development Review*, Vol. 2, no. 11, Dec. 1969, pp. 2–6; 'What Are we Trying to Measure?' in Nancy Basters (ed.) *Measuring Development: The Rolé and Adequacy of Development Indicators* (London, Cass, 1972) pp. 21–36. Professor Seers stresses the importance of eradicating poverty and inequality.
14. See authors mentioned in footnote 13. For a view which stresses 'the more deeply human' aspects of concepts underlying development see Johan Galtung, 'Towards New Indicators of Development', *Futures*, June 1976, pp. 261–5. To do justice to the authors mentioned, i.e. not to categorise them as 'monistic thinkers' (which surely they are not!), it should be stressed that they do include usually all aspects mentioned, but that the emphasis given to them differs.

Chapter 6

1. Developing the function into a Taylor series

$$\frac{dS_n}{dt} = a_1 S_n + a_{11} S_n^2 + \cdots$$

we obtain two basic shapes which the function may take. Retaining the first term of the Taylor series we have

$$\frac{dS_n}{dt} = a_1 S_n,$$

which gives the solution

$$S_n = S_{n_0} e^{a_1 t}.$$

Using the previous notation, we have for the change of population

$$P = P_0 e^{r_p t},$$

where P_0 represents the initial population and r_p the relative rate of change of population (kept constant in the above differential notation, that is, $dP/dt \propto P \therefore dP/dt = c \cdot P$).

However, as was already understood in the 19th century, the above exponential growth path does not hold when applied to growth of a human population (or any other biological population) with limited resources.

Instead, a path must allow for the finite values of the related systems, for instance, the ecological system S_c. The general shape of the behaviour of a population subject to constraints imposed by the related systems can be obtained by retaining two terms of the Taylor series

$$\frac{dP}{dt} = a_1 P + a_{11} P^2.$$

where P is substituted for S_n.

The solution of this equation gives a logistic curve which describes the growth of a population as an exponential trend with a constant (or increasing) r_p up to a point of inflexion, and from this point on with a decreasing r_p. As $r_p \to 0$, $P \to S_c$ (in terms of maximum P supported by S_c), that is, S_c becomes the upper asymptote—a case where the limiting value is given by the maximum carrying capacity of the ecosystem. The sigmoid shape of the logistic curve is given by

$$P = \frac{S_c}{1 + P_0 e^{-r_p t}}$$

2. The subsequent discussion is based on data from T. H. Hollingsworth, 'Population Crisis in the Past', in Bernard Benjamin, Peter R. Cox and John Peel (eds) *Resources and Population* (London, Academic Press, 1973) pp. 99–108.
3. For problems concerning the timing of the Industrial Revolution see Paul Mantoux, *The Industrial Revolution in the Eighteenth Century: An Outline of the Beginnings of the Modern Factory System in England* (London: Methuen, 1970—first published 1928) p. 28.
4. C. Geertz, *Agricultural Involution: the Process of Ecological Change in Indonesia* (Berkeley: University of California Press, 1968); reprinted in Richard Jolly, Emanuel de Kadt, Hans Singer, and Fiona Wilson (eds) Third World Employment (Harmondsworth, Penguin Books, 1973) pp. 238–247.
5. An exception is Finland, with an average rate of 3 per cent in the years 1750–1800.

Chapter 8

1. A general statement of the hypothesis is given in Appendix III, 'Shifting production functions under finite resource constraints'.
2. J. J. Habakuk and M. Postan (eds), *Cambridge Economic History*, vol. 6, part 2 (London: Cambridge University Press, 1966) p. 614.
3. David Landes, 'Japan and Europe: Contrasts in Industrialisation', in William W. Lockwood (ed), *The State and Economic Enterprise in Japan* (Princeton University Press' 1965) p. 162.
4. For a classification of climate zones in Asia and their impact on soil conditions see Andrew M. Kamarck, *Climate and Economic Development*,

Economic Development Institute, International Bank for Reconstruction and Development, Seminar Paper No. 2, Washington, DC: 1972; and Gunnar Myrdal, *Asian Drama*, vol. 3 (Harmondsworth: Penguin Books, 1968) appendix 10, pp. 2121–38.

5. For a discussion of various methods of cultivation applied in Asian monsoon agriculture see Lucien M. Hanks, *Rice and Man: Agricultural Ecology in South-East Asia* (Cornell University Press, 1972).
6. As an example may serve the 'dry zone' around Pagan (Burma) where, for cultural reasons, large forests were slashed around AD 1100.
7. For the data mentioned and further data see E. C. J. Mohr, *The Soils of Equatorial Regions, with Special Reference to the Netherlands East Indies* (Ann Arbor: 1944).
8. 'Availability and Development of Natural Resources in the ESCAP Region', in *Report* and *Selected Papers* of the Regional Seminar on Ecological Implications of Rural and Urban Population Growth, Asian Population Studies Series, no. 10 (Bangkok: United Nations, 1972) pp. 66 and 67.
9. Ibid.

Chapter 9

1. The period of exhaustion may be postponed or perhaps never be reached if recycling constitutes a (technically and economically) feasible solution.
2. Yoichi Kaya and Yutaka Suzuki, *Global Constraints and New Vision for Development* (Tokyo, 1973) mimeo, pp. 8–9.
3. The 'technical' relationship between grade of mineral deposits and the cumulated tonnage of total reserves (at each grade of ore) may be expressed by the Lasky equation

$$\bigcirc = K_1 - K_2 \log \sum,$$

where $\bigcirc$ designates the grade of ore and $\sum$ the cumulated reserve above the grade of $\bigcirc$ (in percentages); K_1 and K_2 are constants to be determined for each deposit.

4. B. J. Skinner, *Earth Resources* (New York: Prentice-Hall, 1969); discussed in Kaya and Suzuki, op. cit., pp. 9 ff.
5. This implies, for instance, that in the future the average Asian grade of ores (not yet competitive) will match that of other mineral producers then being recovered and exploited.
6. *Report* and *Selected Papers* of the Regional Seminar on Ecological Implications of Rural and Urban Population Growth, Asian Population Studies Series, no. 10 (Bangkok: United Nations), pp. 68–70.
7. Y. Kaya and Y. Suzuki, op. cit., pp. 12–14.
8. *Population and Natural Resources*, symposium in Cairo, 1973, prepared by the United Nations Secretariat for the World Population Conference, 1974, preliminary text, pp. 4 and 5.
9. The figure of the ultimate reserves to which the estimate applies is $290 \cdot 10^9$ tons. The estimates are taken from 'Fuels for the Electric Utility Industry, 1971–1985: A Report of National Economic Research Associates to the

Edison Electric Institute, 1972', p. 3, cited in Van Ruyter de Steveninck, *Energy Consumption and Production: Trends and Forecasts*, 1973, mimeo, p. 9.
10. Bank of Indonesia, Jakarta, 1972; for the assessment of this and other resource problems the author benefited from his cooperation in a project for the Indonesian government (BAPPENAS) sponsored by the International Development Centre of Japan: the report has been published as *Study of Economic Development of Indonesia* (Tokyo, Overseas Technical Cooperation Agency, Government of Japan, 1973).
11. J. Darmstadter, 'Population, Resources and the Environment', *Population and the American Future*, vol. 3, 1972, pp. 108 ff.
12. Dennis Gabor, *The Fuel and Energy Crisis*, 1973, mimeo, p. 2.
13. Hubbert M. King, *Resources and Man*, 1969, p. 207.
14. J. W. Brinck, *Eurospectra X*, no. 2, 1971.
15. Steveninck, op. cit., p. 12.

Chapter 10

1. Shigeru Ishikawa, *Agricultural Development Strategies in Asia: Case Studies of the Philippines and Thailand* (Manila: 1970) Asian Development Bank, pp. 30–8. For further discussion on farm-scale size and agricultural ecosystem see Ch. 15.
2. *Environmental Costs and Priorities: a Study at Different Locations and Stages of Development*. United Nations Conference on the Human Environment (Paris: Mouton, 1972) pp. 141 ff.
3. 'Environmental Pollution and Rural and Urban Population Change', in *Report* and *Selected Papers* of The Regional Seminar on Ecological Implications of Rural and Urban Population Growth, Asian Population Studies, Series no. 10 (Bangkok: United Nations, 1971) pp. 121–3.
4. Ibid.
5. 'Man and Ecosystem', in *Report* and *Selected Papers*, op. cit., pp. 41–6.
6. For a first attempt to formulate minimum standards see *Document* of the United Nations Conference on the Human Environment, Stockholm, 1972.

Chapter 11

1. See, for instance, the recent study of 64 developed and less-developed countries in *Population Policies and Economic Development*, a World Bank Staff Report (Baltimore: Johns Hopkins University Press, 1974) pp. 144–5.
2. As suggested in the cited *Document* of The United Nations Conference on the Human Environment, Stockholm, 1972.
3. For a discussion of the problems of discounting future utilities under exhaustible-resource conditions see contributions in H. C. Bos, H. Linnemann, P. de Wolff (eds), *Economic Structure and Development: Essays in*

Honour of Jan Tinbergen (Amsterdam: North Holland Publishing Co., 1973).

Chapter 13

1. For an analytical account of the Malthusian 'low-trap-equilibrium' see the classic study by Harvey Leibenstein, *Economic Backwardness and Economic Growth* (New York: Wiley, 1957).
2. C. Geertz, *Agricultural Involution: the Processes of Ecological Change in Indonesia*, op. cit.
3. See Douglas S. Paauw and John C. H. Fei, *The Transition in Open Dualistic Economies: Theory and South-East Asian Experience.* (New Haven, Conn.: Yale University Press, 1973) pp. 57–76.
4. See Gunnar Myrdal, *Asian Drama*, op. cit., pp. 49–125.

Chapter 14

1. For classical contributions see, in particular, W. A. Lewis, 'Economic Development with Unlimited Supplies of Labour', in *The Manchester School*, vol. 22, May 1954, reprinted in A. N. Agarwala and S. P. Singh (eds), *The Economics of Underdevelopment* (London: Oxford University Press, 1971), pp. 400–49; Gustav Ranis and John C. H. Fei, 'A Theory of Economic Development', in *American Economic Review: Papers and Proceedings, Sept. 1961*, reprinted in Theodore Morgan and George W. Betz (eds.), *Economic Development*; (Belmont: Wadsworth, 1970) pp. 89–98; Gustav Ranis and John C. H. Fei, 'Agrarianism, Dualism, and Economic Development' in Irma Adelman and Eric Thorbecke (eds.), *The Theory and Design of Economic Development*, op. cit. pp. 3–43. For neoclassical contributions see, for instance, Dale W. Jorgenson, 'Testing Alternative Theories of the Development of a Dual Economy', ibid., pp. 45–60; id, 'The Role of Agriculture in Economic Development: Classical versus Neoclassical Models of Growth', in Clifton R. Wharton, Jr. (ed.), *Subsistence Agriculture and Economic Development* (Chicago: Aldine, 1970), pp. 320–48.
2. The neoclassicists argue that the capital-output ratio eventually becomes constant, since the rate of growth of output and the rate of growth of capital tend to the same limit.
3. See, particularly, Albert O. Hirschman, *The Strategy of Economic Development* (New Haven, Conn.: Yale University Press, 1958). The theory of pressure as stimulants of development has also been applied to the agricultural sector; for instance, Ester Boserup, *The Conditions of Agricultural Growth: The Economics of Agrarian Change Under Population Pressure* (London: Allen & Unwin, 1965); and Yujiro Hayami and Vernon W. Ruttan, *Agricultural Development: An International Perspective* (Baltimore: Johns Hopkins University Press, 1971), pp. 61–3.
4. This assumption is implied in both classical and neoclassical theories; an explicit statement can be found in Albert O. Hirschman, op. cit., pp. 35–40.

5. John Maynard Keynes, *Economic Consequences of the Peace* (1918) pp. 16–17, quoted in Joan Robinson, *Economics, An Awkward Corner* (London: Allen & Unwin, 1973) p. 12.
6. See David S. Landes, 'Japan and Europe: Contrasts in Industrialisation', in William W. Lockwood (ed), *The State and the Economic Enterprise in Japan* (Princeton University Press, 1965) pp. 100 ff.
7. See Alexander Gerschenkron, *Economic Backwardness in Historical Perspective* (Cambridge, Mass.: Harvard University Press, 1962) p. 16 ff.
8. *Second Malaysia Plan, 1971–75* (Kuala Lumpur: Government Printer, 1971) pp. 56–9 and 90–2.
9. *The Third Five-Year Economic Development Plan, 1972–76, Gov. of the Republic of Korea* (Seoul, 1971), pp. 13–14.
10. *National Income of Thailand, 1968–69* (Bangkok: Office of the National Economic Development Board, 1970) pp. 110–13.
11. *Four-Year Development Plan, 1974–77* (Manila: Republic of the Philippines, 1973) p. 107.
12. Arthur J. Taylor, *Laissez-faire and State Intervention in Nineteenth-century Britain* (London: Macmillan, 1972), pp. 60–4.
13. For a discussion on the British 'individualistic approach' see L. J. Zimmerman, *Poor Lands, Rich lands: the widening Gap* (New York: Random House, 1965) pp. 108–20.
14. On the role of French, Austrian and other European banks see Alexander Gerschenkron, *Economic Backwardness in Historical Perspective*, op. cit.
15. David S. Landes, 'Japan and Europe: Contrasts in Industrialisation', op. cit., pp. 94–6.
16. Despite the familiar consideration that 'poor people are too poor to be unemployed'.
17. A. Vaidyanathan, *Some Aspects of Inequalities in Living Standards in Rural India* (New Delhi: Planning Commission, 1971) p. 36 ff. Dandekar and Rath's survey supports, by and large, the above findings. They report that 10 per cent of India's rural poor have stayed where they were at the beginning of the 1960s, while the 10 per cent of the urban poor have definitely suffered; see V. M. Dandekar and N. Rath, 'Poverty in India: Dimensions and Trends', *Economic and Political Weekly*, vol. 6, 1971, pp. 39 and 40.

Chapter 15

1. Since savings are subtracted already, the propensity to consume is at unity, or $Y = C$.
2. For a quantitative account of the dual structure in Japan see, for instance, Takao Fukuchi and Noriyoshi Oguchi, 'The Trend of the Dual Structure and the Backwash Effect in Japan', *Economic Studies Quarterly*, vol. 23, no. 2, Aug. 1972, pp. 60–9.
3. For a reform policy which is replete with lofty but unfulfilled promises see J. Eliseo Rocamora, 'Rural Development Strategies: the Philippine Case', in *Approaches To Rural Development In Asia; the South-East Asian Experience*, vol. 2, Proceedings of a seminar organised by the Asian Centre for Development Administration, Kuala Lumpur, 1975, pp. 175–322.

4. For a related discussion see K. Dopfer, 'The Relationship between Population Growth and Economic Development: a Comparison between 18th- and 19th-Century Europe and Developing Countries Today', *Social Science Journal* (Tokyo), no. 12, May 1974, pp. 43–98.
5. N. K. S. Sarkar, *Industrial Structure of Greater Bangkok* (Bangkok: United Nations Asian Institute for Economic Development and Planning, 1974).
6. See J. Bhagwati and S. Chakravarty, 'Contributions to Indian Economic Analysis: a Survey', *American Economic Review*, part 2, supplement, vol. 59, Sept. 1969.
7. Includes not only the availability of adequate 'technology' but also information (newspaper circulation, TV, radio, etc.) and the capacity to pay the costs for a system of widely distributed family-planning stations.
8. For instance, in the previously mentioned *National Income Survey of Thailand*, the capital-output ratio stood at 1·65 in 1966 and at 3·98 in the following year, pp. 122–3.
9. Some positive effect on productivity may be gained by embodied technical progress, however.
10. The hypothetical projections are contained in Bruce F. Johnston, *Agriculture and Economic Development: The Relevance of the Japanese Experience*, Food Research Institute Studies, vol. 4, no. 3 (Stanford University, 1966), pp. 251 ff.
11. *Industrial Development, Asia and the Far East*, United Nations, vol. 1, pp. 149–55.
12. Sometimes the term crude activity rate (expressed usually as a percentage) is used instead. For clarification on terminology see various manuals of the United Nations, and of the International Labour Office, Geneva. An alternative measure is the dependency ratio, as stated earlier in the chapter on population; it is defined as population aged between 0–14 plus population above 65, divided by population between 15–64.
13. See, for instance, Douglas S. Paauw and John C. H. Fei, *The Transition in Open Dualistic Economies: Theory and South-East Asian Experience*, op. cit., p. 229.
14. A case in point is Malaysia. Land frontiers have hardly begun to be exploited; at the time of Malaysian independence in 1957, 78 per cent of land under cultivation was devoted exclusively to export crops and 67 per cent to the economy's major export, rubber; the percentages have not changed much within the last two decades; ibid., pp. 207–8.
15. B. S. Minhas, 'Rural Poverty, Land Redistribution and Economic Strategy', *Indian Economic Review*, vol. 5, April 1970, pp. 97–128.

Chapter 16

1. See in particular the contributions by Jan Tinbergen, e.g. his *Development Planning* (New York: World University Library, 1967).
2. See Amilcar O. Herrera, Hugo D. Scolnik *et al.*, *Catastrophe o Nueva Sociedad? Modelo Mundial Latinoamericano* (Fundacion Bariloche, 1977).

3. The works are, in alphabetical order: Irma Adelman and Cynthia Taft Morris, 'A Factor Analysis of the Interrelationship between Social and Political Variables and *Per Capita* Gross National Product', *Quarterly Journal of Economics*, vol. 79, pp. 555–78; Erik Allardt, 'A Welfare Model for Selecting Indicators of National Development', *Policy Sciences*, no. 4, 1973, pp. 63–74; David E. Christian, 'International Social Indicators: the OECD Experience', *Social Indicators Research*, vol. 1, no. 2, 1974; Jan Drewnowski, *On Measuring and Planning the Quality of Life* (The Hague: Mouton, 1974); J. Galtung *et al.*, 'Measuring World Development', *Alternatives*, no. 1, 1975, pp. 131–58 and 523–55; D. V. McGranahan *et al.*, *Contents and Measurement of Socio-Economic Development: an Empirical Study* (Geneva: United Nations Research Institute for Social Development, 1970); Shlomit Levy and Louis Guttman, 'On the Multivariate Structure of Well-Being', *Social Indicators Research*, vol. 2, 1975, pp. 361–88; Udo E. Simonis, 'Social Indicators for Development Planning', New Asia College Academic Annual, vol. 18, 1976, pp. 221–36; Hiroshi Takamori and Shoichi Yamashita, 'Measuring Socio-economic Development: Indicators, Development Paths, and International Comparisions', op. cit.; Laurence H. Tribe, 'Policy Science: Analysis or Ideology?', *Philosophy and Public Affairs*, vol. 1, no. 1, 1972, pp. 66–110, reprinted in Benefit-Cost and Policy Analysis, An Aldine Annual on Forecasting, Decision-Making and Evaluation (Chicago: Aldine, 1973).
4. For a comprehensive discussion see Montek S. Ahluwalia and Hollis Chenery, 'The Economic Framework', in *Redistribution with Growth*, Hollis Chenery, Montek S. Ahluwalia, C. L. G. Bell, John H. Duloy, Richard Jolly (eds.) (London: Oxford University Press, 1974) pp. 38–51.
5. *Energy and Protein Requirements*, Report of a Joint Food and Agriculture Organisation and World Health Organisation *ad hoc* Expert Committee (Rome: FAO, 1973).
6. See Amartya K. Sen, *Choice of Techniques* (Oxford: Blackwell, 1968); and A. S. Bhalla, 'Investment Allocation and Technological Choice', in *Economic Journal*, vol. 74, 1964, pp. 611 ff.; Gustav Ranis, *Employment and Income Distribution in Developing Countries*, IBRD Staff Working Paper no. 115 (Washington, D.C.: 1971), p. 15 ff.
7. A. S. Bhalla, 'Choosing Techniques: Handpounding vs. Machine Milling of Rice: an Indian Case', in *Oxford Economic Papers*, vol. 17, 1965, pp. 147–57. However, productivity measured in terms of output per hectare of land cultivated shows that small-scale farms are superior to large-scale farms; see, for instance, Dipak Mazumdar, 'Size of Farm and Productivity: a Problem of Indian Peasant Agriculture', *Economica*, vol. 32. On some problems related to statistical validity and significance see Amartya K. Sen, *Employment, Technology and Development* (Oxford, Clarendon Press, 1975) appendix C, pp. 146–51.
8. See Table 16.8.
9. See David Morawetz, *Employment Implications of Industrialisation in Developing Countries: a Survey*, IBRD Staff Working Paper no. 170 (Washington, D.C., 1974) pp. 17 ff.
10. Ronald Soligo, *Factor Intensity of Consumption Patterns, Income Distribution and Employment Growth in West Pakistan*, 1972, mimeo.

Chapter 17

1. Along this line Leibenstein has developed his new Micro-Micro Economics; see particularly his *Beyond Economic Man* (Harvard University Press, 1976) and 'Micro-Micro Theory, Agent-Agent Trade, and X-Efficiency, in *Economics in the Future*, op. cit., pp. 53–68.
2. Gustav Ranis and John C. H. Fei, 'Agrarianism, Dualism and Economic Development', in *The Theory and Design of Economic Development*, op. cit. See also discussion in Part I, Ch. 4; in particular, quotation in fn. 7.
3. For instance, Everett Hagen, *On the Theory of Social Change* (Homewood, Ill.: Dorsey Press, 1962).
4. David C. McClelland, *The Achieving Society* (Princeton University Press, 1962).
5. See for instance, Frederick G. Bailey, *Caste and the Economic Frontier* (Manchester University Press, 1957); Martin H. Ross, *Family Organisation and the Development of Agrarian Capitalism in a North Indian Village*, unpubld. Ph.D. thesis, University of Wisconsin, 1968, quoted in Joseph W. Elder, 'Cultural and Social Factors in Agricultural Development', in: Norman T. Uphoff and Warren F. Ilchman (eds.), *The Political Economy of Development* (Berkeley: University of California Press, 1972) pp. 46–54.
6. For instance, E. Boserup, op. cit.

Chapter 18

1. Although the development of indicators for political variables is still in its infancy, recent research has shown that, at least, there are no principal problems in quantifying and measuring political variables such as representation and participation. For a discussion on the application of indicators in the political contexts see, for instance, Irma Adelman and Cynthia Taft Morris, 'The Measurement of Institutional Characteristics of Nations: Methodological Considerations', in Nancy Baster (ed.), *Measuring Development*, op. cit., pp. 111—36; ibid., *Society, Politics and Economic Development* (Johns Hopkins University Press, 1967); Charles Lewis Taylor, 'Indicators of Political Development', in N. Baster (ed.), *Measuring Development*, op. cit., pp. 103–9. In the following discussion, emphasis will be on the theoretical delineation of the major causal relationships. Not all variables introduced will currently pass a rigorous test when subjected to the requirements of exact (or sufficiently exact) measurability; but as new theoretical constructs are suggested, further development of the statistical indicators and subsequent advances in the measurability of the yet little-considered 'soft' variables may be expected. It should be recalled that it took economists almost 200 years to develop a concept like the GNP, and that the methodological and practical problems with this central category are not diminished after half a century of its development.

   Furthermore, it should be noted that the relevance and validity of a theory when used for strategy purposes are not necessarily dependent on the possibility of exactly measuring it. Although improved measurement will be instrumental for further advances in theory, a successful application of an alternative strategy may not much depend on improvements in exact measurement. This point has been well understood in a recent ESCAP report: 'It is true that not enough is known about the precise relations between psychological, economic, social and political variables, but, to the extent that national goals can be approached through broadly participative processes, precise knowledge is not required. If the people are determining the processes, then they will presumably be shaping them on the basis of their own knowledge of themselves and their communities', cit. from *Review of the Economic and Social Situation in the ESCAP Region and Consideration of Action in Priority Areas* (Bangkok, 1974), pp. 27 and 28.

2. This proposition is in line with frequent demands made, for example, by the United Nations commission for the region, op. cit. Scholars concerned with development planning are increasingly stressing the need to 'redistribute' political representation and participation, delegating decision-making powers to the 'grass roots'; for instance, Albert Waterston, *Resolving the Three-Horned Planning Dilemma* (Washington, D.C., 1971), mimeo; furthermore, Inayatullah, 'A Proposed Conceptual Framework for the Study of Approaches to Rural Development in Asia', in *Approaches to Rural Development in Asia*, op. cit., pp. 1–24; see also other contributions in that volume.
3. For a discussion on 'political resources' see Norman T. Uphoff and Warren F. Ilchman, 'Development in the Perspective of Political Economy', in N. T. Uphoff and W. F. Ilchman (eds.), *The Political Economy of Development*, op. cit., pp. 75–121, particularly pp. 77–82.
4. For a similar (Marxist) view see Yujiro Hayami and Vernon W. Ruttan, *Agricultural Development: an International Perspective*, op. cit., pp. 53–63 and 258–73. See discussion in Ch. 17.
5. A measuring of I_a and I_e may first be attempted along the traditional lines of measurement. A crude indicator would be the average income, viz. in terms of income actually received and income desired. In a subsequent (preliminary) step we could speculate about the extent of dependency between the two variables. In a rare piece of empirical evidence, an Indian case study concludes that the relative increase in income desired (measured as percentage of income actually received) decreases as the income actually received increases, see H. Ganguli, 'Some Factors Influencing Income Aspirations', *Journal of Applied Psychology*, no. 41, 1957, pp. 32 ff.

   However, if the variables I_a and I_e are considered to be a principal driving force that generates political action and induces political change, we certainly must include further explanatory variables (besides income). This suggests that we will have to face the possibility of complex causal interactions among those variables. Hence, for the nature of the problem to be properly stated, the causal structure that allows the relevant causal interactions to be described would have to be further refined (see Fig. 18.2).

Appendix 2

1. The formal exposition suggested is reminiscent of the one used in control theory.

2. The principle of equifinality has been developed first in biology; see Bertalanffy, op. cit., p. 79.

Appendix 3

1. For simplicity, we assume that $r_p = c$ is equal for Asia and the Western countries. dt_A will further decrease as we allow for the fact that $r_{p_A} > r_{p_E}$.

Appendix 5

1. Of course, $\bar{A}_{max}$ sets a maximum only for the volume of activities; it is not necessarily an expression of the 'ultimate state' of a society. Once P and k impose constraints on $\bar{A}$, the social-utility curve may still be shifted upwards by improving the quality of life, by changes in the distribution of welfare entities among social groups (say by changes in income distribution), increasing non-material welfare entities, improvement in the utility derived from 'processes' such as leisure time and the working process (job satisfaction, etc.). Given the historical constraints for an increase in $\bar{A}$, contemporary Asian countries may have to increase the non-commodity-related welfare entities (in order to accomplish an increase in the welfare of their societies) at an earlier development level than did Europe, the United States or Japan.
2. Since we shall revert to this relationship in the later discussion, an explicit statement of the steps yielding this relationship shall be provided. Let the average activities $\bar{A}$ be specified as average income y, and Y and P represent total income and total population respectively. Then we have

$$Y = yP$$

and for the increase

$$Y + \Delta Y = (y + \Delta y)(P + \Delta P)$$
$$\Delta Y = yP + y\Delta P + P\Delta y + \Delta y\Delta P - yP.$$

We write for the relative change

$$\frac{\Delta Y}{Y} = \frac{y\Delta P}{Y} + \frac{P\Delta y}{Y} + \frac{\Delta y\Delta P}{Y},$$

and for the percentage change

$$\frac{100\Delta Y}{Y} = \frac{100\Delta P}{P} + \frac{100\Delta y}{y} + \frac{100\Delta y\Delta P}{yP}.$$

Since the last term is the product of two small increases, the result is negligible; so we drop the last term. We thus have the percentage increase in population plus the percentage increase in *per capita* income

$$\frac{100\Delta Y}{Y} = \frac{100\Delta P}{P} + \frac{100\Delta y}{y}$$

or

$$r_0 = r_p + r_y,$$

where r_0 stands for the percentage change in Y, r_p and r_y for the percentage changes of P and y respectively.

Bibliography

I. Adelman, *Theories of Economic Growth and Development* (Stanford University Press, 1961).

I. Adelman and C. T. Morris, 'A Factor Analysis of the Interrelationship between Social and Political Variables and *Per Capita* Gross National Product', *Quarterly Journal of Economics*, vol. 79.

I. Adelman and E. Thorbecke (eds), *The Theory and Design of Economic Development* (Baltimore: Johns Hopkins University Press, 1969).

A. N. Agarwala and S. P. Singh (eds), *The Economics of Underdevelopment* (London: Oxford University Press, 1971).

M. S. Ahluwalia, 'Inequality, Poverty, and Development', *Journal of Development Economics*, 3, 1976.

E. Allardt, 'A Welfare Model for Selecting Indicators of National Development', *Policy Sciences*, no. 4, 1973.

'Availability and Development of Natural Resources in the ESCAP Region', in *Report* and *Selected Papers* of the Regional Seminar on Ecological Implications of Rural and Urban Population Growth, Asian Population Studies Series, no. 10 (Bangkok: United Nations, 1972).

E. B. Ayal (ed.), *Micro-Aspects of Development*, Praeger Special Studies (New York: Praeger, 1973).

F. G. Bailey, *Caste and the Economic Frontier* (Manchester University Press, 1957).

P. Bairoch, *Le Tiers-Monde dans l'impasse: Le démarrage économique du XVIIIe au XX siècle* (Paris: Gallimard, 1971).

R. E. Baldwin, *Economic Development and Growth* (New York: Wiley, 1972).

P. K. Bardhan, 'On the Minimum Level of Living and the Rural Poor', *Indian Economic Review*, vol. 5, 1970.

N. Baster (ed), *Measuring Development: The Role and Adequacy of Development Indicators* (London: Frank Cass, 1972).

P. T. Bauer and B. S. Yamey, *The Economics of Under-Developed Countries*

(London: Cambridge University Press, 1959).
C. Bell, 'Production Conditions, Innovation and the Choice of Lease in Agriculture', Sankya C, 1976.
C. Bell, 'Alternative Theories of Sharecropping: Some Tests Using Evidence from Northwest India', *Journal of Development Studies*, 13, July 1977.
J. M. Bengoa, 'Recent Trends in Public Health Nutrition', Protein-Calorie Malnutrition Proceedings of 8th International Congress on Nutrition, Prague, 1969, reprinted in *Excerpta Medica*, International Congress Series, no. 213.
B. Benjamin, P. R. Cox and J. Peel (eds), 'Resources and Population, Proceedings of the 9th Annual Symposium of the Eugenics Society, London, 1972' (London: Academic Press, 1973).
R. A. Berry and A. Soligo, 'Rural-Urban Migration, Agricultural Output and the Supply Price of Labour in a Labour Surplus Economy, *Oxford Economic Papers*, vol. 20, 1968.
L. von Bertalanffy, *General System Theory: Foundations Development, Applications* (New York: Braziller, 1975).
J. W. Bews, *Human Ecology* (New York: Russell, 1935).
A. Bhaduri, 'Agricultural Backwardness under Semi-Feudalism', *Economic Journal*, vol. 83, Mar. 1973.
J. Bhagwati and S. Chakravarty, 'Contributions to Indian Economic Analysis: a Survey', *American Economic Review*, part 2, supplement, vol. 59, Sept. 1969.
A. S. Bhalla, 'Choosing Techniques: Handpounding vs. Machine Milling of Rice: an Indian Case', in *Oxford Economic Papers*, vol. 17, 1965.
M. Bhattacharya, 'Urbanisation and Policy Intervention in India', in T. Ichinose (ed), *Asia Urbanising*.
M. H. Billings and A. Singh, 'Mechanisation and Rural Employment with some Implications for Rural Income Distribution, *Economic and Political Weekly*, vol. 5, no. 27, June 1970.
H. C. Binswanger *et al.*, *Die Wohlstandsfalle* (Frankfurt-am-Main: Fischer-Verlag, 1978).
E. Boserup, *The Conditions of Agricultural Growth: the Economics of Agrarian Change under Population Pressure* (London: Allen & Unwin, 1965).
K. E. Boulding, *Economic Development as an Evolutionary System*, Fifth World Congress of the International Economic Association, Tokyo, Aug.–Sept. 1977, mimeo.
J. W. Brinck, *Eurospectra X*, no. 2, 1971.
P. R. Brahmananda, *Explorations in the New Classical Theory of Political Economy* (Bombay: Allied Publishers, 1974).
H. S. Brown, *et al.*, *The Next Hundred Years* (London: Weidenfeld & Nicolson, 1957).
H. J. Bruton, 'Economic Development and Labour Use: A Review', *World Development*. vol. 1, no. 12, Dec. 1973.
P. Chattopadhyay, 'Mode of Production in Indian Agriculture', *Economic and Political Weekly*, 1972.
H. B. Chenery, 'Comparative Advantage and Development Policy', *American Economic Review*, vol. 51, 1961.
H. B. Chenery and M. Syrquin, *Patterns of Development, 1950–1970*, A World Bank Research Publication (London: Oxford University Press, 1975).

H. B. Chenery and L. Taylor, 'Development Patterns Among Countries and Over Time', *Review of Economics and Statistics*, no. 50, Nov., 1968.
K. R. Chopra, *Dualism and Investment Patterns* (Bombay: McGraw-Hill, 1972).
D. E. Christian, 'International Social Indicators: the OECD Experience', *Social Indicators Research*, vol. 1, no. 2, 1974.
C. Clague, 'Capital-Labour Substitution in Developing Countries', *Econometrica*, vol. 37, 1969.
C. Clark, *The Conditions of Economic Progress* (London: Macmillan, 1957).
S. I. Cohen, *Production, Manpower and Social Planning* (Rotterdam: Universitaire Pers, 1975).
Comparative Study of Mortality Trends in ECAFE (ESCAP) Countries, United Nations, ESCAP, Asian Population Studies Series, no. 14 E/CN./11/1108 (Bangkok: United Nations, 1973).
J. Cravioto *et al.*, 'Nutrition, Growth and Neurological Development: An Experimental and Ecologic Study', *Journal of Pediatrics*, vol. 38, no. 2, suppl. 2, Aug. 1966.
H. E. Daly, 'A Marxian-Malthusian View of Poverty and Development', *Population Studies*, Mar. 1971, pp. 25–37.
V. M. Dandekar and N. Rath, 'Poverty in India: Dimensions and Trends, *Economic and Political Weekly*, vol. 6, 1971.
J. Darmstadter, 'Population, Resources and the Environment', in *Population and the American Future*, vol. 3, 1972.
A. K. Dasgupta, *Economic Theory and Developing Countries* (London: Macmillan, 1970).
A. K. Dasgupta, *Planning and Economic Growth* (London: Allen & Unwin, 1965).
B. Dasgupta, 'Calcutta's Informal Sector', *Bulletin of the Institute of Development Studies*, 5, 1973.
P. Deane and W. A. Cole, *British Economic Growth, 1688–1959* (London: Cambridge University Press, 1962).
Demographic Situation in Relation to Factors Effecting Population Change, Second Asian Population Conference. United Nations, Tokyo, 1972 (United Nations publication, POP/APC.2/BP/1, 1972).
R. Diaz, 'Myrdal's Mechanism of Underdevelopment and Development', UN Asian Institute for Economic Development and Planning, *Occasional Papers*, vol. 1, no. 2 (Bangkok: Dec. 1969).
Document of the United Nations Conference on the Human Environment, Stockholm, 1972.
K. Dopfer (ed), *Economics in the Future* (London: Macmillan, 1976).
K. Dopfer, 'The Relationship between Population Growth and Economic Development: a Comparison between 18th- and 19th-Century Europe and Developing Countries Today,' *Social Science Journal* (Tokyo), no. 12, May 1974.
P. Dorner, *Land Reform and Economic Development* (Baltimore: Penguin Books, 1972).
J. Drewnowski, *On Measuring and Planning the Quality of Life* (The Hague: Mouton, 1974).
R. S. Eckaus, 'The Factor-Proportions Problem in Underdeveloped Areas',

American Economic Review, vol. 65, 1955.

E. O. Edwards (ed), *Employment in Developing Nations*, Report on a Ford Foundation Study (New York: Columbia University Press, 1974).

J. W. Elder, 'Cultural and Social Factors in Agricultural Development', in N. T. Uphoff and W. F. Ilchman (eds), *The Political Economy of Development* (Berkeley: University of California Press, 1972).

R. J. Eliseo, 'Rural Development Strategies: the Philippine Case', in *Approaches to Rural Development in Asia: the South-East Asian Experience*, vol. 2 (Kuala Lumpur: Asian Centre for Development Administration, 1975).

Energy and Protein Requirements, Report of a Joint Food and Agricultural Organisation and World Health Organisation ad hoc Expert Committee (Rome: FAO, 1973).

Environmental Costs and Priorities: a Study at Different Locations and Stages of Development, United Nations Conference on the Human Environment (Paris: Mouton, 1972).

'Environmental Pollution and Rural and Urban Population Change', in *Report* and *Selected Papers* of the Regional Seminar on Ecological Implications of Rural and Urban Population Growth, Asian Population Studies Series, no. 10 (Bangkok: United Nations, 1971).

G. Etienne (ed), *India's Agricultural Development*, Special Issue of Studies and Documents, Graduate Institute of International Studies (Geneva: 1975).

G. Etienne, *Bangladesh: Development in Perspective* (Geneva: Asian Center, 1977).

W. P. Falcon, 'The Green Revolution: Generations of Problems', *American Journal of Agricultural Economics*, vol. 52, 1970.

J. C. H. Fei and G. Ranis, *Development of the Labour Surplus Economy: Theory and Policy* (Homewood, Ill.: Irwin, 1964).

G. S. Fields, 'Rural-Urban Migration, Urban Unemployment and Underemployment, and Job-Search Activity in LDCs', *Journal of Development Economics*, 2, 1975.

R. F. Florentino, 'Energy Requirements of Filipinos', *Philippine Journal of Nutrition*, Jan.–June 1966.

Food Habits in Calcutta (Calcutta: Hindustan Thompson Associates, 1972).

Four-Year Development Plan, 1974–77, Republic of the Philippines (Manila: 1973).

T. Frejka, *Alternatives of World Population Growth* (New York: Population Council, 1973) monograph.

B. Frey, *Moderne Politische Oekonomie* (Munich: Piper-Verlag, 1977).

E. Friedmann and M. Selden (eds), *America's Asia: Dissenting Essays on Asian-American Relations* (New York: Random House, 1971).

B. Fritsch, *Die vierte Welt: Modell einer neuen Wirklichkeit* (Munich: Deutscher Taschenbuch-Verlag, 1970).

T. Fukuchi and N. Oguchi, 'The Trend of the Dual Structure and the Backwash effect in Japan', *Economic Studies Quarterly*, vol. 23, no. 2, Aug. 1972.

D. Gabor, *The Fuel and Energy Crisis* (1973) mimeo.

W. Galenson and H. Leibenstein, 'Investment Criteria, Productivity and Economic Development', *Quarterly Journal of Economics*, vol. 80, 1955.

J. Galtung, 'Towards New Indicators of Development', *Futures*, June 1976.

J. Galtung *et al.*, 'Measuring World Development', *Alternatives*, no. 1, 1975.

H. Ganguli, 'Some Factors Influencing Income Aspirations', *Journal of Applied Psychology*, no. 41, 1957.
C. Geertz, *Agricultural Involution: the Processes of Ecological Change in Indonesia* (Berkeley: University of California Press, 1968).
N. Georgescu-Roegen, 'Economic Theory and Agrarian Reforms', *Oxford Economic Papers*, vol. 12, 1960.
A. Gerschenkron, *Economic Backwardness in Historical Perspective* (Cambridge, Mass: Harvard University Press, 1962).
D. V. Glass, 'A Note on the Under-Registration of Births in Britain in the Nineteenth Century', *Population Studies*, vol. 5, no. 1, 1951–2.
D. V. Glass and D. E. C. Eversley (eds), *Population in History: Essays in Historical Demography* (London: Edward Arnold, 1974).
K. Gough and H. P. Sharma, *Imperialism and Revolution in South Asia* (New York: Monthly Review Press, 1973).
J. D. Gould, *Economic Growth in History* (London: Methuen, 1972).
K. Griffin, *The Green Revolution: an Economic Analysis* (Geneva: United Nations Research Institute for Social Development, 1972).
A. Guha, 'Accumulation, Innovation and Growth under Conditions of Disguised Unemployment', *Oxford Economic Papers*, vol. 21, 1969.
S. K. Gupta, *Economic Aspects of Urbanization*, Indian Council of Social Sciences Research (Bombay: Bank of India, 1975), mimeo.
J. G. Gurley, 'Capitalist and Maoist Economic Development, in *America's Asia: Dissenting Essays on Asian-American Relations* (New York: Random House, 1971).
J. J. Habakuk, *American and British Technology in the Nineteenth Century* (London: Cambridge University Press, 1962).
J. J. Habakuk and M. Postan (eds), *Cambridge Economic History*, vol. 4 (London: Cambridge University Press, 1966).
E. Hagen, *On the Theory of Social Change* (Homewood, Ill.: Dorsey Press, 1962).
L. M. Hanks, *Rice and Man: Agricultural Ecology in South-East Asia* (Chicago: Aldine, 1972).
B. Hansen, *Long- and Short-Term Planning in Underdeveloped Countries* (Amsterdam: North-Holland, 1972).
M. Haq, ul, *The Poverty Curtain: Choices for the Third World* (New York: Columbia University Press, 1976).
A. C. Harberger, 'On Measuring the Social Opportunity Cost of Labour', *International Labour Review*, vol. 103, 1971.
J. R. Harris and M. P. Todaro, 'Migration, Unemployment and Development: a Two-Sector Analysis', *American Economic Review*, vol. 60, March 1970.
J. A. Hauser, Bevölkerungsprobleme der Dritten Welt (Berne: 1976).
Y. Hayami and V. W. Ruttan, *Agricultural Development: an International Perspective* (Baltimore: Johns Hopkins University Press, 1971).
F. A. Hayek, 'The Theory of Complex Phenomena', in *Studies in Philosophy, Politics and Economics* (London: Routledge & Kegan Paul, 1967).
Health, Sector Policy Paper (World Bank, 1975).
A. O. Herrera *et al.*, *Catastrophe o Nueva Sociedad? Modelo Mundial Latinoamericano* (Fundacion Bariloche, 1977).
B. Higgins, *Economic Development: Problems, Principles and Policies* (New

York: Norton, 1968).
A. O. Hirschman, *The Strategy of Economic Development* (New Haven, Conn.: Yale University Press, 1958).
T. H. Hollingsworth, 'Population Crisis in the Past', in B. Benjamin, P. R. Cox and J. Peel (eds), *Resources and Population* (London: Academic Press, 1973).
M. R. Hollnsteiner, 'Manila: the Face of Poverty', in T. Ichinose (ed), *Asia Urbanising* op. cit.
J. M. Horby, 'Investment and Trade Policy in the Dual Economy', *Economic Journal*, vol. 78, 1968.
M. Hug, *Education, Manpower and Development in South and South-East Asia* (New York: Praeger, 1975).
S. Hymer and S. Resnick, 'A Model of an Agrarian Economy with Non-Agricultural Activities', *American Economic Review*, Sept. 1969.
T. Ichinose, *Asia Urbanising: Population Growth, Concentration; and the Problems Thereof* (Tokyo: Simul Press, 1976).
Income Distribution, Employment and Economic Development in South-East and East Asia, vols 1–2 (Tokyo: Japan Economic Research Center; Manila: Council for Asian Manpower Studies, 1975).
Industrial Development: Asia and the Far East (Bangkok: United Nations, 1971).
S. Ishikawa, *Agricultural Development Strategies in Asia: Case Studies of the Philippines and Thailand* (Manila: Asian Development Bank 1970).
S. Ishikawa, *Economic Development in Asian Perspective* (Tokyo: Kinokuniya, 1967).
S. Ishikawa and K. Ohkawa, 'Significance of Japan's Experience: Technological Changes in Agricultural Production and Changes in Agrarian Structure', *Agriculture and Economic Development* (Tokyo: Japan Economic Research Centre, 1972).
D. G. Johnson, 'Resource Allocation under Share Constraints', *Journal of Political Economy*, vol. 58, 1972.
B. R. Johnston, *Agriculture and Economic Development: the Relevance of the Japanese Experience*, Food Research Institute Studies, vol. 4, no 3 (Stanford University, 1966).
R. Jolly, E. de Kadt, H. Singer and F. Wilson (eds), *Third World Employment: Problems and Strategy* (Harmondsworth: Penguin Books, 1973).
R. Jolly, 'The World Employment Conference: The enthronement of basic needs', *Overseas Development Institute Review*, 1976.
D. W. Jorgenson, 'The Role of Agriculture in Economic Development: Classical versus Neoclassical Models of Growth', in *Subsistence Agriculture and Economic Development*, R. Clifton Wharton, Jr. (ed) (Chicago: Aldine, 1970).
D. W. Jorgenson, 'Testing Alternative Theories of the Development of a Dual Economy', in I. Adelman and E. Thorbecke (ed), *The Theory and Design of Economic Development* (Baltimore: Johns Hopkins University Press, 1966).
D. W. Jorgenson and L. J. Lau, *An Economic Theory of Agricultural Household Behaviour* (Tokyo: Econometric Society, 1969).
A. M. Kamarck, *Climate and Economic Development*, Economic Development Institute, International Bank for Reconstruction and Development, Seminar Paper no. 2 (Washington, DC: 1972).

C. H. C. Kao, K. R. Anschel and E. K. Eicher, 'Disguised Unemployment in Agriculture', in C. K. Eicher and L. Witt (eds), *Agriculture in Economic Development* (New York: McGraw-Hill, 1964).

G. Kay, *Development and Underdevelopment: a Marxist Analysis* (London: Macmillan, 1975).

Y. Kaya and Y. Suzuki, *Global Constraints and New Vision for Development* (Tokyo, 1973) mimeo.

A. C. Kelley, J. G. Williamson and R. J. Cheetham, *Dualistic Economic Development: Theory and History* (University of Chicago Press, 1972).

A. C. Kelly and J. G. Williamson, 'Sources of Growth Methodology in Low-Income Countries: a Critique', *Quarterly Journal of Economics*, vol. 87, no. 1, 1973.

J. M. Keynes, *Economic Consequences of the Peace*, 1918.

P. Kilby (ed), *Entrepreneurship and Economic Development* (New York: Free Press, 1971).

C. P. Kindleberger, *Economic Development* (New York: McGraw-Hill, 1965).

G. J. Klir, *An Approach to General Systems Theory* (New York: Van Nostrand, 1969).

Medhi-Krongkaew, 'The Determination of the Poverty Band in Thailand', (Bangkok: Thammasat University, Discussion Paper Series, Nr 64).

J. A. Kregel, *The Reconstruction of Political Economy: an Introduction to Post-Keynesian Economics* (London: Macmillan, 1973).

D. Kumar, 'Technical Change and Dualism within Agriculture in India', *Journal of Development Studies*, vol. 7, 1970.

J. H. Kunkel, *Society and Economic Growth* (London: Oxford University Press, 1970).

S. Kuznets, *Modern Economic Growth* (New Haven, Conn: Yale University Press, 1969).

D. S. Landes, 'Japan and Europe: Contrasts in Industrialisation', in W. W. Lockwood (ed), *The State and Economic Enterprise in Japan* (Princeton University Press, 1965).

L. Lefeber, 'Planning in a Surplus Labour Economy', *American Economic Review*, vol. 58, 1968.

L. Lefeber and M. Datta Chaudhuri, *Regional Development Experience and Prospects in South and South-East Asia* (The Hague: Mouton, 1971).

A. D. Lehmann (ed), *Agrarian Reform and Agrarian Reformism* (London: Faber, 1974).

H. Leibenstein, 'Micro-Micro Theory, Agent-Agent Trade, and X-Efficiency', in K. Dopfer (ed.), *Economics in the Future* (London: Macmillan, 1976).

H. Leibenstein, *Beyond Economic Man* (Cambridge, Mass.: Harvard University press, 1976).

H. Leibenstein, 'Allocative Efficiency vs. X-Efficiency', *American Economic Review*, vol. 56, 1966.

H. Leibenstein, *Economic Backwardness and Economic Growth* (New York: Wiley, 1957).

H. Leibenstein, *A Theory of Economic-Demographic Development* (Princeton University Press, 1954).

K. Leisinger, *Arbeitslosigkeit, Direktinvestitionen und angepasste Technologie* (Berne/Stuttgart: Verlag Paul Haupt, 1975).

S. Levy and L. Guttman, 'On the Multivariate Structure of Well-Being', *Social Indicators Research*, vol. 2, 1975.
W. A. Lewis, *Theory of Economic Growth* (London: Allen & Unwin, 1970).
W. A. Lewis, 'Economic Development with Unlimited Supplies of Labour', in *The Manchester School*, vol. 22, May 1954.
H. C. Linnemann, H. Bos and P. de Wolff (eds), *Economic Structure and Development: Essays in Honour of Jan Tinbergen* (Amsterdam: North Holland, 1973).
W. W. Lockwood (ed), *The State and Economic Enterprise in Japan* (Princeton University Press, 1965).
W. W. Lockwood, *The Economic Development of Japan: Growth and Structural Change, 1868–1938* (Princeton University Press, 1954).
D. C. McClelland, *The Achieving Society* (Princeton University Press, 1962).
D. V. McGranahan *et al.*, *Contents and Measurement of Socio-Economic Development: an Empirical Enquiry* (Geneva: United Nations Research Institute for Social Development, 1970).
F. Machlup, *Issues in Economic Semantics* (New York University Press, 1975).
M. Mangahas, 'Income Inequality in the Philippines; a Decomposition Analysis', in *Income Distribution, Employment and Economic Development in South-East and East Asia*, vol. 1 (Tokyo: Japan Economic Research Centre; Manila: Council for Asian Manpower Studies, 1975).
Manpower and Employment in the Context of Economic Development, International Labour Organisation, Second Asian Population Conference, Tokyo, 1972.
P. Mantoux, *The Industrial Revolution in the Eighteenth Century: an Outline of the Beginnings of the Modern Factory System in England* (London: Methuen, 1970).
K. Marsden, 'Toward a Synthesis of Economic Growth and Social Justice', *International Labour Review*, vol. 100, 1969.
D. Mazumdar, 'Size of Farm and Productivity: a Problem of Indian Peasant Agriculture', *Economica*, vol. 32.
G. M. Meier (ed.), *Leading Issues in Development Economics*: Studies in International Poverty (Oxford University Press, 1970).
G. M. Meier and R. E. Baldwin, *Economic Development: Theory, History, Policy* (New York: John Wiley, 1960).
U. Meier, *Oekologie und Entwicklungsländer* (Winterthur: Schellenberg, 1975).
J. W. Mellor, *The New Economics of Growth: a Strategy for India and the Developing World* (Cornell University Press, 1976).
J. W. Mellor, 'The Use and Productivity of Farm Family Labour in Early Stages of Agricultural Development', *Journal of Farm Economics* (Cornell University Press), vol. 45, 1963.
R. F. Mikesell and J. E. Zinser, 'The Nature of Savings Function in Developing Countries: a Survey of the Theoretical and Empirical Literature', *Journal of Economic Literature*, no. 11, 1973.
B. S. Minhas, 'Rural Poverty, Land Redistribution and Development Strategy', *Indian Economic Review*, vol. 5, 1970.
B. R. Mitchell and P. Deane, *Abstract of British Historical Statistics* (London: Cambridge University Press, 1962).
E. C. J. Mohr, *The Soils of Equatorial Regions, with Special Reference to the*

Netherlands East Indies (Ann Arbor, 1944).
D. Morawetz, *Employment Implications of Industrialisation in Developing Countries: a Survey*, IBRD Staff Working Paper no. 170 (Washington, DC, 1974), mimeo.
T. Morgan and G. W. Betz (eds.), *Economic Development* (Belmont: Wadsworth, 1970).
A. T. Mosher, *Creating a Progressive Rural Structure to serve a Modern Agriculture* (New York: Agricultural Development Council, 1969).
H. Myint, *The Economics of the Developing Countries* (New York: Praeger, 1971).
G. Myrdal, *Economic Theory and Underdeveloped Regions* (New York: Harper, 1971).
G. Myrdal, *Asian Drama: an Inquiry into the Poverty of Nations*, vols. 1–3 (Harmondsworth: Penguin Books, 1968).
G. Myrdal, *What is Development?* Paper in honour of the late Professor Ayres, n.d., mimeo.
National Accounts and Development Planning in Low-Income Countries (Paris: OECD, 1974).
National Income of Thailand, 1968–69 (Office of the National Economic Development Board, Bangkok, 1970).
D. M. G. Newbery, 'Public Policy in the Dual Economy', *Economic Journal*, vol. 82, 1972.
D. Nohlen and F. Nuscheler (eds.), *Handbuch der Dritten Welt*, 4 vols. (Frankfurt: Hoffmann, 1974).
G. Ohlin, *Population Control and Economic Development* (Paris: OECD, 1967).
J. K. Onoh, *Strategic Approaches to Crucial Policies in Economic Development* (Rotterdam University Press, 1972).
H. T. Oshima, 'Labour Absorption in East and South-East Asia: a Summary with Interpretation of Postwar Experience', *Malayan Economic Review*, 1971.
H. T. Oshima, *Seasonality, Under-Employment and Growth in South-East Asian Countries*, Technology and Development Institute, East-West Centre, University of Hawaii, 1971, mimeo.
H. T. Oshima, 'Food Consumption, Nutrition and Economic Development in Asian Countries', in: *Economic Development and Cultural Change*, vol. 15, no. 4.
H. Ōtsuka, 'Modernisation Reconsidered, with Special Reference to Industrialisation', in S. Tobata (ed.) *The Modernisation of Japan* (Tokyo: Maruzen, 1966).
D. S. Paauw and J. C. H. Fei, *The Transition in Open Dualistic Economies:* Theory and South-East Asian Experience (Yale University Press, 1973).
I. Palmer, *Food and the New Agricultural Technology* (Geneva: United Nations Research Institute for Social Development, 1972).
G. F. Papanek, 'Economic Growth, Income Distribution, and the Political Process in Less Developed Countries', in Z. Griliches, *et al.* (eds.), *Income Distribution and Economic Inequality* (forthcoming).
G. F. Papanek, 'Growth, Income Distribution and Policies in Less Developed Countries', in Y. Ramati (ed.), *Economic Growth in Developing Countries* (New York: Praeger, 1975).

F. Paukert, 'Income Distribution at Different Levels of Development: a Survey of Evidence', *International Labour Review*, no. 108, 2–3, 1973.

H. B. Peter and J. A. Hauser (eds.), *Entwicklungsprobleme-Interdisziplinär* (Berne/Stuttgart: Verlag Paul Haupt, 1976).

Population and Natural Resources, Symposium in Cairo, 1973, Preliminary Text for the World Population Conference, United Nations, 1974.

Population Aspects of Social Development, Asian Population Studies Series, no. 11 (Bangkok: United Nations, 1972).

Population Policies and Economic Development, a World Bank Staff Report (Baltimore: Johns Hopkins University Press, 1974).

E. Quiogue *et al.*, 'Nutrition Survey of Eight Regions in the Philippines-Dietary Phase', *Philippine Journal of Nutrition*, vol. 22, 1969.

G. Ranis, *Employment and Income Distribution in Developing Countries*, IBRD Staff Working Paper no. 115 (Washington, DC: 1971).

G. Ranis and J. C. H. Fei, 'Agrarianism, Dualism and Economic Development', in I. Adelman and E. Thorbecke (eds.), *The Theory and Design of Economic Development* (Baltimore: Johns Hopkins University Press, 1966).

G. Ranis and J. C. H. Fei, 'A Theory of Economic Development', *American Economic Review: Papers and Proceedings*, Sept. 1961.

W. Rasaputram, 'Changes in the Pattern of Income Inequality in Ceylon', *Marga* 1: 4, 1972.

J. Rawls, *A Theory of Justice* (London: Oxford University Press, 1971).

Report and *Selected Papers* of the Regional Seminar on Ecological Implications of Rural and Urban Population Growth, Asian Population Studies Series, no. 10 (Bangkok: United Nations, 1971).

S. Reutlinger and M. Selowsky, *Undernutrition and Poverty*, IBRD Staff Working Paper no. 202 (Washington, DC: 1975).

L. G. Reynolds (ed.), *Agriculture in Development Theory* (New Haven: Yale University Press).

P. Richards, 'Poverty, Unemployment and Underemployment', in *Tripartite World Conference on Employment, Income Distribution and Social Progress and the International Division of Labour*, vol. 1 (Geneva: International Labour Office, 1976).

J.-P. Rioux, *La revolution industrielle, 1780–1880* (Paris: Éditions du Seuil, 1971).

C. H. Ro, 'The Seoul Phenomenon', in T. Ichinose (ed.) *Asia Urbanising*, op. cit.

J. Robinson, *Economics: an Awkward Corner* (London: Allen & Unwin, 1973).

M. Rokeach, *The Nature of Human Values* (New York: Free Press, 1973).

M. H. Ross, *Family Organisation and the Development of Agrarian Capitalism in a North Indian Village*, unpubl. Ph.D. thesis, University of Wisconsin, 1968.

W. W. Rostow, *The Stages of Economic Growth: a Non-Communist Manifesto* (London: Cambridge University Press, 1960).

Y. Sabolo, 'Sectoral Employment Growth: the Outlook for 1980', *International Labour Review*, vol. 3, no. 5, Nov. 1969.

U. Sandmeyer, *Wahl der industriellen Technologie in Entwicklungsländern* (Diesenhofen: Rügger, 1976).

N. K. S. Sarkar, *Industrial Structure of Greater Bangkok* (Bangkok: United Nations Asian Institute for Economic Development and Planning, 1974).

A. Sasson, *Développement et environment: Faits et perspectives dans les pays industrialisés et en voie de développement* (The Hague: 1975).
A. Sauvy, *General Theory of Population* (London: Methuen, 1974).
S. Schiavo-Campo and H. W. Singer, *Perspectives of Economic Development* (Boston: Houghton Mifflin, 1970).
Second Asian Population Conference, *Population and Food Supply in Asia*, Background Paper, Tokyo, 1972.
Second Malaysia Plan, 1971–75 (Kuala Lumpur: Government Printer, 1971).
D. Seers, 'The Meaning of Development', *International Development Review*, vol. 2, no. 4, Dec. 1969.
T. W. Schultz, *Transforming Traditional Agriculture* (New Haven: Yale University Press, 1964).
M. Selowsky and L. Taylor, 'The Economics of Malnourished Children: an Example of Disinvestment in Human Capital', in *Economic Development and Cultural Change*, vol. 2, no. 1, 1973.
A. Sen, *Employment, Technology and Development, prepared for the International Labour Office* (Oxford: Clarendon Press, 1975).
A. Sen, *Choice of Techniques* (Oxford: Basil Blackwell, 1968).
D. Senghaas, *Weltwirtschaftsordnung und Entwicklungspolitik, Plädoyer für Dissoziation* (Frankfurt-am-Main: Suhrkamp, 1977).
E. S. Shaw, *Financial Deepening in Economic Development* (London: Oxford University Press, 1973).
A. M. Sierers, *The Mystical World of Indonesia* (Baltimore: Johns Hopkins University Press, 1974).
H. Simonis and U. E. Simonis, *Japan* (Wiesbaden: Otto Harrassowitz, 1974).
U. E. Simonis, 'Social Indicators for Development Planning', *New Asia College Academic Annual*, vol. 18, 1976.
H. W. Singer, 'Appropriate Technology for a Basic Human Needs Strategy', *International Development Review*, vol. 19, no. 2, 1977.
H. W. Singer, *Technologies for Basic Needs* (Geneva: I.L.O., 1977).
R. Sinha, Competing Ideology and Agricultural Strategy; Current Agricultural Development in India and China compared with Meiji Strategy', *World Development*, vol. 1, no. 6, 1973.
B. J. Skinner, *Earth Resources* (New York: Prentice-Hall, 1969).
T. C. Smith, *The Agrarian Origins of Modern Japan* (Stanford University Press, 1959).
J. C. Smuts, *Holism and Evolution* (New York: Greenwood, 1961).
R. Soligo, *Factor Intensity of Consumption Patterns, Income Distribution and Employment Growth in West Pakistan*, 1972, mimeo.
D. Soo, *Income Distribution in the ADE Region* (Manila: Asian Development Bank, 1974).
J. E. Spencer and W. L. Thomas, *Asia, East by South: a Cultural Geography* (New York: Wiley, 1971).
E. Staley and R. Morse, *Modern Small Industry for Developing Countries* (New York: McGraw-Hill, 1965).
P. Streeten, *The Limits of Development Studies* (Leeds University Press, 1975).
P. Streeten, *The Frontiers of Development Studies* (New York: John Wiley, 1972).
P. Streeten (ed.), *Unfashionable Economics*: Issues in Honour of Lord Balogh

(London: Weidenfeld & Nicolson, 1970).
F. Stewart, *Technology and Underdevelopment* (Boulder, Colorado: West View Press, 1977).
F. Stewart (ed.), *Employment, Income Distribution, and Development* (London: Frank Cass, 1975).
F. Stewart and P. Streeten, *New Strategies for Development*: Poverty, Income Distribution, and Growth, Oxford Economic Papers, vol. 28, no. 3, 1976.
R. Steppacher, *Surplus, Kapitalbildung und wirtschaftliche Entwicklung: Zur Relevanz der Physiokratie und der institutionellen Oekonomie für das Problem der Kapitalbildung in unterentwickelten Ländern* (Leibefeld/Bern: Lang AG, 1976).
P. V. Sukhatme, 'Human Calorie and Protein Needs and How Far They are Satisfied Today' in B. Benjamin *et al.* (eds.) *Resources and Population*, op. cit.
H. Takamori and S. Yamashita, 'Measuring Socio-Economic Development: Indicators, Development Paths and International Comparisons', in *The Developing Economies*, vol. XI, no. 2, (Tokyo, June 1973).
A. P. Thirlwall, *Growth and Development: with Special Reference to Developing Economies* (London: Macmillan, 1972).
C. P. Timmer and W. P. Falcon, *Solving China's Food Problem*, Food Research Institute Studies, No. 1, 1976.
J. Tinbergen, *Development Planning* (New York: World University Library, 1967).
J. Tinbergen, *Economic Policy: Principles and Design*, (Amsterdam: North Holland, 1967).
G. Tintner, J. K. Sengupta, and E. J. Thomas, 'Applications of the Theory of Stochastic Processes to Economic Development', in I. Adelman and E. Thorbecke (eds.), *The Theory and Design of Economic Development*, op. cit.
M. P. Todaro, 'A Model of Labour Migration and Urban Unemployment in Less-Developed Countries', *American Economic Review*, vol. 59, no. 1, 1969.
M. P. Todaro, *Economics for a Developing World: An Introduction to Principles, Problems and Policies for Development* (London: Longman Group, 1977).
L. H. Tribe, 'Policy Science: Analysis or Ideology?', *Philosophy and Public Affairs*, vol. 1, No. 1, 1972.
S. Tsuru, 'In Place of Gross National Product', in H. and U. E. Simonis (eds.), *Japan: Economic and Social Studies in Development*, op. cit.
S. Tsuru, 'Towards a New Political Economy', in K. Dopfer (ed.), *Economics in the Future*, op. cit.
S. Tsuru, Essays in Economic Development (Tokyo: Kinokuniya, 1968).
N. R. Uphoff and W. F. Ilchman (eds.), *The Political Economy of Development* (Berkeley: University of California Press, 1973).
A. Vaidyanathan, *Some Aspects of Inequalities in Living Standards in Rural India* (New Delhi: Planning Commission, 1971).
J. P. Van Gigch, *Applied General Systems Theory* (New York: Harper, 1974).
B. Ward (ed.), *The Widening Gap* (New York: Columbia University Press, 1971).
Water Supply and Sewerage: Sectoral Programmes and Policies (Washington, DC.: World Bank, 1972).
A. Waterston, 'Resolving the Three-Horned Planning Dilemma (Washington,

D.C.: 1971), mimeo.

Clifton R. Wharton, Jr. (ed.), *Subsistence Agriculture and Economic Development*, (Chicago: Aldine, 1970).

Wickizer and Bennett, *The Rice Economy of Monsoon Asia*, Food Research Institute (Stanford University, 1941).

R. G. Wilkinson, *Poverty and Progress: an Ecological Model of Economic Development* (London: Methuen, 1973).

C. E. A. Winslow, *The Cost of Sickness and the Price of Health, World Health Organisation*, Monograph Series no. 7 (Geneva: 1973).

World and Regional Population Prospects, World Population Conference 1974, Symposium in Cairo, 1973, preliminary text, 60/BP/3.

L. J. Zimmerman, *Poor Lands, Rich Lands: the Widening Gap* (New York: Random House, 1965).

Index

MIX
Papier aus verantwortungsvollen Quellen
Paper from responsible sources
FSC® C105338

If you have any concerns about our products,
you can contact us on
ProductSafety@springernature.com

In case Publisher is established outside the EU,
the EU authorized representative is:
Springer Nature Customer Service Center GmbH
Europaplatz 3, 69115 Heidelberg, Germany

Printed by Libri Plureos GmbH
in Hamburg, Germany